where
to
weekend
around
NEW YORK CITY
Fodor's

Fodor's Travel Publications   New York   Toronto   London   Sydney   Auckland

Fodor's Where to Weekend Around New York City

Editor: Chris Swiac

Editorial Production: David Downing

Editorial Contributors: Gary Allen, Heather Buchanan, Laura Knowles Callanan, Marianne Comfort, Patricia Earnest, Erica Freudenberger, Elizabeth Gehrman, Ann Hammerle, Gail Jaffe-Bennek, Wendy Kagan, Lisa S. Kahn, Shannon M. Kelly, Laura M. Kidder, Diana Niles King, Catherine Warren Leone, Karen Little, Jeremy Olshan, Amy Patton, John D. Rambow, Sarah Sper, Douglas Stallings, Jane E. Zarem

Maps: David Lindroth *cartographer;* Bob Blake and Rebecca Baer, *map editors*

Cover Art: Jessie Hartland

Book Design: Fabrizio La Rocca, *creative director;* Guido Caroti, *art director;* Sophie Ye Chin, *designer*

Production/Manufacturing: Robert B. Shields

Copyright

ISBN 1–4000–1233–3

ISSN 1547–674X

Special Sales

Where to Weekend Around New York City

What are you doing this weekend? Just the word *weekend* implies such promise—a break from the workday rhythm, a bit of downtime, a chance to see friends and family, a good time to be had by all. Two things are certain: there aren't enough weekends, and they're always too short. You can make them feel longer, however, by going away, seeing someplace different, and really leaving the concerns of home life behind. And, surprise, planning a weekend getaway doesn't have to be stressful, regardless of whether you're deciding where to go next month or next weekend. That's where this book comes in.

Where to Weekend around New York City helps you plan trips to 22 destinations within 215 mi of the city. In the dozens of towns we describe, you'll find hundreds of places to explore. Some may be places you know; others may be new to you. This book makes sure you know your options so that you don't miss something that's right around the next bend—even practically in your backyard—just because you didn't know it was there. Maybe you usually spend summer weekends in Montauk. Why not consider Cape May or Block Island for a change, or go in May or October instead? Perhaps your favorite inn is booked solid and you can't wait to get away, or you're tired of eating at the same three restaurants in Rhinebeck. With the practical information in this book, you can easily call to confirm the details that matter and study up on what you'll want to see and do and where you'll want to eat and sleep. Then toss *Where to Weekend around New York City* in your bag for the journey.

Although there's no substitute for travel advice from a good friend who knows your style and taste, our contributors are the next best thing—the kind of people you would poll for weekend ideas if you knew them.

Food writer and editor **Gary Allen** has lived in Ulster County since the 1960s, when he came to the area to attend the State University of New York at New Paltz. His work has appeared in *Gastronomica*, the *Journal of the Association for the Study of Food and Society*, the *Valley Table*, and *Flavor & Fortune*, as well as on food-related Web sites. He teaches food-writing and -history classes at Empire State College and was an instructor at the Culinary Institute of America.

A Sag Harbor native and local journalist, **Heather Buchanan** has written about her area of Long Island's South Fork for various travel publications. She also pens a weekly singles' column for the Hamptons' Independent newspaper chain.

Originally from New Jersey, freelance writer **Laura Knowles Callanan** moved west in the 1970s—to south-central Pennsylvania. She covers the food, arts, and entertainment scenes for area newspapers and other publications.

Freelance writer **Marianne Comfort** lives in northeastern New York and counts Saratoga Springs as a stomping ground. Formerly a reporter for Schenectady's *Daily Gazette*, she regularly contributes to several periodicals, including the *Valley Table*, and often covers agriculture, food, and restaurants. She also cohosts a monthly farm- and food-focused program on WRPI, the radio station for Rensselaer Polytechnic Institute.

Connecticut-based **Patricia Earnest** is a freelance travel writer whose work has appeared in *Modern Bride*, *Woodall's*, *WindCheck*, and *Alaska Magazine*. She also writes for *JAX FAX Travel Marketing Magazine*, a publication for U.S. travel agents.

Following in the footsteps of thousands before her, **Erica Freudenberger** came to the Catskills for a visit and ended up staying. An associate editor at Ulster Publishing, she contributes to the *Woodstock Times* and the *Saugerties Times*.

A weekend in Boston convinced **Elizabeth Gehrman** to leave behind the stresses of New York in 1997. Once a magazine editor and now a freelance writer, the Massachusetts resident has contributed to various magazines and newspapers, including the *Boston Herald* and *Harvard Gazette*, as well as to several Fodor's guides.

Ann Hammerle has lived and worked on Long Island's East End since the late 1970s. She is compiling a photographic essay about Montauk and writing a book about container gardening.

Gail Jaffe-Bennek moved to the mid-Hudson Valley in the early 1980s. A kayaker, hiker, and gardener, she is also copublisher of *AboutTown*, a quarterly community guide covering Northern Dutchess and Southern Columbia counties.

Freelance writer **Wendy Kagan** calls the Hudson Valley home. Her articles have appeared in *Travel and Leisure, Organic Style,* and *Garden Design* magazines, among others, and she previously penned the monthly "Hudson Valley Traveler" column for the *Putnam County News & Recorder*.

Lisa S. Kahn can recall many happy times on Long Island's North Fork, where her family frequently spent summers. A freelance writer since 1988, Lisa pens feature articles for New Jersey's *Star-Ledger* newspaper and special advertising sections for the *New York Times* and *USA Today*. She contributed to *Fodor's How to Take a Road Trip*.

Before moving to Dutchess County, **Diana Niles King** devoted much of her career to writing peppy prose for the cosmetics-fragrance industry. These days she turns her hand to freelance writing and volunteering for the Dutchess Land Conservancy. She is also active in local equestrian pursuits.

New Jersey–based freelance writer **Catherine Warren Leone,** formerly an editor at *Women's Wear Daily* and *W*, writes special sections for the *New York Times*.

Karen Little is a freelance writer who specializes in "how-to" articles, everything from how to use software to how to make the most of a vacation. New York City is the focus of her Web site, www.littleviews.com.

Jeremy Olshan, a freelance writer based in New York City, previously covered city hall for the *Press of Atlantic City* and contributes to publications such as *Newsday*.

Amy Patton is the arts and entertainment editor of the *Southampton Independent*, a Hamptons weekly for which she also writes a column. She has lived in Southampton since 1997.

Native New Englander **Jane E. Zarem** calls Connecticut home but travels widely as a freelance writer. Although she is a regular contributor to *Fodor's Caribbean*, she is quite content to remain close to her roots, which she does for this book.

Contents

How to Use This Book

Our goal is to cover the best sights, activities, lodgings, and restaurants in their category within each weekend-getaway destination. Alphabetical organization makes it easy to navigate through these pages. Still, we've made certain decisions and used certain terms that you need to know about. For starters you can go on the assumption that everything you read about in this book is recommended by our writers and editors. It goes without saying that no property mentioned in the book has paid to be included.

ORGANIZATION

Bullets on the map, which follows How to Use This Book, correspond to the chapter numbers. Each chapter focuses on one getaway destination; the directional line at the start of each chapter tells you how far it is from the city. The information in each chapter's What to See & Do section is arranged in alphabetical order, broken up by town in many cases. Where to Stay and Where to Eat follow, with suggestions for places for all budgets, also arranged alphabetically and usually by town as well. The Essentials section provides information about how to get there and other logistical details.

For ideas about the best places for antiquing, hiking, and one-day trips, flip to the Fodor's Choice listings, which follow the map. Pit Stops are places to pull off the highway, stretch your legs, and grab a snack.

WHAT TO SEE & DO

This book is loaded with sights and activities for all seasons, budgets, lifestyles, and interests, which means that whether you want to rock climb or go antiquing, you'll find plenty of places to explore. Admission prices given apply to adults; substantially reduced fees are almost always available for children, students, and senior citizens.

Where they're available, sightseeing tours are listed in their own section. Sports are limited to area highlights. Biking is an option most everywhere, so we give details only when facilities are extensive or otherwise notable. The same can be said of shopping, but we tell you about shopping standouts, such as Mecox Gardens in Southampton and Winter Sun/Summer Moon in Rhinebeck. Use Save the Date as a timing tool, for events you wish to attend (or perhaps crowds you'd prefer to avoid).

WHERE TO STAY

The places we list—including homey bed-and-breakfasts, mom-and-pop motels, grand inns, chain hotels, and luxury retreats—are the cream of the crop in each price and lodging category.

Baths: You'll find private bathrooms unless noted otherwise.

Closings: Assume that hostelries are open all year unless otherwise noted.

Credit cards: AE, D, DC, MC, V following lodging listings indicate whether American Express, Discover, Diner's Club, MasterCard, or Visa are accepted.

Facilities: We list what's available but we don't specify what costs extra. When pricing accommodations, always ask what's included. The term *hot tub* denotes hot tubs, whirlpools, and Jacuzzis. Assume that lodgings have phones, TVs, and air-conditioning and that they permit smoking, unless we note otherwise.

Meal plans: Hostelries operate on the European Plan (EP, with no meals) unless we specify that they use the Continental Plan (CP, with a Continental breakfast), Breakfast Plan (BP, with a full breakfast), Modified American Plan (MAP, with breakfast and dinner), or the Full American Plan (FAP, with all meals).

Prices: Price categories are based on the price range for a standard double room during high season, excluding service charges and tax. Price categories for all-suites properties are based on prices for standard suites.

WHAT IT COSTS

$$$$	over $225
$$$	$175–$225
$$	$125–$174
$	$90–$124
¢	under $90

WHERE TO EAT

We make a point of including local food-lovers' hot spots as well as neighborhood options, with choices for all budgets.

Credit cards: AE, D, DC, MC, V following restaurant listings indicate whether American Express, Discover, Diner's Club, MasterCard, or Visa are accepted.

Dress: Assume that no jackets or ties are required for men unless otherwise noted.

Meals and hours: Assume that restaurants are open for lunch and dinner unless otherwise noted. We always specify days closed and meals not available. When traveling in off-season, be sure to call ahead.

Prices: The price categories listed are based on the cost per person for a main course at dinner or, when dinner isn't available, the next most expensive meal.

Reservations: They're always a good idea, but we don't mention them unless they're essential or are not accepted.

WHAT IT COSTS

$$$$	over $30
$$$	$22–$30
$$	$15–$21
$	$8–$14
¢	under $8

ESSENTIALS

Details about transportation and other logistical information end each chapter. Be sure to check Web sites or call for particulars.

AN IMPORTANT TIP

Although all prices, opening times, and other details in this book are based on information supplied to us at press time, changes occur all the time in the travel world, especially in seasonal destinations, and Fodor's cannot accept responsibility for facts that become outdated or for inadvertent errors or omissions. So always confirm information when it matters, especially if you're making a detour to visit a specific place.

Let Us Hear from You

Keeping a travel guide fresh and up-to-date is a big job, and we welcome any and all comments. We'd love to have your thoughts on places we've listed, and we're interested in hearing about your own special finds. Our guides are thoroughly updated for each new edition, and we're always adding new information, so your feedback is vital. Contact us via e-mail in care of editors@fodors.com (specifying *Where to Weekend around New York City* on the subject line) or via snail mail in care of *Where to Weekend around New York City,* at Fodor's, 1745 Broadway, New York, NY 10019. We look forward to hearing from you. And in the meantime, have a great weekend.

—The Editors

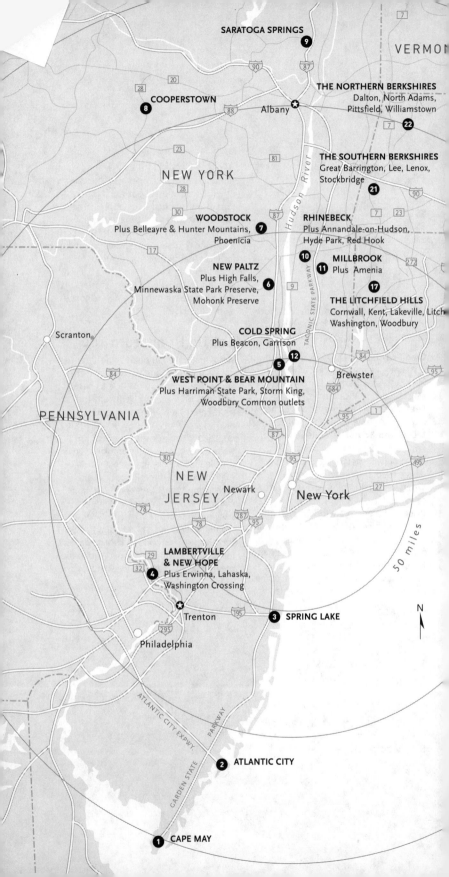

SARATOGA SPRINGS 9

THE NORTHERN BERKSHIRES
Dalton, North Adams,
Pittsfield, Williamstown
22

VERMON

COOPERSTOWN 8

Albany

THE SOUTHERN BERKSHIRES Great Barrington, Lee, Lenox,
Stockbridge
21

NEW YORK

Hudson River

WOODSTOCK 7
Plus Belleayre & Hunter Mountains,
Phoenicia

RHINEBECK
Plus Annandale-on-Hudson,
Hyde Park, Red Hook
10

NEW PALTZ
Plus High Falls,
Minnewaska State Park Preserve,
Mohonk Preserve
6

MILLBROOK
Plus Amenia
11

17

Scranton

THE LITCHFIELD HILLS
Cornwall, Kent, Lakeville, Litch
Washington, Woodbury

COLD SPRING
Plus Beacon, Garrison
5 12

Brewster

WEST POINT & BEAR MOUNTAIN
Plus Harriman State Park, Storm King,
Woodbury Common outlets

PENNSYLVANIA

**NEW
JERSEY**

Newark

New York

50 miles

**LAMBERTVILLE
& NEW HOPE**
Plus Erwinna, Lahaska,
Washington Crossing
4

N

Trenton

3 **SPRING LAKE**

Philadelphia

2 **ATLANTIC CITY**

1 **CAPE MAY**

Pit Stops

Off the major thoroughfares outside the city and beyond the highway rest stops, these places offer a quick bite (and a bathroom). Pit-stop listings are grouped together by thoroughfare, per state (Connecticut, New Jersey, New York).

I–95, CONNECTICUT TURNPIKE

Johnny Ad's
2½ mi southeast of Exit 66, Spencer Plains Road
Lobster rolls are served two ways here: hot and buttered or cold and mixed with mayo. But this seafood shack also serves a respectable chili dog. If you're heading northbound, take U.S. 1 east to get back on Interstate 95. > 910 Boston Post Rd./U.S. 1, Old Saybrook, CT, tel. 860/388–4032. No credit cards.

S&S Dugout
½ mi northwest of Exit 19, Center Street/Southport
Freshly sliced ham, roast beef, and other sandwich makings are piled high at this 1950s eatery and served hot or cold. Seating is at a well-worn counter and in a couple of booths. The eatery stays open until 4 p.m. > 3449 Post Rd./U.S. 1, between Center and Spruce Sts., Southport, CT, tel. 203/255–2579. No credit cards. Closed Sun. No dinner.

GARDEN STATE PARKWAY

Old Time Tavern
2 mi east and north of Exit 82, Route 37 East
Interesting sandwiches (including wraps and grilled vegetable panini), Italian dishes, steaks, and seafood are the lures at this restaurant-taproom. Early birds can get soup-to-dessert meals at bargain prices. Kids get their own menu. > Dover Mall, Rte. 166 north of Rte. 37, Toms River, NJ, tel. 732/349–2387. AE, DC, MC, V.

I–495, LONG ISLAND EXPRESSWAY

American Burger Co.
6 mi north of Exit 49, Route 110
Most of the menu at this gleaming red-white-and-blue, retro-style eatery is devoted to burgers, but you can also order a hotdog or a BLT, or get a veggie burger. The place stays open until 11 PM Sunday through Thursday and until 2 AM Friday and Saturday. > 337 New York Ave., south of Main St./Rte. 25A, Huntington, NY, tel. 631/935–0300. No credit cards.

I–87, NEW YORK STATE THRUWAY

Dallas Hot Weiners
1 mi southeast of Exit 19, Kingston
Hot dogs are the specialty at this narrow spot with a counter and a handful of tables. "One with everything" means a steamed dog on a steamed bun topped with slightly spicy chili sauce, a dab of mustard, and a sprinkling of chopped onions. The sauce livens up fries, too; temper it with ketchup if it's too spicy for you. > 51 N. Front St., off Washington Ave., Kingston, NY, tel. 845/338–6094. No credit cards. Closed Sun.

Fodor's Choice

The towns, sights, activities, and other travel experiences listed on this page are Fodor's editors' and writers' top picks for each category.

ANTIQUING
Cold Spring > Chapter 12
Lambertville & New Hope > Chapter 4
The Litchfield Hills > Chapter 17
Millbrook > Chapter 11
The Southern Berkshires > Chapter 21

FALL FOLIAGE
The Litchfield Hills > Chapter 17
New Paltz > Chapter 6
The Northern Berkshires > Chapter 22
The Southern Berkshires > Chapter 21
West Point & Bear Mountain > Chapter 5
Woodstock > Chapter 7

FISHING
Block Island > Chapter 19
Cape May > Chapter 1
Montauk > Chapter 14
Woodstock > Chapter 7

GARDENS & OUTDOOR SPACES
Cliff Walk, Newport, RI > Chapter 20
Innisfree Garden, Millbrook, NY > Chapter 11
Montgomery Place, Annandale-on-Hudson, NY > Chapter 10
Opus 40, Saugerties, NY > Chapter 7
Stonecrop Gardens, Cold Spring, NY > Chapter 12
Storm King Art Center, Mountainville, NY > Chapter 5

GOLF COURSES
Harbor Pines Golf Club, Egg Harbor Township, NJ > Chapter 2
Howell Park Golf Course, Howell, NJ > Chapter 3
Leatherstocking Golf Course, Cooperstown, NY > Chapter 8
Montauk Downs State Park, Montauk, NY > Chapter 14

Saratoga Spa Golf, Saratoga Springs, NY > Chapter 9
Seaview Marriott Resort & Spa, Galloway Township, NJ > Chapter 2

HISTORIC HOMES & MANSIONS
Boscobel Restoration, Garrison, NY > Chapter 12
The Breakers, Newport, RI > Chapter 20
Chesterwood, Stockbridge, MA > Chapter 21
Emlen Physick Estate, Cape May, NJ > Chapter 1
Franklin D. Roosevelt National Historic Site, Hyde Park, NY > Chapter 10
Huguenot Street houses, New Paltz, NY > Chapter 6
Marble House, Newport, RI > Chapter 20
The Mount, Lenox, MA > Chapter 21
Olana State Historic Site, Hudson, NY > Chapter 10
Vanderbilt Mansion National Historic Site, Hyde Park, NY > Chapter 10

ONE-DAY GETAWAYS
Cold Spring > Chapter 12
Lambertville & New Hope > Chapter 4
New Paltz > Chapter 6
Spring Lake > Chapter 3
West Point & Bear Mountain > Chapter 5

Cape May

169 mi south of New York City

1

Revised by Catherine Warren Leone

THE SOUTHERNMOST POINT IN NEW JERSEY, believed to be the oldest beachfront resort in the country, is a National Historic Landmark. Cape May today retains more than 600 Victorian-era houses, built from the mid-1800s to the early 1900s, which have found new life as bed-and-breakfasts, inns, and restaurants. Take a tour or attend a festival and learn a little about the architecture and the customs of a bygone era.

Guest houses made their appearance here as early as the mid-1700s, and in the 19th century, well-heeled Philadelphians picked Cape May as the place to build their summer cottages, which really were more like mansions. Soon industrialists from New York and Wilmington followed. Grand Victorian houses, encircled by wide verandas and flowering gardens, and elaborate hotels sprang up on tree-lined streets within strolling distance of town and beach. In the 20th century, the area experienced a downturn as visitors headed for Atlantic City and other Jersey Shore towns, which were easier to reach than Cape May. In the 1970s, fledgling entrepreneurs with a passion for the past and a vision for the future began the hard work of restoring the crumbling Victorians and other structures and turning them into charming B&Bs with period antiques and decor.

Cape May sits at the tip of a peninsula with the Delaware Bay to its west and the Atlantic Ocean on the east—a location that allows for a remarkably temperate climate. Because of its strategic position along the Atlantic Flyway, the resort has stellar birdwatching and draws flocks of birders to its naturalist-staffed observatory on the boardwalk at Cape May Point State Park. During the fall migration, from late September to early November, you might spot any of 16 species of hawks stopping to rest for a spell. Sightseeing boats leave Cape May's marina to watch whales and dolphins. Horseshoe crabs are a common shoreline sight.

Walking, trolley, and candlelight tours point out the architectural riches of Cape May's many housing styles: Italianate, Second Empire, Gothic Revival, stick, shingle, Queen Anne, Colonial Revival, and even the odd Federal. By tour's end, you're able to easily spot the tell-tale signs—a cupola here, a turret there—of each type. Many of New Jersey's finest restaurants are at home in these architectural beauties or nearby.

A year-round, largely family-oriented resort, the community has a full schedule of events each month, among them a dressed-to-the-gables Dickensian Christmas in December, as well as an enormous Victorian Week celebration in October. The entire Jersey Shore gets busy in July and August, but Cape May knows what is has and takes full advantage of its Victorian heritage, sponsoring events and specials to keep the crowds coming throughout the year.

The flat-as-a-flounder terrain makes it easy to get around town, country, and beach, whether you're walking, bicycling solo, or pooling energy to peddle a surrey-top four-wheeler. In the process, you can come across plenty of simple pleasures, such as picking up Cape May polished quartz "diamonds" at Sunset Beach as the sun sets and the flag is lowered for the night.

Cape May Kids Playhouse Jugglers, magicians, puppeteers, and clowns turn the Convention Hall into a house of mirth every Monday and Thursday (10 AM and 7 PM) in July and August. > Beach Dr. at Stockton Pl., tel. 609/884–5404 or 800/275–4278, www.capemaymac.org.

Cape May Lighthouse One of the oldest operating lighthouses in the United States, the 1859 beacon marks the southernmost tip of New Jersey and beams its light 24 mi out to sea. Climb up the winding stairs (199) to the top of the 157½-foot-tall structure. From the watch gallery, under the reconstructed lantern, you have views of the Atlantic, Delaware Bay, and Cape May Point State Park. A small museum and gift shop are on-site. > Cape May Point State Park, Lighthouse Ave., tel. 609/884–5404 or 800/275–4278, www.capemaymac.org. $5. Feb. and Mar., weekends 11–3; Apr. and May, daily 10–4; June–Aug., daily 9–8; Sept.–Dec., daily 11–3.

Cape May Point State Park The diverse mix of ocean shoreline, dunes, freshwater coastal marsh and ponds, islands, forests, and fields makes the 235-acre park at the southern end of the Cape May peninsula a mecca for sea and shore birds during the fall migration. Bird-watchers follow in droves. Available surf fishing, marked trails, observation platforms, the Cape May Lighthouse, picnic tables and shelters, a visitors center, and a museum make the park perfect for year-round visits. > Lighthouse Ave., tel. 609/884–2159, www.state.nj.us. Free. Memorial Day–Labor Day, daily dawn–dusk; rest of yr, daily dawn–6 PM.

Emlen Physick Estate Peer into the life of the Victorian elite during a 45-minute tour of the 18-room mansion built in 1879 for Emlen Physick, a nonpracticing physician (courtesy of a family inheritance) who lived with his mother and maiden aunt. The mansion's timber-outline exterior is in stick style, avant-garde for its day. Guides point out original furnishings and discuss period customs. Take time for afternoon tea or a light lunch at the Twining's Tearoom, in the estate's carriage house. Entrance to the adjacent Carriage House Gallery is included in the tour price. The estate is home office to the Mid-Atlantic Center for the Arts (MAC), the nonprofit organization formed in 1970 to save the mansion from the wood pile; it now promotes restoration throughout Cape May. > 1048 Washington St., tel. 609/884–5404 or 800/275–4278, www.capemaymac.org. House tour $8, gallery $2. Mid-June–mid-Sept., daily 9:30–5; mid-Sept.–Dec., daily 11–4; Jan.–mid-Mar., weekends 10–3; mid-Mar.–Apr., Sun.–Fri. 11–3, Sat. 10–5; May–mid-June, daily 10:30–4:30.

Historic Cold Spring Village Craftspeople in date-appropriate costumes demonstrate their trades using traditional tools, methods, and materials at this nonprofit, living-history site. More than 20 buildings, built between 1702 and 1897, make up the farming village on 22 shady acres north of Cape May. > 720 U.S. 9, tel. 609/898–2300, www.hcsv.org. $7. Late June–Sept., Tues.–Sun. 10–4:30.

Nature Center of Cape May Part of the New Jersey Audubon Society, the center has tours, exhibits, and educational activities on 18 acres of beach, meadow, and marsh habitat bordering the man-made Cape May Harbor. > 1600 Delaware Ave., tel. 609/898–8848, www.njaudubon.org. Free. Daily 9–4:30.

WHAT'S NEARBY

Cape May County's Historical Museum & Genealogical Society The circa-1755 John Holmes House holds 300 years of Cape May County history. Furnishings, costumes, textiles, tools, and decorative and practical objects are on display, as well as a collection of old Cape May family bibles and other genealogical references.

> 504 Rte. 9N, Cape May Court House, tel. 609/465–3535, www.cmcmuseum.org. $3.50. Apr.–Oct., Tues.–Sat. 9–3; Nov.–Mar., Sat. 9–3.

Cape May County Park and Zoo A small gem of a zoo covers 85 acres. Take a walking safari on the raised boardwalk bordering the African savanna re-creation, and visit the aviary and reptile houses. The rest of the 128-acre park is filled with picnic areas, playgrounds, bike trails, and a pond for fishing. > 4 Moore St., Cape May Court House, tel. 609/465–5271. Free. Daily 9–dusk.

Leaming's Run Gardens Stroll on a winding path through the 22 theme gardens of annual flowers, all started from seeds. A small museum depicts life in the 1700s (when the Leaming family lived here). There's also a farm with goats, sheep, and chickens. > 1845 Rte. 9N, Swainton, tel. 609/465–5871, www.njsouth.com. $7. Mid-May–mid-Oct., daily 9:30–5.

Sunset Beach Cape May "diamonds" (pebbles of pure, rounded quartz) wash up on the shore at this beach walking distance from the Cape May Lighthouse, and are yours for the taking. Drive—or better yet—bicycle the 3 mi to the south end of Sunset Boulevard for the sunset flag ceremony held from June through September; listen as Kate Smith belts out "God Bless America" and the flag is lowered for the night. Gift shops on the privately owned beach sell the quartz diamonds already cut down and mounted in jewelry. Stop into the on-site Sunset Beach Grille for homemade crab cakes. > Sunset Blvd., Cape May Point, tel. 609/884–7079, www.sunsetbeachnj.com. Free. June–Sept., daily 8:30–dusk; Oct.–May, daily 9–6:30.

Tours

Delaware Bay Lighthouse Adventures From late April to mid-October, the Mid-Atlantic Center for the Arts runs sightseeing cruises around Cape May, boat tours of Delaware Bay and the Cape May Lighthouse (July and August), and a morning cruise to see historic sites on both sides of the Delaware Bay. Boats leave from Miss Chris Fishing Center, at the marina at the entrance to Cape May. > Miss Chris Fishing Center, 2nd Ave. and Wilson Dr., tel. 609/884–5404, www.capemaymac.org.

Historic District Trolley Tours Take a 30-minute tour of the east, west, or beachfront area of Cape May aboard one of the MAC-sponsored red trolleys that ply town streets. Combination trolley/Physick Estate tours are offered, along with garden-theme trolley tours, Romantic Moonlight rides, and Stairway to the Stars, a trolley ride combined with a trip to the top of the Cape May Point Lighthouse to stargaze (remember the mosquito repellent). > MAC Washington Street Mall Information Booth, Ocean St., tel. 609/884–5404 or 800/275–4278, www.capemaymac.org. $6 and up.

Whale Watcher Board a 75-foot catamaran for up-close wildlife viewing with the Cape May Whale Watch and Research Center. An onboard naturalist identifies species of whales, dolphins, and other marine mammals. Complimentary coffee and rolls come with the dolphin breakfast cruise; free pizza and hot dogs are served in the evening. Cruises run from April through November. > 1286 Wilson Dr., tel. 609/898–0055 or 888/531–0055, www.capemaywhalewatch.com. $28.

Sports

BIRD-WATCHING

Cape May Bird Observatory Sixteen species of hawks can be spotted from the Cape May Point Hawk Count platform during fall migration. Educational interns staff the platform, at the far end of the lighthouse in Cape May Point State Park, from September through November. The observatory's educational center, open year-round, leads naturalist-conducted walks that focus on sunset birding, wildflowers, butterflies, and local birding hot spots. > 701 E. Lake Dr., Cape May Point, tel. 609/884–2736, www.njaudubon.org. Free. Daily 9–4:30.

FISHING

Deep-sea and surf fishing are both popular pastimes off Cape May. You can rent equipment, hire a guide, or schedule a class at Bob Jackson's Surf Fishing Center.

South Jersey Deep Sea Fishing Catch flounder, weakfish, bluefish, shark, tuna, and marlin during a half-day, full-day, or night trip (from $300 for four hours) on a South Jersey charter boat. Bait, ice, tackle, and fish cleaning are included. > Rte. 109, tel. 609/884–3800, www.sjmarina.com.

EQUIPMENT **Bob Jackson's Surf Fishing Center** > 719 Cape May, West Cape May, tel. 609/898–7950, www.fishcapemay.com.

GOLFING

Cape May National Golf Club The championship-level 18-hole golf course surrounds a 50-acre bird sanctuary and is open year-round. Considered a leader in design that's sensitive to the environment, the course encompasses natural grasses, wetlands, and ponds. Greens fees are $50–$85. The course is 2 mi south of the intersection of U.S. 9 and Route 47 (Garden State Parkway Exit 4A). > Florence Ave., Erma, tel. 609/884–1563 or 888/227–3874, www.cmngc.com.

KAYAKING

Aqua Trails With your naturalist guide, paddle in sit-on-top kayaks through the diverse ecosystem of Cape May's inland salt marshes. From May through September two daily 1½-hour tours are available ($40); make advance reservations. Aqua Trails also offers kayak rentals and full-moon tours. > 956 Ocean Dr., Cape May, tel. 609/884–5600, www.aquatrails.com.

Shopping

Washington Street Mall Positioned in the heart of Cape May's historic district, this outdoor pedestrian mall's stores occupy old town buildings. Clothing, souvenirs and gifts, toys, and children's togs are just some of the types of merchandise available. > Washington St. between Ocean and Perry Sts., tel. 609/884–5011, www.washingtonstreetmall.com.

Save the Date

MARCH

Sherlock Holmes Weekend The Victorian-era's famous detective stars in a weekend-long murder-mystery event in late March and again in late October. The intrigue starts with a society ball (period costumes welcomed) Friday evening and continues Saturday with a search-for-the-clues tour and luncheon at varying town locations. The mystery is revealed Sunday at brunch, with prizes awarded. > Tel. 609/884–5404 or 800/275–4278, www.capemaymac.org.

APRIL

Cape May's Spring Festival Make it a Victorian spring. Gardens and 19th-century houses are preened and ready to show off during nine days of festivities in late April through early May: private garden walking tours, trolley tulip tours, a Victorian ball, a crafts fair, and brass-band concerts. The town-wide event, which includes the Tulip Festival, is cosponsored by the Mid-Atlantic Center for the Arts and the Chamber of Commerce of Greater Cape May. > Tel. 609/884–5404 or 800/275–4278, www.capemaymac.org.

MAY

Cape May Bird Observatory Spring Weekend Guided walks, boat trips, speakers, and birding are part of this three-day nature festival in mid-May. Count as many bird species as you can and perhaps be the winner in the Cape May Bird Observatory World Series of Birding contest. > 701 E. Lake Dr., Cape May Point, tel. 609/884-2736.

JUNE

Cape May Music Festival The menu of concerts during this five-week festival that starts in early June swings from orchestral and chamber music to jazz, pop, and international beats. Performances are held in the Cape May Convention Hall. > Beach Dr. at Stockton Pl., tel. 609/884-5404 or 800/275-4278, www.capemaymac.org.

SEPTEMBER

Annual Cape May Food and Wine Festival See why the *New York Times* called Cape May "the restaurant capital of New Jersey." You can take classes and seminars taught by local chefs and attend workshops and tours in the kitchens of acclaimed restaurants. Packages including dinner and lunch are available. > Mid-Atlantic Center for the Arts, Emlen Physick Estate, 1048 Washington St., tel. 609/884-5404 or 800/275-4278, www.capemaymac.org.

OCTOBER

Victorian Week Cape May's heritage is on parade in this all-out, town-wide Victorian celebration in mid-October. Tour private, late-1800s homes, attend period dance workshops in preparation for the evening balls, watch vintage-fashion shows with clothing from 1850 to 1960, and listen to brass-band concerts. Daily workshops are held on subjects like craft beer making, antiques and appraisal, and cooking. > Mid-Atlantic Center for the Arts, Emlen Physick Estate, 1048 Washington St., tel. 609/884-5404 or 800/275-4278, www.capemaymac.org.

NOVEMBER

Cape May Autumn Weekend/The Bird Show Commune with nature during hawk, owl, and bat demonstrations, or attend lectures sponsored by the Cape May Bird Observatory the first weekend in November (last weekend in October). The demonstrations take place at Convention Hall; field trips and walks are at the observatory. > 701 E. Lake Dr., Cape May Point, tel. 609/884-2736.

DECEMBER

Annual Christmas Candlelight House Tours Revel in the spirit and warmth of a Victorian Christmas. Festooned to their gingerbread rafters, Cape May's Victorian inns, B&Bs, hotels, and churches welcome you. Self-guided tours on Saturday evenings in December are $22 for adults and $11 for children (3–12). Advance reservations are recommended. > Mid-Atlantic Center for the Arts, Emlen Physick Estate, 1048 Washington St., tel. 609/884-5404 or 800/275-4278, www.capemaymac.org.

Dickens Christmas Extravaganza Gift yourself with the sights and sounds—and tastes and scents—of a Dickens Christmas with three days of Christmas plays, lectures, private-home tours, and period costumes and crafts in early December. You're invited to a Sunday evening innkeeper's dinner and Dickensian feast at the Washington Inn. Packages including activities and double-occupancy accommodations are $600 to $960. > Mid-Atlantic Center for the Arts, Emlen Physick Estate, 1048 Washington St., tel. 609/884-5404 or 800/275-4278, www.capemaymac.org.

WHERE TO STAY

Book as far ahead as possible. Even motels in Cape May require advance reservations, with deposit, and have cancellation fees.

The Abbey Draped in heavy velvet, mammoth windows look down upon carved-wood settees, huge glass-front bookcases, and a harpsichord inside this Gothic Revival B&B in the historic district. Victorian writing desks and plush armchairs are part of the bedroom comforts, along with walnut or brass beds—some four-poster. The adjoining Cottage is beachy counterpoint to the formal main building; rooms have a casual mix of white wicker and greenery. > 34 Gurney St., 08204, tel. 609/884–4506 or 866/884–8800, fax 609/884–2379, www.abbeybedandbreakfast.com. 14 rooms. Fans, refrigerators; no a/c in some rooms, no room phones, no room TVs, no kids under 12, no smoking. Closed Jan.–early Mar. D, MC, V. CP. **$–$$$$**

Angel of the Sea The town's largest B&B, a sprawling 1850s mansion designed for the Philadelphia chemist who invented quinine, dominates Cape May's tranquil northern shore. Angel of the Sea is Disneylike in its gingerbread perfection: flowered wallpaper, beds with ornate headboards, and a flurry of white wicker add to the fairy-tale aura. Some guest rooms have working fireplaces. Curvaceous period antiques, covered in lace doilies, fill the common areas. > 5–7 Trenton Ave., 08204, tel. 609/884–3369 or 800/848–3369, fax 609/884–3331, www.angelofthesea.com. 21 rooms, 6 suites. Cable TV, business services; no room phones, no kids under 8. AE, D, MC, V. BP. **$$–$$$**

Atlas Inn Resort What you find here at beach-central is more a full-service hotel than an inn. The pool, which has a kids' safety area, faces the ocean; there are barbecue grills, an exercise room and sauna, even a baseball-theme restaurant loaded with Babe Ruth memorabilia. Standard and modern, guest rooms have private balconies, many with ocean views. > 1035 Beach Dr., 08204, tel. 609/884–7000 or 888/285–2746, fax 609/884–0301, www.atlasinn.com. 38 rooms, 50 suites. Restaurant, microwaves, refrigerators, cable TV, pool, gym, sauna, bar, laundry facilities. AE, D, MC, V. BP. **$–$$$**

Captain Mey's Inn Vintage corsets and hoop skirts hang on a hat rack in the dining room of this Victorian B&B, a great conversation starter for the T-shirts–and–shorts crowd. The 1890 Colonial Revival house, named for the Dutch discoverer of Cape May, draws you, book and iced tea in hand, to the veranda to sit a spell. Half canopies and dominant, print wallpapers add to the period aesthetic. Walk to the beach (two blocks) from here, or the Washington Mall (half a block). > 202 Ocean St., 08204, tel. 609/884–7793 or 800/981–3702, www.captainmeys.com. 8 rooms. Dining room, some in-room hot tubs, free parking; no TV in some rooms, no kids under 8. AE, MC, V. BP. **¢–$$$**

Carroll Villa Not only do you spend a night in a mansion (Italian villa–style, circa 1882), but the price also buys breakfast downstairs at the Mad Batter, Cape May's popular breakfast spot. Floral prints hang on the walls of the functionally compact guest rooms; headboards are made of carved wood. The family-owned hotel is a half block from the ocean, beach, and promenade. > 19 Jackson St., 08204, tel. 609/884–9619, fax 609/884–0264, www.carrollvilla.com. 22 rooms. Restaurant, in-room VCRs, business services, meeting rooms, free parking. AE, D, MC, V. BP. **$–$$$**

Chalfonte This is the real thing, a Victorian summer hotel (1876) on the boardwalk with striped green awnings and crisp white paint. The Chalfonte keeps it simple and friendly. Room are pleasantly spartan with wood floors and white curtains and bedspreads; some share hallway baths. Children are more than welcome—a supervised kid's dining room has its own menu. Parents dine in the Magnolia Room or on the boardwalk-long veranda. Southern-style fried chicken, smothered pork chops, corn pudding, and flaky biscuits are made by sisters Lucille and Dot, as their mother, Chalfonte's former beloved cook, taught them. > 301 Howard St., 08204, tel. 609/884–8409 or 888/411–1998, fax 609/884–4588, www.chalfonte.com. 70 rooms, 13 with bath. Restaurant, fans, bar, baby-sitting, children's programs (ages 3–8), playground, meeting rooms; no a/c, no room phones, no room TVs. AE, D, DC, MC, V. Closed Columbus Day–late May. MAP. **$$–$$$$**

Congress Hall From its inception in 1816, Congress Hall has had star power: President Benjamin Harrison made it his summer White House, and John Philip Sousa conducted the Congress Hall March on the lawn. Today the white-colonnade, Tuscan-yellow hotel is all breezy chic—sky-high ceilings, titan-size Victorian mirrors, glossy black wicker, and potted palms with attitude. Carpets have vibrant stripes, beds are dressed in white linens, and baths are sybaritic—some with 1920s, big-enough-for-two tubs—stocked with Aveda soaps and lotions. A C. H.-crest terry-cloth robe awaits so you can open the door and retrieve the *New York Times* without incident. > 251 Beach Ave., 08204, tel. 609/884-8421 or 888/944-1816, fax 609/884-6094, www.congresshall.com. 104 rooms, 5 suites. Restaurant, room service, in-room data ports, cable TV, in-room VCRs, pool, gym, spa, beach, bar, lounge, nightclub, shops, concierge, business services, meeting rooms, airport shuttle, free parking; no smoking. AE, D, DC, MC, V. EP. **$$$$**

Mainstay Inn Fourteen-foot ceilings, tall windows, a 13-foot hallway mirror, and black walnut dining-room furniture show a pedigree of money and manners. The two wealthy gamblers who constructed the building in 1872, as a gambling clubhouse for their friends (men only), obviously meant to impress. In 1971, the Mainstay became Cape May's first B&B, and since then has been the archetype for those that followed. You can also stay at the adjoining Cottage, or across the street at the suites-only Officers' Quarters. Guest rooms have Victorian antiques, but the luxury suites—traditional, but more contemporary looking—have hot tubs, kitchens, and fireplaces. > 635 Columbia Ave., 08204, tel. 609/884-8690, www.mainstayinn.com. 9 rooms, 7 suites. Fans, some microwaves, some refrigerators, some in-room hot tubs, free parking; no phones in some rooms, no TVs in some rooms, no kids, no smoking. MC, V. BP. **$$$–$$$$**

Manor House Put a roll in the player piano, take a homemade goodie out of the cookie jar and make yourself at home in a 1905 guest house. When it's time to go out, borrow beach chairs, or one of their supply of bicycles—and helmets—to ride to the beach two blocks away. Sheer white curtains cover the windows of the sunny bedrooms with period furniture; some have wood floors. > 612 Hughes St., 08204, tel. 609/884-4710, www.manorhouse.net. 10 rooms. Dining room, some in-room hot tubs, bicycles, free parking; no room phones, no room TVs, no children under 12, no smoking. D, MC, V. Closed Jan. BP. **$$–$$$**

Montreal Inn This modern, family-oriented, oceanfront hotel has patrons who have been coming for more than 20 years; reservations are taken a year in advance. There's a heated pool, a separate children's pool, an outdoor whirlpool, and a exercise room with sauna; plus there's free on-premises miniature golf, a game room, and activities for the kids in July and August. Every one of the motel-style rooms has a refrigerator and coffeemaker, and efficiency suites have kitchens. Don't feel like cooking? Sit back and have room service delivered. > 1025 Beach Dr., 08204, tel. 609/884-7011 or 800/525-7011, fax 609/884-4559, www.capemayfun.com. 22 rooms, 48 suites. Restaurant, room service, in-room data ports, some kitchenettes, microwaves, refrigerators, cable TV, miniature golf, putting green, pool, wading pool, exercise equipment, hot tub, sauna, Ping-Pong, bar, video game room, laundry facilities, children's programs (ages 3–8), business services, meeting rooms, airport shuttle, free parking, no-smoking rooms. Closed late Oct.–mid-Mar. AE, D, MC, V. EP. **$$**

Mt. Vernon Motel Birders love the Mt. Vernon's location, far-from-the-madding crowd on the western end of Cape May, across from the ocean and within walking distance to Cape May Point Lighthouse and the Nature Conservancy Bird Refuge. The motel is also five blocks from the historic district. All rooms have queen-size beds, wall-to-wall carpeting, and open onto a sundeck. Efficiency units have kitchens. > 1st

Ave. and Beach Dr., 08204, tel. 609/884–4665, www.mtvernonmotel.com. 13 rooms, 12 efficiencies. Restaurant, some kitchenettes, some microwaves, refrigerators, cable TV, pool, wading pool. Closed Nov.–early Apr. No credit cards. EP. **$$–$$$**

Peter Shields Inn White columns rise skyward to the large portico at the entrance of this 1907 Georgian Revival mansion on Cape May's peaceful northern shore. Inside, the wide double staircase in the lobby continues the grandeur. Victorian-era rooms are dressed with massive carved headboards, stuffed chairs, and working fireplaces. Some baths have claw-foot tubs. The restaurant encompasses several different rooms: choose to dine by a large fireplace or on the west sunporch. > 1301 Beach Dr., 08204, tel. 609/884–9090, fax 609/884–9098, www.petershieldsinn.com. 9 rooms. Restaurant, dining room, cable TV, exercise equipment, bicycles; no room phones, no kids under 8, no smoking. AE, D, DC, MC, V. BP. **$$$–$$$$**

The Queen's Hotel The main building housing the Queen's Hotel started life in 1876 as a second-floor gambling parlor with rooms above. Owned by the same people who own the Queen Victoria, rooms are a bit more standardized, but still have the charm of Bradbury and Bradbury wall coverings and elegant wood headboards. In the adjacent building, the two Victorian Lady Rooms are large and romantic, with iron and brass beds and carved-wood antiques. All this and it's just a block from the ocean. > 601 Columbia Ave., 08204, tel. 609/884–1613, fax 609/884–1666, www.queenshotel.com. 8 rooms, 3 suites. Some in-room hot tubs, some microwaves, refrigerators, cable TV, bicycles, business services; no smoking. MC, V. CP. **$$$–$$$$**

Queen Victoria A Victorian B&B that's in two 1880 buildings—Prince Albert Hall and the Queen Victoria—combines the best of two worlds. Although furnishings are antique, and many of the bedrooms have handmade quilts, amenities are modern—310-thread-count sheets, whirlpool tubs, minifridges. For those in search of the peace and quiet of yesteryear, owners will gladly remove the TV from the room. Afternoon tea is served 4–5:30. The ocean is a block away. > 102 Ocean St., 08204, tel. 609/884–8702, fax 609/884–1666, www.queenvictoria.com. 17 rooms, 6 suites. Dining room, fans, some in-room hot tubs, some refrigerators, cable TV, bicycles; no smoking. MC, V. BP. **$$$–$$$$**

The Southern Mansion The stunning Italianate mansion, one of the few large estates to survive Cape May's Great Fire of 1879, now serves as a boutique hotel. Its brightly painted rooms—robin's-egg blue, mustard yellow, deep red—are filled with Victorian antiques, such as ornate fireplace mantels and four-poster beds, as well as modern amenities like phones with data ports. Stroll along the garden path and admire the flowers, especially abundant in May, or visit in December to see the parlors decked out with Christmas trees and garlands appropriate to the Victorian era. > 720 Washington St., 08204, tel. 609/884–7171 or 800/381–3888, fax 609/898–0492, www.southernmansion.net. 24 rooms, 1 suite. Picnic area, room service, in-room data ports, cable TV, massage, business services; no kids under 12, no smoking. AE, D, MC, V. BP. **$$$–$$$$**

Summer Cottage Inn Painted sunflower gold and edged in red, the 1867 Italianate-style inn seems to smile as you enter the gate and approach its veranda ringed by floppy-headed hydrangeas. In every Victorian-dressed room and hallway, a bowl of candy sits on a table. It's an upbeat place, and close to town and beach. > 613 Columbia Ave., 08204, tel. 609/884–4948, www.summercottageinn.com. 9 rooms. Dining room, fans, cable TV in some rooms, piano; no TV in some rooms, no room phones, no children under 14, no smoking. D, MC, V. BP. **$–$$$$**

Virginia Hotel With turndown and room service, a copy of the *New York Times* delivered to your door each morning, and privileges at local golf clubs, the Virginia is a full-service hotel on an intimate scale (24 rooms). Owned by the Congress Hotel group, the Virginia makes a little Victoriana—fringed lamp shades and potted palms—look modern with up-to-date color palettes. Rooms have down comforters and terrycloth bathrobes, as well as Bulgari Parfums soaps and lotions. Its Ebbitt Room Restaurant is one of the town's best. > 25 Jackson St., 08204, tel. 609/884–5700 or 800/732–4236, www.virginiahotel.com. 24 rooms. Restaurant, room service, in-room data ports, some in-room hot tubs, cable TV, in-room VCRs, bar, business services; no-smoking. AE, D, DC, MC, V. CP. **$$$–$$$$**

The Wooden Rabbit An alternative to the elaborate Victorian-style B&Bs in town, the Wooden Rabitt is a cozy, Federal inn (1838). The American antiques decorating the house, such as Windsor chairs, brass chandeliers, and cherrywood four-poster beds have clean lines without undue ornamentation. Handsome Nantucket baskets atop an armoire in the sitting room were woven by Dave McGonigle—he and wife Nancy are the on-site innkeepers. > 609 Hughes St., 08204, tel. 609/884–7293, fax 609/898–0842, www.woodenrabbit.com. 2 rooms, 2 suites. Dining room, in-room VCRs, bicycles; no smoking. MC, V. BP. **$$$–$$$$**

CAMPING

Beachcomber Camping Resort Rent lakefront and wilderness cabins, some with loft spaces, as well as travel trailers sleeping up to six at this 100-acre wooded resort. Ultra-VIP sites (with cable hook-up) are big-rig friendly, and there are plenty of places for smaller RVs and tents. Two spring-fed lakes mean there's one for swimming and one for fishing. The latter is stocked with bass, sunnies, and catfish for catch-and-release fishing. Beachcomber is 4 mi from the Cape May historic district and from Wildwood. > 462M Seashore Rd., 08204, tel. 609/886–6035 or 800/233–0150, fax 609/886–0289, www.beachcombercamp.com. 500 campsites, 50 tent/pop-up sites, 150 RV sites. Flush toilets, full hook-ups, partial hook-ups (electric and water), dump station, drinking water, laundry facilities, showers, fire pits, grills (cabins only), picnic tables, snack bar, electricity, public telephone, general store, ranger station, playground, pool, swimming (lake). Reservations essential in summer. MC, V. Closed Nov.–early Apr. ¢

WHERE TO EAT

Axelsson's Blue Claw Restaurant Head to the waterfront early and catch a Blue Claw martini (gin or vodka, Dry Sack sherry, and flamed orange peel) at the bar. Try the fresh oysters, the blue-claw crab cakes, or the specialty of the house, the fisherman's kettle (a medley of seafood sautéed, sauced, and served in a copper pot) for dinner. > 991 Ocean Dr., tel. 609/884–5878. No lunch. D, DC, MC, V. **$$$**

Black Duck on Sunset Named after a frequent flier in local skies, the Black Duck is in the center of the small town of West Cape May, near the Audubon observatory. White walls, wicker paddle ceiling fans, and black-and-white photos of old Cape May lend an island sensibility. An infusion of Asian and Latin flavors sparks the classic dishes on its contemporary American menu. > 1 Sunset Blvd., West Cape May, tel. 609/898–0100. MC, V. BYOB. No lunch, no dinner Tues. **$$–$$$**

Ebbitt Room White starched tablecloths, sleek ebony chairs, and arching potted palms banish any notion of chaos in the world. At the Ebbitt Room in the Virginia Hotel, the fireplace burns year-round, a pianist plays, and the menu dazzles with contemporary dishes like mushroom-crust tuna seasoned with curry and cilantro. > 25 Jackson St., tel. 609/884–5700. No lunch. AE, D, DC, MC, V. **$$$–$$$$**

410 Bank Street The Cape May newspaper, *Exit Zero,* described Bank Street's cuisine as part Key West, part French Caribbean, part New Orleans. Mesquite-grilled fish steaks, home-smoked cowboy steak, and bayou oyster stew are flavorful stand-outs. Dine on the veranda or in the garden courtyard of the 1850s cottage. > 410 Bank St., tel. 609/884–2127. Closed Nov.–Apr. No lunch. AE, MC, V. $$$–$$$$

Frescos This hot-property, Italian restaurant serves dishes inspired by those of the tables of Tuscany, Venice, and places around the Mediterranean. Try the jumbo crab-meat ravioli appetizer and follow it with linguini and fresh clams. The enclosed porch is the favorite spot to sit and enjoy the wines by the bottle. > 412 Bank St., tel. 609/884–0366. Closed Nov.–Apr. No lunch. AE, MC, V. $$–$$$

Lobster House Its own private fishing fleet delivers fresh sea fare seven days a week to the Lobster House. Cape May salts, a petite and salty oyster, are harvested from the restaurant's beds in Delaware Bay. Dine inside on checked tablecloths, at the raw bar, or outside on the dock for the full maritime show. > Fisherman's Wharf, on Shillenger Landing Rd., tel. 609/884–8296. No lunch Sun. AE, D, MC, V. $$–$$$$

Mad Batter The only thing "mad" about this spot, which is credited with starting Cape May's restaurant renaissance in the 1970s, is the wild popularity of its bountiful American breakfasts and brunches. Be prepared to wait. Or book a table for lunch or dinner. Request the porch to watch the action on Jackson Street and sample the lump crab cakes or the grilled nut-and-honey chicken breast. > Carroll Villa, 19 Jackson St., tel. 609/884–5970, www.madbatter.com. AE, MC, V. Closed Jan. $$–$$$

Union Park An oil painting hangs over the fireplace mantle, wall sconces add soft light, and extravagant bouquets of flowers dress the room. You could be dining at your sophisticated auntie's house circa 1870, but would she have had a chef of the Union Park caliber preparing New American dishes like fennel-seared Chilean sea bass, or pomegranate duckling? The restaurant is in the Hotel Macomber. > 727 Beach Ave., tel. 609/884–8811. BYOB. Closed Jan. and weekdays in Feb. No lunch. AE, MC, V. $$$

Washington Inn Pull out your good shoes and jacket, you're dining in an 1840s Victorian plantation home that's romantic enough for the O'Hara's of Tara. The Washington Inn has five dining areas, one of which is a wine cellar where 10,000 bottles await the uncorking. Start with rock shrimp and lobster bisque, followed by twin fillets of veal. > 801 Washington St., tel. 609/884–5697. Reservations essential. No lunch. AE, D, DC, MC, V. $$–$$$

Water's Edge Only a psychic could have predicted that Cape May's hippest restaurant would be located on the quiet northern shore of Beach Avenue. Peach walls are the backdrop for modern art (for sale), and view-framing windows overlook the ocean. Its oft-praised, inventive American dishes pair the classic with the exotic: grilled loin lamb chops with pesto couscous. Caviar by the ounce—along with iced vodka—makes a gala first course. Breakfast is also served. > Pittsburgh Ave. and Beach Ave., tel. 609/884–1717. Closed Jan.–mid-Feb.; weekdays in Nov. and Dec.; Tues. and Wed. in Oct. and Mar. AE, D, DC, MC, V. $$$–$$$$

ESSENTIALS

Getting Here

Traveling by car gives you freedom of choice—when to leave and where to stop, as well as what you hope is the most time-efficient and comfortable mode of travel. Driving to Cape May is fairly simple: basically you get on the Garden State Parkway (GSP) southbound and take it to the end. If you're staying in town, however, you don't need a car to get around; you can rent a bicycle or walk. From late June to late August, a direct New Jersey Transit bus runs daily to Cape May from Manhattan.

During the peak summer season, do your best to avoid the beach "rush" hours—try not to leave for Cape May on Friday afternoon or Saturday and Sunday mornings, or return Sunday evening.

BY BUS

From late June to late August, a NJ Transit express bus from the Port Authority Terminal in Manhattan to Cape May departs almost hourly. It arrives at the Cape May Transportation Center bus depot. The round-trip fare is about $53; travel time is 3½ to 5 hours.

Within Cape May, the Cape Area Transit bus loops through the town's major attractions; it services downtown, Beach Drive, and the Coast Guard base and marina area, and runs daily from Memorial Day through Labor Day and on weekends in fall. Day passes are $4, and a single ride is $1.

LINES **Greyhound** > Tel. 212/231–2222, www.greyhound.com. **NJ Transit** > Tel. 973/762–5100, 800/772–2222 in NJ, www.njtransit.com.

DEPOTS **Cape May Transportation Center** > 609 Lafayette St., Cape May, tel. 609/884–9562.

BY CAR

The main road serving the Jersey Shore is the GSP, a north–south toll road that ends in Cape May. The frequency of toll plazas and their slowing effect on traffic is a major headache. Having an E-ZPass tag can eliminate waiting in toll-booth lines to toss the coins into the basket. On a more relaxing note, the shore section of the GSP runs through untouched pine barrens and green fields.

From Manhattan, take the Lincoln or Holland tunnel to the New Jersey Turnpike (I–95) southbound. Take Exit 11 to the GSP and continue south to the end of the parkway (approximately 133 mi). Take Route 109 south, cross the Cape May Bridge (no toll), and continue straight, on Lafayette Street, which leads to the center of Cape May.

Visitor Information

The Mid-Atlantic Center for the Arts, a nonprofit organization that promotes preservation of the town's heritage, sponsors many of the towns events and tours. Contact them for information on upcoming festivities. The county and town chambers of commerce both provide visitor packets upon request and can help with lodging.

CONTACTS **Cape May County Chamber of Commerce** > 13 Crest Haven Rd., Cape May Court House, 08210, tel. 609/465–7181, www.capemaycountychamber.com. **Chamber of Commerce of Greater Cape May** > 609 Lafayette St., 08204, tel. 609/884–5508, www.capemaychamber.com. **Mid-Atlantic Center for the Arts** > Emlen Physick Estate, 1048 Washington St., tel. 609/884–5404 or 800/275–4278, www.capemaymac.org.

Atlantic City

125 mi south of New York City

2

Revised by Jeremy Olshan

ATLANTIC CITY IS A TOWN OF FORTUNE WINNERS, losers, and tellers. Chance has always been the game of choice on the hotel-laden streets that inspired Monopoly, even if casino gambling wasn't legalized here until 1978. Some 33 million visitors arrive at this capital of wheeling and blackjack dealing each year, most hoping to leave with their community chests a little fuller.

In its century and a half, Atlantic City has had more highs and lows than the tide, and with an array of development under way, it's poised to reinvent itself yet again. Founded on a barren barrier island in 1854 to provide an escape from the summer heat for Philadelphia's masses, the resort had become the preferred retreat of card-sharps, newlyweds, rumrunners, beauty queens, and mobsters by the early decades of the 20th century. Unlike staid Newport and Cape May, Atlantic City opened its arms to all kinds and classes. Whether you were Joe Millionaire or Joe Six-Pack, there were good times to be had.

Atlantic City arguably invented the weekend getaway. It's also the birthplace of the boardwalk, the Ferris wheel, the amusement pier, saltwater taffy, the picture postcard, and—in what began as a ploy to lure visitors to town after Labor Day—the Miss America Pageant.

Built in 1870 to keep beachgoers from tracking sand into the hotels, the Boardwalk became a showcase for all manner of ballyhoo, from the famous diving-horse show on the Steel Pier to performances by entertainers like Frank Sinatra to absurdities such as the world's largest typewriter and tire. Visitors continue to pay for the privilege of being pushed up and down the Boardwalk in wicker rolling chairs, past the mishmash of fortune-tellers, souvenir shops, casinos, and beach bars.

By the 1960s cheap air travel to more-exotic destinations left the city nearly forgotten. The legalization of gambling and the opening of Resorts Casino Hotel in 1978 revitalized the resort, although many of its once grand hotels were demolished. The casinos were a tremendous success, even if the resort never became the "Monte Carlo at the Jersey Shore" that some of gambling's early proponents envisioned.

In an effort to compete with the growing scale and glitz of Las Vegas's leisure palaces as well as the opening of casinos in Connecticut, Atlantic City is experiencing a third major wave of development, which began with the opening of the Borgata hotel–casino in 2003, and is adding new retail and entertainment venues and other noncasino attractions.

You don't need to step into a casino to enjoy the area, though; you can get a dose of wildlife at the Edwin B. Forsythe National Wildlife Refuge in Brigantine, or golf at one of the area's dozen or so courses. The region is also home to the Marine Mammal Stranding Center and Sea Life Museum, which rescues and returns stranded marine animals to their natural environments; the Ocean Life Center at Gardner's Basin; and the Wetlands Institute near Stone Harbor. And, aside from the all-night drinking and gambling, the attraction that first put the resort onto the map continues to be one of its most popular: the beach.

The Visitor Welcome Center, about 1 mi east of the toll plaza on the Atlantic City Expressway, has information about the Boardwalk attractions, Historic Gardner's Basin, the Historic Village of Smithville, the national wildlife refuge, and other activities within a short drive of "America's Favorite Playground."

WHAT TO SEE & DO

Absecon Lighthouse The 1857 lighthouse was designed by George Meade, stands 171 feet tall, and is the oldest man-made tourist attraction on the Jersey shore. You can tour the adjacent lightkeeper's house and climb to the top for a great view of Atlantic City. In winter, call ahead to check that the lighthouse is open. > Pacific and Rhode Island Aves., tel. 609/449–1360, www.absewonlighthouse.org. $4. Early Sept.–June, Thurs.–Mon. 11–4; July and Aug. daily 10–5.

Boardwalk Part thoroughfare, part three-ring circus, the Boardwalk is center stage for every imaginable oddity. Conceived in 1870 as a way to allow Victorian-era visitors to experience nature without getting sand in their shoes, the Boardwalk became *the* place to see or be seen. Named for Alexander Boardman, the promenade's inventor—and not as you might think, for its wooden boards—the 4-mi-long Boardwalk begins in Atlantic City's Inlet section (at Maine Avenue), and heads south into neighboring Ventnor, where it continues for another 1½ mi (to Jackson Avenue). Saltwater taffy was invented on the Boardwalk in 1883, as legend has it, when a storm flooded a candy dealer's wares. The Boardwalk's attractions include amusement piers, museums, arcades, bars, restaurants, carnival games, and miniature golf. The **Steel Pier,** which once hosted the best music acts of the day as well as the famed diving-horse show, is now home to rides and carnival games. On the **Central Pier** you can ride go-carts or fire paintball rounds at human targets. Aside from strolling up and down the boards, the traditional way to experience the Boardwalk is to be pushed in a rolling chair. These wicker chairs evolved from the wheelchairs that infirm visitors used back when the city's promoters' claimed the salty ocean air could cure all diseases. Despite medical evidence to the contrary, after a long stroll on the Boardwalk, you might have to agree.

Boardwalk Hall The 456-foot-long, 310-foot-wide, and 137-foot-tall architectural wonder was once the largest open-air space in the world. Opened in 1929, the main hall has hosted the Miss American Pageant since 1940 and is now also home to the Boardwalk Bullies, the city's minor-league ice-hockey team. It's also the city's largest venue for concerts and other events and it houses the world's largest pipe organ. > 2301 Boardwalk, between Mississippi and Florida Aves., tel. 609/348–7000, www.boardwalkhall.com.

Garden Pier A spot of culture in Atlantic City, the Garden Pier is home to both the **Atlantic City Historical Museum** and the **Atlantic City Art Center.** With its vast collection of photographs and kitschy memorabilia, the museum tells the story of the resort's rise from barren sand dune to "Queen of Resorts." The art center houses galleries and regularly hosts concerts and readings. > Boardwalk and New Jersey Ave., tel. 609/347–5844. Free. Daily 10–4.

Gardner's Basin Once a home to pirates, privateers, and whalers, this site is now a restored maritime village and waterfront park complete with historic vessels, a museum, and two restaurants. The **Ocean Life Center** (www.oceanlifecenter.com) is an interactive facility with 10 themed exhibits and eight aquariums. > 800 N. New Hampshire Ave., tel. 609/348–2880. $7. Daily 10–5.

Ripley's Believe It or Not! Museum Occupying a building that seems ready for the wrecking ball, this showcase of absurdities and its Odditorium fit right into the Boardwalk scene. However, as one chair pusher put it, "Believe it or not, it costs 10 bucks to get in there." > 1441 Boardwalk, at New York Ave., tel. 609/347–2001, www.ripleys.com. $10.95. Memorial Day–Labor Day, daily 10–10; rest of yr, weekdays 11–5, weekends 10–8.

THE CASINOS

Atlantic City Hilton The Hilton, on the south end of the casino district, is staid and sane as casinos go. The 60,000-square-foot gaming space, with Italian marble and scenic murals, isn't as flashy as its cousins and actually aims for elegance. > Boston and Pacific Aves., tel. 609/347–7111 or 800/257–8677, www.hiltonac.com.

Bally's Atlantic City When you land at Park Place and the Boardwalk you know you're standing on prime real estate. The property, which includes the historic 1860 Dennis Hotel, is actually several casinos in one. Bally's has a six-story-high escalator, twin waterfalls, and tropical plants. The attached **Wild Wild West Casino** is a themed frontier town with 17 animatronic prospectors and other sordid characters. The casino also has 12 restaurants and 2 lounges. In 2002 Bally's merged with the Claridge Casino Hotel, which occupies one of the few grand old hotels left from the city's heyday. > Park Pl. and Boardwalk, tel. 609/340–2000, www.ballysac.com.

Borgata Hotel Casino & Spa Parker Brothers may have to rejigger the Monopoly board to reflect this newcomer. The hottest property in town is now not on the Boardwalk but in the Marina district, way on the other side of the city. The $1.1 billion casino-hotel, the first addition to Atlantic City since 1990, exists on a scale more akin to Las Vegas than anything in these parts. Glitzy yet trendy, Borgata encompasses a 125,000-square-foot casino and 3,650 coinless slot machines. The architecture and interior design, a blend of modern elements and old-Italy motifs, combined with Borgata's big-name restaurants and clubs pull in a younger crowd (on average) than the other area casinos. > 1 Borgata Way, tel. 609/317–1000, www.theborgata.com.

Caesars Atlantic City Hotel/Casino Where else can you see a replica of Michelangelo's *David* surrounded by slot machines? Caesar's invented the theme casino, and here as in Las Vegas it continues to be a pantheon of gaudiness. In the main lobby and the Temple Bar, the ceiling is a faux night sky, and Caesar and Cleopatra themselves make regular appearances. There are few low-stakes tables in this high-rolling 125,000-square-foot Roman empire. > 2100 Pacific Ave., tel. 609/348–4411, www.caesarsac.com.

Harrah's Atlantic City Casino Hotel Off in the Marina District, near the Borgata and Trump Marina, Harrah's has a distinct, perhaps mellow, vibe compared with the other casinos in town. It's known as a haven for slot players. The hotel also has seven restaurants, several shops, and a large theater. > 777 Harrah's Blvd., tel. 609/441–5000, www.harrahs.com.

Resorts Atlantic City When it opened in 1978, Resorts was Atlantic City's first casino and, for a time, the world's most profitable. A remnant of the city's grand hotels, Resorts has a classy, understated art-deco style. At this writing, extensive renovations and a new hotel tower were in the works. > 1133 Boardwalk, tel. 609/344–6000, www.resortsac.com.

Sands Casino Hotel If you're looking for lower stakes tables in Atlantic City, the Sands is a good bet. Known for affordable options like the Epic Buffet, the property has fewer frills and offers cheaper thrills than some of its competitors. The location, in the heart of the casino district on the Boardwalk, is prime, however. The Copa Lounge is a classic venue for singers, bandleaders, and other acts. At this writing, plans to expand the gambling and entertainment space were under way. > Indiana Ave. and Brighton Park, tel. 800/227–2637, www.acsands.com.

Showboat Atlantic City Filled with hypercolor murals that offer no place for weary eyes to rest, the Showboat spins the Mardi Gras theme into an almost psychedelic experience. Instead of big-name acts, New Orleans jazz bands and other performers constantly troll the casino. The northernmost casino on the Boardwalk, the Showboat is just south of the Garden Pier. > Delaware Ave. and Boardwalk, tel. 609/343–4000, www.harrahs.com.

Tropicana Casino The house may always win, but this casino takes risks and doesn't take itself too seriously. Where else can you play tic-tac-toe against a live chicken or win the chance to spend 60 seconds in the Fortune Dome, in which thousands of dollars blow about as you scramble to catch as many bills as you can. The casino also has one of the better poker rooms in Atlantic City. At this writing, the Tropicana plans to open the Quarter—a retail-and-entertainment complex with restaurants and an IMAX theater—by 2005. > Brighton Ave. and Boardwalk, tel. 609/340–4000, www.tropicana.net.

Trump Marina Hotel Casino On the outside Trump Marina looks outmoded, but the casino successfully markets itself toward a younger crowd, with the bars and clubs it offers and the big-name rock bands it books. The hotel runs the adjacent state marina and is one of the only casinos in town you can arrive by yacht. > Huron Ave. and Brigantine Blvd., tel. 609/441–2000 or 800/365–8786, www.trumpmarina.com.

Trump Plaza Hotel and Casino Elegant, and understated by Trump standards, the Plaza attracts higher-end bettors but does offer some lower-stakes tables. Its prime location, at the center of the Boardwalk and at the mouth of the Atlantic City Expressway, makes the hotel a great base for casino hopping. > Mississippi Ave. and Boardwalk, tel. 609/441–6000, www.trumpplaza.com.

Trump Taj Mahal Casino Resort With its huge chandeliers and elephant motif, the Taj is, without question, the most over-the-top, outrageous, and gaudy property in Atlantic City. The sprawling casino has the area's most popular poker room and nightlife options such as the Casbah and Xanadu dance clubs. The casino is also directly across from the Steel Pier. > 1000 Boardwalk, at Virginia Ave., tel. 609/449–1000 or 800/825–8786, www.trumptaj.com.

WHAT'S NEARBY

Edwin B. Forsythe National Wildlife Refuge, Brigantine Division Nearly 40,000 acres of coastal habitats—including 3,000 acres of woodland—are protected in this refuge. Peregrine falcons and bald eagles are among the winged visitors. You can take an 8-mi wildlife drive, or walk the Leeds Eco-Trail, a ½-mi loop through salt marsh and woodlands, or the Akers Woodland Trail, an easy ¼ quarter mi. To get here from Atlantic City, head west on U.S. 30, then right on U.S. 9. After about 5 mi, make a right onto Great Creek Road. > Great Creek Rd. and U.S. 9, Oceanville, tel. 609/652–1665, http://forsythe.fws.gov. $4 per vehicle. Daily dawn–dusk.

Historic Town of Smithville This enclave of restaurants and shops specializing in Early American antiques is centered on the 1787 Smithville Inn. Special events are held throughout the year. To get here from Atlantic City, take the Atlantic City Expressway to northbound U.S. 9. > 615 Moss Mill Rd., Smithville, tel. 609/652–4040. Free.

Lucy, the Margate Elephant Built in 1881 as a publicity stunt to sell real estate in what was then known as "South Atlantic City," Lucy is a 6-story-tall, 90-ton elephant. Before being designated a National Historic Landmark, this palatial pachyderm even had a stint as a hotel. You can tour the elephant's innards and climb to the top of its howdah for a view of the ocean. The elephant is 3 mi south of Atlantic City. > 9200 Atlantic Ave., at Decatur Ave., Margate, tel. 609/823–6473, www.lucytheelephant.org. $4. Apr.–mid-June, weekends 10–4; mid-June–Labor Day, Mon.–Thurs. 10–8, Fri. and Sat. 10–5.

Marine Mammal Stranding Center and Museum The center is on call to rescue stranded dolphins, seals, sea turtles, and whales that travel up this way and into New York Harbor. Museum exhibits relate to marine life. To get here from Atlantic City, cross the Brigantine Bridge to Atlantic-Brigantine Boulevard. > 3625 Atlantic-Brigantine Blvd., tel. 609/266–0538, www.mmsc.org. $1 suggested donation. Memorial Day–Labor Day, daily 11–5; rest of yr, weekends noon–4.

Noyes Museum A small showcase for the arts of southern New Jersey, the museum exhibits contemporary American and folk art, crafts, and a superb bird-decoy collection. To get here from Atlantic City take U.S. 30 west to northbound U.S. 9 and proceed through Absecon for about 4½ mi to Lily Lake Road. > Lily Lake Rd., Oceanville, tel. 609/652–8848, www.noyesmuseum.org. $3. Wed.–Sun. 11–4.

Renault Winery Established in 1864, Renault is the oldest vineyard in the United States. It has, along with tours, tastings, and a museum, an elegant restaurant and a wine café. To get here from Atlantic City head west on U.S. 30 for approximately 16 mi, then turn right on North Bremen Avenue. > 72 N. Bremen Ave., Egg Harbor City, tel. 609/965–2111, www.renaultwinery.com. $2. Weekdays 11–4, Sat. 11–8, Sun. noon–4.

Storybook Land The 20-acre theme park, about 10 mi west of Atlantic City, has 50 larger-than-life buildings and displays illustrating the tales of popular childhood stories—perfect for the under-eight set. There are also rides and a picnic area. Santa takes residence in mid-November. > 6415 Black Horse Pike, Egg Harbor Township, tel. 609/641–7847 or 609/646–0103, www.storybookland.com. $14.95. Apr., weekends 11–5; May and June weekends 11–5, weekdays 11–3; July and Aug., daily 10–5:30; Sept. and Oct. weekends 11–5, Thurs. and Fri. 10–3; call for hrs for rest of yr.

Tours

Atlantic City Cruises From morning cruises to moonlight dance parties, these voyages combine great views of the city's skyline from the ocean and bay as well as a little history. Departing from Gardner's Basin, the line runs half a dozen hour-long cruises throughout the day, from May through October, starting at 10:30 AM. > 800 N. New Hampshire Ave., tel. 609/347–7600, www.atlanticcitycruises.com. $15–$20.

Atlantic City Jitney Jitneys have been an Atlantic City tradition since 1915. (*Jitney* is slang for a nickel, the original cost of a ride.) The jitneys cover most of the 48-block city, including landmarks such as the Absecon Lighthouse, Gardner's Basin, and the Convention Center, and run round the clock. > 201 Pacific Ave., tel. 609/344–8642, www.virtualac.com/jitney. $1.50.

Sports

BASEBALL

Atlantic City Surf The city's minor-league team has called the 5,900-seat Sandcastle stadium home since 1998. The season runs mid-May to mid-September. > 545 N. Albany Ave., Atlantic City, tel. 609/344–8873, www.acsurf.com.

GOLF

Greater Atlantic City Golf Association A coalition of area golf courses and hotels, the group offers local stay-and-play packages. > 1742 Mays Landing, Egg Harbor Township, tel. 800/465–3222, www.gacga.com.

Harbor Pines Golf Club The five sets of tees here have great views and 17 acres of water. The course winds through 520 acres of dense pine forest with most holes so private you feel you're playing on your own estate. Greens fees are $70. > 500 St. Andrews Dr., Egg Harbor Township, tel. 609/927–0006, www.harborpines.com.

The Links at Brigantine Beach Right over the Brigantine Bridge, the 18-hole, par-72 course is just a long putt away from the casinos. The links-style course has ocean views and a flat, nearly treeless terrain. Greens fees are $35. > 1075 North Shore Dr., off Roosevelt Blvd., Brigantine, tel. 609/266–1388 or 800/698–1388, www.brigantinegolf.com.

Seaview Marriott Resort & Spa The resort has two 18-hole, par-71 championship courses: the 6,247-yard Bay Course, which has Atlantic City–skyline views, and the 6,731-yard, parkland-set Pines Course. Greens fees are $49–$129. > 401 S. New York Rd., Galloway Township, tel. 609/652–1800, www.seaviewgolf.com.

ShopRite LPGA Classic The only Ladies Professional Golf Association (LPGA) event played in New Jersey takes place at the Seaview Resort in Absecon in late June. > Seaview Marriott Resort & Spa, 401 S. New York Rd., Absecon, tel. 609/383–8330, www.shopritelpga.org.

HOCKEY

Boardwalk Bullies The city's minor-league hockey team plays in Boardwalk Hall. Even if you're not a hockey fan, it's worth a trip to sit in the renovated 1929 venue, home of the Miss America pageant. The season runs from October to early April. > 2301 Boardwalk, between Mississippi and Florida Aves., Atlantic City, tel. 609/348–7825, www.boardwalkbullies.com.

Save the Date

MARCH

Atlantique City Spring Festival Covering 10½ acres of floor space in Atlantic City's Convention Center, this is the world's largest indoor antiques-and-collectibles show, with dealers from around the country and overseas. A fall festival is held the third week in October. > Tel. 800/526–2724, www.atlantiquecity.com.

JUNE

NJ Fresh Seafood Festival Held the second weekend of June in Gardner's Basin, the festival includes seafood samples, live music, and amusement games and rides. > Tel. 609/347–4386, www.njseafoodfest.com.

Spring Fling, Chevy Thing Antique Chevrolets are on display in Historic Smithville during this one-day event, which includes food and entertainment. It's usually held on a Saturday or Sunday in the middle of the month. > U.S. 9 and Moss Mill Rd., Smithville, tel. 609/748–6160 or 215/321–8835, www.smithvillenj.com.

AUGUST

Wedding of the Sea The local Catholic tradition, commemorating the Bible's story of the appearance of the Virgin Mary to the fishermen of Venice and always celebrated on August 15, regularly draws 10,000 faithful to the Atlantic City Boardwalk. The bishop of the Diocese of Camden leads his choir down to the water, where he tosses a wreath into the ocean, symbolizing the marriage of the city and the sea. > Tel. 609/344–8536.

SEPTEMBER
Festival Latino-Americano Celebrate Hispanic culture in Gardner's Basin with enter-tainment, dancing, food, and crafts. This festival is usually held on the second weekend in September. > Tel. Hispanic Alliance of Atlantic County 609/822–8584, www.haac.org.

SEPTEMBER–OCTOBER
Miss America Week and Pageant Held at Boardwalk Hall, this event is more than just pretty faces on the big televised night; the whirlwind week of activities includes the Miss America Parade. > Tel. 609/344–5278, www.missamerica.org.

OCTOBER
Atlantique City Fall Festival The third weekend in October, the Atlantic City Conven-tion Center hosts this huge antiques-and-collectibles show, which is also held on the last weekend in March. > Tel. 800/526–2724, www.atlantiquecity.com.

WHERE TO STAY

Atlantic City–Boardwalk Days Inn The oceanfront motel has sweeping water views and beach access. It's adjacent to the Tropicana Casino and an easy walk to several other casinos. The pool has a great view of the ocean. > Boardwalk and Morris Ave., 08401, tel. 609/344–6101 or 800/544–8313, fax 609/348–5335, www.daysinn.com or www.atlanticcitydaysinn.com. 105 rooms. Restaurant, room service, in-room data ports, cable TV, pool, bar, free parking, no-smoking floors. AE, D, MC, V. EP. $–$$
Atlantic City Hilton Rooms at this Boardwalk property are bright, airy, and unclut-tered; many have ocean views. The hotel has a fun beach bar on the Boardwalk; the highly regarded Peregrines' restaurant; several casual and fancy eateries; and a spa. The theater here presents major musical acts such as Daryl Hall and John Oates, Tr-isha Yearwood, and Kenny Rogers. > Boston and Pacific Aves., 08401, tel. 609/347–7111 or 800/257–8677, fax 609/340–4858, www.hiltonac.com. 804 rooms, 200 suites. 6 restaurants, coffee shop, room service, cable TV, golf privileges, indoor pool, health club, hair salon, hot tub, massage, sauna, spa, steam room, bar, concert hall, shops, laundry service, business services, meeting rooms, parking (fee), no-smoking rooms. AE, D, DC, MC, V. EP. $$–$$$$
Atlantic City's Howard Johnson Hotel The oceanfront hotel is steps from the Boardwalk, next to Tropicana Casino, and two blocks from the Atlantic City Hilton. Many rooms have balconies. > Chelsea Ave. and Boardwalk, 08401, tel. 800/695–4685, fax 609/344–0878, www.hojoboardwalk.com. 121 rooms. Restaurant, in-room safes, cable TV, indoor pool, gym, hot tub, sauna, bar, video game room, laundry service, business services, meeting rooms, free parking, no-smoking rooms. AE, D, MC, V. EP. $–$$$
Bally's Atlantic City Rooms come in a variety of styles at this beachfront property: the main building, the 1860 Dennis Hotel, incorporates traditional and contemporary interior schemes; Claridge Tower rooms are bright and airy; and Bally's Tower rooms echo art deco. The spa facilities, with a multitiered complex of mosaic-tile whirlpools and an atrium pool with water-aerobics classes, are exceptional. > Boardwalk at Park Pl., 08401, tel. 609/340–2000 or 800/225–5977, fax 609/340–4713, www.ballysac.com. 1,753 rooms, 100 suites. 21 restaurants, room service, some refrig-erators, cable TV, golf privileges, 2 pools (1 indoor), health club, hair salon, hot tub, sauna, spa, steam room, bar, casino, dry cleaning, laundry service, business services, meeting rooms, parking (fee), no-smoking rooms. AE, D, DC, MC, V. EP. $$–$$$$
Borgata Hotel Casino & Spa The Borgata has raised the bar in Atlantic City. Floor-to-ceiling windows and oh-so-tasteful furnishings grace the standard rooms, which

are large and have a spacious bathroom with a shower for two. Suites all have entertainment centers, wet bars, and bathrooms with deep tubs and his-and-her vanity sets. The spa here is the biggest in Atlantic City, and the restaurants include Suilan by Susanna Foo (the famed Philly restaurateur) and an outpost of New York City's Old Homestead steak house. > One Borgata Way, 08401, tel. 609/317–1000 or 866/692–6742, fax 609/317–1100, www.theborgata.com. 2,002 rooms, 402 suites. 11 restaurants, room service, in-room data ports, some minibars, cable TV, pool, gym, hair salon, hot tub, spa, 2 bars, casino, comedy club, concert hall, nightclub, theater, shops, dry cleaning, laundry service, concierge, meeting rooms, parking (fee), no-smoking rooms. AE, D, MC, V. EP. **$$$$**

Caesars Atlantic City Hotel/Casino The numbers at this beachfront property are impressive: 120,231 square feet; 1,138 rooms; 24 casinos; 3,595 slot machines; a theater seating 1,100 that offers "world-class entertainment"; and on and on. Rooms are luxurious and many have breathtaking ocean views. > 2100 Pacific Ave., 08401, tel. 609/348–4411 or 800/443–0104, fax 609/347–8089, www.caesars.com. 1,144 rooms, 186 suites. 11 restaurants, room service, in-room data ports, cable TV, golf privileges, pool, health club, hair salon, hot tub, spa, steam room, 4 bars, piano bar, casino, concert hall, shops, dry cleaning, laundry service, concierge, concierge floor, business services, meeting rooms, parking (fee), no-smoking rooms. AE, D, DC, MC, V. EP. **$$–$$$$**

Comfort Inn–Boardwalk The beach and the casinos are 100 yards from this Comfort Inn. Smaller than many other area hotels, it prides itself on offering personal attention to its guests. Each room has a Jacuzzi tub for two. > 154 S. Kentucky Ave., 08401, tel. 609/348–4000, fax 609/348–0072, www.comfortinn.com. 80 rooms. In-room data ports, in-room hot tubs, some microwaves, some refrigerators, cable TV, laundry facilities, free parking, no-smoking rooms. AE, D, DC, MC, V. CP. **¢–$**

Flagship Resort The modern, 32-story, all-suites condo hotel across from the Boardwalk offers respite from the casino action and faces the island of Brigantine and the Absecon Inlet. Each suite has a private balcony (some have Boardwalk and water views) and a wet bar. > 60 N. Main Ave., 08401, tel. 609/343–7447 or 800/647–7890, fax 609/343–1608, www.flagshipresort.com. 300 suites. Restaurant, some kitchenettes, microwaves, refrigerators, cable TV, indoor pool, health club, hot tub, billiards, video game room, laundry facilities, free parking, no-smoking rooms. AE, D, MC, V. CP. **$$–$$$**

Harrah's Atlantic City Casino Hotel In the marina district, this 16-story, four-tower property has rooms with high ceilings, elegant wood furniture, and tasteful fabric flourishes. The hotel features live entertainment, including top Broadway productions and celebrity vocalists. > 777 Harrah's Blvd., 08401, tel. 609/441–5000 or 800/242–7724, fax 609/348–6057, www.harrahs.com. 1,622 rooms, 60 suites. 6 restaurants, coffee shop, room service, cable TV, pool, health club, hair salon, paddle tennis, shuffleboard, bar, casino, shops, dry cleaning, laundry facilities, meeting rooms, parking (fee), no-smoking rooms. AE, D, DC, MC, V. EP. **$$–$$$$**

Holiday Inn–Boardwalk The hotel, in the city's central business district, overlooks the Boardwalk and the beach, and many guest rooms have ocean views. > Chelsea Ave. and Boardwalk, 08401, tel. 609/348–2200, fax 609/348–0168, www.holiday-inn.com. 216 rooms, 4 suites. Restaurant, in-room data ports, cable TV, pool, bar, dry cleaning, laundry facilities, Internet, business services, free parking, no-smoking rooms. AE, D, DC, MC, V. EP. **¢–$$$**

Quality Inn Atlantic City One of Atlantic City's best lodging values is half a block from the Boardwalk and has a 17-story modern guest wing above a Federal-style base. Handsome Colonial reproductions furnish rooms. > S. Carolina and Pacific Aves., 08401, tel. 609/345–7070 or 800/356–6044, fax 609/345–0633, www.qualityinnatlanticcity.com.

199 rooms, 4 suites. Restaurant, in-room data ports, some in-room hot tubs, some minibars, cable TV, video game room, laundry facilities, meeting rooms, free parking, no-smoking rooms. AE, D, DC, MC, V. CP. $$–$$$

Sheraton Atlantic City Convention Center Hotel The 16-story art-deco hotel, connected to the convention center by an enclosed walkway, showcases Miss America Pageant memorabilia in display windows. A grand circular staircase leads to the Miss America–theme Shoe Bar as well as restaurants and meeting rooms. Rooms are available with both city and bay views. > 2 Ocean Way, 08401, tel. 609/344–3535 or 800/325–3535, fax 609/348–4336, www.sheraton.com. 482 rooms, 20 suites. Restaurant, room service, in-room data ports, in-room safes, cable TV, pool, gym, outdoor hot tub, spa, bar, shop, concierge, concierge floor, business services, convention center, parking (fee), some pets allowed, no-smoking rooms. AE, D, MC, V. EP. $$$

Tropicana Casino Bright colors mix with bold patterns in some rooms and subdued prints in others. Some rooms have water views. The atmosphere here is slightly frantic and sometimes chaotic, but the hotel offers a few escapes from the busy casino scene, such as the 20th-floor Top of the Trop bar and a stand-up comedy club. > Brighton Ave. and Boardwalk, 08401, tel. 609/340–4000 or 800/257–6227, fax 609/343–5211, www.tropicana.net. 1,283 rooms, 342 suites. 5 restaurants, room service, in-room data ports, cable TV, 2 pools (1 indoor), health club, hair salon, hot tub, massage, 2 bars, casino, comedy club, concert hall, shops, dry cleaning, laundry service, business services, meeting rooms, parking (fee), no-smoking floors. AE, D, MC, V. EP. $$$–$$$$

Trump Marina Hotel Casino With helicopter service and the state's largest marina at its disposal, the hotel caters to a sophisticated clientele. Luxurious touches include marble and mahogany trim, crystal chandeliers, and plush carpeting. The hotel hosts major sporting and entertainment events. > Huron Ave. and Brigantine Blvd., 08401, tel. 609/441–2000 or 800/777–8477, fax 609/345–7604, www.trumpmarina.com. 728 rooms, 57 suites. 8 restaurants, room service, in-room data ports, some in-room hot tubs, cable TV with movies, in-room VCRs, 2 tennis courts, pool, wading pool, gym, hair salon, hot tub, massage, basketball, 2 bars, casino, concert hall, nightclub, showroom, shops, dry cleaning, laundry service, business services, meeting rooms, parking (fee), no-smoking rooms. AE, D, DC, MC, V. EP. $$–$$$$

Trump Plaza Hotel and Casino Visible from anywhere in town, this white tower is the first hotel at the mouth of the expressway. It's close to trains and buses and right on the Boardwalk. Ultramodern guest rooms have lots of mirrors, and suites have jet tubs. One side of the hotel overlooks the ocean; the other overlooks the city. > Mississippi Ave. and Boardwalk, 08401, tel. 609/441–6000 or 800/677–7378, fax 609/441–2603, www.trumpplaza.com. 904 rooms, 142 suites. 12 restaurants, room service, in-room data ports, some in-room hot tubs, some refrigerators, cable TV with movies, 2 tennis courts, pool, gym, hair salon, hot tub, massage, shuffleboard, 3 bars, casino, shops, dry cleaning, laundry service, business services, meeting rooms, parking (fee), no-smoking rooms. AE, D, DC, MC, V. EP. $$$–$$$$

Trump Taj Mahal Casino Resort The extravagantly decorated, over-the-top Taj has rooms overlooking the ocean or the city, and suites with master bedrooms, living rooms, dining areas, and hot tubs. > 1000 Boardwalk, 08401, tel. 609/449–1000 or 800/825–8786, fax 609/449–6818, www.trumptaj.com. 980 rooms, 224 suites. 7 restaurants, coffee shop, pizzeria, room service, some in-room hot tubs, some minibars, some refrigerators, cable TV, indoor pool, gym, hair salon, hot tub, massage, steam room, bicycles, 3 bars, lounge, casino, concert hall, nightclub, showroom, shops, dry cleaning, laundry service, concierge floor, business services, convention center, parking (fee), no-smoking rooms. AE, D, DC, MC, V. EP. $$$$

WHAT'S NEARBY

Clarion Bayside Resort The two-story bayfront complex is 2 mi from the casinos and loaded with amenities. Rooms overlook either the pool, the bay, or the Atlantic City skyline. The golf shop offers packages to nine area courses, along with free shuttle service. > 8029 Black Horse Pike, West Atlantic City 08232, tel. 609/641–3546 or 800/999–9466, fax 609/641–4329, www.clarionac.com. 110 rooms. Restaurant, room service, in-room data ports, in-room safes, some microwaves, some refrigerators, cable TV with movies, golf privileges, 6 tennis courts, pro shop, pool, wading pool, gym, massage, sauna, billiards, bar, shop, laundry facilities, Internet, business services, meeting rooms, airport shuttle, free parking, no-smoking rooms. AE, D, DC, MC, V. ¢–$$

Comfort Inn–North About 3 mi northeast of Atlantic City's Boardwalk, this seven-story hotel is convenient to the casinos but less expensive than the beachfront hotels. Some rooms have views of the city skyline. > 539 E. Absecon Blvd., Absecon 08201, tel. 609/641–7272, fax 609/641–1239, www.comfortinn.com. 205 rooms, 2 suites. In-room data ports, some refrigerators, cable TV, exercise equipment, business services, meeting rooms, free parking, no-smoking rooms. AE, D, DC, MC, V. CP. ¢–$$

Fairfield Inn by Marriott This comfortable chain hotel is about 5 mi from the beach and casinos and offers free weekend shuttle service to the Tropicana Casino. Some rooms have city-skyline views. To get here from Atlantic City, head west on U.S. 30. > 405 E. Absecon Blvd., Absecon 08201, tel. 609/646–5000, fax 609/383–8744, www.fairfieldinn.com. 200 rooms. In-room data ports, some refrigerators, cable TV with video games, pool, laundry service, business services, meeting rooms, free parking, no-smoking rooms. AE, D, DC, MC, V. CP. $–$$

Hampton Inn On U.S. 30 in Absecon, the inn is 4 mi from the Atlantic City International Airport and fewer than 10 mi from many area attractions, including the Boardwalk and casinos. Rooms, from singles to king-deluxe configurations, are furnished with antique reproductions and subdued colors. > 240 E. White Horse Pike, Absecon 08201, tel. 609/652–2500, fax 609/652–2212, www.hamptoninn.com. 129 rooms. Restaurant, in-room data ports, cable TV, pool, hot tub, laundry facilities, business services, airport shuttle, free parking, no-smoking rooms. AE, D, DC, MC, V. CP. ¢–$$

Seaview Marriott Resort & Spa If the 670-acre property has a country-club feel to it, that's because it got its start in 1914 as the Seaview Country Club and offers such refined diversions as golf and tennis. Rooms, a classy blend of traditional fabrics and wood furniture, avoid going overboard with frills. The spa is an Elizabeth Arden Red Door facility. > 401 S. New York Rd., Galloway Township 08205, tel. 609/652–1800, www.seaviewgolf.com. 260 rooms, 37 suites. 2 restaurants, room service, in-room data ports, minibars, cable TV with movies and video games, 2 18-hole golf courses, 6 tennis courts, pro shop, 2 pools (1 indoor), health club, sauna, spa, steam room, lobby lounge, recreation room, business services, meeting rooms, no-smoking rooms. EP. $$$

WHERE TO EAT

Angeloni's In the traditionally Italian Ducktown section of Atlantic City, this restaurant serves family-style beef, veal, and seafood dishes. The *braciole* (rolled veal stuffed with sausage and cheese) is popular. The Italian restaurant's wine list is extensive. > 2400 Arctic Ave., tel. 609/344–7875. AE, D, DC, MC, V. $–$$$

Angelo's Fairmount Tavern Locals flock to this unassuming Ducktown favorite, decorated with New York Yankees and other sports memorabilia. Open since 1935, the restaurant is known for Italian standards as well as steaks and seafood. > 2300 Fairmount Ave., tel. 609/344–2439. AE, D, MC, V. No lunch weekends. **$–$$$**

Brighton Steakhouse Lots of dark wood and leather help to create a subdued atmosphere at this classic steak house in the Sands Casino Hotel. The chateaubriand for two gets many orders, as do lobster and shrimp dishes. Six different desserts are offered each month, along with 21 wines by the glass. Call for hours, which change monthly. > Sands Casino Hotel, Indiana Ave. and Brighton Park, tel. 609/441–4300. AE, D, DC, MC, V. **$$–$$$$**

Chef Vola's Small, intimate, and exclusive, this Italian restaurant draws many regulars. The steak, veal, and homemade pasta dishes earn high marks, as does the service. > 111 S. Albion Pl., tel. 609/345–2022. Reservations essential. No credit cards. Closed Mon. No lunch. **$$–$$$$**

Dock's Oyster House Owned and operated by the Dougherty family since 1897, the city's oldest restaurant serves seafood in a setting of wood and stained glass engraved with nautical scenes. Try the pan-seared ahi tuna and fresh soft-shell crab. A children's menu is available. > 2405 Atlantic Ave., tel. 609/345–0092. AE, DC, MC, V. Closed Dec. and Jan. No lunch Mon. **$$–$$$$**

Grabel's The restaurant is known for standards such as veal chops, steak, jumbo shrimp, and crab cakes. Between courses you can hit the large dance floor. A piano bar is part of the scene Thursday through Sunday. Kids get their own menu. > 3901 Atlantic Ave., tel. 609/344–9263. AE, DC, MC, V. No lunch. **$–$$$**

Irish Pub and Inn Enjoy live Irish music nightly at this informal spot serving pub fare such as corned-beef sandwiches, turkey dinners, and beef stew. The $1.95 lunch special is one of the city's great bargains. The bar is open 24 hours, and you can order dinner until 7:30 AM. > 164 St. James Pl., tel. 609/344–9063. No credit cards. **¢**

Knife and Fork Inn The historic Flemish building that holds this restaurant started as a private gentlemen's club in 1912 and in 1927 was sold to the Latz family, which still owns it. Seafood, from bouillabaisse and crab cakes to lobster preparations—shines here, and filet mignon satisfies landlubbers. > 29 S. Albany Ave., tel. 609/344–1133. AE, D, DC, MC, V. **$$–$$$$**

Le Grand Fromage The French bistro serves updates of classics like steak frites and veal Oscar (asparagus, crab meat, and hollandaise sauce) in a building dating to the early 20th century. > 25 Gordon's Alley, tel. 609/347–2743. AE, MC, V. Closed Sun. and Mon. **$$$**

Los Amigos In the dim back room of this small bar–restaurant two blocks from the Boardwalk casinos, you can tuck into such south-of-the-border-inspired specialties as Mexican pizza and burritos and wash them down with margaritas. > 1926 Atlantic Ave., tel. 609/344–2293. AE, DC, MC, V. **$–$$**

Mama Mott's With candles, chandeliers, and plenty of red and gold, this center-city spot could be in Little Italy. Seafood takes center stage here. Flounder Orleans is dressed with sweet and hot peppers, onions, and white-wine sauce; *zuppa di pesce* mixes all sorts of shellfish with marinara and serves it atop linguine. The menu also includes plenty of veal and chicken dishes. Live piano music fills the air Saturday night. > 151 S. New York Ave., tel. 609/345–8218 or 800/293–0805. AE, DC, MC, V. No lunch. **$$–$$$$**

Old Waterway Inn The fireplace is always going at this waterfront restaurant 2 mi from the Venice Park section of the Boardwalk. The charbroiled steak here has a following; more-adventurous preparations include pan-seared red snapper with green coconut-curry sauce. An enclosed patio dining area overlooks the water. A children's menu is available. > 1700 W. Riverside Dr., tel. 609/347–1793. AE, DC, MC, V. Closed Jan. No lunch. **$$–$$$**

Peregrines' A standout among Atlantic City's well-established casino restaurants, this small contemporary-Continental restaurant is elegant and friendly. Ingredients on the à la carte and prix fixe menus tend toward such luxuries as Belon oysters from France and truffles from Belgium. > Atlantic City Hilton, Boston and Pacific Aves., tel. 609/347–7111. AE, D, DC, MC, V. Closed Mon.–Wed. No lunch. $$$$

Scannicchio's One of Atlantic City's most popular eateries, this intimate, candlelit, classic Italian restaurant offers eight fish specials daily and an extensive pasta menu. Filet mignon stuffed with crab, shrimp, and scallops is one of the most requested dishes. Homemade cannoli is a must for dessert. Reservations are essential on weekends. > 119 S. California Ave., tel. 609/348–6378. AE, MC, V. No lunch. $–$$$

White House Sub Shop The place claims to have made more than 17 million overstuffed sandwiches since 1946. Celebrities seem to love it; check out the photos on the walls. > 2301 Arctic Ave., at Mississippi Ave., tel. 609/345–1564 or 609/345–8599. Reservations not accepted. No credit cards. ¢–$

WHAT'S NEARBY

Harley Dawn Diner Settle in for meat loaf that tastes homemade, mashed potatoes, and fresh seafood at this old-fashioned diner 30 mi west of Atlantic City. Pies are baked daily. You can get breakfast here, too. A kids' menu is available. > 1402 Black Horse Pike, Folsom, tel. 609/567–6084. AE, D, DC, MC, V. ¢–$$

Ram's Head Inn One of New Jersey's top restaurants, this pastoral yet formal retreat is 8 mi from Atlantic City. It's filled with the works of local artists and soft piano music plays as you enjoy drinks by the fireplace. In season, you can dine outdoors in a flower-filled courtyard with a fountain. Try creamy chicken potpie with dumplings in a copper kettle, glazed crisp roasted duckling with rice, and Maryland crab imperial in a pastry crust. > 9 W. White Horse Pike, Absecon, tel. 609/652–1700. Jacket required. Closed Mon. No lunch weekends. AE, D, DC, MC, V. $–$$$

Renault Winery A guitarist sets the mood at this elegant 1864 winery, where six-course seafood, poultry, and beef meals are served with appropriate wines. For lunch, check out the winery's Garden Café, which offers lighter fare. Sunday brunch is available. To get here from Atlantic City, take U.S. 30 west for about 30 mi. > 72 N. Bremen Ave., Egg Harbor City, tel. 609/965–2111. Reservations essential. AE, D, DC, MC, V. $$$$

ESSENTIALS

Getting Here

Railroads put Atlantic City on the map, but this has long since become a car and bus town; some 350,000 buses and millions of cars arrive in the resort each year. Aside from the Greyhound and New Jersey Transit bus lines, dozens of smaller services may have stops right around your corner. Many of them comp you $20 worth of chips when you arrive at the casino.

BY BUS

New Jersey Transit, Greyhound, and Academy Bus lines leave for Atlantic City from the Port Authority terminal, so departures are frequent. Buses often stop directly at certain casinos before proceeding to the Atlantic City bus station. Some Atlantic City casino-hotels offer direct service to their properties; ask your hotel for specifics.

In summer, expect heavy afternoon and evening traffic southbound on Friday and northbound on Sunday.

LINES **Academy Bus Lines** > Tel. 732/291–1300 or 800/442–7272, www.academybus.com. **Greyhound** > Tel. 609/345–6617 or 800/231–2222, www.greyhound.com. **New Jersey Transit** > Tel. 800/582–5946, www.njtransit.com.

DEPOTS **Atlantic City Municipal Terminal** > Atlantic and Michigan Aves., tel. 609/345–6617.

BY CAR

The main road serving the Jersey Shore is the Garden State Parkway (GSP), a north–south toll road that ends in Cape May. From New York City, Interstate 80 and the New Jersey Turnpike (toll) connect with the GSP. Proceed to Exit 38 of the parkway and take the Atlantic City Expressway east.

Visitor Information

CONTACTS **Atlantic City Convention Center & Visitors Authority** > 2314 Pacific Ave., 08401, tel. 800/262–7395, www.atlanticcitynj.com.

Spring Lake

60 mi southwest of New York City

3

By Karen Little

ONE AND A HALF MILES of prime Jersey Shore beach and a noncommercial boardwalk line the eastern edge of the village of Spring Lake. Two sparkling-clean beach houses mark the north and south ends of the village, which is scattered with stunning mansions, some old and some new. A few blocks from the shore you find a one-of-a-kind shopping district—with no chain stores at all—and a green lake park.

In the early 1900s, Spring Lake was primarily a resort town, with mammoth ocean-front hotels catering to wealthy Philadelphians and New Yorkers. Through the years, it has evolved into a year-round community, one dedicated to providing a high quality-of-life standard to local residents: hotels and restaurants have been systematically weaned, liquor licenses reduced, and a balance struck between resident and tourist needs. Although the village fills up during peak season, it manages to avoid becoming overrun or rowdy.

Come to the village to swim and surf, to stroll and lounge, and to shop. Many residents are expert at surfing the Atlantic. If that seems too daunting, consider taking up body surfing, which can easily be mastered in a weekend; lessons are available locally. At a minimum, wave bobbing is something every age group can do. Remember that the ocean water is moody, and lifeguards are on duty only from June through August. Tides are rougher in September, when it's still warm outside, and later on into the year.

Spring Lake is a great walking destination, whether you stroll along the beach or away from the ocean. You can start your weekend walk in Divine Park, which includes Spring Lake (approximately 1⅓ mi around) and plenty of picnic spots; two wood bridges, green lawns, old-growth trees, swans, and large, white gazebos provide endless backdrops for pictures. Afterward head to Ocean Avenue, parallel to the boardwalk, and proceed northward. The coastline and the avenue's many magnificent mansions will have you turning your head left and right. Then take either Tuttle or Ludlow Avenue away from the shore and toward the business district.

Anchoring the north end of the Third Avenue shopping street is the Spring Lake Community Center, a beautiful old building containing a theater and a library. A creative array of local merchants makes shopping here distinct. Most store owners are year-round residents and professionals in their field—designers, fashion stylists, artists, chefs, candy makers, jewelers, writers, and surfers. Prices for even the finest merchandise are reasonable, selections of boutique items are good (although stores are small and some digging may be required), and proprietors are well informed. Among the shops are two homemade candy stores, plus an open-all-year ice-cream shop. It's worth a brief detour off the Garden State Expressway just to sample the sweets.

Spring Lake's quiet nature and its proximity to New York City are big draws. Weekend lodging requires advance reservations year-round, with popular rooms booked six months to a year in advance. From June to August even weekdays are usually reserved ahead. The rest of the year, last-minute weekday access is possible. Rates drop significantly off season, early fall being a both a bargain and a pleasure.

WHAT TO SEE & DO

Dan's Kitchen Catering and Cooking School Master chefs host classes for adults and children. Topics include elegant entertaining, Venetian cooking, and children's pasta making. Classes are usually held weekdays. > 524 Brighton Ave., Suite 9, tel. 732/449-7665. $15 one-hour class.

Divine Park Spring Lake, as the name suggests, is a spring-fed, ½-mi-long lake running northwest to southeast inside Divine Park. You can paddle along the calm water in a rented boat or kayak. By sidewalk, Divine Park's perimeter is approximately 1⅓ mi, but two picturesque wood bridges cut across the lake. The park is nicely landscaped all around, with a large, white gazebo at the far northwest end. > Passaic and 5th Aves. Free.

Spring Lake Boardwalk A 1½-mi boardwalk lines the town's Atlantic Ocean beach. Two large beach houses stand, one on each end, with 100-foot-long by 33-foot-wide saltwater pools inside. From June through August, you need a badge to access the beach and beach houses—but use of the saltwater pools themselves is limited to residents and their guests. A beach badge is usually provided by your lodging, or you can buy one at either beach house. > Ocean Ave., tel. 732/449-8005. Badge $6 June-Aug.

Spring Lake Community House Built in the early 1900s as a family mansion, the community house was donated to the town in 1923. Today it houses the Spring Lake Theater Company and the Children's Theater Workshop and Dance School and hosts civic events. On the northeast side is the town library, featuring a dark, European reading room with a huge fireplace to warm by in winter, and a book-lined gallery. > 1501 3rd Ave., tel. 732/449-4530. Mon.-Sat. noon-3.

Spring Lake Theatre Company The company produces six events (plays, musicals, or reviews) per year, staged in April through August and in December. Shows ($15-$20) take place at the old, acoustically balanced Spring Lake Community House theater. > 3rd Ave. and Madison Ave. S, tel. 732/449-4530, www.springlaketheatre.com. Box office Sept.-May, Mon.-Sat. noon-3; June-Aug., Mon.-Sat. 11-5.

St. Catharine Roman Catholic Church This domed neoclassical church dominates the southwest side of Spring Lake. Inside look for the gilded vaults and the intricately painted rotunda depicting religious figures. > 215 Essex Ave., tel. 732/449-5765. Free. Mon.-Thurs. 6:45 AM-4 PM, Sat. 6:45 AM-6:30 PM, Sun. 6:45 AM-4 PM.

Sports

BOATING & KAYAKING

You can choose between two bodies of water upon which to boat: try ocean kayaking, or take a rowboat out on gentle Spring Lake in Divine Park. Weekend Outfitters rents canoes, rowboats, and ocean kayaks.

RENTALS **Weekend Outfitters** > 219 Morris Ave., Spring Lake, tel. 732/449-0062, www.springlake.net/fun.

GOLF

Howell Park Golf Course Bent-grass fairways, usually associated with private clubs, are one of the draws at this 6,964-yard, 18-hole, par-72 course 15 mi east of Spring

Lake. Nonresident greens fees are $45–$55. > Preventorium Rd., Howell, tel.
732/938–4771, www.monmouthcountyparks.com.

Shark River Golf Course Although only 6,200-yards long, the 18-hole, par-71 course
includes short par 4s; long, challenging par 5s; and a natural mix of par 3s. Nonresident greens fees are $41–$49. The course is in Neptune, about 6 mi northwest of
Spring Lake. It's closed from late December to mid-March. > 320 Old Corlies Ave.,
Neptune, tel. 732/922–4141, www.monmouthcountyparks.com.

SURFING

The ocean waves at Spring Lake make for good surfing and body surfing. Bring your
own board, or rent locally. If you're a novice, make sure to get expert advice or training before going out on your own. You can even get someone to go out in the water
with you. The 3rd Avenue Surf Shop, owned and operated by life-long Jersey surfer T.
R. Deveney, gives advice, sells pro gear, provides class referrals and workshops, and
rents wet suits, surf boards, beach chairs, and umbrellas; check the surf and swimming report while you're here. Weekend Outfitters has picnic food, beach chairs, and
umbrellas for sale, as well as bikes, boats, and surfing-equipment rentals.

RENTALS **3rd Avenue Surf Shop** > 1206 3rd Ave., Spring Lake, tel. 732/449–1866,
www.3rdavesurf.com. **Weekend Outfitters** > 219 Morris Ave., Spring Lake, tel.
732/449–0062, www.springlake.net/fun.

Shopping

Stores and restaurants in the Third Avenue business district are owned and operated
by residents—there are no chain stores. The result is diversity and surprising selections. Shops include one of New Jersey's few remaining independent bookstores, a
surf hut, decorating and furniture stores, antiques stores, art and framing galleries
(many of which carry paintings and prints by local artists). Women's boutiques are
especially popular and well-stocked. Goods include one-of-a-kind designer purses,
dresses, and jewelry, in addition to sports clothing and swim suits. Owners, including
several well-regarded fashion-industry consultants, know their stuff and take time to
help you.

Dreamkeeper The selection of dressy-yet-comfortable clothing by popular designers
comes in extra-small to plus sizes. Dreamkeeper also sells one-of-a-kind jewelry and
small crafts produced by well-known artisans. > 304 Morris Ave., Spring Lake, tel.
732/974–0184.

Irish Centre A large, friendly place, the Centre sells Irish imports—sweaters, capes,
pottery, and collectibles. Numerous special events here let you meet Irish artists,
painters, print-makers, and potters. > 1120 3rd Ave., Spring Lake, tel. 732/449–6650.

Jean Louise Homemade Candies Stand just outside the candy kitchen in this small
shop, smell the ambrosia, listen to the candy makers' chatter, and then order the succulent fresh creams (such as dark chocolate filled with orange or peanut butter),
chocolate-coated fruit, and finely molded candy. > 1205 3rd Ave., Spring Lake, tel.
732/449–2627.

Karen's Boutique This very small women's boutique is noteworthy in that it's one of
the few outlets anywhere to carry Ladybeads jewelry, which is fashioned out of antique Venetian crystal. On weekends, you may see the boutique's flirty and sophisticated clothing modeled at noon fashion shows in the restaurant at the Breakers. Just
have lunch to attend. > 1212 3rd Ave., Spring Lake, tel. 732/449–7536.

Landmark Books Owner and published historian Patricia Colrick is an independent
bookseller. She sponsors author visits, hosts children's story hours, and stocks books
about New Jersey's ocean lore as well as general-interest subjects. Antique publica-

tions and books about photography are two other specialties. > 1201 3rd Ave., Spring Lake, tel. 732/449–0804.

Susan Murphy's Homemade Ice Cream Take a short walk past the train station to savor rich, creamy ice cream: brown sugar–caramel, tiramisu, cherry vanilla. > 601 Warren Ave., Spring Lake Heights, tel. 732/449–1130.

Third Avenue Chocolate Shoppe The shop makes offbeat, playful candy creations, as well as traditional sweets, plus it sells small children's toys. Try the crisp and nutty chocolate turtles, which, unlike others, won't hold your teeth for ransom. > 1118 3rd Ave., Spring Lake, tel. 732/449–7535.

Weekend Outfitters Choose from such items as baked Brie-and-apple sandwiches, fresh-fruit salad, and bruschetta to make up your picnic lunch from Weekend Outfitters. It packs your feast in a basket complete with linens and china. Twenty-four-hour advance reservation is required. Consider renting a boat from here, too, and eat your picnic while floating on the lake. > 219 Morris Ave., Spring Lake, tel. 732/449–0062.

WHERE TO STAY

The Breakers on the Ocean The only elevators in town whisk you to upper stories and great views of the ocean. Ask for a room with a direct view and an extra-large whirlpool tub, or, as a second choice, a side-view room with a jet tub. Vast outdoor porches and a large freshwater pool make this hotel feel like a mansion. Both restaurants have fabulous water views. > 1507 Ocean Ave., 07762, tel. 732/449–7700, fax 732/449–0161, www.breakershotel.com. 72 rooms. 2 restaurants, snack bar, room service, some in-room hot tubs, refrigerators, cable TV, some in-room VCRs, pool, piano bar, convention center, no-smoking rooms. AE, D, MC, V. EP. $$$–$$$$

The Hewitt Wellington Originally a 19th-century Victorian hotel, the Hewitt Wellington is now a condominium that rents its large rooms whenever owners aren't present. Furnishings throughout are elegant and understated—less frilly than the many area bed-and-breakfasts. The best of the two-room suites have private porches. Staying here puts you next to Spring Lake and three blocks from the ocean. Off the wraparound porch is Whispers restaurant, which preserves the Victorian aesthetic while serving contemporary cuisine. > 200 Monmouth Ave., 07762, tel. 732/974–1212, fax 732/974–2338, www.hewittwellington.com. 12 rooms, 17 suites. Restaurant, in-room data ports, cable TV with VCR, pool, Internet, business services, meeting rooms; no kids under 12, no smoking. AE, D, MC, V. EP. $$$–$$$$

Normandy Inn This multicolor painted lady, circa 1889, has red rooftops and a central, square tower. The interior is filled with period antiques, including stain-glass lamps throughout, ladies' handiwork from the 1800s in the dining room, and intricate carved-wood furniture. Floral wallpapers and area rugs complement the Victorian pieces. The largest rooms are the most comfortable; on the other end of the spectrum, the tiny tower room (Room 200) feels a bit like the crows nest of an old schooner, looking out at the ocean a half block away. > 21 Tuttle Ave., 07762, tel. 732/449–7172, fax 732/449–1070, www.normandyinn.com. 17 rooms, 1 suite. Dining room, some in-room hot tubs, cable TV, bicycles, business services; no smoking. AE, D, MC, V. BP. $$$

Ocean House Bed and Breakfast Hotel Salmon outer walls, striped window awnings, and a two-sided porch characterize the bright and breezy resort hotel built in 1878. Brightly colored guest rooms—blue-green, dusky blue, daffodil yellow, powder pink, magenta—coordinate with floral bedspreads on white iron, four-poster, and brass beds. Antiques fill the attractive common rooms—look for the original switchboard in the main lobby and try to imagine what this inn was like when first opened. The Ocean House is one block from Spring Lake and one block from the ocean. > 102 Sussex Ave., tel. 732/449–9090, fax 732/449–9092, www.theoceanhouse.net. 30 rooms, 9 suites. Dining room, fans, cable TV, bicycles; no kids under 10, no smoking. AE, MC, V. CP; BP Sat. **$$$–$$$$**

Sea Crest by the Sea Only half a block from the ocean, this beautiful inn spoils you. Awake smelling elaborate baked goods and custards that are part of breakfast and afternoon tea. Homemade cordials and chocolates arrive in the evening. Expect a fireplace, a jet tub for two, flowers, wine, a rubber ducky, and fluffy bathrobes in every room. Many rooms have Victorian furnishings and lace. The Norwegian Wood suite has three rooms under sloping eves—one room has a wood ceiling and a spa tub surrounded by windows. > 19 Tuttle Ave., 07762, tel. 732/449–9031 or 800/803–9031, fax 732/974–0403, www.seacrestbythesea.com. 3 rooms, 5 suites. In-room hot tubs, refrigerators, cable TV, bicycles, meeting rooms; no kids, no smoking. AE, MC, V. BP. **$$$$**

Spring Lake Inn A big front porch and unusual, angular-shape guest rooms make staying here a memorable experience. Most rooms are painted in bold, solid hues, tempered by light floral bedspreads and lace curtains. Some rooms have queen-sized sleigh beds, and all have gas fireplaces. Homemade baked goods are a specialty, with breads and jam served with breakfast and fresh cookies for afternoon snacks. At breakfast, ask for the inn's version of bananas Foster—thick French toast stuffed with cream cheese, flavored with rum extract, and topped with bananas. The inn is a block from the boardwalk's south beach house and two blocks from Spring Lake. > 104 Salem Ave., 07762, tel. 732/449–2010, www.springlakeinn.com. 15 rooms. Dining room, some in-room hot tubs, some refrigerators, cable TV with VCR, croquet, shop; no room phones, no kids, no smoking. AE, D, MC, V. BP. **$$$–$$$$**

Victoria House Bed & Breakfast The first thing you notice when you walk into this 1882 Queen Anne is a beautiful stained-glass window at the base of the stairway and the scent of freshly baked goods in the air. With extras such as fireplaces and featherbeds, the suites and deluxe rooms are the best bets here. All rooms have refined, antique wood bureaus, rockers, mantels, or bedsteads. Breakfast is served in a formal dining room by candlelight or, weather permitting, in an enclosed porch that leads to a traditional English garden. The Victoria is close to Spring Lake and four blocks from the ocean. > 214 Monmouth Ave., tel. 732/974–1882 or 888/249–6562, fax 732/974–2132, www.victoriahouse.net. 6 rooms, 2 suites. Dining room, fans, some in-room hot tubs, some refrigerators, cable TV with VCR, bicycles; no kids, no smoking. AE, MC, V. BP. **$$$–$$$$**

WHERE TO EAT

The Breakers on the Ocean Stop in the lounge before dinner to enjoy a cocktail and listen to the piano player. Then head into the pastel hotel dining room, which overlooks the ocean. You might try veal Parmigiana, a tender New York strip steak, or flounder *marechiare* (with shrimp). Both service and food are first class, yet the restaurant is casual enough that you may wear nice shorts and deck shoes. Breakfast and lunch are served on a long, sunny enclosed veranda near the pool. Lunch choices include burgers, club sandwiches, and pizza. > 1507 Ocean Ave., tel. 732/449–7700. AE, MC, V. **$$–$$$$**

Cucina Cafe This six-table, deli-style café sells fresh, high-quality food, such as salmon encrusted with pistachios, crisp salads, sandwich wraps, and baked goods. Although the chef is Italian, he sometimes cooks thick, tender Irish pork chops smothered in a secret sauce and sauerkraut, which is excellent. Eat in if a table is available, or buy food for a picnic or to take back to your room. > 219B Morris Ave., tel. 732/974–3433. MC, V. ¢

Sister's Cafe The owners here take pride in developing unusual, top-quality dishes, borrowed from different regions. If it's on the changing menu the day you arrive, don't miss the grilled porterhouse veal chop with chili-honey glaze. Sister's also has a flair for vegetarian dishes. In addition to lunch and dinner in the storefront restaurant, you can have breakfast on Saturday; Sunday service is limited to brunch. > 1321 3rd Ave., tel. 732/449–1909. Closed Mon. No dinner Sun. MC, V. $$–$$$

Spring Lake Gourmet Pizzeria and Restaurant Order large, cracker-crisp pizzas by the slice or pie at this pizzeria with dinette tables. The white pizza is delicious, as is anything with the Italian sausage. Or you might try the fried calamari, then choose your favorite pasta combined with your favorite sauce to make a meal. > 1110 3rd Ave., tel. 732/449–9595. MC, V. BYOB. $

Tom Bailey's Market Head to this spot for take-out, New York–delicatessen style: Tom Bailey's specialties are grilled fresh fish and prime-beef sandwiches. There's a selection of cheese, fruit, and desserts, too. The old brass cash register, as well as the Rock-Ola Juke Box with its bubbling, colored lights, are worth seeing even if you don't need food. > 1323 3rd Ave., tel. 732/282–0920. D, MC, V. ¢–$

Whispers Evening meals in this renowned 40-seat, Victorian restaurant are perfectly romantic. Sink into red tufted chairs under ornate crystal chandeliers and relax. The owner personally handles reservations, welcomes diners, and oversees the staff. The contemporary menu changes weekly, but always emphasizes seafood, especially fresh New Jersey sea scallops. In addition to fish, consider the rack of lamb or the grilled, barrel-cut, filet mignon. > The Hewitt Wellington, 200 Monmouth Ave., tel. 732/974–9755. Reservations essential. Closed Tues. Nov.–Memorial Day. AE, MC, V. BYOB. $$$–$$$$

Who's on Third Deli and Grill Eat at the old-fashioned lunch counter or in the spacious dinette area, for hearty and reasonably priced meals. In summer, the deli stays open later and has entrées such as succulent pot roast. Who's on Third is open for breakfast, too. > 1300 3rd Ave., tel. 732/449–4233. MC, V. ¢–$$

ESSENTIALS

Getting Here

Reaching Spring Lake by either bus and or car takes about an hour if traffic is with you—but traffic problems can add time to your trip. Taking the train (1½ hours) may take a little longer but is more reliable. The village is easily walked, so there's no need for a car once you arrive.

BY BUS

You might reach Spring Lake by bus in an hour, but traffic jams on the Garden State Parkway and the New Jersey Turnpike often add hours to arrival and departure times. Spring Lake is serviced by Academy charter buses. Round-trip tickets are $20, and buses leave Port Authority in Manhattan nearly once an hour from 8 AM–11:30 PM. Buses leaving Spring Lake run once every one to two hours from 5:15 AM–9:30 PM. A schedule is posted outside the Spring Lake Railroad Plaza bus station. You must call and prebook your tickets.

LINES **Academy Bus Lines** > Tel. 800/442–7272, www.academybus.com.
DEPOTS **Spring Lake Railroad Plaza** > Railroad Plaza at Warren Ave., no phone.

BY CAR

If conditions are good, and traffic is light, travel to Spring Lake takes about an hour from New York City. Traffic out of the city on weekdays from 5 PM to 6:30 PM can add at least an hour to your time. Re-entering New York on Sunday evening, even until midnight on nice weekends, also can add an hour. Returning the Sunday after a holiday weekend, especially after 2 PM, can add two or more hours to the journey.

Starting southbound on the New Jersey Turnpike, follow the cars-only lane to Exit 11, and the GSP. Take the GSP south for approximately 30 mi to Exit 98, Route 34. Note that only a single, small sign announces SPRING LAKE prior to the exit. Merge onto Route 34 south and follow it through the roundabout, to the third exit, Route 524 (Allaire Road) and travel approximately 3 mi to the fork. Turn right (east) on Ludlow Avenue. Continue about ½ mi to Third Avenue and turn right (south).

At this point, you've entered the village at its northern edge. Travel south on Third Avenue, through the business district. Directly ahead four blocks is Spring Lake itself. To your left (east) three blocks is the ocean. The focus of this getaway is primarily the area to the east of Third Avenue.

Traffic along the beach can be infuriatingly slow, especially in summer and on late-spring and early-fall weekends, and parking can be tight. Most inns and B&Bs have off-street parking.

BY TRAIN

Commuting by train from New York to Spring Lake takes a reasonable 1½ hours; the timetable is stable, and you don't have to worry about traffic. New Jersey Transit trains leave from Manhattan's Penn Station; you want the Jersey Coast line. Once in Spring Lake, call your lodging for a cab, or else walk. The village is small—the longest walk from the station is only 1½ mi. The train schedule is posted outside the station.

LINES **New Jersey Transit** > Tel. 800/772–2222, www.njtransit.com.
STATIONS **Spring Lake Railroad Plaza** > Railroad Plaza at Warren Ave., no phone.

Visitor Information

The volunteer Spring Lake Chamber of Commerce has a map and guide to Spring Lake, as well as a high-quality area map, all of which you can order online or by phone, or pick up at the office (open Monday through Saturday, 11–3). The Spring Lake Merchants Association can send you a town booklet or help with lodging arrangements. Leave a message; all calls are returned.

CONTACTS **Greater Spring Lake Chamber of Commerce** > 302–304 Washington Ave., Suite 104, Spring Lake 07762, tel. 732/449–0577, www.springlake.org. **Spring Lake Merchants Association** > 1212 3rd Ave., Spring Lake 07762, tel. 732/449–2172, www.springlakemerchants.org.

Lambertville & New Hope

67 mi west of New York City

4

Updated by Laura Knowles Callanan

ALTHOUGH THEY FACE EACH OTHER across the Delaware River, Lambertville and New Hope are not twins. New Jersey's Lambertville is the calmer, and smaller, of the two towns, whereas New Hope is the brasher older sister. Classic American scenery surrounds both, and together they offer a getaway destination where you can slow down to enjoy a leisurely pace or rev up to jostle with the crowds and people watch just by crossing the bridge.

Federal row houses, proud Victorians, and an abundance of art galleries, antiques shops, quirky boutiques, restaurants, cafés, and bed-and-breakfasts populate Lambertville's tree-lined streets, which are charming but avoid being cutesy. In the self-described "Antiques Capital of New Jersey," you can find collectibles from the 1950s, books from the early 1900s, and furniture and decorative pieces from the 1700s. Lambertville's roots are blue-collar, however, and this working-class past has contributed to the complex texture of this small city, where old buildings are reincarnated again and again.

Much busier and more commercial, New Hope, in Bucks County, remained rural until the 20th century, its land given over to woods, mills, and farms. In the late 1800s an art colony took root, and in the 1930s New York luminaries, including writer Dorothy Parker and lyricist Oscar Hammerstein II, began to make the area their home. In intervening years, Bucks County—and especially New Hope—has become known for its art galleries, antiques shops, summer theater, and B&Bs. Shops sell everything from fine examples of Early American craftsmanship to fun kitsch.

You'd do well to explore Lambertville and New Hope on foot, as weekend traffic can really back up and parking spaces are hard to come by, especially in summer, fall, and before the winter holidays. With many of their most interesting sights, restaurants, and shops clustered near the Delaware, both cities are eminently walkable. After you've had your fill, you may explore the surrounding areas by car or take a leisurely drive along the river. One of area's chief pleasures doesn't involve commerce at all: the towpaths along the canals on either side of the river are bucolic retreats for biking, running, or just strolling.

Point Pleasant, to the north of New Hope, is reminiscent of England's Cotswolds, with roads that resemble corkscrews, bridge-keeper lodges, and gorgeous vistas. In tiny Lumberville, a bit to the south, you can picnic along the Delaware Canal or on Bull's Island, accessible by footbridge. The bucolic river town of Erwinna is a few miles north of Point Pleasant. West of New Hope, on U.S. 202, is Lahaska, the region's center for shopping. Its Peddler's Village, a group of 75 stores, can be a rewarding place to search for antiques and fine reproduction furniture, handcrafted chandeliers, hand-woven wicker, and homespun fabrics.

A few miles to the south is where George Washington made his historic Revolutionary War crossing of the Delaware, an event that's reenacted every Christmas.

Area inns and restaurants occupy former houses, barns, and mills built up to a half century before the Revolution, and many of these display plaques stating that GEORGE WASHINGTON SLEPT HERE. If you want to secure a place to sleep, plan and reserve early—as much as three months ahead for summer and fall weekends.

WHAT TO SEE & DO

LAMBERTVILLE

David Rago Auctions Really three auction houses in one, this place specializes in 20th-century furnishings and decorative arts. Textiles, religious icons and statuary, pottery and ceramics, jewelry, Nakashima tables, and art-deco furniture are among the items that might be brought to the block. Call, or check the Web site, for the auction schedule. > 333 N. Main St., tel. 609/397-9374, www.ragoarts.com.

Holcombe–Jimison Farmstead Museum Displays include farming equipment, a country kitchen, a rural post office, a doctor–dentist office, and blacksmith, print, and carpentry shops. From spring through fall, the herb garden showcases old-fashioned varieties. The museum is just north of Lambertville center on Route 29. > Rte. 29 at last exit of U.S. 202 toll bridge, tel. 609/397-2752 or 908/782-6653. Donations suggested. May–Oct., Sun. 1–4, Wed. 9–noon.

Marshall House This house, run by the Lambertville Historical Society, offers a look at mid-19th-century Lambertville. Inside are furnishings from 1843, quilts, and a display devoted to shad fishing. Group tours can be arranged by appointment year-round. > 62 Bridge St., tel. 609/397-1898. Donations suggested. Apr.–Oct., weekends 1–4; guided walking tours on 1st Sun. at 2.

Washington Crossing State Park In 1776, General George Washington and his troops landed at Johnson's Ferry, now a site in the park, from which they marched to Trenton in the wee hours of December 26. The surprise attack on the Hessian soldiers there led to a pivotal victory for the Continental Army. The 1,770-acre park, about 8 mi south of Lambertville, includes the **Johnson Ferry House** (tel. 609/737-2515, Wed.–Sat. 10–4, Sun. 1–4), an early-18th-century farmhouse–tavern thought to have been used at least briefly by Washington and his officers at the time of the famous crossing. The visitor center–museum contains more than 600 artifacts from the Revolutionary War era. Nature and hiking trails lace the grounds. > Rtes. 29 and 546, Titusville, NJ, tel. 609/737-0623, 609/737-9303 visitor center–museum, www.state.nj.us/dep/parksandforests. Parking $5 Memorial Day–Labor Day (free rest of yr). Park daily 8–4:30; visitor center Wed.–Sun. 9–4:30.

NEW HOPE

Bucks County Playhouse One of New Hope's original gristmills houses New Hope's theater company, which stages revivals of Broadway musicals. The season runs from April through December. > 70 S. Main St., tel. 215/862-2041, www.buckscountyplayhouse.com.

Parry Mansion The eight rooms of this 1784 stone house are filled with furnishings that date from 1775 to 1900, representing more than a century of changing tastes in wall decoration, upholstery, and accessories. Built by lumber-mill owner Benjamin Parry, the house was occupied by five generations of his family. > S. Main and Ferry Sts., tel. 215/862-5652, www.parrymansion.org. $5. May–Dec., Fri.–Sun. 1–5.

Washington Crossing Historic Park The park encompasses the point from which General George Washington and his 2,400 soldiers crossed the icy Delaware River on the nigh.   .mas 1776 to march to Trenton. Taking the Hessian soldiers there by surprise, Washington's men captured the base, scoring an important victory against the British in the Revolutionary War. The park is divided between a lower and an upper section. In the **Lower Park,** 7 mi south of New Hope on Route 32 and near the junction of Route 532 in Washington Crossing, the Memorial Building displays a reproduction of Emanuel Leutze's famous painting of the crossing. (The original hangs in New York's Metropolitan Museum of Art.) The McConkey Ferry Inn, near the Memorial Building, is where Washington and his staff had Christmas dinner while waiting to cross the river. In the **Upper Park,** on Route 32 about 5 mi north of the Memorial Building, is Bowman's Hill Tower; Washington used the hill it stands on as a lookout point. You can get a much better view of the countryside than he did by riding the elevator up the 110-foot-tall memorial tower, named after a surgeon who sailed with Captain Kidd. The tower is open April through November, Tuesday through Sunday 10–4:30. The 100-acre **Bowman's Hill Wildflower Preserve** (tel. 215/862–2924, www.bhwp.org), ½ mi north of Bowman's Hill Tower, showcases hundreds of species of wildflowers, trees, shrubs, and ferns native to Pennsylvania. You may take a guided tour, offered April through October for $3 per person, or follow the short loop trails. Also here is the Thompson-Neely House, an 18th-century farmhouse furnished just as it was when the Colonial leaders sat in the kitchen and planned the Trenton attack. > Rte. 32, Washington Crossing and New Hope, tel. 215/493–4076, www.phmc.state.pa.us. $5. Tues.–Sat. 9–5, Sun. noon–5.

ERWINNA

Tinicum Park The busy park has 126 acres for hiking, picnicking, and fishing. On weekend afternoons from May through September (or by appointment), you can tour the **Erwin-Stover House** (tel. 215/489–5133), an 1800 Federal house with later additions. > River Rd./Rte. 32, tel. 215/757–0571, www.buckscounty.org. Free. Daily sunrise–sunset.

Tours

Bucks County Carriages The horses that pull the carriages for these 20-minute tours are "parked" at the Logan Inn in New Hope, near the bakery in Lahaska's Peddler's Village, and at the Lambertville Station. Daytime and evening rides are available depending on the season and departure point. > Tel. 215/862–3582.

Coryell's Ferry Ride and Historic Narrative A paddle wheeler takes passengers on a half-hour sightseeing ride on the Delaware River. Tours are offered from mid-April through October. > 22 S. Main St., New Hope, tel. 215/862–2050.

Ghost Tours of New Hope On Saturday nights from June through November, this tour operator leads a one-hour lantern-led walk that explores haunting area locations. In October, additional tours are given Friday nights and on Halloween. > Main and Ferry Sts., New Hope, tel. 215/957–9988.

New Hope Canal Boat Company Beginning in 1832, coal barges traveled the Delaware Canal. Now the canal is a part of a state park, and you can ride one of the boat company's mule-pulled barges. From April through October, the one-hour narrated tours ($8) float past gardens, Revolutionary-era cottages, and artists' workshops. A barge historian and folk singer entertain aboard the 60-passenger boat. > New and S. Main Sts., New Hope, tel. 215/862–0758, www.canalboats.com.

Wings of Gold Balloon Rides The hot-air balloon flights that Wings of Gold organizes last either 30 or 60 minutes. The balloons, which depart from Lahaska as well as Newtown or Richboro, leave within two hours of sunrise or sunset, when the winds are best. Trips are $100–$175 per person. > Tel. 215/244–9323, www.wingsofgold.biz.

Sports

BIKING

With towpaths on both sides of the Delaware River and numerous bridges connecting the two sides, this area is a favorite of bikers. A popular route loops through Lumberville, about 8 mi north of New Hope. Cross the pedestrian bridge to Bulls Island Recreation Area; go south on the New Jersey side along the Delaware and Raritan Canal to Stockton; cross back over the river to Centre Bridge (PA) and head up the Delaware Canal towpath again to Lumberville. You can start this looping ride anywhere along the route.

You can extend this loop into a longer ride (30-mi) that goes through Washington Crossing Historic Park, heads 7 mi north to New Hope, proceeds northward to Centre Bridge and Lumberville, crosses the Delaware to Bulls Island Recreation Area, and then picks up the towpath going south toward Stockton and Lambertville, continuing through Lambertville and Titusville, and into Washington Crossing State Park. (In New Hope, after you arrive at Odette's restaurant, go through Odette's parking lot to Main Street, which you should cross and proceed up the stairs to pick up the towpath again.)

TUBING

Bucks County River Country Canoe and Tube Each year more than 100,000 people—from toddlers to grandparents—negotiate the Delaware on this company's inner tubes. From April through October, a bus transports people upriver to begin three- or four-hour tube or raft rides down to the base. Wear sneakers (expect them to get wet) and lots of sunscreen; life jackets are available at no charge. Reservations are required for the trips, which cost around $18 per person for an inner tube and $22 for a raft on weekends. River Country also rents rafts and kayaks. > Byron Rd. at Rte. 32, Point Pleasant, PA, tel. 215/297–5000, www.rivercountry.net.

Shopping

Many shops not listed here dot a 4-mi stretch of U.S. 202 between Lahaska and New Hope (in Pennsylvania) as well as some of the intersecting country roads. Stores are generally open on weekends, with weekday hours by appointment only: it's best to call first.

LAMBERTVILLE

A Mano Gallery The focus is on handcrafted gift items and home furnishings: wood and iron furniture, jewelry, copper home accessories, ceramic plaques, glass pieces, and wearable art, to name a few. > 36 N. Union St., tel. 609/397–0063.

America Antiques & Designs Decorative arts, eclectic 19th- and 20th-century artifacts, and furniture are part of the mix here. > 5 S. Main St., tel. 609/397–6966.

Broadmoor Antiques The 10 galleries at this location are packed with decorative and antique items. > 6 N. Union St., tel. 609/397–8802.

Coryell Street Antiques Proprietor Charles A. Buttaci displays an ever-changing selection of fine art, period antiques, paintings, grandfather clocks, and Kentucky rifles inside a Victorian house. > 51 Coryell St., tel. 609/397–5700. Closed Mon.–Wed.

Golden Nugget Antique Flea Market Dozens of vendors set up their wares at this flea market. > 1850 River Rd., tel. 609/397–0811. Closed Mon., Tues., Thurs., and Fri.

Orchard Hill Collection The store carries a fine collection of Dutch Colonial antiques and handcrafted furniture. > 22 N. Union St., tel. 609/397–1188.

The Urban Archaeologist Italian and Greek objects for the house and garden are the highlights here. > 63 Bridge St., tel. 609/397–9588.

NEW HOPE

Farley's Bookshop The store's crowded shelves hold plenty of choices, including a good selection of books about the area and children's volumes. > 44 S. Main St., tel. 215/862–2452.

Golden Door Gallery Specializing in works by Bucks County painters, sculptors, and printmakers, the Golden Door also displays work by artists from other parts of the country. > 52 S. Main St., tel. 215/862–5529. Closed Mon.

Hobensack & Keller Antique (real and faux) garden ornaments, salvaged wrought-iron fencing, and Oriental rugs are among the finds. > 57 W. Bridge St., tel. 215/862–2406.

Katy Kane Head here for high-quality antique, vintage, and designer clothing; accessories; and fine linens. The shop is open by appointment only. > 34 W. Ferry St., tel. 215/862–5873.

Olde Hope Antiques Hooked rugs, Pennsylvania German textiles, hand-painted furniture, American portraits, and folk art are on offer at this beautifully arranged space, open by appointment only. > 6465 U.S. 202, tel. 215/297–0200.

Pink House Antiques Magnificent 18th- and 19th-century European furnishings and textiles are for sale at this antiques store. > 80 Ferry St., tel. 215/862–5947.

LAHASKA

Peddler's Village In the early 1960s, Earl Jamison bought a 6-acre chicken farm, moved local 18th-century houses to the site, and opened a collection of specialty shops and restaurants. Today the 75 shops in the 42-acre "village" peddle books, cookware, toys, leather goods, clothes, jewelry, contemporary crafts, art prints, candles, and other decorative items. The Grand Carousel, a restored 1922 Philadelphia Toboggan Company creation, still operates. Children love the games and rides of Giggleberry Fair. > York Rd., tel. 215/794–4000.

Penn's Purchase Factory Outlet Stores The 40 stores here sell merchandise at 20%–60% off regular retail prices. The brands represented include Adidas, Coach, Easy Spirit, Izod, Nine West, Orvis, and Nautica. Peddler's Village is across the road. > 5881 York Rd., at U.S. 202, tel. 215/794–0300.

Save the Date

APRIL

Annual Shad Festival On the last weekend of the month of April, Lambertville celebrates its favorite fish, marking the arrival of spring's warm weather. The festival includes musical performances and the showing of works by local artists and craftspeople. At Lewis Fishery, New Jersey's only commercial fishery, you can watch shad being hauled in. > Tel. 609/397–9066, www.lambertville.org.

DECEMBER

Washington's Crossing Reenactment Past and present seem to merge during the annual Christmas Day reenactment of George Washington's crossing of the Delaware River. Locals don Colonial uniforms and brave the elements in small boats, leaving from Washington Crossing Historic Park on the Pennsylvania side and arriving at Washington Crossing State Park on the New Jersey side. At nearby restaurants later in the day, you may discover troops, still in uniform, enjoying their holiday fare. > Tel. 215/493–4076 or 609/737–9303, www.state.nj.us/dep/parksandforests.

WHERE TO STAY

The area has relatively limited lodging options for families; larger inns, hotels, and motels are the best bets.

ERWINNA

Evermay on-the-Delaware A cream-color clapboard Victorian is the centerpiece of this property along the Delaware River. Rooms are housed in several buildings. Interiors are traditional, with fresh flowers, antique furniture, and subdued prints in the guest rooms. A pre-dinner sherry or afternoon tea is served in the stately parlor of the main house, which has twin fireplaces. The restaurant serves highly regarded contemporary American fare. > 889 River Rd., PA 18920, tel. 610/294–9100, www.evermay.com. 15 rooms, 1 suite, 1 cottage. Restaurant, in-room data ports, some in-room hot tubs; no room TVs, no kids, no smoking. MC, V. CP. **$–$$$**

Golden Pheasant Inn Rooms at this intimate 1857 inn all have four-poster beds, overlook the canal and the Delaware River, and often book months in advance. Bright colors are juxtaposed against ruffled and lace trimmings. The restaurant serves French and French-inspired dishes in a pretty setting. > 763 River Rd., PA 18920, tel. 610/294–9595 or 800/830–4474, fax 610/294–9882, www.goldenpheasant.com. 6 rooms, 1 suite. Restaurant, in-room data ports, some kitchenettes, cable TV, some pets allowed (fee); no smoking. AE, D, DC, MC, V. CP. **$–$$**

LAHASKA

Ash Mill Farm An 18th-century fieldstone manor house set on 10 acres just south of Lahaska serves as country B&B. High ceilings, ornate moldings, and deep-sill windows add character to the parlor; guest rooms have family antiques, reproductions, and thoughtful extras, such as hair dryers and down comforters on canopy or four-poster beds. The porch has a view of resident sheep. > 5358 York Rd., Holicong, PA 18928, tel. 215/794–5373, www.ashmillfarm.com. 3 rooms, 2 suites. Dining room, some fans, cable TV, Internet; no kids under 10. MC, V. BP. **$$**

Barley Sheaf Farm Once the home of George S. Kaufman, who cowrote such classic plays as *The Man Who Came to Dinner* and *You Can't Take It with You,* this 30-acre property includes a 1740 fieldstone house, a duck pond, a pool, and a meadow full of sheep. Bedrooms have country antiques, and brass and four-poster beds. A hearty breakfast is served on the sunporch. Barley Sheaf Farm is 1 mi west of Lahaska. > 5281 York Rd., Holicong, PA 18928, tel. 215/794–5104, fax 215/794–5332, www.barleysheaf.com. 8 rooms, 7 suites. Dining room, some in-room hot tubs, some microwaves, some refrigerators, cable TV, pool, badminton, croquet, business services, meeting rooms; no kids under 8, no smoking. AE, MC, V. BP. **$–$$$**

Golden Plough Inn The main building of this inn has 22 spacious rooms, many with four-poster beds, rich fabrics, and cozy window seats. Some have a fireplace or whirlpool bath. Buildings housing other rooms are scattered around Peddler's Village and include an 18th-century farmhouse and a carriage house. > Peddler's Village, U.S. 202 and Street Rd., Lahaska, PA 18931, tel. 215/794–4004, fax 215/794–4000, www.goldenploughinn.com. 42 rooms, 24 suites. Restaurant, some in-room hot tubs, refrigerators, cable TV, shops, no-smoking rooms. AE, D, DC, MC, V. CP. **$–$$$**

LAMBERTVILLE

Historic Lambertville House Rooms in this former stagecoach stop, built in 1823, are furnished with a mix of antiques and period pieces. Most have whirlpool tubs, and some rooms have fireplaces. The handsome stone building overlooks Lambertville's small downtown; it's also steps away from North Union Street's antiques shops and the bridge to New Hope. On the first floor is Left Bank Libations, a cozy bar with an inviting outdoor warm-weather porch. > 32 Bridge St., Lambertville 18938, tel. 609/397–0200 or 888/867–8859, fax 609/397–0511, www.lambertvillehouse.com. 20 rooms, 6 suites. Dining room, in-room data ports, in-room hot tubs, cable TV, bar, meeting rooms; no smoking. AE, MC, V. BP. $$–$$$

Inn at Lambertville Station At this small, contemporary hotel, rooms overlook the Delaware River and are decorated with antiques and antique-reproduction furnishings. Suites have sitting areas and gas fireplaces. > 11 Bridge St., Lambertville 08530, tel. 609/397–8300 or 800/524–1091, fax 609/397–9744, www.lambertvillestation.com. 37 rooms, 8 suites. Restaurant, in-room data ports, in-room hot tubs, cable TV, bar, lobby lounge, laundry service. AE, MC, V. BP. $$–$$$

Martin Coryell House Bed & Breakfast The rather formal inn is classically decorated, with a chinoiserie mural, a hand-painted dining-room ceiling inspired by a New Orleans ballroom, and rich wallpapers. Romantic touches—such as whirlpool tubs for two or claw-foot tubs, fireplaces, and plush feather beds—fill the rooms. > 111 N. Union St., Lambertville 08530, tel. 609/397–8981, fax 609/397–0755, www.martincoryellhouse.com. 3 rooms, 3 suites. Dining room, some in-room hot tubs, cable TV, Internet; no kids under 12, no smoking. AE, MC, V. CP. $$–$$$$

Stockton Inn Immortalized in a Rodgers and Hart song about "a small hotel with a wishing well," the Stockton has a circa-1710 main house as well as three other buildings with guest rooms, mostly suites. Several have a canopy bed and fireplace. The restaurant serves traditional American cuisine. > 1 Main St., Stockton, NJ 08559, tel. 609/397–1250, fax 609/397–8948, www.stocktoninn.com. 4 rooms, 7 suites. Restaurant, some refrigerators, cable TV, bar; no smoking. AE, MC, V. CP. $–$$

Woolverton Inn More than 300 acres of farm- and woodland surround this stunning stone manor beside the Delaware River, creating a secluded hideaway. Antiques, in-room CD players, and fluffy feather beds are among the many fine touches here; some rooms have a whirlpool bath and a fireplace. Amelia's Suite is all opulence, with red damask bedding and a crystal chandelier. Stockton's Hideaway, tailored but textured, has a window seat overlooking a garden. Accommodations in the 1860s carriage house and in two barns have private entrances and outdoor sitting areas. > 6 Woolverton Rd., Stockton, NJ 08559, tel. 609/397–0802, fax 609/397–0987, www.woolvertoninn.com. 7 rooms, 6 suites. Dining room, some fans, some in-room data ports, some in-room hot tubs, some refrigerators, steam room, hiking, meeting rooms; no room TVs, no kids under 12, no smoking. AE, MC, V. BP. $$–$$$$

NEW HOPE

Best Western New Hope Inn A few minutes from the center of New Hope, this Best Western is the place to consider when the B&Bs are booked or you want to stay only one night. The hotel is nicely outfitted, and the amenities here make this a good option for families. > 6426 Lower York Rd., 18938, tel. 215/862–5221 or 800/467–3202, fax 215/862–5847, www.bwnewhope.com. 159 rooms. Restaurant, in-room data ports, cable TV with video games, tennis court, pool, gym, bar, playground, dry cleaning, laundry facilities, business services, some pets allowed (fee), no-smoking rooms. AE, D, DC, MC, V. ¢–$

Hotel du Village A large early-1900s stone mansion that once served as a boarding school has been transformed into an inn with the feel of an English manor house. Guest rooms have country furniture, quilts, and elegant artwork. > 2535 River Rd., 18938, tel. 215/862–9911, fax 215/862–9788, www.hotelduvillage.com. 19 rooms. Restaurant, 2 tennis courts, pool, bar; no room phones, no room TVs, no smoking. AE, DC. CP. **$**

Logan Inn George Washington is said to have stayed at this early-1700s inn on at least five occasions. Rooms are decked out with patterned wall coverings, upholstery, and rugs, and have swagged windows, original and reproduction Colonial and Victorian furnishings, and canopy beds; some have river views. > 10 W. Ferry St., 18938, tel. 215/862–2300, www.loganinn.com. 16 rooms. Restaurant, in-room data ports, cable TV. AE, D, DC, MC, V. Closed Jan. CP. **$$–$$$**

Mansion Inn Even the English gardens at this elegant 1863 Victorian inn feel private. Inside, Depression glass, local artwork, antiques, and comfortable furniture fill the high-ceilinged yellow and beige sitting rooms. Guest rooms have antique pieces, plush linens, and modern baths; some have fireplaces, canopy beds, and whirlpool tubs. > 9 S. Main St., 18938, tel. 215/862–1231, fax 215/862–0277, www.themansioninn.com. 2 rooms, 5 suites. Restaurant, some in-room hot tubs, cable TV, pool; no TV in some rooms, no smoking, no kids under 16. AE, MC, V. BP. **$$–$$$$**

Wedgwood Inn The B&B includes an 1870 Victorian with a porch and gabled roof as well as a Federal-style 1840 stone manor house and the 1870 Aaron Burr House, all amid lush gardens. Rooms may have Wedgwood pieces, a fireplace, or a four-poster or canopy bed; those in the Aaron Burr House are a bit more countrified than the others, with lace or floral bedspreads. Breakfast is served on the sunporch, gazebo, or in your room. Tennis and pool privileges are available. > 111 W. Bridge St., 18938, tel. 215/862–2570, www.new-hope-inn.com/wedgwood. 15 rooms, 4 suites. Some fans, some in-room hot tubs, cable TV, concierge, meeting rooms, some pets allowed; no TV in some rooms, no smoking. AE, MC, V. CP. **¢–$$**

WHERE TO EAT

ERWINNA

Evermay on-the-Delaware The cream-color clapboard Victorian mansion is as popular for its contemporary fare as it is for its stylish B&B accommodations. On Friday and Saturday, there's one seating, at 7:30. Dinner is prix fixe; $68 includes six courses and a glass of champagne. Most items are set, but you do get to choose between two entrées—pan-seared salmon in beurre blanc or roast loin of lamb in mint demiglacé, for example. A four-course dinner ($45) is offered Sunday, with multiple seatings from 5 to 7:30. > 889 River Rd., PA, tel. 610/294–9100. MC, V. Closed Mon.–Thurs. No lunch. **$$$$**

Golden Pheasant Inn At this intimate inn, one of the prettiest places along the Delaware Canal, you may dine beneath the stars in the solarium. The tavern room has a working fireplace, gleaming copper cooking vessels, and pierced-tin chandeliers. Depending on the season, the menu, built on traditional French food, might list roasted pheasant in apple–Calvados sauce or sautéed scallops in lobster-and-wine sauce. Brunch is available Sunday. > 763 River Rd., PA, tel. 610/294–9595. AE, D, DC, MC, V. Closed Mon. and Tues. No lunch. **$$–$$$$**

LAMBERTVILLE

DeAnna's You have three dining options here: a bohemian main dining room with colorful, overstuffed cushions; a more formal dining room; and, in warm weather, a covered outdoor patio. The restaurant is known for its homemade ravioli and other pasta dishes; Gorgonzola cream sauce is a specialty. > 18 S. Main St., Lambertville, tel. 609/397–8957. No credit cards. Closed Mon. No lunch. BYOB. $–$$

Full Moon The menu at this funky, casual eatery includes Asian, Cajun, and Mediterranean dishes. At lunch there's hearty meat loaf, along with such vegetarian offerings as cheese-topped Portobello mushrooms sautéed with onions and peppers in pesto olive oil. Dinner, served Friday and Saturday, might include seafood bisque, baked artichoke, or grilled pork chops seasoned with Cajun spices. > 23 Bridge St., Lambertville, tel. 609/397–1096. No credit cards. Closed Tues. No dinner Sun.–Thurs. $–$$

Hamilton's Grill Room The casually elegant Grill Room has earned a fine reputation for its simply prepared, Mediterranean-inspired meat and fish dishes. The open grill, the centerpiece of the main dining room, figures heavily in the kitchen's preparations. Entrées might include grilled duck with dates and almonds or grilled tuna with avocado chutney, for example. > 8½ Coryell St., Lambertville, tel. 609/397–4343. Reservations essential. AE, MC, V. No lunch. BYOB. $$–$$$

The Lambertville Station The restaurant, in an 1867 stone building—a former train depot designed by Thomas Ustick Walter, architect of the U.S. Capitol's dome—serves American dishes in Victorian-style dining rooms. Classics include roasted pork loin in onion gravy and Atlantic salmon with lemon-dill sauce. The pub serves sandwiches and snacks. Sunday brunch is popular. > 11 Bridge St., Lambertville, tel. 609/397–8300. AE, MC, V. $$–$$$

Stockton Inn Murals and fireplaces add to the coziness of the dining rooms at this inn. In warm weather, you may choose to eat outdoors by waterfalls and a pond. The food is largely American but draws on other cuisines. Roast pork tenderloin is glazed with maple syrup, wrapped in prosciutto, and served with port sauce; grilled swordfish is spiced with Jamaican jerk seasoning and accompanied with passion-fruit coulis. Brunch is offered on Sunday. > 1 Main St., Stockton, NJ, tel. 609/397–1250. AE, MC, V. $$–$$$

LUMBERVILLE

Black Bass Hotel The excellent restaurant at this long-standing inn serves contemporary dishes such as lobster bouillabaisse and grilled, cumin-rubbed pork chop. An outdoor deck with tables overlooks the Delaware River. > Rte. 32, tel. 215/297–5770. AE, DC, MC, V. $$–$$$$

NEW HOPE

Havana Bar and Restaurant Grilled specialties are what stand out amid the American and contemporary fare here. Options include sesame onion rings, a grilled eggplant-and-Brie sandwich, and an updated hamburger with Gorgonzola and spiced walnuts. Jazz, blues, and dance bands enliven the bar Thursday through Sunday nights; Monday is karaoke night. Havana's Main Street view, especially from the patio, makes this spot ideal for people watching. > 105 S. Main St., tel. 215/862–9897. AE, D, DC, MC, V. $–$$

Hotel du Village The restaurant, in a former school, serves French-country fare. Dishes include tournedos Henri IV, a beef fillet with béarnaise sauce; sweetbreads with mushrooms in Madeira sauce; and fillet of sole in curried butter. The dining room is

Tudor in style; you also may eat on the sunporch. Desserts are extravagant. > 2535 N. River Rd., tel. 215/862–9911. AE, DC. Closed Mon. and Tues. No lunch. **$$–$$$**

La Bonne Auberge Inside a pre-Revolutionary farmhouse, La Bonne Auberge serves classic French cuisine in a formal setting. Some specialties include rack of lamb and poached Dover sole with champagne-and-lobster sauce. The four-course prix fixe menu ($50, available Wednesday and Thursday) is a good deal. The restaurant is within a development called Village 2; travel directions are provided when you call for a reservation. > Village 2, off Mechanic St., tel. 215/862–2462. Reservations essential. Jacket required. AE, MC, V. Closed Mon. and Tues. No lunch. **$$$–$$$$**

Logan Inn A restored 1727 inn is home to elegant Colonial dining rooms as well as an enclosed Garden Room, which has a wall of stained glass, and a tavern. When the weather cooperates, patio dining is popular. The multiple-personality menu ranges from contemporary dishes, such as broiled grouper with Jamaican jerk spicing and mango-papaya salsa, to pasta and other Italian preparations as well as Continental fare. In addition to lunch and dinner, this friendly place also serves a bar menu throughout the day. > 10 W. Ferry St., tel. 215/862–2300. AE, D, DC, MC, V. Closed Jan. **$–$$$**

Martine's The beam ceiling, plaster-over-stone walls, and fireplace make Martine's look like an English pub. The eclectic menu includes filet mignon au poivre, pasta, duckling, and a steamed seafood mélange. The French onion soup is a winner. Outdoor dining is on a small patio. > 7 E. Ferry St., tel. 215/862–2966. AE, MC, V. **$$–$$$**

Mother's At one of New Hope's most popular dining spots, it's the desserts—including chocolate-mousse pie and apple-walnut cake—that really stand out. The menu is extensive, covering homemade soups, pastas, and unusual pizzas. In summer meals are also served in the garden. Expect to wait; it's often crowded here. > 34 N. Main St., tel. 215/862–9354. AE, D, MC, V. **$$–$$$**

Odette's In 1961 Parisian actress Odette Myrtil Logan converted this former canal lock house into a restaurant that resembles a French country bistro. The Continental menu, which changes seasonally, might include pine nut–crusted swordfish or roasted rack of veal. Sunday brunch is buffet style. Entertainment consists of a nightly session around the piano bar, legendary among local show-tune buffs, plus regular appearances by nationally known cabaret performers. > S. River Rd. ½ mi south of Bridge St., tel. 215/862–2432. AE, DC, MC, V. Reservations essential. **$$–$$$**

ESSENTIALS

Getting Here

Lambertville and New Hope are completely manageable without a car if you stay in town and don't plan to explore the surrounding areas. If you do want to wind through pastoral back roads and take in some rural scenery, or if you plan to do a lot of antiques shopping (and buying), a car is a must. Whether you come by car or bus, traffic can be an issue. Still, car is always the faster option.

BY BUS

Trans-Bridge buses leave for Lambertville and New Hope from Manhattan's Port Authority Bus Terminal four to nine times daily. The trip to Lambertville is scheduled to take an hour and 40 minutes to 2 hours and 25 minutes, but takes longer in traffic. New Hope is another 10 minutes or so farther. Round-trip peak tickets cost $27.55 to either location.

LINES **Trans-Bridge Lines** > Tel. 800/962–9135 or 610/868–6001, www.transbridgebus.com.

BY CAR

From New York, take Interstate 95 or U.S. 1/U.S. 9 south to Interstate 78 west (toward Clinton) and proceed to Interstate 287 south. Then take U.S. 202 south through Flemington to Route 179 south, which takes you to Lambertville. When you reach the traffic light at the bottom of a steep hill, turn right onto Bridge Street. To get to New Hope, continue on Bridge Street across the Delaware River.

Visitor Information

CONTACTS **Bucks County Conference and Visitors Bureau** > 3207 Street Rd., Bensalem, PA 19020, tel. 215/639–0300 or 800/836–2825, www.bccvb.org. **Lambertville Area Chamber of Commerce** > 239 N. Union St., Lambertville, NJ 08530, tel. 609/397–9066, www.lambertville.org. **New Hope Information Center** > 1 W. Mechanic St., New Hope, PA 18938, tel. 215/862–5880 automated menu, 215/862–5030 travel counselor, www.newhopepa.com.

West Point & Bear Mountain

West Point is 50 mi north of New York City

5

By Wendy Kagan

VAST, RUGGED PARKLANDS and captivating Revolutionary War history surround and define the Hudson River shores at West Point and Bear Mountain State Park. The Gothic facades of the United States Military Academy at West Point, like some medieval fortress, lend an imposing aspect to the river's narrowest, deepest, and perhaps most striking, section. George Washington once considered West Point to be the nation's key strategic defense position, and the site remains a tremendous seat of power, history, pageantry, and patriotism. Touring the academy's grounds, you walk in the footsteps of the presidents, war heroes, and astronauts who trained here as cadets.

South of the citadel is the mountain that some say resembles the profile of a reclining bear. Bear Mountain presides over the eponymous, four-season state park, which has trails for hiking, biking, and cross-country skiing; lakes and streams for boating and fishing; a public swimming pool and playgrounds; and an ice rink. A beautiful weekend can attract swarms of picnickers, but the commotion rarely extends beyond the lawns and into the wooded trails, which the park shares with adjacent Harriman State Park—a rambling wilderness of mountain peaks, dense forests, and beach-fringed lakes. A 21-mi stretch of the Appalachian Trail, including its first completed section, snakes through both parks, crossing nine peaks before crossing the Hudson River via the Bear Mountain Bridge.

A few miles north of West Point, in Cornwall, the majestic granite dome known as Storm King inspired many 19th-century Hudson River school painters. The American environmental movement gained tremendous momentum here in the early 1960s, when locals fought Con Edison's plans to erect a power plant that would desecrate the mountainside. Eschewing industry, the state opened a park in Cornwall, but severe forest fires—which triggered the detonation of unexploded ammunition from the military academy—led to its closure in 1999. The park has since reopened to the public, so you can hike the storied peak, which dips its toes in the river. Or you can simply drive along its perimeter. Carved into the granite, Storm King Highway (Route 218) hugs the tree-lined rock face, winding in and out of the foliage to reveal stunning Hudson vistas. Nearby, colossal modern sculptures pepper the meadows and fields of the renowned Storm King Art Center.

A drive upriver takes you to Newburgh, where George Washington kept his headquarters and residence toward the close of the Revolutionary War. Although the city lost much of its original architecture to urban renewal, Newburgh retains the largest historic district in the state, with elaborate Italianate mansions and fanciful Queen Anne Victorians lining Montgomery, Grand, and Liberty streets. Although the city's interior is rather rough, the waterfront area has rebounded, thanks partly to the bevy of restaurants, bars, and shops that opened at Newburgh Landing in 2000. A parade of tour boats departs from here, and piers, pathways, and alfresco tables make it a prime spot from which to ogle valley views.

WHAT TO SEE & DO

Bear Mountain State Park The mass of pinkish-grey granite known as Bear Mountain looms over this enormously popular 5,067-acre park, which hugs the Hudson River at the northern end of the Palisades Interstate Parkway. The park's varied terrain affords hiking, road biking, and cross-country skiing, and boat rentals and fishing are available on Hessian Lake, and small craft can moor at a dock on the river. Of the three picnic areas, the prettiest edges the lake. Open to the public are the Bear Mountain Inn and its restaurant, a swimming pool, an ice rink (rentals $3 plus $2 deposit), merry-go-round, playground, and playing fields. The **Trailside Museums & Wildlife Center** (open daily year-round, 10–4:30) consists of a nature trail with outdoor exhibits and animal enclosures, as well as four museum buildings with exhibits interpreting such themes as Colonial and Native American history, geology, and wildlife. To enter the park, take the Palisades Interstate Parkway to Exit 19 and follow signs. Parking fills up quickly on weekends, so plan accordingly. > Rte. 9W, Bear Mountain, tel. 845/786–2701, http://nysparks.state.ny.us. Free; parking $6, museum $1, pool $2. Daily 8 AM–dusk.

Harriman State Park Miles of hiking trails and biking roadways link this park with contiguous Bear Mountain State Park, with which it is considered one unit of the Palisades Interstate Park system. Nearly 10 times as large as its neighbor, the park encompasses more than 46,000 acres in the Ramapo Mountains of the Hudson Highlands. Mostly vast, pristine wilderness in which are scattered 31 lakes, ponds, and reservoirs, the park has several recreational areas, including three beaches (at lakes Welch, Sebago, and Tiorati); two camping facilities; fishing areas; and cross-country skiing, hiking, and bridle trails. In a wooded valley, the **Anthony Wayne Recreation Area** (Exit 17 off the Palisades Parkway) has picnic areas with fireplaces, playing fields, and access to hiking and skiing trails. The Silver Mine area (Exit 18 off the parkway) has lakeside picnic grounds and biking roads, as well as boat-launch sites and fishing. A visitors center, in the parkway median between exits 16 and 17, sells trail maps and books. > Palisades Interstate Parkway Exits 15–18, tel. 845/786–2701, http://nysparks.state.ny.us. Free; parking $6 (beach parking $7). Daily 8 AM–dusk.

United States Military Academy at West Point Occupying the western shore of one of the most scenic bends in the Hudson River, the academy sits on some 16,000 acres of training grounds, playing fields, and buildings constructed of native granite in the Military Gothic style. The oldest continually garrisoned post in the U.S. Army, the citadel was founded in 1778 and opened as a military academy in 1802. Distinguished graduates include Robert E. Lee, Ulysses S. Grant, and Douglas MacArthur. The world's oldest and largest military museum, the **West Point Museum** in Olmstead Hall showcases a vast collection of uniforms, weapons, flags, American military art, and other memorabilia. **Fort Putnam**, built in 1778 and a key component of West Point's defense during the Revolutionary War, was restored in the 1970s. Campus visits are by bus tour only (bring photo ID), but you do get a chance to step off the bus, look at a few memorials and cannons up close, and perhaps glimpse cadets in action. Individuals are also allowed on campus for sporting and cultural events, including football games, theater presentations, parades, and concerts. You can visit the museum and visitors' center without taking the tour. Tours aren't given during graduation week (usually late May) and on Saturdays of home football games. > Rte. 9W 5 mi north of Bear Mountain State Park, Highland Falls, tel. 845/938–2638, www.usma.edu. Tour $7, museum and Visitors Center free. Visitors Center daily 9–4:45, museum daily 10:30–4:15.

WHAT'S NEARBY

Newburgh Landing Newburgh's revitalized waterfront is a lively spot where you may stroll, catch a tour boat, and sample the creations of the riverfront restaurants. The cluster of businesses here, which also includes bars and a day spa, definitely benefits from the breezy marina setting and panoramic Hudson Highlands views. Torches has an expansive bar and floor-to-ceiling windows; it also lays claim to one of the biggest aquariums in the country—a 5,700-gallon tank filled with exotic fish. > Front and 4th Sts., Newburgh.

Storm King Art Center More than 100 sculptures by major international artists—including David Smith, Alexander Calder, and Isamu Noguchi—are spread out on 500 acres of hills, fields, meadows, and woodlands. The relationship between art and nature is a focus point for the center. For the best overview of the grounds and collection, ride the shuttle (wheelchair-accessible), which runs every half hour. Free "Highlights of the Collection" walk-in tours are offered daily at 2 and summer evenings at 5:30. Designated picnic areas have tree-shaded tables. Whether or not you picnic, consider bringing bug repellent. > Old Pleasant Hill Rd., Mountainville, tel. 845/534–3115, www.stormking.org. $9. Apr.–late Oct., Wed.–Sun. 11–5:30 (late May–Labor Day Sat. until 8 PM); late Oct.–mid-Nov., Wed.–Sun. 11–5.

Washington's Headquarters State Historic Site From April 1782 to August 1783, General George Washington made his military headquarters and home in this Dutch fieldstone house, where he attended to the final years of Revolutionary War activity. Ongoing guided tours show how Washington, his wife, Martha, and his aides-de-camp lived and worked here as the war drew to a close. Filled with period furniture and reproductions, the house opened to the public in 1850, becoming the first official historic site in the United States. A monument to peace, the Tower of Victory was erected here in the late 1880s. A small museum, containing artifacts collected over 150 years, opened adjacent to the house in 1910. > 84 Liberty St., Newburgh, tel. 845/562–1195, http://nysparks.state.ny.us. $3. Mid-Apr.–Oct., Mon. and Wed.–Sat., 10–5; Sun. 11–5.

Woodbury Common Premium Outlets More than 220 designer outlets fill this sprawling shopping complex in Central Valley, about 20 minutes north of Bear Mountain. Many of the top fashion retailers are here, including Giorgio Armani, Gucci, J. Crew, and Donna Karan. Beyond clothing, the goods range from shoes and leather goods to housewares and jewelry, with outlets for Nike, Kenneth Cole, and Williams-Sonoma. Deals can be found but don't expect everything to be a bargain. One of the most popular destinations in the state, the center draws about 10 million visitors a year. The parking lots fill quickly and traffic can be a tangle on weekends (and certain holidays). > 498 Red Apple Ct. (off Rte. 32, Exit 16 of I–87), Central Valley, tel. 845/928–4000 or 845/928–6840, www.premiumoutlets.com/woodburycommon.

Tours

Between Bear Mountain and Newburgh, the Hudson River winds through some of the most enchanting scenery on the East Coast, complete with picturesque river towns, poetically named peaks, and even a crumbling castle. In a single afternoon you can drink it all in from the deck of a riverboat. Three cruise operators, each with its own itinerary, schedule, and amenities, tour the region.

Hudson Highlands Cruises Departing from West Point's South Dock, the World War I-era ferryboat *Commander* takes you north past Constitution Island and Storm King Mountain to Pollepel Island for a view of the ruins of Bannerman's Castle before returning to West Point 90 minutes later. From May through October, cruises leave weekdays at 12:30 and on the first Sunday of the month. Tickets, $13, are payable at the dock. Reservations are recommended. > South Dock, West Point, tel. 845/534–7245, www.commanderboat.com.

Hudson River Adventures On weekends from May through October, the company's *Pride of the Hudson,* a modern yacht, departs from Newburgh Landing for one to two cruises a day. The two-hour sightseeing cruise takes you south past the ruins of Bannerman's Castle on Pollepel Island and passes Cold Spring and Storm King Mountain before turning back at West Point. A special cruise to Pollepel Island operates twice a month and includes commentary about the castle, which was built to store munitions at the beginning of the 20th century, but the cruise doesn't land at the island. Tickets are $15; advance ticket purchase is recommended. > Newburgh Landing, Front and Fourth Sts., Newburgh, tel. 845/220–2120, www.prideofthehudson.com.

River Rose Cruises *The River Rose* is a double-decker New Orleans paddle-wheel boat—with a fully stocked snack and wine bar—that first saw service in the 1980s on the Mississippi River. Cruises leave once daily on weekends from mid-April through October; dinner and Sunday-brunch cruises are available. The two-hour round-trip cruise to West Point leaves the dock at 2. Tickets, payable at the dock, are $15. Reservations are recommended. > Newburgh Landing, Front and Fourth Sts., Newburgh, tel. 845/562–1067, www.riverrosecruises.com.

Sports

BIKING

Bear Mountain and Harriman State Parks Some 55 mi of roadways snake through these two linked parks, giving you numerous options for biking expeditions. Expect a vigorous ride through hilly areas; you'll be rewarded with fine lake and river views. Popular routes include Seven Lakes Drive east from the Palisades Interstate Parkway and Perkins Memorial Drive to the Hudson River; Tiorati Brook Road off Tiorati Circle; and Arden Valley Road. Many park roads are closed to truck traffic and have 40 mph speed limits. > Palisades Interstate Parkway, Exits 15–19, tel. 845/786–2701, http://nysparks.state.ny.us.

CROSS-COUNTRY SKIING

Bear Mountain State Park The 1777E Trail begins near the ice rink and merry-go-round, cutting an approximately 5-mi loop through the park's Doodletown area. Marked but not groomed, the trail follows an old woods road; mostly flat and fairly wide open, it's suitable for beginner to intermediate skiers. To get there, go to the south end of parking lot No. 2, pass through the stone tunnel, and look for a white trail marker with red lettering. Equipment rentals aren't available. > Rte. 9W, Bear Mountain, tel. 845/786–2701, http://nysparks.state.ny.us.

Harriman State Park Many miles of marked, ungroomed trails crisscross this vast park, so bring a map and keep your bearings. At Lake Sebago (Exit 18 off the Palisades Interstate Parkway), you can pick up a trail near the "fishermen's parking lot." Crossing Seven Lakes Drive, this trail follows peaceful, traffic-free Wood Town Road to Pine Meadow Lake and Lake Wanoksink. The terrain here can vary and is suitable for all levels. Alternately, pick up one of many trails starting near the Anthony Wayne Recreation Area (Exit 17 off the parkway). Beachy Bottom Road is one of several wood roads fit for intermediate-level skiing. The park doesn't offer gear rentals. > Palisades Interstate Parkway, Exits 17 and 18, tel. 845/786–2701, http://nysparks.state.ny.us.

HIKING

Throughout the hiking trails of this region is evidence of old iron mines, active here from Colonial times through the Civil War. In Bear Mountain and Harriman state parks, abandoned shafts, pits, and dumps from these mines are a fascinating aspect of many hikes. Take care to stick to the trails and resist the temptation to explore the old mines, which can be unstable and dangerous.

Bear Mountain State Park The first completed section of the Appalachian Trail (AT) opened in Bear Mountain in 1923; today this section is only a small piece of the 2,160-mi trail that stretches from Georgia to Maine. The moderately vigorous, two-hour trek up Bear Mountain is popular with day-hikers. Begin just past the southern side of the Bear Mountain Inn, following the white AT blazes, which first lead you along a paved road. The trail then splits off to the right, ascending amid open woods. At the peak you may climb to the top of Perkins Memorial Tower for panoramic views of four states (New York, New Jersey, Connecticut, and Pennsylvania) and even glimpse the New York City skyline. > Rte. 9W off Palisades Interstate Parkway Exit 19, Bear Mountain, tel. 845/786–2701, http://nysparks.state.ny.us.

Black Rock Forest Preserve and Consortium Peaceful, less-traveled hiking trails traverse this 3,750-acre preserve just north of Storm King in Cornwall. In the 1800s loggers cut down the old-growth forest here to make way for farms. By the next century a restoration project was under way to bring the forest back, and the preserve remains an important educational and research site. Black Rock, the forest's highest peak, can be accessed from a number of trails. The Stillman Trail ascends through mountain laurel to the summit, which affords views of Storm King, the Schunnemunk Mountains, and the Shawangunks. > Rte. 9W, Cornwall, tel. 845/534–4517, www.blackrockforest.org.

Harriman State Park Scores of trails weave through this enormous park, giving you countless choices for easy, moderate, or vigorous hikes. Stop at the Visitors Center, in the median between exits 16 and 17 of the Palisades Interstate Parkway, and pick up a trail map before you go. Popular routes include the Pine Meadow Trail, a 2½-mi loop that begins at the Reeves Meadow Visitors Center, and the Harriman-Iron Mine Trail, a moderately vigorous 3-mi hike from the Lake Skannatati parking area. The latter trail passes the site of the Pine Swamp iron mine, which dates from the 1830s. > Palisades Interstate Parkway, Exits 15–18, tel. 845/786–2701, http://nysparks.state.ny.us.

Storm King State Park At the heart of this 1,900-acre park is Storm King Mountain, which is veined with hiking trails, many with spectacular views. The park is undeveloped, so there are no toilets and parking is limited. Hikers must heed posted warnings and restrictions and stick to marked trails here because unexploded artillery shells from the neighboring military academy might be found off trails in area B of the park, in the south. (In 1999 severe forest fires set off the unexploded ordnance, or UXO, which apparently would land in the park whenever a particular target range at the military academy was overshot, and resulted in a three-year closure of the park.) > Off Rte. 9W between Cornwall and the United States Military Academy at West Point, tel. 845/786–2701, http://nysparks.state.ny.us.

Save the Date

FEBRUARY

George Washington's Birthday Celebration Lectures, live music, military and craft demonstrations, and family programs honor Washington's birthday during this three-day extravaganza over Presidents' Day weekend. > Washington's Headquarters, 84 Liberty St., Newburgh, tel. 845/562–1195, http://nysparks.state.ny.us.

JUNE

The General's Lady Celebrate the birthday of Martha Washington in early June, with craft demonstrations, food vendors, and live music. > Washington's Headquarters, 84 Liberty St., Newburgh, tel. 845/562–1195, http://nysparks.state.ny.us.

RiverFest Live music, food, and crafts are part of this riverfront celebration in Cornwall-on-Hudson, usually held in early June. > Cornwall Landing (off Shore Rd.), tel. 845/534–7581, www.cornwallny.com.

AUGUST

Kites Over the Hudson Free kites are distributed to the first 150 children at this festival on the grounds of Washington's Headquarters, usually held late in the month. > Washington's Headquarters, 84 Liberty St., Newburgh, tel. 845/562–1195, http://nysparks.state.ny.us.

SEPTEMBER–DECEMBER

Army Football The Black Knights season runs from early September to early December. The last game is always against the Naval Academy team, a rivalry that dates to the 1890s, and is never at home. Each season Army plays at least five games at home (mostly in the afternoons), on Michie Stadium, which many sports fans consider one of the top college-football venues in the United States. Arrive three hours before kick-off to see the Cadet Parade. > Michie Stadium, United States Military Academy at West Point, Rte. 9W 5 mi north of Bear Mountain State Park, Highland Falls, tel. 877/849–2769 ticket office, www.goarmysports.com.

DECEMBER

Washington's Headquarters by Candlelight Tour the historic site at Christmastime to see the 18th-century holiday decorations and costumed interpreters. Live music and hot spiced cider add to the festivities, which take place on two weekend evenings in mid-December. > Washington's Headquarters, 84 Liberty St., Newburgh, tel. 845/562–1195, http://nysparks.state.ny.us.

WHERE TO STAY

Bear Mountain Inn A convenient setting and inexpensive room rates are the draw at this family-friendly place within Bear Mountain State Park. Constructed in 1915 of native stone and timber found on the site, the Main Inn has 12 rooms, a restaurant and bar, and a vast, rustic lobby with a fireplace, a cathedral ceiling, and exposed chestnut-log posts and beams. About a mile away, on the other side of Hessian Lake, are two additional buildings called the Stone Lodges. These have large windows (some with lake views) but get traffic noise from nearby highways. Overlook Lodge, in a quiet wooded area, has 24 spacious, serviceable rooms and a lobby with Hudson River vistas. With the inn undergoing a major renovation that is expected to last through 2005, you may want to request a room in one of the stone lodges. > Rte. 9W, Bear Mountain 10911, tel. 845/786–2731, fax 845/786–2543, www.bearmountaininn.com. 60 rooms. Restaurant, some cable TV, pool, lake, boating, fishing, hiking, cross-country skiing, bar, playground, meeting rooms, no-smoking rooms. AE, D, MC, V. CP. ¢–$

The Thayer Hotel Elegant accommodations and ethereal Hudson River views ennoble this imposing brick-and-granite hotel on the grounds of the United States Military Academy at West Point. Sleek marble floors, iron chandeliers, and portraits of military leaders bedeck the main lobby, whereas dark, regal furnishings and prints of river scenes adorn guest rooms. Request an odd-numbered room for river vistas or an even-numbered room for commander's-eye views of the academy. Corner rooms are particularly spacious. You pass through two security checkpoints on your way to the hotel, which has long housed military officers and their guests. > 674 Thayer Rd., West Point 10996, tel. 845/446–4731 or 800/247–5047, fax 845/446–0338, www.thethayerhotel.com. 117 rooms, 8 suites. Restaurant, room service, in-room data ports, cable TV with video games, hair salon, lounge, comedy club, business services, meeting rooms, no-smoking rooms. AE, D, DC, MC, V. EP. **$$$$**

WHAT'S NEARBY

Cromwell Manor Inn After you arrive at this stately Greek Revival mansion and pass through the grand columns of the portico, any hint of formality dissolves away as the innkeepers greet you with a plate of fresh-baked cookies. Combining manor-house elegance with bed-and-breakfast-style warmth, this 1820 architectural treasure sits regally amid lawns, gardens, and a patio with sunset views. Many rooms have four-poster beds with sheer panels or crocheted canopies; cavernous marble bathrooms accessorize the suites, which are plush. Windows give way to pastoral vistas without another house in sight—except the 1764 Chimney's Cottage, which contains four bedrooms filled with period antiques. > 174 Angola Rd., Cornwall 12518, tel. 845/534–7136, fax 845/534–0354, www.cromwellmanor.com. 10 rooms, 3 suites. Dining room, Internet; no room phones, no room TVs, no kids under 7; no smoking. AE, MC, V. BP. **$$–$$$$**

The Inn at Painter's Funky artwork fills the guest rooms and public spaces of this inn above a popular local restaurant. A slightly disheveled, East Village flavor prevails here. Simple furnishings reminiscent of the 1970s are a backdrop for the eclectic paintings, multimedia works, and bright murals; even radiators are used as canvases. Request a room with a wall mural, such as Room 5, which has a Hudson River landscape on one wall, or Room 8, which has a Hopper-esque street scene. Motel prices make these bohemian digs one of the area's best deals. > 266 Hudson St., Cornwall-on-Hudson 12520, tel. 845/534–2109, fax 845/534–8428, www.painters-restaurant.com. 6 rooms, 1 suite. Restaurant, room service, bar, laundry service; no room phones, no smoking. AE, D, DC, MC, V. EP. **¢–$**

Sebago Cabin Camp Rustic cabins, built in the 1930s, offer a step up from tent camping on the grounds by Lake Sebago in Harriman State Park. Ranging from two to four bedrooms (each with two military cots), the cabins have heat, electricity, refrigerators, and hot plates, but no running water. Bathrooms are communal. Also available are two furnished cottages with private bathrooms and full kitchens. The site has swimming, tennis courts, rowboat rentals, and a recreation hall with kids' activities. Rangers are on duty all night and make Saturday bonfires. From late June through Labor Day, rentals are by the week only (cabins $190–$310, cottages $580–$640). To get here take Exit 16, Lake Welch Drive, off the Palisades Interstate Parkway. > Seven Lakes Dr., off Lake Welch Drive, Harriman State Park 10911, tel. 845/351–2360 information, 800/456–2267 reservations, http://nysparks.state.ny.us. 36 cabins with shared baths, 2 cottages. Picnic area, some kitchens, refrigerators, 2 tennis courts, lake, boating, fishing, basketball, hiking, playground, laundry facilities; no a/c, no room phones, no room TVs, no smoking. MC, V. Closed mid-Oct.–mid-Apr. EP. **¢–$$**

Stockbridge Ramsdell House on Hudson Every bedroom in this rambling 1870 Queen Anne Victorian commands sweeping views of the Hudson River, with some windows framing scenes of Bannerman's Island and the Beacon-Newburgh Bridge. Among the spacious rooms, Beau Rivage has a high canopy bed and private enclosed porch, and Ferry Crossing has an outdoor deck with top-of-the-world vistas. The multicourse breakfast fuels a day's worth of sightseeing. Wander the block to see the 19th-century mansions, but if you stray too far west you'll come to rough-around-the-edges inner Newburgh. > 158 Montgomery St., Newburgh 12550, tel. 845/562–9310, www.stockbridgeramsdell.com. 5 rooms. Dining room, cable TV, in-room VCRs; no room phones, no smoking. AE, D, MC, V. BP. **$$–$$$**

Storm King Lodge A vast, light-filled great room with exposed beams, comfy couches, and a massive hearth welcomes you to this white-clapboard country B&B. Rolling lawns and a peaceful feng shui garden surround the early-1800s carriage house, which was converted to a guest house in the 1920s. The covered back porch—often a setting for breakfast or an evening drink amid candlelight—looks out over the Storm King Art Center's sculpture-strewn meadows across the thruway. Up-stairs guest rooms have higher ceilings and are bright; the Lavender Room has a fire-place, rocker, and wide-board floors. > 100 Pleasant Hill Rd., Mountainville 10953, tel. 845/534–9421, fax 845/534–9416, www.stormkinglodge.com. 4 rooms. Kitchenette, piano; no room phones, no room TVs, no smoking. AE, MC, V. BP. **$$–$$$**

CAMPING

Beaver Pond Campgrounds Adjacent to Lake Welch in Harriman State Park, the campground occupies an open area dotted with trees. Man-made Lake Welch has the largest beach—½-mi long—in the park and is popular for swimming, fishing, boat-ing, and picnicking. Some 14-by-14-foot platforms for free-standing tents are avail-able. Access is from Route 106 off the Palisades Interstate Parkway (Exit 14). > 800 County Rte. 106, Stony Point 10980, tel. 845/947–2792 information, 800/456–2267 reservations, http://nysparks.state.ny.us. 73 regular tent sites, 55 platform tent sites, 12 RV sites without hook-ups. Flush toilets, dump station, running water, showers, fire pits, grills, picnic tables, public telephone, swimming (lake). Reservations essen-tial. MC, V. Closed mid-Oct.–mid-Apr. **¢**

WHERE TO EAT

Cub Room Restaurant Seasonal outdoor dining on a covered porch gives you a bird's-eye view of the boaters on Hessian Lake at this casual eatery within Bear Mountain State Park. The varied menu covers all the bases, from burgers and pastas to barbecued ribs and Parmesan-encrusted salmon. Some dishes err on the greasy side, but the service is cheerful and attentive, and weekends bring a steady stream of families, inn guests, and hungry hikers. > Bear Mountain Inn, Rte. 9W off Palisades Interstate Parkway Exit 19, Bear Mountain, tel. 845/786–2731. AE, D, MC, V. Closed Mon. and Tues. Jan.–Mar. **$–$$**

The Thayer Hotel With its buffet of almost unimaginable abundance, the legendary Sunday champagne brunch ($26 prix fixe) lures crowds to the hotel's dining room. Pastries, salads, pastas, quiches, and even omelet, waffle, and beef-carving stations amount to a veritable food orgy. In summer, angle for a table on the outdoor terrace above the treetops, where you can savor the panoramic Hudson River views. Inside, the chandelier-lit dining room doubles as a dance hall on Saturday nights. Dinner specialties include rack of lamb, stuffed shrimp, and the house pasta dish, fettuccine with artichokes, black olives, and tomatoes. > 674 Thayer Rd., West Point, tel. 845/446–4731 or 800/247–5047. Reservations essential. AE, D, DC, MC, V. **$$–$$$**

WHAT'S NEARBY

Cafe Pitti Riverfront tables under a mandarin-orange canopy make for a relaxed meal at this small café, perfect for lunch, dessert, or a light bite in warm weather. When the air is nippy, head inside to the slightly cramped but warm space. The chairs are rick-ety and the service can be slow, but all is forgiven upon the arrival of the authentic Italian fare. Try a warm panini with brie, arugula, and truffle oil, or a thin-crusted, pro-sciutto-topped pizzetta from the wood-burning oven. Tiramisu and cappuccino cake pair well with a selection of dessert wines and ports. > 40 Front St., Newburgh, tel. 845/565–1444. AE, MC, V. ¢–$

Gasho of Japan Housed in a 400-year-old samurai farmhouse—shipped to America from Japan and reconstructed onsite in Central Valley—this hibachi chophouse claims to deliver both "steak and theater." Skillful chefs slice, dice, flip, and grill your dinner before your eyes, while kimono-clad servers fetch appetizers and umbrella-topped specialty drinks. Proximity to Woodbury Common Premium Outlets makes this a convenient post-shopping spot. > 365 Rte. 32, Central Valley, tel. 845/928–2277. AE, D, DC, MC, V. $–$$$

Il Cena'colo The flavors of Tuscany take center stage at this highly regarded eatery, tucked into an unlikely corner of commercial Newburgh. You'll want to toss the menu aside in favor of the exhaustive list of daily specials, many of which appear with regularity. Fresh buffalo mozzarella, porcini mushrooms, and sun-dried tomatoes pop up in many dishes; the osso buco is a signature dish, and the pasta with shaved black truffles has acquired nearly a cult following. For dessert, don't miss the chocolate soufflé cake. The cordial waitstaff, outfitted in ties and crisp white aprons, presides over the softly lit dining room, which has a pressed-copper ceiling and blonde-wood beams. > 228 S. Plank Rd., Newburgh, tel. 845/564–4494. Reservations essential. Closed Tues. No lunch. AE, D, DC, MC, V. $$–$$$

Painter's Down-home cooking with creative twists keeps the locals coming back to this well-liked tavern. Beyond burgers and steaks, the extensive menu mixes in Southern favorites (such as buttermilk fried chicken with coffee-cream gravy) and other inspired choices (like the veggie-filled "Dragon Bowl" of Chinese noodles and silky peanut sauce). Berry-red ceilings, steel I-beams, and quirky paintings adorn the spacious dining room. Art and revelry spill over into the bar/gallery on weekends. The service can be uneven and the volume high, but the casual crowd and families don't seem to mind. > 266 Hudson St., Cornwall-on-Hudson, tel. 845/534–2109. AE, D, DC, MC, V. $–$$

ESSENTIALS

Getting Here

By far the best way to get to and around the West Point/Bear Mountain area is to drive. Public transportation to the region is limited, especially because a commuter train line doesn't service the area. You can take a bus from Port Authority, but you sacrifice mobility once you're here; significant distances separate the area's attractions and local bus service is infrequent. Weekend traffic notwithstanding, the bus to Bear Mountain takes 1½ hours, as opposed to a car ride of about an hour.

BY BUS

On weekdays, only two daily Shortline buses leave for West Point/Bear Mountain from Manhattan's Port Authority Bus Terminal, with three return buses. On weekends service increases to five buses a day, with four return buses. The round-trip ride costs $22.35 to Bear Mountain (the stop is at the Bear Mountain Inn), $26.55 to West Point (the Visitors Center and Thayer Gate). Some buses continue on to Cornwall and Newburgh. Shortline also offers special day-trip and overnight packages to Bear Mountain State Park, West Point, and Woodbury Common Premium Outlets; call for information.

LINES **Shortline** > Tel. 800/631–8405, www.shortlinebus.com.

BY CAR

Traveling by car dramatically increases the range of sites you'll be able to see in the West Point/Bear Mountain area. With your own wheels, you can bed down at an inn or B&B tucked into the countryside and also explore the scenic Hudson Highlands. A drive along the Storm King Highway (Route 218, off Route 9W), a windy, river-hugging road sliced into the granite mountainside, delivers jaw-dropping views taking in Highland Falls to Cornwall-on-Hudson.

To get to the West Point/Bear Mountain region, take the George Washington Bridge to the Palisades Interstate Parkway. Drive north about 35 mi to the end of the parkway, following signs to Bear Mountain. You pass several exits for recreational areas within Harriman State Park, as well as the park's visitors center, which is in the parkway median between exits 16 and 17. After the parkway ends, veer right to follow U.S. 6. After about 3 mi you come to a traffic circle. Take the first right off the circle to enter Bear Mountain State Park. To continue north to West Point, take the third right off the circle to Route 9W north. Take the first "West Point/Highland Falls" exit, and follow signs to the military academy.

Visitor Information

CONTACTS **City of Newburgh Visitors Center** > Rte. 9W between South and 3rd Sts., Newburgh 12550, tel. 845/565–5559. **Greater Cornwall Chamber of Commerce** > 286 Main St., Cornwall, 12518, tel. 845/534–7826, www.cornwallnychamberofcommerce.org. **Orange County Chamber of Commerce** > 30 Matthews St., Suite 111, Goshen, 10924, tel. 845/291–2136 or 800/762–8687, www.orangetourism.org. **Palisades Parkway Tourist Information Center** > Palisades Interstate Parkway between Exits 16 and 17, tel. 845/786–5003, www.pipc.org.

New Paltz

85 mi north of New York City

6

By Gary Allen

AS YOU ENTER THIS SMALL COLLEGE TOWN from the thruway, the appeal of New Paltz becomes apparent immediately. There, in the distance beyond a main street of casual eateries and quirky shops, rise the craggy cliffs of the Shawangunk Mountains—or the Gunks, as they're known casually. Atop a prominent ledge sits Sky Top Tower, a landmark for miles around. The rolling lands below are carpeted with lush greens in spring and summer; fall turns them into a tapestry of jewel tones. In winter the Shawangunks' beauty is stark but alluring nonetheless.

With steep faces of white quartzite conglomerate that reach more than 2,000 feet above sea level at some points, the Shawangunks are a premier destination for rock climbers in the northeast. Hikers can take in the views from cliff-top trails, high above the Wallkill River valley, and, in autumn, see migrating birds and monarch butterflies flutter by at eye level. Minnewaska State Park Preserve and the Mohonk Preserve, both easily reached from New Paltz, together cover more than 18,000 acres of popular spots for picnicking, mountain biking, cross-country skiing, and other recreational activities, as well as for hiking and rock climbing.

The magnificent natural setting and abundant outdoor activities are draws for repeat visitors as well as new residents, but the village itself has its own charms. Many serious students of the arts first lured to the area by the State University of New York (SUNY) at New Paltz end up staying here after graduation. These artists, craftspeople, writers, and musicians have helped make New Paltz an energetic place with diverse shopping and dining and a vibrant cultural scene.

Founded in 1677 by Huguenots who received a patent from the Colonial governor, New Paltz is also one of the oldest communities in the United States. The settlers originally wanted to build on the flats, on the west side of the Wallkill River, but rethought that plan after the Native Americans warned them about the river's spring floods. Building on the higher, eastern bank was an excellent decision: buildings dating to the early 1700s still stand throughout town. Several serve as bed-and-breakfasts today, so you can experience them personally.

Fertilized by those annual floods, the flats constitute rich farm land, and New Paltz retains much of its agricultural nature today. Apple orchards, farms, and vineyards are found throughout the region; many allow you to pick your own pumpkins or fruit. Local produce and other Hudson Valley ingredients make their way onto menus at area restaurants, many of them staffed or owned by graduates and students of the Culinary Institute of America, which is just across the Hudson River.

Autumn weekends are especially busy, thanks to the fall-foliage spectacle as well as SUNY events that bring students' parents to town. If you plan to visit in fall, book a room at least a couple of months in advance. Even if New Paltz lodgings aren't all booked, consider places in the nearby small villages of High Falls, Rosendale, and Stone Ridge. And pick up produce for home Sunday morning, so you don't get stuck on the long line of cars snaking along Route 299 and Main Street late Sunday afternoon.

WHAT TO SEE & DO

Adair Vineyards Tastings are offered in this small winery's centuries-old Dutch barn. The mountain views provide a pleasant backdrop for a picnic. > 52 Allhusen Rd., tel. 845/255–1377. Free. May, Nov.–Dec., Fri.–Sun. 11–5; June–Oct., daily 11–6.

Country Charm Farm On the first three weekends in October, you can take the kids on a 20-minute hayride and let them pick their own pumpkins (while you admire the views and gardens) and pose with the scarecrow collection. Barn sales, loaded with collectibles and bric-a-brac, begin the first Friday in October. > 201 DuBois Rd., tel. 845/255–4321, www.countrycharmfarm.com. Hayride $1. Oct., weekends 10–4:30.

Huguenot Street A National Historic Landmark, the street includes six stone houses that date to before 1720 and are among the oldest in the United States. Indeed, parts of the Jean Hasbrouck, Abraham Hasbrouck, and Bevier-Elting houses were built in the 1680s, soon after the founding of New Paltz, in 1677. Another building, the French church, is a reconstruction of the 1717 structure, which was torn down in the early 19th century. The Huguenot Historical Society owns the buildings, many of which contain original furnishings and architectural details, and runs tours of them. The 55-minute tour includes an orientation, one house, and the church; the longer tour, nearly two hours, includes two additional houses. Tours begin on the hour during the week and on the half hour on weekends. The tour office is in the 1705 DuBois Fort, on Huguenot Street between Broadhead Avenue and North Front Street. > 64 Huguenot St., tel. 845/255–1889 or 845/255–1660, www.hhs-newpaltz.net. Short tour $7, long tour $10. Tours May–Oct., Tues.–Sun. 9–4.

Mohonk Mountain House Even if you don't stay at this grand Victorian resort, you can spend the day here. The 2,200-acre property includes Lake Mohonk, 85 mi of hiking trails, a 9-hole golf course, extensive gardens, and a restaurant and is adjacent to Mohonk Preserve. If you come for breakfast, lunch, or dinner, admission to the grounds and the house (off limits to day visitors who don't eat here) is included. Meal reservations are required, even for breakfast and lunch. > 1000 Mountain Rest Rd., tel. 845/255–1000, www.mohonk.com. $12 weekends, $10 weekdays. Daily dawn–1 hr before sunset.

Rivendell Winery Tastings of Rivendell wines are offered alongside more than 50 other New York State wines. You may also picnic on the grounds and pick up local foods at the deli counter here. > 714 Albany Post Rd., tel. 845/255–2494, www.rivendellwine.com. Free. Daily 10–6.

State University of New York at New Paltz The college, which long has attracted artistic students, presents the community with a host of cultural offerings on its 216-acre campus. At the **Samuel Dorsky Museum of Art** (tel. 845/257–3844), 19th- and 20th-century photographs and American and European paintings, along with a core collection of works on paper, are focal points. Public concerts are part of **PianoSummer at New Paltz Festival/Institute**; Vladimir Feltsman is the program's artistic director. Also seasonal: the **New Paltz Summer Repertory Theatre,** which mounts comedies, dramas, and musicals in Parker Theatre. > 75 S. Manheim Blvd./Rte. 32S, tel. 845/257–2121, 845/257–3880 box office, www.newpaltz.edu.

Trapeze Club at Stone Mountain Farm From May through September, the center offers several two-hour trapeze classes each week on a 350-acre farm. All levels, from beginner to expert, are welcome; flyers may be as young as four years old. Classes are limited to 10 students; call to reserve a spot. > 475 River Rd. Extension, tel. 845/658–8540, www.trapeze-club.org.

WHAT'S NEARBY

A. J. Snyder Estate The estate includes the Widow Jane Mine, cement kilns, and parts of the Delaware and Hudson Canal. The museum concentrates on the local cement industry and showcases antique sleighs and carriages. > Rte. 213, Rosendale, tel. 845/658–9900. $2. May–Oct., weekends 1–4; or by appointment.

Delaware and Hudson Canal Museum The small museum, in a former church, traces the history of an important waterway that, from 1828–98, connected Pennsylvania's coal mines to the Hudson. Canal boats also carried bluestone for New York City's sidewalks, and Rosendale cement for the Brooklyn Bridge. A brochure outlines a walking tour of landmark locks. > Rte. 6A/Mohonk Rd. off Rte. 213, High Falls, tel. 845/687–9311, www.canalmuseum.org. $3. May–Oct., Mon. and Thurs.–Sat. 11–5, Sun. 1–5.

JMW Auction Gallery Auctions are held at least every few months, and more frequently in summer. They're usually scheduled for Saturday and may include antique furniture, arts-and-crafts pieces, old coins, wrought-iron outdoor dining sets, wicker chairs, and decorative items. The assortment is hit or miss, but half the fun is looking for that one treasure. Call, or check the Web site, for an auction schedule. > Fann's Shopping Center, 1157 Rte. 32, Rosendale, tel. 845/658–8586 or 845/339–4133, www.jmwauction.com.

Locust Lawn Josiah Hasbrouck—a lieutenant in the Revolution and U.S. Congressman during the presidential terms of Jefferson, Madison, and Monroe—built the 1814 Federal-style mansion, which has an impressive three-story central hall. Exhibits include 18th- and 19th-century furniture and an ox cart used to carry supplies to the Continental army at Valley Forge. Nearby is **Terwilliger House** (1738), a Huguenot-era stone building with period furnishings. > 400 Rte. 32, Gardiner, tel. 845/255–1660 Huguenot Historical Society, www.hhs-newpaltz.net. $7. By appointment.

Minnewaska State Park Preserve The park encompasses 12,000 acres in the Shawangunk Mountains. Much of the terrain is wooded and rocky, but you also come across trickling streams, gushing waterfalls, and spectacular valley views. Lake Minnewaska is its jewel; the park also includes Awosting Lake. A network of historic carriageways, now used by hikers, mountain bikers, horseback riders, and cross-country skiers, and other trails veins the land. Swimming is restricted to designated areas; scuba divers must be certified. Boating is allowed with a permit. Nature programs include walks and talks. The entrance to the **Peter's Kill Escarpment,** where you may rock climb, is 1 mi east of the main entrance. > U.S. 44/Rte. 55 5 mi from Rte. 299, tel. 845/255–0752, http://nysparks.state.ny.us. $6 per vehicle. Daily 9–dusk.

Mohonk Preserve The 6,400-acre preserve has more than 60 mi of hiking trails and carriageways and four trailheads: **Visitor Center,** on U.S. 44/Route 55; **West Trapps,** about 1⅓ mi east of the visitor center; **Coxing,** 1 mi off Clove Road (about ¼ mi east of West Trapps); and **Spring Farm,** on Mountain Rest Road near the entrance to the Mohonk Mountain House. The mountain views are spectacular. A visit to the preserve, which accommodates picnickers, walkers, hikers, bikers, rock climbers, and horseback riders, gives you access to the adjacent Mohonk Mountain House grounds (with some restrictions) and the Minnewaska State Park Preserve. > Mohonk Preserve Visitor Center, 3197 U.S. 44/Rte. 55, ½ mi west of Rte. 299, Gardiner, tel. 845/255–0919, www.mohonkpreserve.org. $6 weekdays, $8 weekends and holidays. Daily sunrise–sunset. Visitor center Tues.–Sun. 9–5.

Rosendale Theatre An early-1900s firehouse was converted to a movie theater in 1949—and few changes have been made to it since. Instead of a concession counter, two ancient vending machines discharge candy. Movies run the gamut from action blockbusters to small foreign films and, occasionally, first runs. Call for movie times. > 401 Main St., Rosendale, tel. 845/658–8989. $5.

Tours

Hudson Valley Pottery Trail Of the 10 pottery studios featured on this self-guided tour, three are in High Falls and one is in Stone Ridge. For a free brochure outlining the route, send your request with a self-addressed, stamped business-size envelope. The Web site also shows the route. > Box 433, High Falls, 12440, www.potterytrail.com.

Shawangunk Wine Trail Adair and Rivendell are the two New Paltz–area wineries included on this wine trail. It starts 5½ mi west of the village center, at Rivendell Winery, and continues through 60 mi of scenic countryside. > Rivendell Winery, 714 Albany Post Rd., New Paltz, tel. 845/255–2494, www.rivendellwine.com or www.shawangunkwinetrail.com.

Sports

CROSS-COUNTRY SKIING

Minnewaska State Park Preserve The park has 27 mi of carriage trails (8 mi ungroomed) available for cross-country skiing. Winter scenery here includes frosted cliffs and frozen lakes and waterfalls. > U.S. 44/Rte. 55 5 mi west of Rte. 299, tel. 845/256–0579, 845/256–0752 trail conditions, http://nysparks.state.ny.us. Daily 9–dusk.

Mohonk Mountain House The 2,200-acre property of this Victorian resort includes 38 mi of cross-country-skiing trails. Equipment is available only to resort guests. > 1000 Mountain Rest Rd., tel. 845/255–1000, www.mohonk.com.

Mohonk Preserve Approximately 25 mi of groomed trails lace the preserve and lead to spectacular views. > Mohonk Preserve Visitor Center, 3197 U.S. 44/Rte. 55, ½ mi west of Rte. 299, tel. 845/255–0919, www.mohonkpreserve.org.

Williams Lake Hotel The old-style resort, on 600 rolling wooded acres with a lake, has 7 mi of groomed and backcountry trails, some lit at night. You can rent skis, boots, and poles on site. > Binnewater Rd. 2 mi north of Rte. 213, Rosendale, tel. 845/658–3101 or 800/382–3818, www.willylake.com.

EQUIPMENT **Rock & Snow** > 44 Main St., New Paltz, tel. 845/255–1311, www.rocksnow.com.

HIKING

Some area trails are rather challenging, but less demanding options, including those for casual walkers, are plentiful.

Minnewaska State Park Preserve Crystalline streams and mountain-top lakes highlight 27 mi of carriage trails and 30 mi of footpaths. > U.S. 44/Rte. 55 5 mi west of Rte. 299, tel. 845/256–0579, http://nysparks.state.ny.us.

Mohonk Preserve Hikers can use more than 100 mi of carriageways and paths and are allowed access to the trails of the Minnewaska State Park Preserve and the Mohonk Mountain House Resort. A popular route at the latter starts from the lake and leads through a maze of giant boulders and up the Lemon Squeeze (not for claustrophobic or tall people); the rewards are cool winds and spectacular cliff-top views. > Mohonk Preserve Visitor Center, 3197 U.S. 44/Rte. 55, ½ mi west of Rte. 299, tel. 845/255–0919, www.mohonkpreserve.org.

MOUNTAIN BIKING
The area has an extensive network of well-maintained trails that are peppered with jaw-dropping views.

Minnewaska State Park Preserve The 27 mi of carriage trails open to bikers here are hilly, sometimes quite steep, and have a gravel or rocky surface. The carriageways may take you through woods and meadows, around lakes and beaches, and to ledges with panoramic views. On weekends, the earlier in the day you go, the better. > U.S. 44/Rte. 55 5 mi west of Rte. 299, tel. 845/256–0579, http://nysparks.state.ny.us.

Mohonk Preserve The preserve's 25 mi of carriage roads connect to those of the Mohonk Mountain House resort and the Minnewaska State Park Preserve. The carriage trails, mostly covered in shale, are hilly and sometimes steep but are interspersed with level stretches. Weekends are crowded. > Mohonk Preserve Visitor Center, 3197 U.S. 44/Rte. 55, ½ mi west of Rte. 299, tel. 845/255–0919, www.mohonkpreserve.org.

RENTALS **Bicycle Depot** > 15 Main St., New Paltz, tel. 845/255–3859, www.bicycledepot.com. **Bistro Mountain Store** > 3124 U.S. 44/Rte. 55, at Rte. 299, New Paltz, tel. 845/255–2999. **Table Rock Tours & Bicycles** > 292 Main St., Rosendale, tel. 845/658–7832, www.tablerocktours.com.

ROCK CLIMBING
The long ridge of the Shawangunk Mountains offers plenty of cliffs for climbers of all abilities. Because the Gunks are a major draw for climbing enthusiasts, routes can be extremely crowded on weekends, especially on some of the more accessible cliffs, such as the Trapps and Near Trapps areas.

If you want climbing instruction, use a guide accredited by the American Mountain Guide Association. Note that in order to give climbing classes in Mohonk Preserve, guides must be registered with the preserve. Check with the preserves and local outfitters for guide recommendations.

Minnewaska State Park Preserve Rock climbing is restricted to the lower Peter's Kill Escarpment, a west-facing escarpment, ½-mi long, with a talus area offering excellent bouldering. In order to climb here you first must obtain a climbing permit, on the day you plan to use it, from the office next to the Peter's Kill parking area. The park limits the number of permits it hands out. > U.S. 44/Rte. 55 4 mi west of Rte. 299, tel. 845/256–0752, http://nysparks.state.ny.us.

Mohonk Preserve More than 1,000 technical rock-climbing routes attract 40,000-plus climbing visits each year. A small camping area is available (for climbers only) near Trapps Bridge. > Mohonk Preserve Visitor Center, 3197 U.S. 44/Rte. 55, ½ mi west of Rte. 299, tel. 845/255–0919, www.mohonkpreserve.org. Daily dawn–dusk. Visitor center Tues.–Sun. 9–5.

EQUIPMENT **Eastern Mountain Sports** > 4124 U.S. 44/Rte. 55, Gardiner, tel. 845/255–3280 or 800/310–4504, www.emsclimb.com. **Rock & Snow** > 44 Main St., New Paltz, tel. 845/255–1311, www.rocksnow.com.

Shopping

Shopping in New Paltz is eclectic, largely aimed at students, creative individuals (of all ages), and outdoors enthusiasts. The mix includes unusual imports, antiques, arty items, and sportswear, at mostly reasonable prices. Nearly all the shops are on or near Main Street and within easy walking distance of one another. Farm stands are outside the village center, so you need a car to get to them. High Falls, about 9 mi northwest of New Paltz, has a clutch of interesting shops.

Ariel Booksellers Regional books and remainders are among the strengths of this airy bookstore. Readings include well-known—and, often, local—authors, such as Gail Godwin and Valerie Martin. > 3 Plattekill Ave., New Paltz, tel. 845/255–8041.

Handmade and More Specializing in crafts and jewelry, the store also carries toys, clothing, and a selection of quirky cards. > 6 N. Front St., New Paltz, tel. 845/255–6277; Water Street Market, 10 Main St., New Paltz, tel. 845/255–1458.

Jenkins-Lueken Orchards More than 20 varieties of apples, from Macoun and Red Delicious to Empire and Ida Red, as well as other produce, are sold at this farm stand. You can pick pumpkins, and the apple cider, made on the premises, is fresh and good. > Yankee Folly Rd. at Rte. 299, New Paltz, tel. 845/255–0999. Closed Apr.–mid-Aug.

Toscani & Sons Toscani's prepares fresh cheeses, sausages, and antipasti; sells Italian imported foods and kitchen equipment; and makes good sandwiches ("the Gourmet" combines prosciutto, mozzarella, tomatoes, and olive oil). The days leading up to Christmas and Easter are incredibly busy. > 127 Main St., New Paltz, tel. 845/255–6770. Closed Mon.

Wallkill View Farm Market The farm stand sells local produce, cheeses, baked goods, jams and preserves, maple syrup, garden supplies, fresh-pressed apple cider, and pumpkins you can pick yourself. > 15 Rte. 299, New Paltz, tel. 845/255–8050. Closed Dec. 23–wk before Easter.

Water Street Market An unassuming pedestrian mall includes antiques stores, craft and art galleries, cafés, clothing boutiques, and custom-furniture and other specialty shops. > 10 Main St., New Paltz, tel. 845/255–1458.

Save the Date

MAY
Woodstock/New Paltz Art and Crafts Fair The juried art-and-crafts fair, held Memorial Day weekend, showcases potters, photographers, jewelry designers, and other artists from across the nation. The food is better than usual fair fare, with many vegetarian and unusual dishes. The fair returns Labor Day weekend. > Ulster County Fairgrounds, Libertyville Rd., tel. 845/679–8087 or 845/246–3414, www.quailhollow.com.

AUGUST
Colonial Street Festival Huguenot Street's stone houses and church are open for tours during this one-day event. Weaving, quilting, butter churning, musket firing, sheep shearing, and African-American storytelling are demonstrated. Shuttles leave from the SUNY parking lots, off Route 32 South. > Huguenot St., New Paltz, tel. 845/255–1660 or 845/255–1889, www.hhs-newpaltz.net.

Ulster County Fair Livestock, local-crafts, pig races, and amusement rides constitute a genuine old-fashioned county fair. > Ulster County Fairgrounds, Libertyville Rd., New Paltz, tel. 845/255–1380, www.ulstercountyfair.com.

AUGUST–SEPTEMBER
Woodstock/New Paltz Art and Crafts Fair The fair is held on Labor Day weekend as well as on Memorial Day weekend. (See description above.) > Ulster County Fairgrounds, Libertyville Rd., New Paltz, tel. 845/679–8087 or 845/246–3414, www.quailhollow.com.

SEPTEMBER
Taste of New Paltz Nosh and nibble at this one-day event during which area restaurants, farm markets, breweries, and wineries sell tasting portions. Activities include music acts, children's games, as well as pony and other rides. > Ulster County Fairgrounds, Libertyville Rd., New Paltz, tel. 845/255–0243, newpaltzchamber.org.

Shopping in High Falls

NEAR THE INTERSECTION of Route 213 and Bruceville Road in the tiny village of High Falls (about 9 mi northwest of New Paltz) is a cluster of old buildings with interesting shops and a couple of restaurants, including the highly regarded DePuy Canal House.

Food is the focus at the **New York Store** (103 Main St., High Falls, tel. 845/687–7779), an offshoot of the DePuy Canal House restaurant. In addition to a small assortment of prepared foods and baked goods, the store carries a smattering of chocolates and candies, spreads and preserves, cheeses, flavored oils, and batter mixes—all from New York State. Gift baskets are a specialty.

At appropriately named **Linger** (8 Second St., off Rte. 213, High Falls, tel. 845/687–7907), you may indeed want to stay awhile to browse through the diverse collection of home furnishings and decorative items (most new, some antique), bath-and-body lotions and potions, garden accessories, and affordable jewelry. The owners, a husband-and-wife team, also run the furniture store downstairs.

Lounge (8 Second St., off Rte. 213, High Falls, tel. 845/687–9463) carries Mitchell Gold–brand couches, chairs, and other furnishings, as well as accessories such as lamps and rugs. Can't find the sofa you want? Pick a style, length, and material, and have it delivered.

Antiques fill the warren of rooms at the **Barking Dog** (7 Second St., off Rte. 213, High Falls, tel. 845/687–4834), in business since 1984. You won't find the ubiquitous here. The shop specializes in country pieces, such as pine tables and cupboards, and folk art, and also offers old prints and paintings. Half-price sales are usually held during the weeks surrounding Presidents' Day and Labor Day. For about three weeks in May and sometimes in November, the store showcases its stock of vintage linens, textiles, and clothing (call for details). Nearly all items here date to before the 1920s.

The inventory at **Cathouse Antiques** (136 Bruceville Rd., ½ mi off Rte. 213, High Falls, tel. 845/687–0457) favors the 1940s, but items from the 1930s and '50s are here, too. Kitchen items and housewares in bright hues mingle with collectibles, glass and pottery pieces, and some furniture.

The **Green Cottage** (1204 Rte. 213, High Falls, tel. 845/687–4810), 50% florist, creates interesting bouquets and carries small gift items such as ceramic vases, prettily packaged soaps, sculptural candles, handcrafted jewelry (one of the owners has a jewelry studio), children's books, and a few toys. The mix changes seasonally. Garden gear is featured in summer.

Birds—wild birds, in particular—are the theme at the **Bird Watcher's Country Store** (Rte. 213, High Falls, tel. 800/947–2347), about ½ mi west of High Falls center. In addition to bird feeders, seed, houses, and baths, the store has chimes, field guides, window ornaments, and weathervanes.

WHERE TO STAY

Days Inn The single-story motel is 2 mi east of SUNY New Paltz and convenient to shopping and restaurants. The thruway entrance is less than ½ mi away. > 601 Main St./Rte. 299, 12561, tel. 845/883–7373, www.daysinn.com. 20 rooms. In-room data ports, cable TV, no-smoking rooms. AE, D, DC, MC, V. CP. ¢–$$$

Lefevre House Bed & Breakfast Contemporary European paintings, many of them for sale, fill this 1870 pink-and-white gingerbread Victorian. The name of each room— Red Hot, Am I Blue, Purple Rain, and Green with Envy—corresponds to its color scheme. Although bold, the palettes tend toward rich jewel tones rather than headache-inducing primary colors. Beds, some king-size four posters, have Frette sheets and Versace comforters and shams. Until bathroom renovations are completed (expected by April 2004), rooms have to share baths. (The owners also plan to add three guest rooms.) Breakfast is served in the formal dining room or on the wraparound porch, which has a perfectly framed view of Sky Top Tower. The house is within walking distance of the college. > 14 Southside Ave., 12561, tel. 845/255–4747 or 845/430–5689, fax 845/255–0808, www.lefevrehousebedandbreakfast.com. 3 rooms, 1 suite. Dining room, some in-room hot tubs, some kitchenettes, cable TV, outdoor hot tub; no room phones, no smoking. AE, D, DC, MC, V. BP. $$$

Mohonk Mountain House The rambling Victorian-era hotel—a jumble of gables, towers, chimneys, porches, and turrets—sits at the edge of a mountain-top lake. The resort's 2,200 acres encompass private woodland and elaborate gardens and offer a wealth of options for recreation, including 85 mi of hiking trails. Antiques fill the guest rooms, which are luxurious and spacious. Choice accommodations, in the towers, have original Victorian woodwork, working fireplaces, and balconies. Breakfast and lunch are served buffet-style; dinner is a formal affair for which men (and boys 12 and older) are required to wear jackets. > 1000 Mountain Rest Rd., 12561, tel. 845/255–1000 or 800/772–6646, fax 845/256–2180, www.mohonk.com. 269 rooms, 6 suites, 4 cottages. 3 restaurants, room service, in-room data ports, 9-hole golf course, putting green, 6 tennis courts, gym, spa, boating, fishing, croquet, hiking, horseback riding, lawn bowling, shuffleboard, cross-country skiing, ice-skating, library, children's programs (ages 2–12), laundry facilities, Internet; no a/c, no room TVs. AE, DC, MC, V. Cottages closed mid-Oct.–mid-May. FAP; EP in cottages. $$$$

Mountain Meadows Bed & Breakfast Linger over breakfast by the pool, which faces the Shawangunk cliffs, or in the country kitchen. Later you may throw some horseshoes or shoot some pool. Frills and florals adorn furnishings in the guest rooms. > 542 Albany Post Rd., 12561, tel. 845/255–6144 or 845/527–8359, www.mountainmeadowsbnb.com. 4 rooms. Pool, outdoor hot tub, badminton, billiards, croquet, horseshoes, Ping-Pong, recreation room, laundry facilities; no room phones, no room TVs, no smoking. No credit cards. BP. $$

Nieuw Country Lloft Fireplaces, beamed ceilings, wide-board floors, local 18th-century antiques, and original wood paneling characterize this stone-and-brick house that Aaron Burr once visited. The suite is spacious and uncluttered, a clean take on country decor, and includes reading chairs and a fireplace. Because there's only one room, the pond, herb garden, woods, and meadows are all yours. You do have the option to book another room for friends, however. The village center is about 4 mi north of the B&B. > 41 Allhusen Rd., 12561, tel. 845/255–6533, www.nclbedandbreakfast.com. 1 suite. Dining room, fan, pond; no room phones, no room TVs, no kids, no smoking. No credit cards. BP. $$

Super 8 Motel Not even ½-mi from the thruway entrance and on the edge of the village, this two-story chain property offers reasonable rates and no surprises. > 7

Terwilliger La., at Main St., 12561, tel. 845/255–8865 or 800/800–8000, fax 845/255–1629, www.super8.com. 67 rooms, 2 suites. Restaurant, in-room data ports, some microwaves, some refrigerators, cable TV; no-smoking rooms. AE, D, DC, MC, V. CP. $–$$$

WHAT'S NEARBY

Baker's B&B On frosty days you can cuddle up by one of the woodstoves or by the fireplace in this antiques-filled 1780 stone farmhouse in the Rondout Valley. Breakfast, served in front of a fireplace or out on the deck, includes homemade jams and jellies and home-smoked salmon or trout. > 24 Old King's Hwy., Stone Ridge, 12484, tel. 845/687–9795 or 888/623–5513, fax 845/687–4153, www.bakersbandb.com. 5 rooms, 1 suite. Dining room; no room phones, no room TVs, no kids under 12, no smoking. MC, V. BP. $

Captain Schoonmakers B&B Guest rooms, each with a private balcony and a canopy or brass bed, are in an 1810 carriage house at this B&B. Breakfast, including eggs from the owners' hens, is served amid antiques in front of the fireplace in the 1760 stone main house. The library leads to the solarium and, just beyond, 10 acres of gardens, woods, waterfalls, and a trout stream. > 913 Rte. 213, at Mossy Brook Rd., High Falls, 12440, tel. 845/687–7946, www.captainschoonmakers.com. 4 rooms. Fishing, library; no room phones, no room TVs, no kids under 10, no smoking. No credit cards. BP. $$

Hardenbergh House Antiques fill this six-gabled Victorian B&B with high ceilings and floral wall coverings. The Grand Room is lush with patterned and textured fabrics; a salmon-and-sage palette is the focal point in the Asia Room. Both rooms have a cast-iron bathtub. The house is on 3 acres with huge trees and a small pond. Your host, a baker trained at the Culinary Institute, prepares breakfast. > 118 Maple Hill Dr., Rosendale, 12472, tel. 845/658–9147, fax 845/658–3845, www.hardenberghouse.com. 2 rooms. Dining room, cable TV, pond; no room phones, no kids under 13, no smoking. MC, V. CP. $$

The Inn at Stone Ridge The 18th-century Dutch stone mansion sits amid 40 landscaped acres in the village of Stone Ridge, about 12 mi northwest of New Paltz. Period antiques, including an old billiard table, furnish the parlors, library, and guest rooms. The suites are especially spacious. Suite 9 has a fireplace, a sitting area, and a dining table for six; Suite 3 has two bedrooms, a dining table for four, and a sitting area with a TV. Room 10 has a balcony with private access. The inn frequently hosts weddings, often in a massive tent in back. A well-respected restaurant and an intimate bar occupy the first floor. > U.S. 209, Stone Ridge, 12484, tel. 845/687–0736, fax 845/687–0112, www.innatstoneridge.com. 3 rooms, 2 suites. Restaurant, some in-room data ports, some in-room hot tubs, lake, billiards, bar, library, some pets allowed; no TV in some rooms, no smoking. AE, D, DC, MC, V. BP. $$$

The Locktender Cottage The small historic house sits beside a lock of the old Delaware and Hudson Canal in the center of High Falls, about 9 mi northwest of New Paltz. Across the street is the highly regarded DePuy Canal House restaurant, which is where you check in, and quirky antiques and gift shops are a few doors away. In the rooms, pale walls dilute flowery bedspreads and curtains. The Chef's Quarters suite, under the eaves, has a kitchenette, dining area, and laundry facilities. Two additional suites are across the street, in a building next to the Canal House. One has a full kitchen and a screened-in porch. > Rte. 213, High Falls 12440, tel. 845/687–7700, fax 845/687–7073, www.depuycanalhouse.net. 2 rooms, 3 suites. Some in-room hot tubs, some kitchenettes and kitchens, some cable TV, some pets allowed (fee); no smoking. AE, MC, V. CP. $$

Minnewaska Lodge Cathedral ceilings, Arts-and-Crafts styling, and towering windows with views of white cliffs or deep forests contribute to the delight of this lodge. Works and photographs by local artists add interest. Some guest rooms have balconies. A Culinary Institute–trained chef prepares breakfast. > 3116 U.S. 44/Rte. 55, Gardiner, 12525, tel. 845/255–1110, fax 845/256–0629, www.minnewaskalodge.com. 26 rooms, 1 suite. Dining room, in-room data ports, gym; no smoking. AE, MC, V. CP weekdays, BP weekends. **$$$**

The 1712 House at Hardenbergh Pond You pass a duck- and goose-filled pond before you reach the unmarked driveway of this lodge a little more than ½-mi off U.S. 209. The house, built in the mid-1990s, blends wood from the property with Catskill bluestone. Guest rooms have hand-crafted quilt-covered beds (including four posters and canopies), small tables with a couple of chairs, VCRs, and lace-fringed windows. Breakfast is served by the dining-room fireplace, in the kitchen, on the deck, or in your room. > 93 Mill Dam Rd., Stone Ridge, 12484, tel. 845/687–7167, www.1712house.com. 5 rooms, 1 suite. Dining room, in-room data ports, some in-room hot tubs, cable TV, in-room VCRs, pond; no kids, no smoking. AE, D, MC, V. BP. **$$$**

The Sheeley House Built in the 1830s, this quiet brick Italianate B&B has two dining rooms, a sitting room, a porch, and a grand piano. In the spacious Rose Room, which can accommodate up to four people, white bedding offsets floral garlands. The Gold Room is also airy and uncluttered. > 6 Fairview Ave., High Falls, 12440, tel. 845/687–4360, fax 845/687–4360, www.thesheeleyhouse.com. 4 rooms, 2 with shared bath; 1 cottage. No credit cards. Dining room, piano; no room phones, no kids under 13, no smoking. BP weekends, CP weekdays. **$–$$**

CAMPING

Yogi Bear's Jellystone Park at Lazy River A this campground with riverside, meadow, and wooded sites, you can fish for smallmouths and panfish along a half mile of Wallkill River shoreline, rent kayaks and pedal carts, and play miniature golf as well as a slew of other sports and games. > 50 Bevier Rd., Gardiner, 12525, tel. 845/255–5193, 800/610–3433 reservations, www.lazyriverny.com or www.campjellystone.com. 80 full hook-ups, 90 partial hook-ups, 30 tent sites, 16 cabins. Flush toilets, full hook-ups, partial hook-ups (electric and water), dump station, drinking water, laundry facilities, showers, fire pits, grills, picnic tables, snack bar, electricity, public telephone, general store, 3 playgrounds, 2 pools. Reservations essential. D, MC, V. Closed mid-Oct.–Apr. **¢–$**

WHERE TO EAT

The Gilded Otter A gleaming copper brewery, live music, tasty pub grub and more-substantial food, and views of the Gunks—what could be better after a day of rock climbing or hiking? Just don't expect much quiet on weekends. Two brews to try: New Paltz Crimson Lager and Stone House Irish Stout. Among the more unusual dishes here is pizza topped with caramelized pear, bacon, onions, gorgonzola, fontina, mozzarella, and mesclun. > 3 Main St., tel. 845/256–1700, www.gildedotter.com. D, DC, MC, V. **¢–$$**

Harvest Café & Restaurant You can have a leisurely meal on a deck with umbrella-shaded tables or in a warm, casually sophisticated dining room at this eatery in the Water Street Market complex. The fare is up-to-the-minute American; carrot-ginger soup, brie-and-grape salad, and pan-seared crab cakes with wasabi sour cream are good bets. Sunday brunch starts at 9:30 here. > Water Street Market, 10 Main St., tel. 845/255–4205. MC, V. **$–$$**

Hokkaido Japanese Restaurant Sample sushi and other tidbits beneath handcrafted Japanese lanterns at this informal spot. Spider rolls, hot crisp-fried soft-shell crabs in cool nori-wrapped sushi rice, are a delight. > 18 Church St., tel. 845/256–0621. AE, D, MC, V. No lunch weekends. **$–$$$**

La Stazione Dim lighting and dark mahogany trim lend romance to this Italian restaurant in a converted railroad station. For starters consider "La Stazione," a small pizza topped with artichokes, black olives, ham, and onions, or a bowl of escarole and creamy cannellini beans; garlic-laced tomato-sauced clams are a savory main course. Crowds flock to the $7.95 prix fixe dinner, offered Monday and Tuesday. > 5 Main St., tel. 845/256–9447. AE, D, MC, V. **$–$$$**

Loft Restaurant An airy loft, sloping skylights, and a simple but elegant American menu define this eatery. Featured entrées include lobster ravioli in creamy tomato sauce and duck roasted with a black currant–and–brandy glaze. > 46 Main St., tel. 845/255–1426. AE, D, MC, V. Closed Mon. and Tues. **$–$$**

Main Course Formica tables in a strip-mall storefront don't excite your appetite? The menu certainly will. Rosemary-scented pastry caps chicken potpie; smoked-salmon napoleon incorporates wonton crisps, wasabi, guacamole, and organic greens; and orecchiette mingle with artichoke hearts, mushrooms, spinach, and walnut pesto. > Eckerds Plaza, 232 Main St., tel. 845/255–2650 or 845/255–2600. AE, D, MC, V. Closed Mon. **¢–$**

Main Street Bistro Low-priced food, many vegetarian dishes (including veggie-burger versions called Hendrix and Day Tripper), crowded little tables, and a big selection of coffees, teas, and juices—it's a classic student hangout. If you're nostalgic about the '60s, or just want breakfast (served daily), the Bistro is the place to go. > 59 Main St., tel. 845/255–7766, www.mainstreetbistro.com. D, MC, V. No dinner Mon.–Wed. **$**

McGillcuddy's Restaurant & Tap House A lively sports-bar ambience, a good beer menu, tasty food, and generous portions make this a popular spot. Choose from 14 kinds of chicken wings. The "Inferno" wings are hotter than hot. ("Get the fire extinguisher," says the description in the menu—and it's not kidding.) > 84 Main St., tel. 845/256–9289. AE, D, MC, V. **$–$$**

Mohonk Mountain House The three 19th-century dining rooms at this family-owned Victorian resort provide elegant backdrops for dishes like pan-seared tournedos of filet mignon, made modern with blue-crab succotash and lemon-peppercorn butter, and smoked breast of duck, which comes with field greens, New Zealand figs, and maple-cognac vinaigrette. Dinner is prix fixe ($47–$50) only and includes tax and tip. Come early to enjoy the grounds. > 1000 Mountain Rest Rd., tel. 845/256–2056. Reservations essential. Jacket required. AE, D, MC, V. **$$$$**

Ristorante Locust Tree A historic building houses this formal Italian restaurant, where dishes such as roast of "pasture-raised" veal with creamy polenta and truffle sauce or seared Hudson Valley foie gras with figs, prosciutto, and port sauce display the kitchen's love for organic, local ingredients and regional Italian cuisines (the chef hails from northern Italy). The menu changes daily, and tasting menus, $48–$70 depending on the number of courses, are available. Part of the restaurant inhabits a stone Dutch Colonial with fireplaces, beamed ceilings, and hand-carved woodwork that dates to 1759. (The addition was built in the late 1920s.) > 215 Huguenot St., tel. 845/255–7888. Reservations essential. Jacket required. DC, MC, V. Closed Mon. and Tues. No lunch. **$$–$$$**

WHAT'S NEARBY

Chefs on Fire In the former wine cellar of the DePuy Canal House, this is a casual and tasty offshoot of the elegant main restaurant. Flavors are more Italian than they are upstairs, and dishes include frittatas, panini, pasta, and pizza (including a top-ping of arugula, cannellini beans, and bacon). Breads and pastries, baked here, are also available at the New York Store, next door. Sunday brunch is served 11:30–2. > Rte. 213, High Falls, tel. 845/687–7778. AE, MC, V. Closed Mon. and Tues. **$–$$**

DePuy Canal House The food at this 1797 stone tavern, a National Historic Land-mark, is eclectic and elaborate. Chef-owner John Novi opened the place in 1969 and, in 1984, was referred to as "the father of new American cooking" in a *Time* magazine article. After all these years he still manages to be creative. The menu is seasonal and often incorporates Hudson Valley ingredients. You might find chicken-and-fish con-sommé with salmon-mousse wonton or sautéed lobster with steamed spinach, caramelized-shallot beurre blanc, and mango salsa. The restaurant has five antiques-jammed dining rooms; you can also dine at a balcony table overlooking the kitchen. Sunday brunch is available. > Rte. 213, High Falls, tel. 845/687–7700. Reservations es-sential. AE, MC, V. Closed Mon.–Wed. and late Jan.–mid-Feb. No lunch. **$$$–$$$$**

The Egg's Nest Playfully cluttered and wildly painted, the Egg's Nest is fun, whether for a casual meal or a couple of drinks. "Praeseux" are house favorites—crisp, pizza-like dishes with various toppings baked on flour tortillas. The Thanksgiving sandwich layers turkey breast with provolone cheese and apple-walnut stuffing on whole-wheat bread dipped in egg batter. Pasta dishes, wraps, soups, and chili also are offered. > Rte. 213 at Bruceville Rd., High Falls, tel. 845/687–7255. No credit cards. **¢–$**

The Inn at Stone Ridge At this restaurant in an 18th-century stone mansion–inn, you can dine on regional produce and specialties, quaff local beers and ales, or sip something from the wine cellar. Redefined American dishes are the specialty—mulled butternut-squash soup; smoked duck–and–spinach salad with pancetta vinaigrette; pork tenderloin with smoked bacon and horseradish on apple-potato pancake. Fur-nishings in the main dining room have a refined-country appeal; you may also sit in the more casual Jefferson Room or Tavern. > U.S. 209, Stone Ridge, tel. 845/687–0736. AE, D, DC, MC, V. Closed Mon. and Tues. **$$–$$$**

Mountain Brauhaus Restaurant Time (fortunately) has not changed this family-style restaurant. The wood paneling and Alpine decor complement the menu, which in-cludes sauerbraten, schnitzels, wursts, and *kassler ripchen* (smoked pork chops). The selection of German beers, in bottles and on tap, is excellent. > U.S. 44/Rte. 55 and Rte. 299, Gardiner, tel. 845/255–9766. AE, D, MC, V. Closed Mon. and Tues. **$–$$**

The Would The white-tablecloth restaurant is in what was once a resort catering to Italian families from New York City, and boccie is still played here on summer evenings. The food is no throwback, however; organic produce and poultry blend with ingredients and techniques from around the world. Pineapple-soy glaze sweetens pan-seared Hudson Valley duck breast, for example, and papaya-wasabi sauce and shrimp cakes accompany sautéed scallops. In winter a fireplace warms the dining room. > 120 North Rd., west of Rte. 9W, Highland, tel. 845/691–9883. Reservations essential. AE, MC, V. Closed Mon. and Tues. **$$–$$$**

ESSENTIALS

Getting Here

Car and bus are the most convenient ways to get here, but traveling by car al-lows you to explore rural back roads and byways as well as area parks and pre-serves. Taxi service is available at the New Paltz bus station. Trains aren't a practical option because they stop in Poughkeepsie, on the other (east) side of the Hudson River, and because you'd still have to take a bus (and a taxi to the bus station) to get here.

BY BUS

Adirondack Trailways leaves the Port Authority bus terminal for New Paltz several times daily (between 7 AM and 11:30 PM). The trip is scheduled to take an hour and 35 minutes but may be longer, depending on traffic. The bus stops in Rosendale as it continues on to Kingston. Rush-hour and Friday-evening buses are crowded. A round-trip ticket costs $35.30. Taxi service is available at the bus station in New Paltz (Glenn Stagecoach Ltd., 845/255–1550). Mohonk Mountain House has its own limo service.

LINES **Adirondack Trailways** > Tel. 800/858–8555, www.trailways.com.

DEPOTS **New Paltz Bus Station** > 139 Main St., at Prospect St., New Paltz, tel. 845/255–6520, 845/331–0744 tickets and schedule.

BY CAR

The easiest way to get here is to take the New York State Thruway to Exit 18. Turn left onto Route 299, which is called Main Street in the village.

Parking spaces on Main Street are metered and often occupied. They also can be difficult to get in and out of. Free public lots are on Plattekill Avenue (behind Ariel Books) and near the intersection of Chestnut and Main streets. Metered parking is free during the holiday shopping season.

When driving, be on the lookout for deer—plentiful in these parts—especially in the evenings. You can see deer on the edges of Route 299 west of the village, near apple orchards, and in the wooded areas off U.S. 44/Route 55. You may also see them between exits 17 and 18 of the thruway, as you head south.

Visitor Information

The New Paltz Chamber of Commerce is open 9–5 on weekdays and 10–3 on weekends.

CONTACTS **New Paltz Chamber of Commerce** > 124 Main St., New Paltz, 12561, tel. 845/255–0243, www.newpaltzchamber.org. **Ulster County Tourism** > 10 Westbrook La., Kingston, 12401, tel. 800/342–5826, www.ulstertourism.info.

Woodstock

105 mi north of New York City

7

By Erica Freudenberger

WOODSTOCK—THE VERY NAME STRAINS beneath the baggage of its illustrious history. An arts colony and a haven for eccentricity, it's also the almost mythical wellspring of alternative American culture and home to many of the now deified promulgators of the seemingly endless phenomenon of the 1960s. In having its name usurped for a seminal music festival in 1969—actually held in faraway Bethel—Woodstock has inadvertently been called upon to define an entire generation, or at least the amber-tinted soul of its lost youth. That's a lot to ask of a small town in upstate New York.

Woodstock sits within the mountainous Catskill Park, a vast area of public and private lands and immense beauty that encompasses the nearly 300,000-acre Catskill Forest Preserve, which the state intends to keep "forever wild." To the north and west of Woodstock are the undulating Catskill Mountains and their fecund valleys. Hundreds of years ago, the verdant flora, abundant natural resources, and copious edible and fur-bearing fauna lured a smattering of Native Americans to the region. The Europeans who later settled here established farms, logging operations, and quarries. By the mid-19th century, a burgeoning coterie of New York City–bred artists was following the trail to this alluring region via yesteryear's superhighway, the Hudson River.

In 1903, Ralph Radcliffe Whitehead, in league with Bolton Brown and Hervey White, inaugurated the Byrdcliffe Art and Crafts Colony, attracting dreamers, rogues, and artists. By the time the estranged White created Maverick, his own egalitarian artistic colony, a pattern was established. Bohemians flocked to the area, mingling with farmers and transforming the sleepy hamlet. Licentious behavior and cultivated autonomy were the rule of the day and continued for decades.

Woodstock's main street hugs the town green, where angst-ridden teenagers, musicians, political protesters, and the occasional pet parade convene. Although eclectic shops, art galleries, and a pervasive eccentricity help maintain the town's status as a countercultural magnet, the scene has mellowed considerably. These days you're more likely to spot Land Rovers than VW buses in town, where aging hippies and baby boomers, families, and celebrities share sidewalks with out-of-towners. To enjoy Woodstock's charm, don't overlook the details—the gently gurgling brooks, the odd homegrown bench here and there, the twinkling lights that come on at dusk—and consider visiting in winter or spring, when crowds thin out and traffic eases.

As Woodstock's cachet has grown, so has the value of its real estate. As a result, many artists, finding themselves priced out, have moved to neighboring communities. Boiceville, a brief jaunt west of Woodstock via Route 28, is one such hamlet. At the northwest end of the Ashokan Reservoir, it's less developed than Woodstock and thus retains more of a rural sensibility. Not even 3 mi north of Boiceville is Mount Tremper, home of the acclaimed Zen Mountain Monastery. There's no precious shopping district here, just a few good restaurants worth checking out.

Further into the mountains is Phoenicia, 16 mi west of Woodstock. Since the 1990s, when hipsters discovered the hamlet—formerly boondocks—Phoenicia has been undergoing a transformation. The number of creative individuals who have found the natural world narcotic and have settled here, establishing funky boutiques and fine restaurants, is growing. From Phoenicia it's an easy trip through the High Peaks area to the Hunter and Belleayre ski resorts.

WHAT TO SEE & DO

Byrdcliffe Ralph Radcliffe Whitehead, a wealthy Englishman under the sway of William Morris and John Ruskin, decided to create a utopian arts colony. His friend and conspirator Bolton Brown, an artist, suggested Woodstock; after a visit in 1902, Whitehead agreed. Here is the result: 300 acres swaddling 35 buildings, the only intact Arts and Crafts colony remaining on U.S. soil. Although Whitehead was considered dictatorial, his early efforts laid the groundwork for Woodstock's transformation into a colony of the arts. John Dewey, Thomas Mann, naturalist John Burroughs, and Isadora Duncan all fell under Byrdcliffe's spell. Artists, writers, composers, and dance and theater companies still call it home when they participate in its residency programs. Pamphlets in the mailbox outside the barn outline a self-guided walking tour. > Upper Byrdcliffe Rd., off Glasco Tpke., tel. 845/679–2079, www.woodstockguild.org. Free.

Center for Photography at Woodstock If you come here, you're entering hallowed ground: what was once the Espresso Café, where Bob Dylan, Janis Joplin, and others entertained countercultural dreamers, remains indelibly imprinted on the town. Now a gallery space for photography, the center aims to provoke serious consideration of the medium, offering a dynamic series of exhibits, lectures, and workshops. > 59 Tinker St., tel. 845/679–9957, www.cpw.org. Free. Wed.–Sun. noon–5.

Colony Cafe You can hang with hipsters on the upper mezzanine, checking out the tables below. A roaring fireplace at one end and a mesmerizing stage at the other anchor the large open room. Local and national performers come here; after the first time, they always come back. Doors open at 7 nightly except Wednesday, when the place is closed; admission varies. Choose from beer, wine, espresso, and desserts. > 22 Rock City Rd., tel. 845/679–5342, www.colonycafe.com.

Karma Triyana Dharmachakra A giant golden Buddha resides in the colorful shrine room of this Tibetan Buddhist monastery, inviting you to meditate or wander the grounds. Tours are given weekends at 1:30; stroll around to discover a fishpond, guesthouse, and solitary-retreat cabins. Because this is a religious center, you aren't allowed in the shrine room wearing shoes, hats, or revealing garments. Introductory instruction in *shinay* (mind-calming) meditation is also available. Call for the schedule or to make an appointment. The monastery is about 3 mi north of the center of town. > 335 Meads Mountain Rd., tel. 845/679–5906 Ext. 10, www.kagyu.org. Free. Daily 6 AM–6 PM.

Woodstock Artists Association Gallery With three spaces able to run concurrent exhibitions, this gallery exercises its commitment to showing—and collecting—area artists' works in all media. One space has monthly group exhibits; another features solo shows of contemporary artists; and the Phoebe and Belmont Towbin Wing is devoted to art from the permanent collection. > 28 Tinker St., tel. 845/679–2940. Free. Thurs.–Mon. noon–5.

Woodstock Artists Cemetery Dead artists of all kinds reside here: poets, musicians, writers, painters, sculptors, dancers, and bons vivants. Many of the stones, in keeping with the wishes of their buried subjects, tell artfully rendered stories that reverberate in the bones of the living who pause overhead. Look for the grassy knoll behind the Evergreen Cemetery to commune with the spirits of Woodstock. (The cemetery is on a hill behind the parking lot of the Colony Cafe, which is at 22 Rock City Road.) > No phone. Free.

Woodstock Guild A nonprofit arts organization with more than 600 members, the guild has been serving artists in the mid-Hudson Valley since 1939. Steward of the Byrdcliffe Arts Colony, the guild also oversees the **Fleur de Lis Gallery,** which showcases the works of 90-plus artisans, and hosts performing, visual, and literary artists at its **Kleinert/James Arts Center.** > 34 Tinker St., tel. 845/679–2079, www.woodstockguild.org. Free. Call for open days and hrs.

Woodstock Playhouse WDST, Woodstock's independent radio station, books topnotch acts that demonstrably enjoy performing at this outdoor venue. You can expect to interact with the performers—if you're not pulled onto the stage, the performers may work their way through the crowd to you. Seating is stadium-style, but you'll be hard-pressed to remain in your seat. > Rtes. 212 and 375, tel. 845/679–4101, www.woodstockplayhouse.org.

WHAT'S NEARBY

Catskill Corners Marketplace A darkened 60-foot silo, once used to store grain and animal feed, houses an enormous kaleidoscope. From the silo, wander through the cobblestoned courtyard of this retail complex, past the upscale boutiques, to the kaleidoscope museum and see what intricate minds can make happen with beads, glass, oil, and mirrors. > 5340 Rte. 28, Mount Tremper, tel. 845/688–5800, www.catskillcorners.com. Kaleidoscope and museum $8. Mid-Sept.–May, Wed.–Mon. 10–5; June–mid-Sept., daily 10–7.

Elena Zang Gallery Meander through the terraced sculpture garden, past the babbling brook, several inspired birdhouses, and other delightful art objects, to the studio of Elena Zang and Alan Hoffman, creators of minimalist functional pottery. Down the hill is the gallery space, where blond-wood floors and an infusion of light set off the contemporary art on the walls. Mary Frank, Judy Pfaff, and Joan Snyder are some of the contemporary luminaries exhibiting here. > 3671 Rte. 212, Shady, tel. 845/679–5432, www.elenazang.com. Free. Daily 11–5.

F-S Tube and Raft Rentals This tubing outfitter offers a 4-mi run down the Esopus Creek. A lower 3-mi course encounters milder rapids and is more appropriate for families. Note that children must be at least nine years old to go tubing. > 4 Church St., Phoenicia, tel. 845/688–7633, www.catskillpark.com/fs.html. Tube and transport $10. Memorial Day–3rd wk in Sept., daily 9–6.

Opus 40 The late Harvey Fite put 37 years into the making of this 6-acre outdoor sculpture, created in the rock bed of an abandoned bluestone quarry. The architectural creation is an assemblage of curving bluestone walkways, swirling terraces, and finely fitted ramps around pools, trees, and fountains. The **Quarryman's Museum** contains 19th-century tools. Opus 40, 6 mi east of Woodstock, is sometimes closed for special events, so call ahead. > 50 Fite Rd., Saugerties, tel. 845/246–3400, www.opus40.org. $6. Memorial Day–Columbus Day, Fri.–Sun. noon–5.

Town Tinker A red barn stands guard as you enter Phoenicia. It's here that you find everything you need to spend a day riding the rapids or drifting on the currents of the Esopus. You can rent tubes for beginner and advanced routes on the Esopus Creek between Shandaken and Mount Pleasant. Don't feel like hiking back? Get out at a designated spot for a ride to Phoenicia on the Catskill Mountain Railroad. Children must be older than 12, and only strong swimmers should consider this. > 10 Bridge St., Phoenicia, tel. 845/688–5553, www.towntinker.com. Tube and transport $15. Mid-May–Sept., daily 9–6.

Upstate Art A blue-sequined sign lures you inside this gallery. Upstairs, six brightly lighted rooms exhibit contemporary regional artists. Nita Friedman has been running the gallery since the late 1990s, and has created a place where lively openings draw local artists out of their homes in the surrounding wooded hills. > 60 Main St., Phoenicia, tel. 845/688–9881. Free. Call for hrs or to make an appointment.

Zen Mountain Monastery The monastery resides in a four-story bluestone–and–white oak church on 230 acres bordered by the Beaverkill and Esopus rivers. The building, constructed by Norwegian craftsmen at the turn of the 20th century, includes a 150-person meditation hall, a dining hall, and resident and guest quarters. The only way to visit is to partake in introductory Zen instruction, offered Wednesday evening and as weekend retreats, or in the Sunday session of services, *zazen* (or sitting) meditation, and lunch. > South Plank Rd., off Rte. 212, Mount Tremper, tel. 845/688–2228, www.mro.org. Wed. free; Sun. $5 donation. Wed. 7:30 PM–9 PM, Sun. 8:45 AM–noon.

Sports

CANOEING & KAYAKING

Esopus Creek The Class II–III creek, which parallels Route 28 in and around Phoenicia, is a popular spot for canoeing and kayaking. Regulated by the state's Department of Environmental Conservation, releases from the nearby Schoharie Reservoir help to maintain optimal conditions for recreational use of the creek waters—and create some awesome rapids.

RENTALS **Cold Brook Canoes** > 4181 Rte. 28, Boiceville, tel. 845/657–2189.

FISHING

The Esopus Creek, which runs along part of Route 28 west of Woodstock, is one of the most productive wild-trout streams in the Northeast. Although the number of fish—mostly wild rainbow and brown trout, but also brook trout—in the Esopus is impressive, most fish average only about 7 or 8 inches in length. An especially productive area of the Esopus is just south of Boiceville, near the Ashokan Reservoir, where you also may catch smallmouth bass and walleye. For fishing regulations, license fees, seasons, and other specific information, contact the regional headquarters of the New York State Department of Environmental Conservation in Albany (518/474–2121) or in New Paltz (845/256–3000) before your trip.

EQUIPMENT **Ed's Fly Fishing & Guide Services** > 69 Ridge Rd., Shokan, tel. 845/657–6393. **Phoenicia Fish & Game Association** > 5419 Rte. 28, Mount Tremper, tel. 845/688–2508.

HIKING

Catskill Park, designated a state treasure in 1904, spans Ulster, Green, Delaware, and Sullivan counties. It encompasses 700,000 acres of public and private land, and some of the wildest country south of Maine, with bears, coyotes, rattlesnakes, and other creatures. About 60% of the land is privately owned; the nearly 300,000 acres of state land within the park is called the Catskill Forest Preserve. The park has 200 mi of marked trails, campgrounds, ponds, lakes, and mountains; 98 peaks over 3,000 feet make for inspired hiking.

Devil's Path The trail, in the Westkill Mountain Wilderness area of the Catskills, winds through the Stony Clove mountain pass and around natural rock formations. Follow the red trail markers for the scenic 7-mi hike to the summit of Westkill Mountain (3,880 feet). The trailhead is at the north end of the parking lot at the Devil's Tombstone Campground, at Diamond Notch Lake. To get here from Route 28 in Phoenicia, take Route 214 north for 9 mi. > Off Rte. 214, Hunter, tel. 607/652–7365, 607/652–5076, 607/652–5063, www.dec.state.ny.us/website/outdoors.

Overlook Mountain Looming over Woodstock, this mountain has inspired generations of landscape artists as well as several rock musicians. The 3,140-foot peak offers one of the best views in the Catskills, on clear days taking in five neighboring states. On the way up the 2½-mi dirt road, an almost constant ascent, you see the ruins of the Overlook Mountain House, a once-grand hotel; an old fire tower is at the top. To get here from the Woodstock town green, turn onto Rock City Road. Proceed to the four-way stop, after which the road becomes Meads Mountain Road. Continue for another 2½ mi. The Overlook trailhead, and parking for it, are on the right, across the road from Karma Triyana Dharmachakra. > Off Meads Mountain Rd., Woodstock, tel. 845/256–3000, www.catskillcenter.org.

Slide Mountain Stretching over 47,500 acres, the **Slide Mountain Wilderness** is the largest and most popular wilderness area in the Catskills. The area includes the range's highest peak, Slide Mountain (4,190 feet), and encompasses several forest preserves. Its 35 mi of hiking trails, all restricted to foot travel, give entrance to the beautifully remote interior, taking you over lofty peaks with spectacular views. The most straightforward way up Slide Mountain is via the Woodland Valley–Denning and Burroughs Range trails, accessed from the Slide Mountain Trailhead parking area, on Route 47, west of Woodstock. You trek 2.7 mi and climb 1,780 feet to the summit, where a plaque commemorates naturalist and poet John Burroughs. > Off Rte. 47 10 mi south of Big Indian, tel. 607/652–7365, 607/652–5076, 607/652–5063, www.dec.state.ny.us/website/outdoors.

Tremper Mountain Two trails lead you to the summit (at 2,740 feet), where an early-20th-century fire tower stands. The red-blazed Phoenicia Trail, the much shorter but steeper of the two, begins off Route 40 about 1 mi southeast of Phoenicia and climbs the western side of the mountain for 2¾ mi to the summit. To get to the trailhead, take Route 212 west from Woodstock to Mount Tremper, where you turn right onto Route 40 and continue for 2½ mi to the parking area. The 4.2-mi Willow Trail starts just west of the post office in the village of Willow (about 7 mi west of Woodstock). > Tel. 607/652–7365, 607/652–5076, 607/652–5063, www.catskillcenter.org.

MOUNTAIN BIKING

Full-day rentals at Overlook Mountain Bikes are $35 for a dual-suspension bike and $30 for a hard tail.

Jockey Hill Off Route 28 about 6 mi southeast of Woodstock is one of the best-kept mountain-biking secrets in the Catskills. The area encompasses nearly 20 mi of trails with single-track loops; they vary in length and level of difficulty (few are for beginners) and all include obstacles such as rocks and logs. > Jockey Hill Rd., West Hurley. *EQUIPMENT* **Overlook Mountain Bikes** > 93 Tinker St., Woodstock, tel. 845/679–2122.

Shopping

Be it Buddhas, baubles, or books, the Woodstock area has it. Some shops in Woodstock are hippie holdovers, such as Candlestock; other shops appeal to neo-hippies and seekers of Asian inspiration.

Belleayre & Hunter Mountains

AT THE FOOT of the Catskills, Woodstock can be used as a base for the Belleayre and Hunter ski resorts, 27 mi to the west and 19 mi to the north, respectively. Both mountains are in the Catskill Forest Preserve, the state-land portion of Catskill Park, and offer activities throughout the year—from mountain biking to festivals.

Belleayre Mountain Ski Center. Belleayre, in the Catskill Forest Preserve about 30 mi west of Woodstock, has one section for expert skiers and another for intermediates and novices. Of the 38 trails that vein the peak's 171 acres of skiable terrain, 22% are for beginners and 58% are for intermediate skiers; the vertical drop is 1,400 feet. The resort, owned by the New York State Department of Environmental Conservation, has 96% snowmaking capability, eight lifts, and 9.2 km of cross-country trails. Skiing and snowboarding instruction and rentals are available. Full-day peak-season lift tickets are $42. From late April to October, the upper, lower, and cross-country areas offer biking tracks for beginners to experts; lifts aren't equipped for bikes, so you have to ride in both directions. From late May through August, you may also swim, boat, and fish at Pine Hill Lake ($6 per car), where pedal boats, rowboats, and kayaks are for rent. A lift ($8 per person) can take you to the summit, from which you can hike or ride the lift back down. The resort hosts crafts, music, and other festivals. > Off

Rte. 28, Highmount, tel. 845/254–5600 or 800/942–6904, www.belleayre.com.

Hunter Mountain. The sprawling resort has 53 trails on 240 acres where you may ski, snowboard, snow tube, and snowshoe. Hunter, in the Catskill Forest Preserve about 29 mi north of Woodstock, is known for it's full snowmaking capability, a tremendous boon when natural conditions are less than optimal. The 3,200-foot peak offers a 1,600-foot vertical drop; 11 lifts move you up the slope. Fifteen of the trails are set aside for beginners, 8 are designed for double-black-diamond skiers, and about 16 are for intermediates. Full-day lift tickets are $51. Rentals and instruction are available. From May to early October, mountain bikers take over. The single-track trails run through dense forest and cross streams. A chairlift transports bikers to the summit. Throughout summer and fall, music and other festivals are held here. To get to Hunter from Woodstock, take Rock City Road north and turn right onto Glasco Turnpike. Proceed for 1½ mi and turn left onto West Saugerties Road. After just more than 4½ mi, turn left onto Platte Clove Road and proceed to Route 23A, about 9 mi. > Rte. 23A, Hunter, tel. 518/263–4223, 800/486–8376, 866/486–8376, www.huntermtn.com.

Fabulous Furniture Soapbox-derby entries mingle with sculpture at this interesting place 8 mi west of Woodstock; around back, owner Steve Heller does unimaginable things to rotting or dead wood and old Cadillacs and other cars. Inside are the amazing results: custom-made tables with tree-trunk bases, lamps, menorahs, and mirrors. > Rte. 28, Boiceville, tel. 845/657–6317. Closed Mon. and Tues.

Golden Notebook A this venerable Woodstock institution, open since 1978, the friendly staff helps you navigate the eclectic mix of local lore, children's books, fiction, and other titles. Wander through the labyrinth and you come across the Golden Bough, a gift shop that carries the full line of Woodstock Chimes, tabletop fountains, and children's toys. > 29 Tinker St., Woodstock, tel. 845/679–8000.

Loominus Scarves, shawls, jackets, vests, hats, and pillows fashioned from piles of lush chenille fill the front of the store. Behind the counter, women work sewing machines, trying to keep pace with orders from Barneys and Bergdorf. > 3257 Rte. 212, Bearsville, tel. 845/679–6500. Closed Sun.

Mirabai Incense tickles your nose as you enter this decidedly spiritual bookstore. Crystals give way to books, tapes, and a myriad of other objects to help the flow of your chi. > 23 Mill Hill Rd., Woodstock, tel. 845/679–2100.

Morne Imports Garden gnomes occupy the front window of this general store, and camping and hunting gear hangs precariously above their heads. The store sells everything you need to tackle nature, from fishing rods and hand-tied flies to hunting knives. > 52 Main St., Phoenicia, tel. 845/688–7738.

The Tender Land The home goods at this sophisticated country-housewares shop are artfully displayed. After browsing here, head down the street to Tender Land Home, a complementary contemporary store filled with small—and easily transportable—delights. Chic pottery and luscious pillows, window treatments, and rugs make you want to move in. > 45 Main St., Phoenicia, tel. 845/688–2001. Closed Wed.

Woodstock Wool Company Two former Condé Nast graphic designers revamped the old post office into a 3,000-square-foot tribute to wool—this is not your grandmother's knitting store. A multitude of classes and groups has turned this sleek contemporary space into Woodstock's living room. A boisterous young crowd attends monthly karaoke-knitting sessions. > 105 Tinker St., Woodstock, tel. 845/679–0400.

Save the Date

JUNE–SEPTEMBER

Maverick Concert Series Hervey White broke with Ralph Whitehead to form his egalitarian enclave for the arts, Maverick, in the woods outside Woodstock. In order to subsidize his dream, White staged a music and dramatic festival in 1915, thus beginning the country's oldest continuously running summer chamber-music series. Every summer since has seen a confluence of world-class musicians, drawn by superlative acoustics in a chapel renowned by audiophiles. An open-admission policy reflects its beginnings as a collaborative colony of artists; the faithful gather early to secure good seats. The season runs from late June to early September. > 1 mi from junction of Rte. 375 and Maverick Rd., Woodstock, tel. 845/679–8217, www.maverickconcerts.org.

AUGUST

Woodstock Poetry Festival Hordes of literati descend upon Woodstock, armed with words, for this festival. Poet Laureates and Pulitzer Prize winners inspire the aspiring, read to the faithful, and hold workshops praising the muse during the last weekend in August. Venues include the Colony Cafe, the Maverick Concert Hall, and the Center for Photography at Woodstock. > Box 450, Woodstock 12498, no phone, www.woodstockpoetryfestival.com.

SEPTEMBER

Hudson Valley Garlic Festival The last weekend of September finds upwards of 40,000 people making a pilgrimage to Saugerties for a celebration of the stinking rose: garlic. Although you find much of the usual fair fare here—crafts booths, frieddough stands, live musical performances—one vast section of the festival is devoted to farmers, arts and craftspeople, and food vendors all providing tributes to garlic. You may learn about growing your own, or savor garlic soup and ice cream. > Cantine Field, Saugerties, tel. 845/246–3090, www.hvgf.org.

JAS The village of Saugerties closes off its streets to car traffic for one day on the first weekend in September for this celebration of jazz and the arts. (JAS stands for Jazz and Art at Saugerties.) Three stages of live music get people dancing to Latin and other jazz varieties; restaurants serve food outdoors; and local artists, including photographers and sculptors, line the streets with booths showing their works. > Main and Partition Sts., Saugerties, tel. 845/246–2321.

Woodstock Film Festival Cinephiles flock to Woodstock for five autumnal days, when Hollywood converges with the fiercely independent for this well-regarded film festival. Celebrity-led seminars, film screenings, and raucous parties—most in Woodstock—find you pressing the flesh until morning. Straddling the line between glitz and homegrown, the festival strives to remain true to its underdog roots, closing with the Maverick Award, given to individuals who combine challenging professional work with social activism. > Tel. 845/679–4265, www.woodstockfilmfestival.com.

OCTOBER

Oktoberfest The Hunter Mountain ski resort stands in for the Alps during the first two weekends of October, celebrating German and Austrian music, food, and dance. Watch men imitate courting rituals of the wood grouse during traditional Schuhplattler dances; after a couple of beers, you may be tempted to try it yourself. Kids get free pumpkins. > Rte. 23A, Hunter, tel. 518/263–4223, 800/486–8376, 888/486–8376, www.huntermtn.com.

WHERE TO STAY

Twin Gables The Victorian B&B, in the center of Woodstock, has served lodgers since the 1940s. Patterned wallpaper provides a backdrop for period furnishings and local artists' works. Several bedrooms share hall bathrooms. Shops, restaurants, and live-music venues are within strolling distance. > 73 Tinker St., 12498, tel. 845/679–9479, fax 845/679–5638, www.twingableswoodstockny.com. 9 rooms, 6 with shared bath. No room phones, no room TVs, no smoking. AE, D, MC, V. CP. $

The Wild Rose Inn Beyond a white picket fence and a pleasant amble from central Woodstock is this rose-focused 1898 Victorian. Most rooms are draped in damask and organza swags and bedding. A dramatic, antique walnut-burl bed takes center stage in the Honeysuckle Rose Suite, which has a private entrance. The Sweetheart Room is the smallest of the accommodations, but the others are large. Complimentary brandy, truffles, and fruit add to the sweetness. The Continental breakfast is substantial. > 66 Rock City Rd., 12498, tel./fax 845/679–8783, www.thewildroseinn.com. 2 rooms, 3 suites. Dining room, in-room hot tubs, cable TV; no room phones, no smoking. MC, V. CP. $$–$$$

Woodstock Country Inn Hidden in a meadow of wildflowers several hundred yards from the quiet main road 2 mi west of Woodstock center, this B&B offers peaceful seclusion. The house includes paintings by Woodstock artist Jo Cantine, whose home this originally was, as well as hand-painted furnishings. The guest rooms keep frills to a minimum, instead offering simple luxuries such as 300-thread-count sateen sheets, mountain views, a porch or deck, and private entrances. Breakfast is lavish and consists of organic fare. > Cooper Lake Rd., 12498, tel. 845/679–9380, www.woodstockcountryinn.com. 3 rooms, 1 suite. Some cable TV, some kitchenettes, pool; no room phones, no TV in some rooms, no kids under 12, no smoking. MC, V. BP. $$$–$$$$

Woodstock Inn on the Millstream Tall pines stand sentinel at this motel-style lodging, creating a private haven a short walk from the center of Woodstock. After splashing in the swimming hole, you can relax on the landscaped lawn. In the rooms, more like B&B lodgings than motel units, hanging flower planters adorn front porches and quilts cover beds. The Continental breakfast spread is more bountiful you might expect. > 48 Tannery Brook Rd., 12498, tel. 845/679–8211 or 800/420–4707, fax 845/679–4550, www.woodstock-inn-ny.com. 11 rooms, 5 studios. Some kitchenettes, cable TV with movies, Internet; no room phones. AE, MC, V. BP. $–$$

WHAT'S NEARBY

Emerson Inn & Spa You're cosseted from the minute you pull up to this 1870s Victorian building. Before you know it, your car is parked, your luggage delivered to your room, and you're accepting a flute of champagne. Persian, Victorian, West Indies Colonial, African, and Asian decorative schemes are manifested in tailored leopard-print curtains, Asian and African artifacts, fringed lampshades, and embroidered pillows. Bedrooms have cordless phones and Frette linens. One suite has a sauna; the duplex has two bathrooms and an indoor hammock. Fine china and crystal dress tables in the dining room, where breakfast and dinner (included in the rates) are served. At the serene spa, which is open to the public, you may indulge in everything from algae wraps to shiatsu. > 146 Mount Pleasant Rd., Mount Tremper 12457, tel. 845/688–7900 or 800/525–4800, fax 845/688–2789, www.theemerson.com. 20 rooms, 4 suites. Dining room, in-room data ports, some in-room hot tubs, exercise equipment, spa, mountain bikes, concierge, meeting rooms; no TV in some rooms, no kids under 13, no smoking. AE, D, DC, MC, V. MAP. $$$$

Lodge at Catskill Corner Antler chandeliers and a folksy mural greet you in the lobby; a welcome basket of fruit and wine awaits in your room. Plaid blanket–draped Adirondack twig beds and log walls are part of the country-cabin look. Some rooms have fireplaces and views of Esopus Creek. Access to the spa facilities at the Emerson Inn, the lodge's nearby sister property, is $15. > 5368 Rte. 28, Mount Tremper 12457, tel. 845/688–2828, www.thelodgeusa.com. 12 rooms, 15 suites. Restaurant, in-room data ports, in-room safes, some in-room hot tubs, refrigerators, cable TV, baby-sitting, some pets allowed (fee); no smoking. AE, D, MC, V. CP. $$$

Onteora the Mountain House Spectacular Catskills vistas leave you breathless at this B&B, the former summer home of mayonnaise magnate Richard Hellman. A massive stone fireplace presides over the great room, a truly great space with a soaring ceiling. Oriental rugs, scattered across wide-plank honey-colored floors, cushion your every step, and Asian antiques and American pieces share an elegant coexistence. A couple of rooms have fireplaces, and one has a window seat with dazzling valley views. You may play billiards in the cavernous game room, or sweat it out in the sauna. Weekend reservations for May through August usually book up a year in advance. > 96 Piney Point Rd., Boiceville 12412, tel./fax 845/657–6233, www.onteora.com. 4 rooms, 1 suite. Some in-room hot tubs, sauna, billiards, hiking; no a/c, no room phones, no room TVs, no kids under 12, no smoking. D, MC, V. Closed Sun. May–Oct. BP. $$–$$$$

Saugerties Lighthouse Bed and Breakfast A 1/2-mi hike from a small parking lot near a Coast Guard station brings you to this romantic hideout, a restored lighthouse overlooking the Hudson River 10 mi east of Woodstock. Downstairs is a Victorian-style parlor. Accommodations are simple and rustic—you make up your own bed at night, and the shared bathroom has a composting toilet—but the two bedrooms are bright and have expansive views. Be sure to climb to the lantern house, which looks across the river at the Clermont estate. Outdoor decks make for idyllic picnics; at low tide stairs lead to a beach. > Off Mynderse St., off Rte. 9W, Saugerties 12477, tel. 845/247–0656, www.saugertieslighthouse.com. 2 rooms with shared bath. Beach, some pets allowed (fee); no a/c, no room phones, no room TVs. AE, D, MC, V. Closed Mon. and Tues. BP. $$

The Villa at Saugerties Occupying a 1929 Mediterranean-style house on 4 gloriously landscaped and wooded acres, this B&B forgoes froufrou for a contemporary sensibility. The Flat, the largest and most modern of the rooms, has a birch platform bed and naked knotty-planked floors. Furniture is kept to a minimum in the Grange, the smallest of the rooms, which has burnt-red walls. All beds are dressed in 310-thread-count Egyptian-cotton sheets. Common areas include a stone fireplace, floor-to-ceiling paintings, and a breakfast nook with a picture window. The B&B is 7 mi east of Woodstock. > 159 Fawn Rd., Saugerties 12477, tel./fax 845/246–0682, www.thevillaatsaugerties.com. 4 rooms. Cable TV, pool; no room phones, no smoking. MC, V. BP. **$–$$**

CAMPING

Devil's Tombstone Campground The campground, one of the oldest in the state, attracts hikers, who access the popular Devil's Path trail at the north end of the campground parking lot. The terrain here, about 3 mi south of the Hunter Mountain ski resort, is mountainous and rocky. Within the campground sits the Devil's Tombstone, a large boulder typical of the area's natural rock formations, that came down the mountain many centuries ago either in a landslide or via glacier. Sites are wooded, with limited facilities (no electricity, hook-ups, or showers). Self-contained RVs are welcome. > Rte. 214, Hunter 12442, tel. 845/688–7160, 800/456–2267 reservations, www.dec.state.ny.us. 24 tent sites. Flush toilets, running water, grills, picnic tables, public telephone, playground. Reservations essential. MC, V. Closed early Sept.–late May. ¢

Kenneth L. Wilson Campground At this campground, about 5 mi from the center of Woodstock and part of the Catskill Forest Preserve camping system, tall pine trees surround sites, which are near a lake with a sand beach. The lake includes chain pickerel, yellow perch, bullheads, white sucker, shiners, and sunfish. Fishing licenses are available at the campground, as are rowboat, canoe, paddleboat, and kayak rentals. The grounds, originally several farms, lie in the valley of Little Beaver Kill, a tributary of the Esopus Creek. Each site has a picnic table and grill. Self-contained RVs are welcome. > 859 Wittenberg Rd., Mount Tremper 12457, tel. 845/679–7020, 800/456–2267 reservations, fax 845/679–6533, www.dec.state.ny.us. 76 tent sites. Flush toilets, showers, dump station, grills, picnic tables, public telephone, swimming (lake). Reservations essential. MC, V. Closed Columbus Day–Apr. ¢

Woodland Valley State Park Campground The woodsy sites here, with trails leading to Wittenberg and Cornell mountains, are a favorite with hikers. Some sites are next to Woodland Valley Stream, which teams with fish. Fishing licenses are available at the campground. Self-contained RVs are welcome. > 1319 Woodland Valley Rd., Phoenicia 12464, tel. 845/688–7647. 72 tent sites. Flush toilets, dump station, showers, picnic tables, public telephone. Reservations essential. MC, V. Close mid-Oct.–mid-May. ¢

WHERE TO EAT

Blue Mountain Bistro A barn with rough-hewn beams and siding from a corncrib makes for a cozy yet elegant atmosphere. The zinc tapas bar includes duck liver pâté, Moroccan carrot salad, and other goodies. Local wisdom holds that you can't get a bad meal here. Try mushroom *panzerotti* (pizzalike tart), jumbo sea scallops with wild-mushroom risotto, or moules Marseillaise, and see if you don't agree. Herb gardens border the outdoor patio. Thursday is Moroccan night, when dinner is prix fixe and includes a belly-dancing class and performance. A children's menu is available. > 1633 Glasco Tpke., tel. 845/679–8519, www.bluemountainbistro.com. Reservations essential. AE, D, DC, MC, V. Closed Sun. and Mon. **$$–$$$**

Bread Alone Java, pastries, and handmade bread beckon from the window of this centrally located café where Woodstockers go to wake up. You can get all the gossip while waiting in line for a latte. If you're pressed for time or want to grab something to go, this is the place to duck in, grab soup and sandwich, and keep going. > 22 Mill Hill Rd., tel. 845/679–2108. MC, V. No dinner. **¢–$**

Gypsy Wolf Cantina The low-slung turquoise building beckons you inside, where multicolored geckos march across the ceiling, wolf masks eye a coop of ceramic chickens, and red chili-pepper lights enhance the playful vibe. But the Mexican food here, from hearty taco-enchilada combo plates to chiles rellenos, is seriously delicious. > 261 Tinker St., tel. 845/679–9563. MC, V. Closed Mon. No lunch. **$$**

Heaven Celebrities who weekend in Woodstock bring their kids here for breakfast, and supermodels gaze longingly at enticing cookies the size of large plates. Artfully arranged shelves by the entrance display condiments and delicacies, and chocolate Buddhas reflect upon your selection. For lunch consider endive-and-watercress salad with artichoke hummus or curried egg salad with dried apricots and currants. The Yin Yang BLT includes avocado and sprouts, and grilled granola-dusted banana and peanut butter comes on whole-wheat bread. > 17 Tinker St., tel. 845/679–0011. MC, V. No dinner. **¢–$**

Joshua's At one of the oldest eateries on Woodstock's main street, the unassuming interior gives no hint of the wonders that come out of the kitchen. The inventive Middle Eastern menu has zucchini flat cakes and tangy Cosmic Curry Chicken, which is served over brown-rice pilaf. Joshua's Smorgasbord brings together hummus, baba ghanouj, tabbouleh, dolma, and salad. > 51 Tinker St., tel. 845/679–5533. AE, MC, V. Closed Wed. in Jan.–Mar. **$$–$$$**

Landau Grill An outdoor dining area overlooks the main drag, giving you a glimpse of the perpetual parade outside. A steady stream of regulars holds down bar stools while noshing on burgers, pasta, and sesame-crusted tuna. The summer tiki bar satisfies raw-bar appetites. A kids' menu is available. > 17 Mill Hill Rd., tel. 845/679–8937. MC, V. **$–$$**

Taco Juan's The laid-back storefront eatery began as a humble stand behind the infamous Espresso Café. You can help yourself to utensils and sort your dirty dishes when you're done. A rogue's gallery of Woodstock characters lines one wall. Nothing beats the enormous wet-tofu burrito; a scoop of Jane's homemade ice cream is the perfect chaser. Park benches outside provide front-row seats for watching bongo players on the village green. > 31 Tinker St., tel. 845/679–9673. Reservations not accepted. No credit cards. **¢–$**

WHAT'S NEARBY

Bear Cafe Rock stars and actors find their way to this streamside restaurant 3 mi west of Woodstock, where a horseshoe bar adjoins two dining areas, one outdoors. Sit on the west side of the restaurant for an unfettered view of the Sawkill stream. The patio is about as close to the water as you can get without falling in. The kitchen prepares American fare, such as its signature filet mignon, dressed with port-garlic sauce and Stilton. You can wash it all down with a selection from the outrageous wine list, which includes 200 bottles from almost every·continent and ranges from

$25 to $1,500. > 295A Tinker St., Bearsville, tel. 845/679–5555. Closed Tues. No lunch. MC, V. **$–$$$**

Catskill Rose Architectural glass blocks flank a magenta door, hinting at the funky art-deco motif inside; herb gardens line the restaurant's perimeter, with brightly painted window boxes above. If you prefer to eat alfresco, head for the periwinkle tables and chairs on the brick courtyard. Fresh seafood and smoked duck exemplify this energetic restaurant. A dedication to innovation and fresh ingredients mandates a seasonal change of menu. > 5355 Rte. 212, Mount Tremper, tel. 845/688–7100, www.catskillrose.com. Closed Mon.–Wed. No lunch. D, DC, MC, V. **$$**

La Duchesse Ann As you pull into the gravel driveway and climb the steps of this 1850s Victorian, visions of grandma's house dance in your head. Crushed velvet and floral paper cover the walls, and period antiques grace dark rooms. Diners come from miles around to savor French dishes such as *cotriade bretonne* (fish stew), rack of lamb, and Black Angus steak with peppercorn-cognac cream sauce in formal surroundings with a glowing fireplace. Brunch is served Sunday. > 1564 Wittenberg Rd., Mount Tremper, tel. 845/688–5260, www.laduchesseanne.com. AE, D, MC, V. Closed Wed. **$$–$$$**

The Little Bear The wall of windows overlooking the Saw Kill inspires thoughts of feng shui as you ponder the extensive menu. Try chicken (or tofu) with honey walnuts or the vegetable–shark fin soup for two. Hunan shredded pork with black-bean sauce is one way to indulge carnivorous tendencies. The chef keeps it healthful by refusing to yield to the seduction of MSG, and the alert staff keeps things moving. > 295B Tinker St., Bearsville, tel. 845/679–8899. AE, MC, V. **¢–$$**

New World Home Cooking Co. Colorful accents and artwork adorn this lively restaurant 3½ mi east of the center of Woodstock. A large bar and a sapphire–and–stainless steel open kitchen are focal points. The eclectic menu includes a sampler with creole-mustard shrimp, Spanish manchego cheese, Sicilian olive-salad crostini, smoked Maine mussels, roasted chorizo, and pickled vegetables. Also here: chicken Punjabi, Thai barbecued fish, and Cajun peppered shrimp. The pan-blackened string beans will have you humming zydeco. Everything is prepared without "zappers" (deep-fat fryers) or MSG, and a kids' menu is available. Live music gets the joint jumping Friday nights. > 1411 Rte. 212, Saugerties, tel. 845/246–0900, www.newworldhomecooking.com. No lunch Tues. and Wed. AE, D, DC, MC, V. **$–$$$**

Spotted Dog Firehouse Restaurant The vintage fire engine jutting out of the facade signals that this is a kid-friendly place. You pass a video-game room on the way to the hostess station, which is fashioned from the lower half of an engine's cab. Six booths and a play area compose the body of the authentic fire truck parked in the center of this casual eatery. Consider the charbroiled sirloin steak with cabernet-garlic sauce and Portobello sticks. The menu's extensive selection of Mexican dishes includes the popular Frisbee quesadilla with barbecued pork. At this writing, the restaurant is closed for renovations, so call before heading out to eat here. > 5340 Rte. 28, Mount Tremper, tel. 845/688–7700, www.catskillcorners.com. Call for hrs. AE, D, MC, V. **¢–$$$**

Sweet Sue's French doors open into a bright, airy space filled with white wooden booths, marble-top café tables, and a stainless-steel counter where trays of fresh muffins cool. Folksy renditions of the house specialties decorate one wall; a blackboard announcing scrumptious specials resides on another. Robert DeNiro haunts here, as do other area glitterati. You'll see why when you tuck into the Blue Monkey, a stack of blueberry-banana buttermilk pancakes. Pumpkin-crusted tofu over polenta and sautéed kale topped with roasted–red pepper sauce are served alongside hot meat-loaf sandwiches and other comfort food. Efficient, friendly service caters to your needs. Take a note from the locals and stay a while—they come armed with newspapers and books. Reservations are essential on weekends. > 33 Main St., Phoenicia, tel. 845/688–7852. No credit cards. Closed Tues. and Wed. ¢–$

ESSENTIALS

Getting Here

If you're coming up for a relaxing weekend and expect to do little more than hang out at an in-town B&B and wander about the hamlet, bus is a viable option. If your heart is set on exploring the Catskills, winding along back roads, and searching out yard sales, then a car is imperative; public transportation is infrequent and limited and therefore not practical.

BY BUS

Adirondack Trailways leaves Port Authority four times a day (10–5). Additional buses are scheduled Friday, at 6 and 7 PM. The later in the day you leave Friday, the more difficulty you'll have finding a seat and the more likely you are to encounter traffic. Three buses return to the city from Woodstock Sunday; the first bus leaves at 11:50 AM. The trip is scheduled to take just over 2½ hours; the one-way fare is $22.05. The bus drops you off at the village green, in the heart of Woodstock; you may purchase tickets at H. Houst & Son hardware store (2–6 Mill Hill Rd.), down the street from the bus stop. Bicycles must be boxed for transport.

The bus also drops off in Mount Tremper, in front of La Duchesse Anne, on Wittenberg Road; the Zen Mountain Monastery is a short stroll away. Adirondack Trailways also serves Phoenicia, Saugerties, and the Hunter and Belleayre ski resorts.

LINES **Adirondack Trailways** > Tel. 800/858–8555, www.trailways.com.

BY CAR

Driving here gives you the most flexibility to explore the area and its natural riches. Expect the drive from the city to take close to 2½ hours; leaving during rush hour, especially Friday evening, can add an hour of travel time.

To get to Woodstock, take the New York State Thruway (Interstate 87) north to Exit 19, for Kingston. After the tollbooth, take the Route 28 west exit off the traffic circle, toward Pine Hill. (The speed limit on this four-lane road is 45 mph; police monitor Route 28, especially on weekends, looking to catch speeders.) Proceed about 6 mi to Route 375 and turn right. After 3 mi of twists and turns, you arrive in Woodstock. At the intersection of routes 375 and 212, turn left for the center of town. Street parking can be difficult to find on weekends, but municipal parking is usually available. Continuing westward on Route 212 from Woodstock takes you to Mount Tremper, past interesting homes and artist's studios. To get to Saugerties, turn right at the intersection of routes 375 and 212 (instead of left for Woodstock), or stay on the thruway until Exit 20.

The scenery is splendid pretty much anywhere you drive in the area, but be on the lookout for deer, especially at night. You may even spot them on the thruway shoulder.

Visitor Information

A tourist-information kiosk on Rock City Road, just off Woodstock's village green, is staffed from May through November, Thursday through Sunday about 11–6.

CONTACTS **Ulster County Tourism** > 10 Westbrook La., Kingston 12401, tel. 800/342–5826, www.ulstertourism.info. **Woodstock Chamber of Commerce and Arts** > 21 Tinker St., Woodstock 12498, tel. 845/679–8025, http://woodstockchamber.com.

Cooperstown

215 mi northwest of New York City

8

By Karen Little

BREEZY COOPERSTOWN SITS in upstate New York's thickly wooded Mohawk Valley, with the Adirondacks to the northeast and the Catskills to the southeast. A resort area since the mid-1800s, Cooperstown today is largely known for its Baseball Hall of Fame and other sights related to the national pastime. However, with its cultural attractions and other diversions, the village is commanding enough to engage you even if you're not a fan of baseball.

The village was founded in 1786 by William Cooper on the southern shore of Otsego Lake, also known as Lake Glimmerglass. William was the father of novelist James Fenimore Cooper (1789–1851), who set some of his epics in this region. By the late 19th century, word about the village and its lake spread, as New York's wealthy began building vacation homes upstate. The community is full of civic structures and residences from this period—many of them stately, most of them well preserved. Indeed, many of Cooperstown's accommodations occupy refurbished historic mansions run by highly dedicated innkeepers and are a big draw for visitors.

The story goes that Abner Doubleday (1819–93), an area native who went on to West Point and a distinguished military career, created the game of baseball here in 1839. Although many scholars believe that this is only a legend, it's one that's stuck. When thinking of Cooperstown, you can't help but think of the sport. Home to the National Baseball Hall of Fame and Museum as well as a baseball diamond named for Mr. Doubleday, the village draws fans of the game who feel they need to make the pilgrimage at least once in their lives—though often they return with families in tow. Both sights, as well several shops and restaurants, are along a four-block stretch of Main Street, roughly between Chestnut and Fair streets.

And then there's the sparkling Otsego Lake. As you travel east along its 20-mi circumference, you pass through virgin forests and along bluffs with fantastic views. Glimmerglass State Park and the adjacent Hyde Hall, an early-19th-century mansion that's open to the public, are on the northeastern shore of the lake. Continue north and you eventually come to the renowned Glimmerglass Opera, which stages four productions each summer. Driving west and then south brings you to a district with motels and a marina as well as to the Fenimore Art Museum, the Farmer's Museum, and the Leatherstocking Golf Course.

In summer and autumn, Cooperstown swells with visitors; all told, a third of a million people visit the village annually. Be sure to book accommodations in advance. That's really the only thing you need do with any urgency. Stays here are about strolls through the village, unhurried sightseeing, lazy boat rides, and time spent reading or chatting quietly with innkeepers on a breezy porch.

Inns and bed-and-breakfasts on the village's lake side are very large; most were built in the mid-1800s. Places to the southeast are newer; some are small B&Bs where spare bedrooms (usually only two) accommodate guests.

WHAT TO SEE & DO

Brewery Ommegang The affinity with *all* things Belgian, not just the beer, is palpable at this brewery, an elegant, white wooden structure with an unusual round wing that has slitlike windows and would probably be called Romanesque if it were built of stone. Brews include Hennepin Farmhouse Ale, Ommegang Abbey Ale, and Rare Vos Ale. Tours and tastings are possible throughout the year. In warmer months, the staff makes waffles according to a traditional recipe. The brewery also hosts several seasonal events and has a gift shop filled not only with brewery-related items but also with crafts, glassware, cheeses, and chocolates. > 656 Rte. 33, tel. 800/544–1809. Tours $4. Memorial Day–Labor Day, daily 11–6; rest of yr, daily noon–5.

Doubleday Field One glance at the brick entrance, just south of the Baseball Hall of Fame, will have you whistling "Take Me Out to the Ballgame" for the rest of the day. Local leagues play at this diamond, which opened around 1939 and can seat about 9,000 people in its bleachers. It's also used for the Baseball Hall of Fame Game held each summer, exhibition games, and other area events. > Main St., tel. 607/547–7200 or 888/425–5633, www.baseballhalloffame.org.

Farmers' Museum The 10 acres on which this museum is set have been dedicated to farming in one way or another since the days of James Fenimore Cooper. Stone structures that were once part of an actual farm now contain permanent and changing exhibits on agriculture, homemaking, and other aspects of farm life. Docents in period costumes mill about a village created with buildings that date from the 18th and 19th centuries and were moved here from several upstate communities. You can also inspect the livestock in the barns, wander through vegetable patches and herb gardens, and play with such historic toys as stilts and hoops and sticks. > Lake Rd. off Rte. 80, tel. 607/547–1500 or 888/547–1450, www.farmersmuseum.org. $9. May–Oct., daily 10–5.

Fenimore Art Museum Native, folk, fine, and decorative American art is displayed in a brick neoclassical mansion that dates from the 1930s. Paintings of landscapes and everyday scenes enlighten you on what this country was like in the 19th century. Sculptor John H. I. Browere's (1792–1834) bronze busts were made from life masks, so they truly depict such luminaries as Thomas Jefferson and Dolley and James Madison. Furniture, portraits, other items shed light on James Fenimore Cooper and his family. Traveling exhibits are eclectic: one that explored the history of high-heel shoes was held concurrently with another that had paintings of America's Western frontier. Photography and modern works by contemporary artists have been showcased, and so have Norman Rockwell illustrations. There's also an ever-changing roster of lectures, specialty tours, and book signings as well as a gift shop and a café. > Lake Rd., off Rte. 80, tel. 607/547–1400 or 888/547–1450, www.fenimoreartmuseum.org. $9. June–Sept., daily 10–5; Apr., May, and Oct.–Dec., Tues.–Sun. 10–4.

Glimmerglass Opera Area opera devotees staged a performance of *La Bohème* at the local high school in 1975. Twelve summers later the company that they went on to form was successful enough to merit its own space. In 1987 Glimmerglass held its first production in the 900-seat **Alice Bush Opera Theater,** whose walls can be rolled back (but are closed for performances). The company presents four shows during its July–August season. Picnics on the grounds are a good way to spend time before a performance. Tickets are $28–$92 weekdays and $56–$100 on weekends. > 7300 Rte. 80, tel. 607/547–5704, www.glimmerglass.org.

Glimmerglass State Park Enjoy average summer temperatures of 72°F in the deep woods of this state park on Otsego Lake 8 mi north of the village of Cooperstown. In warm months, you can swim, hike, and fish. There's a concession stand as well as 80 campsites. In winter you can snowshoe, snow-tube, cross-country ski, and ice fish. > 1527 County Hwy., tel. 607/547–8662 park, 800/456–2267 reservations, http://nys-parks.state.ny.us/parks. $6 per vehicle. Daily 8 AM–dusk.

Heroes of Baseball Wax Museum It's great to read about and trade cards of your favorite players, but this museum puts you face-to-face with them. Thirty-odd baseball legends are immortalized here. When your interest in all that wax starts to wane, you can slug it out in the virtual-reality batting cage, buy a team pennant or jersey in the gift shop, or grab some lunch in the café. > 99 Main St., tel. 607/547–1273, www.baseballwaxmuseum.com. $7.95. May–Oct., daily 9 AM–10 PM.

Hyde Hall Its legacy is as remarkable as its architecture: from the time it was built in 1819 until it was sold to New York State in 1964, Hyde Hall remained in the same family. Money from estates in here, in Europe, and in the Caribbean enabled George Clarke (1768–1835), a prominent figure in Colonial New York, to finance what is, according to many historians, the largest residence built in this country before the Civil War. Ongoing restoration projects—and the chance to question artisans about their work—add texture to a tour of the 50-room mansion. The property adjoins Glimmerglass State Park on the north end of Otsego Lake. > Mill Rd., tel. 607/547–5098, www.hydehall.org. $7. Mid-Apr.–Oct., Tues.–Thurs. 10–4.

National Baseball Hall of Fame and Museum The ball that Babe Ruth hit for his 500th home run and Shoeless Joe Jackson's shoes are among the memorabilia that helps to make this shrine to America's favorite pastime so beloved. Plaques bearing the pictures and biographies of major-league notables line the walls in the actual hall of fame. The museum also has multimedia displays, exhibits geared to children, and a research library with photos, documents, and videos. > 25 Main St., tel. 607/547–7200 or 888/425–5633, www.baseballhalloffame.org. $9.50. Labor Day–Memorial Day, daily 9–9; rest of yr, daily 9–5.

Sports

BOATING & FISHING

C. P.'s Charter Service From May through October, the company offers 90-minute boat tours of Otsego Lake for as many as 20 people. Vessels can pick you up from many places along the shore, and trips include free soft drinks. Rates vary. C. P.'s also conducts excursions to fish for bass, carp, perch, salmon, trout, and other types of game fish. Prices are $160 for four-hour trips for two people and $250 for full-day trips; if you have more than two people in your group add another $30 per person onto the fees. > 574 Rte. 29, Richfield Springs, tel. 315/858–3922, www.cooperstownfishing.com.

GOLF

Leatherstocking Golf Course The par-72, 6,416-yard course, designed by Devereux Emmet in 1909 and part of the Otesaga resort, has a championship green that runs along Otsego Lake's southwestern shore, starting right in Cooperstown. There's an on-site pro shop as well as a practice facility down the road. Greens fees are $70–$80. You can arrange individual lessons or take part in two- or four-day weekday or weekend training sessions (fees include hotel accommodations) through the Leatherstocking Golf School. The resort also offers a variety of golf packages for those who just want to get out there and play. > 60 Lake St., tel. 607/547–9931 or 800/348–6222, www.otesaga.com.

HORSEBACK RIDING

Hidden Valley Ranch On 560 or so acres just 20 mi northwest of Cooperstown, this working ranch offers trail rides for all skill levels. It also has cabins for rent; a riding school; and trails for hiking, mountain biking, and cross-country skiing. Ride prices per person range from $35 for an hour to $150 for a full day. Riding vacations that include accommodations are also a possibility. > 204 Twomey Rd., West Winfield, tel. 315/822–3841, www.hiddenvalleyvacations.com.

Save the Date

MAY
Wool Festival and Heritage Plant Sale The Farmers' Museum has demonstrations of herding, shearing, spinning, and weaving. There's also a sale of seeds, plants, and garden goodies. > Lake Rd., off Rte. 80, tel. 607/547–1450, www.farmersmuseum.org.

JUNE–AUGUST
Baseball Hall of Fame Weekend The National Baseball Hall of Fame inducts new members during a ceremony held on the grounds of Clark's Sport Center. The event, which may be scheduled for any weekend between June and August, is free. > 25 Main St., tel. 607/547–7200 or 888/425–5633, www.baseballhalloffame.org.

AUGUST
Cooperstown Chamber Music Festival National and international groups perform at this festival, which is held at the Farmers' Museum throughout the entire month. > Lake Rd., off Rte. 80, tel. 607/547–1450, www.cooperstownmusicfest.com.

SEPTEMBER
Autumn Harvest Festival The Farmers' Museum celebrates a fall and the harvest weekend every year around mid-September. > Lake Rd., off Rte. 80, tel. 607/547–1450, www.farmersmuseum.org.

DECEMBER
Candlelight Evening Buildings in the traditional village at the Farmers' Museum are decorated for the holidays and lit by hundreds of candles. Sleighs or wagons pulled by draft horses add to the experience. Special holiday beverages and food are served. > Lake Rd., off Rte. 80, tel. 607/547–1450, www.farmersmuseum.org. $9.

WHERE TO STAY

If you want to be within walking distance of the Baseball Hall of Fame, shops, and restaurants, opt for a place on or just off Main Street. Properties on Lake Street, including the Otesaga resort, often have both lake and mountain vistas. Chestnut Street, from approximately the outer edge of the village to Lake Street, is a main highway with many inns—often with large, landscaped yards—on either side. Most of these places offer full breakfasts, usually in lavishly set dining areas. Lodgings on Route 80 are well outside the village.

Angelholm Bed and Breakfast This impeccable 1805 Federal home is just off Main Street and adjacent to Doubleday Field. Innkeeper Dan Lloyd loves kids and baseball, as evidenced by his ever-full cookie jar and his baseball-card collection. Rooms have elegant wallpapers or traditional Colonial paint schemes, baths (some with clawfoot tubs), lace curtains, and large beds. > 14 Elm St., 13326, tel. 607/547–2483, www.angelholmbb.com. 5 rooms. Dining room, library, piano; no smoking. AE, D, MC, V. BP. $$

Barnwell Inn The owners of this 1850 mansion are opera lovers, and the inn tends to book up with other opera buffs during the local company's July–August season. The house, on a tree-lined, flower-filled yard created from three city lots, includes rooms painted in salmon pink, malachite green, burgundy, or pale yellow. Each guest room is unique, and a coach-house apartment—a good value—has a bedroom, a living area, and a kitchenette. Breakfast includes fresh berry pies and fruit crisps as well as such standard fare as quiche. Note that a dog also resides here. > 48 Susquehanna Ave., 13326, tel. 607/547–1850, www.barnwellinn.com. 2 rooms, 2 suites, 1 apartment. Dining room, fans, some kitchenettes, cable TV, piano; no kids under 2. MC, V. BP. $$–$$$

Bay Side Inn & Marina Otsego Lake is the focal point at this well-run motel, which has its own beach with docks, paddleboats, canoes, and gazebos—there's even a water-side swing set. The central building has large guest rooms, a sweeping porch, a lounge, and a room with pinball machines. There are also 11 freestanding cottages, the largest of which can accommodate 10 people. > 7090 Rte. 80, Cooperstown 13326, tel. 607/547–5856, www.cooperstown.net/bayside. 29 rooms, 11 cottages. Picnic area, refrigerators, cable TV, beach, boating, recreation room, playground; no smoking. Closed Nov.–Apr. AE, D, MC, V. EP. $$–$$$

Bryn Brooke Manor Atop a hill off Lake Street, this old mansion has lake and mountain vistas and provides a country-manor-house experience. The resident dog and cats pay you visits in the spacious public rooms, which have wood details, paneling, and floors. In the dining room, the windows open so wide that you feel like you're on a porch. Guest rooms are done in dusty pastels, whites, and florals. Quilts cover queen-size beds, and baths have plush robes and hair dryers. Some rooms adjoin others. The innkeeper, a baseball expert, can help you plan walks and other activities. Note that to reach the B&B, you need to walk up a steep hill. > 6 Westridge Rd., 13326, tel. 607/544–1885, www.brynbrookemanor.com. 4 rooms. Dining room, in-room data ports, in-room VCRs, pool; no smoking. MC, V. BP. $$

Cooper Inn With white moldings, delicate plaster- and woodwork, and a flying staircase, the interior of this 1812 brick inn is as Federal as its exterior. A stay here gets you access to all the facilities at the nearby Otesaga resort—including discounted greens fees—as well as to those at a sports center down the road. > 15 Chestnut St., 13326, tel. 607/547–2567 or 800/348–6222, www.cooperinn.com. 15 rooms. Dining room, in-room data ports, cable TV; no smoking. AE, MC, V. CP. $$$

Cooperstown Motel The owners of this bargain motel—representing three generations of one family—are very knowledgeable about the area and, like so many folks in Cooperstown, about baseball. The motel, ½ mi from the Baseball Hall of Fame. is one of the few area lodgings with rooms for smokers. > 101 Chestnut St., 13326, tel. 607/547–2301, www.cooperstownmotel.com. 40 rooms. Cable TV, no-smoking rooms. No credit cards. EP. ¢

Diastole Bed and Breakfast The breathtaking views from the huge porch of this hilltop B&B 3 mi from the village center are of woods and Otsego Lake's western shore. Shaker pieces are used throughout the house. The largest guest room, outfitted with Early American as well as Shaker furnishings, is impeccable. The property encompasses miles of private hiking trails, and you can arrange horseback riding with a nearby outfitter. > 276 Van Yahres Rd., 13326, tel. 607/547–2665, www.cooperstownchamber.org/diastole. 5 rooms. Dining room, some in-room hot tubs, hiking; no kids under 6, no smoking. No credit cards. BP. $–$$$$

Green Apple Inn This 1854 Colonial Revival mansion near Otsego Lake has Victorian-style guest rooms, some with clawfoot bathtubs. Porches and an atrium facing a beautiful yard are great places to read in warmer months; on colder days, you can curl up by a fireplace in one of the public areas. It's an easy walk to the museums just outside the village or to Main Street. > 81 Lake St., 13326, tel. 607/547–1080, www.greenappleinn.com. 4 rooms. Dining room, cable TV, Internet; no kids under 8, no smoking. MC, V. BP. $–$$$

Inn at Cooperstown Rocking chairs are set all along the front porch, which runs the width of this glorious Second Empire building (circa 1874) near Main Street. Guest rooms are uncluttered, making them seem even roomier than they already are. Crisp clean walls, king- and queen-size beds, and wall-to-wall carpeting lend modernity. Pastel quilts in traditional patterns and period reproductions are nods to this inn's history and its place on the National Register of Historic Places. > 16 Chestnut St., 13326, tel. 607/547–5767, www.innatcooperstown.com. 17 rooms, 1 suite. Dining room, some refrigerators, Internet; no room phones, no room TVs, no smoking. AE, MC, V. CP. **$$$**

Lake Front Motel Rooms are large and tidy at this professionally-run dock-side motel. Rooms have lake or park views. Don't feel bad if you can't snag one with a water view; just head to the restaurant's patio, where you can eat while watching boats drift by. With so much lake activity, you tend to forget that the Baseball Hall of Fame is just over a ball's throw away. > 10 Fair St., 13326, tel. 607/547–9511, www.lakefrontmotelandrestaurant.com. 44 rooms. Restaurant, cable TV, lake, dock, fishing; no smoking. AE, MC, V. EP. **$–$$$**

Landmark Inn An expansive front lawn rolls from Chestnut Street to the sheltered entry of this truly grand 1856 Italianate mansion. Common areas are large and sunny. Shiny wood floors and attractive furnishings are prevalent throughout. Beds and chairs are so plump you can't resist flopping onto them as soon as you enter your room. Many rooms have special showers or tubs; one has an 11-head shower. Full breakfasts are served in a formal dining room. > 64 Chestnut St., 13326, tel. 607/547–7225, www.landmarkinnbnb.com. 9 rooms. Dining room, some in-room hot tubs, refrigerators, cable TV, in-room VCRs, Internet; no smoking. AE, D, MC, V. BP. **$**

Otesaga Resort Hotel There's something almost collegiate about the stately Otesaga—maybe it's all the brick, or perhaps it's the Greek Revival–style cupola or the neoclassical entryway. The same studied grace runs throughout the interior. But it would be hard to hit the books here, thanks to such distractions as the Leatherstocking Golf Course and fishing or canoeing on Otsego Lake. The water view from the circular back porch alone is enough take you far from the everyday world. You can eat in the main dining room or the less formal Hawkeye Bar & Grill; in warmer months you can also grab an alfresco bite at a patio by the lake and another by the greens. > 60 Lake St., 13326, tel. 607/547–9931 or 800/348–6222, www.otesaga.com. 136 rooms. Restaurant, dining room, in-room data ports, in-room safes, cable TV, 18-hole golf course, 2 tennis courts, pool, lake, gym, boating, fishing, lobby lounge, lounge, concert hall, business services, meeting rooms. Closed mid-Nov.–mid-Apr. MAP. AE, D, DC, MC, V. **$$$$**

Overlook Bed and Breakfast There's no sign up out front, so upon arrival you feel as if you're walking up to the doors of a house—a very big Victorian one—owned by friends. Everything is polished and tidy, not to mention true to the period in which this house was built. Home-baked items are highlights of the breakfast buffet. All the in-town sights and shops are within walking distance. > 8 Pine Blvd., 13326, tel. 607/547–2019, http://members.aol.com/overlookbb. 4 rooms, 2 with bath. Dining room, fans; no a/c, no room TVs, no smoking. No credit cards. CP. **$$**

Stables Inn The Stables is in the heart of town, right near the Baseball Hall of Fame and above a store catercorner to T. J.'s Place, a popular baseball-themed restaurant that's affiliated with the inn. (The full breakfast is served at T. J.'s.) Guest quarters are all suites with queen and twin-size beds as well as such amenities as microwaves and coffeemakers. > 124 Main St., 13326, tel. 607/547–4040, www.tjs-place.com. 5 suites. Restaurant, cable TV, microwaves, refrigerators; no smoking. AE, MC, V. BP. **$–$$$**

Tunnicliff Inn This 1802 Federal-style hotel is one of Cooperstown's oldest brick structures. It was used first as a general store before being transformed, in 1848, into a hotel. A restaurant with an old-fashioned tap room adjoins the hotel, which is near the Baseball Hall of Fame and other village sights. > 34 Pioneer St., at Main St., 13326, tel. 607/547–961, www.cooperstownchamber.org/~tunnicliff. 17 rooms. Restaurant, dining room, cable TV, Internet; no smoking. AE, D, MC, V. EP. **$$–$$$**

White House Inn The 1835 Greek Revival sits on ½ acre near the village's main sights. Behind the inn are the carriage house, pool, and tree-lined, landscaped yard. Public areas have Oriental rugs and rich palettes. Guest rooms feel more casual, thanks to pastel color schemes, country quilts, and touches of floral. Rooms can be combined to accommodate groups of up to six. > 46 Chestnut St., 13326, tel. 607/547–5054, fax 607/547–1100, www.thewhitehouseinn.com. 6 rooms, 1 carriage house. Dining room, cable TV, pool; no smoking. AE, D, MC, V. BP. **$$–$$$$**

CAMPING

Glimmerglass State Park On Otsego Lake's northeast edge, this park has a shoreline as well as deep woods, an inland pond, picnic tables, trailer and tent campsites, and clean facilities. There's a limit of one hard-wheeled camping equipment (trailer or boat) per site. Leashed pets are allowed, but you must have proof of rabies vaccination. > 1527 County Rte. 31, Cooperstown 13326, tel. 607/547–8662, www.reserveamerica.com. 80 sites. Flush toilets, dump station, showers, fire pits, food service, grills, picnic tables, public telephone, playground, swimming (lake). MC, V. ¢

WHERE TO EAT

Café Milano Big windows frame this sunny corner restaurant, which specializes in Northern Italian fare. Shrimp Milanese, wrapped in bacon and baked, is a specialty. Flourless chocolate-espresso cake is a grand finale. > 22 Chestnut St., at Main St., tel. 607/544–1222. AE, MC, V. **$–$$$**

Fenimore Café The café at the Fenimore Art Museum serves tasty salads, soups, and other light fare and has a view across gardens and lawns to Otsego Lake. It's a great place to come just for lunch, which includes sophisticated dishes such as heirloom-tomato gazpacho topped with goat cheese. It's also the perfect spot to grab a cappuccino and something sweet after touring the museum. > Lake Rd., off Rte. 89, tel. 607/547–1400 or 888/547–1450. Reservations not accepted. AE, D, MC, V. No dinner. **¢–$**

Hawkeye Bar & Grill The Otesaga's classic restaurant–pub spills out onto a lakeside patio. The dinner menu includes an exceptionally fresh seafood dish that tops linguine with lobster, clams, shrimp, and scallops, as well as such casual fare as burgers and Caesar salad. Note that although the resort closes in winter, the grill is open throughout the year. > Otesaga Resort Hotel, 60 Lake St., tel. 607/547–9931. AE, MC, V. Closed Sun. and Mon. late Nov.–mid-Apr. No lunch Sat. Nov.–mid-Apr. **$–$$$**

Hoffman Lane Bistro The sunny, alley bistro is 1½ blocks from the Baseball Hall of Fame. You can eat your lunch or dinner on the patio or in brightly painted dining rooms. The dinner menu includes good salads and pasta dishes as well as such classics and meat loaf with pan gravy. > 2 Hoffman La., tel. 607/547–7055. AE, MC, V. **$$–$$$**

James Fenimore Cooper Room Part of the Tunnicliff Inn, this sparkling restaurant is quite cozy. Hallways to the guest areas are closed off, so that diners (no more than

30) can enjoy a peaceful and intimate dinner. The food and service are impeccable. Dishes range from regional American fare to Continental classics and contemporary preparations. One hearty choice: a grilled 12-ounce strip steak atop sautéed Portobello and shiitake mushrooms and a pool of mustard cream sauce. Downstairs is the Pit, a historic pub where many baseball player and fan has raised a glass. The bartender is full of good stories about serving the baseball greats. > 34–36 Pioneer St., tel. 607/547–9611. AE, D, MC, V. No lunch. $$–$$$

Lake Front Restaurant You can watch life on the lake go by from this shipshape casual dockside restaurant that's part of a motel complex. Prime rib is a favorite here, and seafood au gratin—lobster, shrimp, and scallops smothered in a white wine–cream sauce and cheddar cheese—is rich. > 10 Fair St., tel. 607/547–8188. Closed Oct.–Apr. MC, V. $$

Otesaga Resort Hotel Main Dining Room In the Otesaga's luxurious main dining room, elegant jabots frame massive windows. The kitchen prides itself on the high quality of its ingredients, including fish that comes fresh from Boston, and breads are baked on the premises. Dinner is prix fixe, which includes four courses. The ever-changing menu lists contemporary dishes such as an appetizer of corn tortellini with Madeira sauce as well as classics like Black Angus beef medallions in cognac-mushroom cream sauce. > 60 Lake St., tel. 607/547–9931. Jacket required. AE, MC, V. Closed late Nov.–mid-Apr. $$$$

T. J.'s Place The large, family-style restaurant is filled with baseball memorabilia. The menu includes everything from omelets to burgers to Italian dishes. A bar, plasma-screen TV, and gift shop provide additional distractions. > 124 Main St., tel. 607/547–4040. AE, MC, V. No dinner. $–$$

ESSENTIALS

Getting Here

The best way to get to Cooperstown is by car. You can take a bus, but the trip will eat up most of a day. If you don't have a car and can't rent one in the city, arrange for a car rental in Albany, to which you can travel by bus or train. Even if you do drive from the city, consider making this a three- or four-day trip.

BY BUS

Some tour operators arrange special season bus trips to Cooperstown, usually during fall-foliage season or the year-end holidays. Check with your travel agent for more information. Greyhound has limited service to Cooperstown from New York City's Port Authority, and the trip ($49 one way) takes pretty much all day. Greyhound has much more frequent service to Albany, where you can rent a car (at the bus depot) and continue west 70 mi, a drive that takes a little over an hour. Adirondack Trailways also services Albany, a three-hour bus trip.

LINES **Adirondack Trailways** > Tel. 800/858–8555, www.trailways.com. **Greyhound Bus** > Tel. 800/231–2222, www.greyhound.com.

BY CAR

The drive to Cooperstown from New York City takes about four hours from the George Washington Bridge. The last portion of trip is along winding, hilly, country roads. Have a detailed map or maps to guide you. Note that cell phones don't always work in the area.

Follow Interstate 87 (the New York State Thruway) north to Route 23 and travel west over the top of the Catskill State Park, approximately 70 mi to Interstate 88. Head northeast about 5 mi to Route 28 and take it through Portlandville and Milford to Cooperstown.

In-town parking is limited. There are, however, three free color-coded lots south of town. The blue and red lots are off Route 28; the yellow one is on Route 80. A trolley takes you among the lots and town; it also stops at sights within town, and the $2 ticket allows you to ride it all day. It runs every 20 minutes or so daily from 8:30 AM to 9 PM late June through early September and weekends 8:30 AM–9 PM late May 'til late June and early September through early October.

BY TRAIN
Amtrak makes 10-odd trips a day between New York and Albany, where you may rent a car from one of the agencies in the train station.
LINES **Amtrak** > Tel. 800/872–7245, www.amtrak.com.

Visitor Information

The Cooperstown Chamber of Commerce has a free 120-page book on the area; you can access the booklet on the chamber's Web site or have a copy mailed to you. Chamber staffers can also make lodging referrals if you arrive in town without reservations.
CONTACTS **Cooperstown Chamber of Commerce** > 31 Chestnut St., Cooperstown 13326, tel. 607/547–9983 or 877/867–4737, www.cooperstownchamber.org.
Otsego County Chamber of Commerce > 12 Carbon St., Oneonta 13820, tel. 877/568–7346, www.otsegocountychamber.com.

Saratoga Springs

180 mi north of New York City

9

Revised by Marianne Comfort

MINERAL-WATER SPRINGS FIRST BROUGHT Native Americans and, later, American settlers to this area just south of the Adirondack foothills—and they continue to attract visitors today.

Gideon Putnam opened the first inn and commercial bathhouse here in 1791, to cater to early health-seekers eager to drink from and bathe in the supposedly restorative waters. By the 1870s, Victorian society had turned Saratoga Springs into one of the country's principal vacation resorts, and the city became known as the "Queen of Spas."

In 1909, after the commercial exploitation of the mineral springs diminished their flow and even dried up some wells, New York State developed the Spa State Reservation (now called Saratoga Spa State Park) to protect against excessive pumping. Today you may sample the naturally carbonated waters of more than a dozen active springs, which were created by complex geological conditions centuries ago. A "tasting tour" brochure (available from the Saratoga Visitor Center) guides you to the springs in the Congress Park and High Rock Park areas, which are downtown, and in Saratoga Spa State Park, at the south end of the city. The springs differ, offering water rich in iron or sulfur or with minute quantities of radon gas (considered beneficial by some European and Japanese travelers). Geysers, or spouters, spray water out of a couple of springs. You can tell which springs are more popular than others by the number of people lined up waiting to fill their plastic jugs.

Some of the spa treatments that were enjoyed by members of Victorian society are available today, with contemporary twists. A few bathhouses, two of them built in the 1930s, offer massages, aromatherapy, and body wraps in addition to traditional mineral-water baths.

But the Victorians came to take part in other pleasures as well. A casino and grand hotels entertained and pampered this wealthy set for a few decades, and by the 1890s the city had become a horse-racing hot spot, with the Travers Stakes a highlight of the racing season. These days, thoroughbred racing has surpassed the springs as a draw, and the Travers, first run in 1864, remains a high point of the racing season.

The other major draw is the Saratoga Performing Arts Center, on the state-park grounds. For a few summer weeks, it's the residence of the Philadelphia Orchestra and the New York City Ballet; the open-air venue also hosts big-name jazz, rock, and pop concerts.

While here, you can enjoy walks through neighborhoods of restored mansions in the Italianate, Greek Revival, Queen Anne, and Second Empire styles. The city did experience a gradual, decades-long decline that started in the Depression and worsened after World War II, during which the race track closed for three years, but a revitalization effort in the latter half of the 20th century reversed the slide. The effort resulted in the restoration of many historic homes and turned the downtown into a thriving district of shops and restaurants, which it remains today. Broadway is more lively any time of year than most cities' downtowns, and the high-quality restaurants along a several-block stretch and its side streets regularly draw residents from throughout New York's Capital Region. In summer, especially during the six-week thoroughbred racing season (which starts in late July), sidewalks are crowded with people strolling from shop to restaurant to bar or enjoying a meal or coffee and pastries at an outdoor table, likely with street musicians nearby.

Some deluxe bed-and-breakfasts—renovated old inns, boarding houses, and private homes—have front porches perfect for quiet observation of these street scenes. The people watching is especially rich during the racing season, but so are lodging rates, which soar during this peak period.

Beyond the city are several American Revolution sites. The Revolution's Battle of Saratoga, actually fought in nearby Stillwater, halted the British invasion from Canada and turned the war in the rebels' favor, thus securing the area a place in U.S. history books.

WHAT TO SEE & DO

Caffè Lena Recognized as the country's oldest folk-music venue, this upstairs coffeehouse opened in 1960 and hosted Bob Dylan and Arlo Guthrie early in their careers. The tradition continues thanks to staff members as well as volunteers who together work the shows, a mix of well-known musicians and newcomers. Admission starts at $1 for open-mike nights, and similar programs and can top $25 for big-name acts. > 47 Phila St., tel. 518/583-0022, www.caffelena.com. Wed.–Sun.; call for schedule.

Children's Museum of Saratoga At this museum with hands-on exhibits geared for kids three to nine years old, youngsters may slide down a fire pole to a pretend fire truck or imagine they're slinging hash in a model diner. > 69 Caroline St., tel. 518/584-5540, www.childrensmuseumatsaratoga.org. $5. July–Labor Day, Mon.–Sat. 9:30–4:30; rest of yr, Tues.–Sat. 9:30–4:30, Sun. noon–4:30.

Congress Park Italian gardens, ponds, fountains, and statuary punctuate wide lawns at this park in the heart of the city. Fifty cents buys you a ride on a **carousel** with 28 horses that were carved and painted about a century ago. Crowds gather outside the Italianate Canfield Casino, a former gambling hall within the park, to watch the tuxedo set enter one of the August balls. The 1870s building also houses the **Historical Society Museum of Saratoga Springs** (tel. 518/584-6920, $4), where exhibits of Victorian furnishings, paintings, original gambling paraphernalia, and historic documents bring the city's history alive. From Memorial Day weekend through Labor Day, the museum is open Monday through Saturday 10–4 and Sunday 1–4; the rest of the year it's closed Monday and Tuesday. > Broadway between Circular and Spring Sts. Free.

Crystal Spa The spa taps into water from the **Rosemary Spring**, on property it shares with the Grand Union Motel. The original motel owner built a gazebo and then drilled water underneath (in 1964) to honor his wife, who had just delivered their 12th child. The family-run, cash-only business offers everything from an aromatherapy sauna for $18 to a package of several treatments for $160. > 120 S. Broadway, tel. 518/584-2556, www.thecrystalspa.com. Sept.–June, Fri.–Tues. 8:30–4:30; July, Thurs.–Tues. 8:30–4:30; Aug., daily 8:30–5:30.

Lincoln Mineral Baths The bathhouse, in a grand building at the entrance to Saratoga Spa State Park, offers a slew of treatments, from massages to body wraps and facials. A mineral bath is $18, a half-hour massage $40. > 65 S. Broadway, tel.

518/584–2011 or 518/583–2880, www.gideonputnam.com. July and Aug., daily 9–4; June and Sept., Wed.–Mon. 9–4; Oct.–May, Wed.–Sun. 9–4.

National Museum of Dance Five galleries house photographs, videos, costumes, and archives that explore the history and development of dance as an art form. The Hall of Fame honors top dancers, choreographers, and costumers. You may even watch dancers rehearsing in the performing-arts studios. > 99 S. Broadway, tel. 518/584–2225, www.dancemuseum.org. $6.50. Late May–late Oct., Tues.–Sun. 10–5; late Oct.–late May, weekends 10–5.

National Museum of Racing and Hall of Fame Exhibits, including memorabilia from famed horse Seabiscuit, relate the story of thoroughbred racing in the United States. In the Hall of Fame, video clips of races bring to life the horses and jockeys enshrined here. For an additional fee you may take a tour of the training track. > 191 Union Ave., tel. 518/584–0400, www.racingmuseum.org. $7. Mon.–Sat. 10–4:30, Sun. noon–4:30 (during the race meet, daily 9–5).

9 Maple Ave Live jazz comes to this 40-seat club every Friday and Saturday evening. The centerpiece of the hand-built mahogany bar is a porcelain tap head thrown by potter Regis Brodie. The club claims to offer the largest selection of single malt scotches in New York State. > 9 Maple Ave., tel. 518/583–2582, www.9mapleavenue.com.

Roosevelt Baths The historic bathhouse in Saratoga Spa State Park, closed for renovations at this writing, is scheduled to reopen by spring 2004. Plans call for 42 treatment rooms and a 1,300-square-foot fitness center. > Saratoga Spa State Park, Saratoga Springs, tel. 518/584–3000 or 800/732–1560.

Saratoga Automobile Museum America's love affair with the car is celebrated in this museum in a former bottling plant in Saratoga Spa State Park. Included are three galleries and an orientation theater. Changing exhibits display classic and racing cars. > 110 Ave. of the Pines, tel. 518/587–1935, www.saratogaautomobilemuseum.org. $7. May–early Nov., daily 10–5; early Nov.–Apr., Tues.–Sun. 10–5.

Saratoga County Arts Council Changing exhibits in this 2,000-square-foot art gallery and theater–performance space showcase works by local as well as nationally known artists. At the theater here, the **Saratoga Film Forum** shows mostly arthouse movies (tickets $6) Thursday and Friday nights in fall, winter, and spring. > 320 Broadway, tel. 518/584–4132, www.saratoga-arts.org. Free. Mon.–Wed. and Fri. 9–5, Thur. 9–8, Sat. 11–5.

Saratoga Harness Racing Museum and Hall of Fame The museum, on the grounds of Saratoga Raceway, displays antique horseshoes, high-wheeled sulkies (the two-wheeled vehicles used for harness racing), and horse-related artwork. > 352 Jefferson St., tel. 518/587–4210, www.saratogaraceway.com. Free. July and Aug., Tues.–Sat. 10–4; Sept.–June, Thurs.–Sat. 10–4.

Saratoga Lake You may fish, rent boats from one of several marinas, learn to water ski, or just watch weekend sailboat races at this 8½-mi-long, 1½-mi-wide lake. **Brown's Beach** (712 Rte. 9P, tel. 518/587–8280, www.brownsbeach.com), the only public beach on Saratoga Lake, is open June through Labor Day ($4). It's about 7 mi east of downtown Saratoga Springs.

Saratoga Performing Arts Center SPAC is the summer home of the New York City Ballet and the Philadelphia Orchestra. The open-air venue, with both assigned amphitheater seats and lawn seating, also hosts the Freihofer's Jazz Festival and concerts by big-name pop acts. > Saratoga Spa State Park, 108 Ave. of the Pines, between U.S. 9 and Rte. 50, tel. 518/587–3330, www.spac.org. Box office early May–Sept., Mon.–Sat. 10–6.

Saratoga Race Course Top jockeys compete for six weeks (starting in late July) each year at the nation's oldest thoroughbred track. Breakfast at the track has become a tradition, with a buffet meal served 7–9:30, while the horses go through their morning workouts. You also can bring your own breakfast and sit in the stands for the free show. Afterward, get a behind-the-scenes look at the track with a free tram tour of the backstretch. The gates open at 11 AM on weekdays (except Tuesday) and 10:30 on weekends. Most first races of the day have a 1 PM post time. > 262 Union Ave., tel. 518/584–6200, www.nyra.com. Grandstand $3, clubhouse $5. Late July–early Sept., Mon. and Wed.–Fri.; call for schedule.

Saratoga Raceway The action here is in the form of harness racing, and it's offered year-round. The air-conditioned clubhouse has a restaurant, but food concessions are options, too. > Nelson Ave., tel. 518/584–2110, www.saratogaraceway.com. Free. Call for schedule.

Saratoga Spa State Park Developed for the study and therapeutic use of the mineral springs here, this 2,200-acre park is now listed on the National Historic Register. It is home to the Gideon Putnam Hotel, the Saratoga Performing Arts Center, the Lincoln and Roosevelt baths, the Spa Little Theatre, and eight active springs. Recreational facilities include walking trails, 36 holes of golf, two pools, clay and asphalt tennis courts, picnic facilities, an ice-skating rink, and 12 mi of cross-country skiing trails. > S. Broadway and Rte. 50, tel. 518/584–2535, http://nysparks.state.ny.us. $6 per vehicle (May–Sept.). Memorial Day–Columbus Day daily 8 AM–dusk; limited access in winter.

Skidmore College This four-year coeducational college, founded in 1903, sponsors year-round cultural events and entertainment and is the summer home of the New York State Writer's Institute. The **Frances Young Tang Teaching Museum and Art Gallery** (tel. 518/580–8080, http://tang.skidmore.edu, $5 suggested donation) contains galleries large enough for oversize works and innovative installations, a 150-seat presentation room, and multimedia classrooms for lectures and film screenings. The rooftop is the setting for summer concerts. The museum is open Tuesday through Friday 10–5 and weekends noon–5. > 815 N. Broadway, tel. 518/580–5000, www.skidmore.edu.

Yaddo Artists, writers, and musicians from all over the United States come to this highly regarded artists' colony to work. The estate was built in 1899 by philanthropist Spencer Trask as a gift to his wife, Katrina. Although you can't visit the house, you can tour the grounds, which include a formal rose garden with fountains and an informal rock garden. From mid-June through the racing season, tours are offered at 11 on weekends. > Union Ave., tel. 518/584–07446, www.yaddo.org. Grounds free, tours $3. Daily dawn–dusk.

WHAT'S NEARBY

National Bottle Museum The state-chartered museum's extensive collection of bottles dates to the 1700s. On site is a glassworks that sometimes hosts a sale of contemporary art-glass pieces. The museum is 7 mi south of Saratoga Springs. > 76 Milton Ave., Ballston Spa, tel. 518/885–7589, http://family.knick.net/nbm. $2 suggested donation. June–Sept., daily 10–4; Oct.–May, weekdays 10–4.

Saratoga National Historical Park/Battlefield The Battle of Saratoga, fought 12 mi southeast of Saratoga Springs at this site in 1777, is recognized as the turning point in the American Revolution. The visitor center at the Route 32 entrance provides historic information and an orientation to the park, which encompasses the battlefield and two sites in the nearby villages of Schuylerville and Victory. Ten stops along a 9½-mi tour road through the battlefield explain the battle and its significance. Re-enactments and other living-history programs are scheduled throughout summer. The road is popular with bicyclists in warm-weather months and, when closed to traffic in winter, with cross-country skiers. The **John Neilson House,** the only structure standing on the battlefield that was here in the time of the Battle of Saratoga, might have served as headquarters for Benedict Arnold. It's open sporadically; if you spot a park ranger nearby, ask to have a look inside.

The 155-foot **Saratoga Monument** (53 Burgoyne St., Victory) commemorates the British surrender on Oct. 17, 1777. The obelisk was built from 1877 to 1883 and has three niches commemorating generals Philip Schuyler, Horatio Gates, and Colonel Daniel Morgan. The fourth niche, where a statue of Benedict Arnold would have gone, has been left empty deliberately and cannot be entered. The monument is open from late May to Labor Day, Wednesday through Friday 9:30–4:30. The **General Philip Schuyler House** (1072 U.S. 4, Schuylerville) was the general's country home before its destruction by the British in 1777. Schuyler and his soldiers rebuilt it in 29 days. The house includes some original furnishings. It's open from late May through Labor Day, Wednesday through Friday 9:30–4:30; tours are given every half hour. > Visitor center, 648 Rte. 32, Stillwater, tel. 518/664–9821 Ext. 224, www.nps.gov/sara. Visitor center free, tour road $5 per vehicle. Visitor center daily 9–5; tour road Apr.–mid-Nov., daily dawn–dusk.

Sports

GOLF

Saratoga National Golf Club The 2½-story Victorian-style clubhouse and mile-long access road edged with ponds and stone walls gives the impression of an exclusive private club. But the 18-hole course, built on 400 acres of hills and wetlands in the style of the 1920s and '30s, is open to anyone willing to pay greens fees that top $100 in-season. > 458 Union Ave., Saratoga Springs, tel. 518/583–4653, http://golf-saratoga.com.

Saratoga Spa Golf This public 18-hole course in Saratoga Spa State Park has a championship layout. Weekend greens fees of $25 make it a good value. The park also has a 9-hole course that's suitable for beginners. > Saratoga Spa State Park, 60 Roosevelt Dr., Saratoga Springs, tel. 518/584–2008, 518/584–3137 Ext. 7, www.saratogaspagolf.com.

Shopping

Chain stores have been encroaching on the small clothing boutiques and gift shops that make wandering down Broadway and its side streets so interesting, but the majority of storefronts are still unique to the city. Antiques stores draw visitors to nearby Ballston Spa.

Ballston Spa Antique Center More than 30 dealers sell everything from furniture and jewelry to clocks, postcards, and railroad memorabilia at this center about 7 mi south of Saratoga Springs. > 217–221 Milton Ave., Ballston Spa, tel. 518/885–6746.

Designers Studio The gallery carries pottery, jewelry, kitchenwares, leather handbags, decorative pieces, and other items from top artisans. > 492 Broadway, Saratoga Springs, tel. 518/584–1977.

Lyrical Ballad Bookstore Out-of-print books, first editions, and antique prints are the specialties of this antiquarian bookseller. > 7–9 Phila St., Saratoga Springs, tel. 518/584–8779.

Saratoga Farmer's Market The market's three covered pavilions are a social gathering spot on Wednesday 3–6 and Saturday 9–1, in season. The variety of produce, poultry, and meats from area farms, baked goods, and jams (from local berries) is good. > High Rock Park, High Rock Ave., off Lake Ave., Saratoga Springs, no phone. Closed mid-Dec.–early May.

Soave Faire Although the store specializes in framing and art and office supplies, it's also the place to buy any type of hat you might want to wear to the track or a picnic on the polo grounds. > 449 Broadway, Saratoga Springs, tel. 518/587–8448.

Save the Date

JUNE

Freihofer's Jazz Festival Some of the hottest jazz musicians stop here for two days of music to kick off summer. > Saratoga Performing Arts Center, 108 Ave. of the Pines, between U.S. 9 and Rte. 50, Saratoga Springs, tel. 518/587–3330, www.spac.org.

JUNE–JULY

Lake George Opera Festival Free pre-opera talks provide some background on the operas performed here for two weeks at the start of the summer. The season also includes the annual musical champagne-and-strawberries cruise on Lake George, 27 mi north. > Spa Little Theatre, 19 Roosevelt Dr., off Ave. of the Pines, Saratoga Springs, tel. 518/587–3330, www.lakegeorgeopera.org.

JULY

New York City Ballet The ballet company brings a repertoire of full-length performances and short pieces to the Saratoga Performing Arts Center for more than two weeks each year. Dress up in your evening best and bring an elaborate picnic supper for the gala, an annual fund-raiser that concludes with dancing to live music and fireworks. > Saratoga Performing Arts Center, 108 Ave. of the Pines, between U.S. 9 and Rte. 50, Saratoga Springs, tel. 518/587–3330, www.spac.org.

Saratoga County State Fair The weeklong traditional county fair, held at the fairgrounds 8 mi south of Saratoga Springs and run by the Saratoga County Agricultural Society, includes live-animal and gardening exhibits, craft and antiques vendors, and carnival rides. > Saratoga County Fairgrounds, Prospect St. and Fairground Ave., Ballston Spa, tel. 518/885–9701, www.saratogacountyfair.org.

JULY–AUGUST

Saratoga Polo Club The club hosts a weeks-long world-class polo competition, with renowned picnics and tailgate parties, at Whitney and Skidmore fields, off Route 9N. > Denton and Bloomfield Rds., Saratoga Springs, tel. 518/584–8108, www.saratogapolo.com.

AUGUST

Alabama/Saratoga Breeder Cup This third leg of the Triple Tiara, the counterpart to the Triple Crown for three-year-old fillies, is scheduled in the middle of the month. A chili cook-off is part of the fun. > Saratoga Race Course, 262 Union Ave., Saratoga Springs, tel. 518/584–6200, www.nyra.com.

Fasig-Tipton Horse Auction North America's oldest thoroughbred auction spans three evenings. Reservations are required to see sales of yearlings that may turn out to be the next Funny Cide or Man-O-War, both of which were purchased here. > Fasig–Tipton Pavilion, East Ave., Saratoga Springs, tel. 518/584–4700.

Philadelphia Orchestra Programs in this three-week summer residency may feature big-name performers such as pianist Emanuel Ax, soprano Kathleen Battle, or conductor Marvin Hamlisch, with works by Johannes Brahms, Ludwig van Beethoven, Cole Porter, and Sergei Prokofiev, among others. > Saratoga Performing Arts Center, 108 Ave. of the Pines, between U.S. 9 and Rte. 50, Saratoga Springs, tel. 518/587–3330, www.spac.org.

Saratoga Chamber Music Festival A celebration of music written for ensemble groups is offered for several days through the Saratoga Performing Arts Center but presented at the more intimate Spa Little Theatre, next door. > Spa Little Theatre, 19 Roosevelt Dr., off Ave. of the Pines, Saratoga Springs, tel. 518/587–3330, www.spac.org.

Travers Stakes The nation's oldest, Grade 1 stakes horse race is usually scheduled on the Saturday before Labor Day weekend. Post time is at 12:30 PM, earlier than for other race days. > Saratoga Race Course, 262 Union Ave., Saratoga Springs, tel. 518/584–6200, www.nyra.com.

Whitney Handicap The first Saturday of the month at the Saratoga Race Course features one of thoroughbred racing's most prestigious handicaps. > 262 Union Ave., Saratoga Springs, tel. 518/584–6200, www.nyra.com.

WHERE TO STAY

High-season prices jump considerably—even as much as 50%—during the racing season, which runs from late July to early September.

Adelphi Hotel The impressive lobby of one of the city's original late-19th-century hotels has slightly worn divans, elaborately stenciled walls and ceilings, and trompe l'oeil details. The grand staircase leads to three floors of guest rooms and common spaces, including a second-story piazza overlooking Broadway. Bedroom styles—from Victorian and French country to Adirondacks and Arts and Crafts—are diverse. The bar, which spills off the lobby and into a courtyard, is a favorite evening gathering spot for drinks and desserts. > 365 Broadway, 12866, tel. 518/587–4688, fax 518/587–0851, www.adelphihotel.com. 21 rooms, 18 suites. Café, cable TV, pool, lounge, meeting rooms. MC, V. Closed Nov.–Apr. CP. **$$–$$$$**

Adirondack Inn Courtyards, gazebos, picnic areas with gas grills, and cottages and motel-like buildings are scattered around 3½ acres at this budget option a few blocks from Broadway. > 230 West Ave., 12866, tel. 518/584–3510, fax 518/584–7010, www.adirondackinn.com. 44 rooms, 9 cottages. Picnic area, some microwaves, refrigerators, cable TV, pool, some pets allowed, no-smoking rooms. AE, D, MC, V. Closed Nov.–Mar. EP. **¢–$**

Batcheller Mansion Inn The ornate architectural details of this High Victorian Gothic stunner include dormer windows crowned with clamshell arches and a mansard roof of alternating bands of red and gray slate. The common spaces include porches, a living room, and a dining room that seats 20. Two long, plush velvet couches invite lingering in the library. Some of the smaller rooms are tucked under the slope of the roof; on the other end of the size spectrum, the Diamond Jim Brady suite has a regulation-size pool table, a jet tub for two, and a king bed. Congress Park is across the street. > 20 Circular St., 12866, tel. 518/584–7012 or 800/616–7012, fax 518/581–7746, www.batchellermansioninn.com. 4 rooms, 5 suites. Dining room, some in-room hot tubs, in-room data ports, refrigerators, cable TV, piano, library; no kids under 14, no smoking. AE, MC, V. BP (racing season and weekends), CP. **$$$–$$$$**

Chestnut Tree Inn The Victorian-style inn has a wide front porch with antique wicker furnishings and a yard with small tables and lounge chairs. The decor in most rooms relies on floral fabrics, with mauve and purple repeating throughout the house. In the bedrooms, solid-painted walls balance the flourishes. > 9 Whitney Pl., 12866, tel. 518/587–8681 or 888/243–7088, www.chestnuttreeinn.net. 7 rooms. Dining room; no room TVs, no smoking, no kids during racing season. MC, V. Closed Nov.–Apr. CP. **$–$$$**

Eddy House The 1847 Federal Colonial house is said to have been the first B&B in the city. Furnishings include antique pieces; a patio and screened porch offer views of the 1½ acres. > 4 Nelson Ave. Extension, 12866, tel. 518/587–2340. 4 rooms with shared baths. Dining room, cable TV, badminton, boccie, library; no room phones, no kids, no smoking. No credit cards. Closed Nov.–Apr. BP. ¢–$

Gideon Putnam Hotel & Conference Center A product of the public-works projects of the 1930s, this Georgian Revival–style brick hotel sits amid the 2,200 acres of Saratoga Spa State Park. Tall windows look out onto front and back gardens, and the interior scheme sticks to a gracious, traditional style. The Sunday brunch buffet of hot and cold entrées is a favorite among locals and visitors alike. > 24 Gideon Putnam Rd., 12866, tel. 518/584–3000 or 800/732–1560, fax 518/584–1354, www.gideonputnam.com. 99 rooms, 22 suites. Restaurant, café, in-room data ports, cable TV, 4 tennis courts, pool, gym, spa, bicycles, ice-skating, bar, lounge, baby-sitting, dry cleaning, laundry service, concierge, Internet, business services, meeting rooms, no-smoking rooms. AE, D, DC, MC, V. EP. $$$

Grand Union Motel The one-story motel, built in the 1950s, shares its address with the Crystal Spa. Lobby highlights include an oval mirror, a fireplace, and lithographs from Saratoga's former Grand Union Hotel, North America's largest hotel in the 1880s. Some rooms are paneled and have a sitting area and a large, tiled tub. > 120 S. Broadway, 12866, tel. 518/584–9000, fax 518/584–9001, www.grandunionmotel.com. 64 rooms. Picnic area, in-room data ports, some refrigerators, cable TV, pool, some pets allowed (fee), no-smoking rooms. AE, MC, V. EP. $

Inn at Saratoga At this 1848 inn, Victorian-inspired rooms with dark wood furniture and tailored swags include such modern conveniences as high-speed Internet access. The four suites, in the Brunelle Cottage in the back, have heated floors. Your room key grants access to the fitness facilities at the YMCA. > 231 Broadway, 12866, tel. 518/583–1890 or 800/274–3573, fax 518/583–2543, www.theinnatsaratoga.com. 38 rooms, 6 suites. Restaurant, in-room data ports, cable TV, lounge, Internet, meeting rooms; no smoking. AE, D, DC, MC, V. BP. $$

Prime Hotels & Conference Center–Saratoga Springs This five-story hotel offers a 24-hour business center and self-serve computerized check-ins (and -outs) both curbside and at a lobby kiosk. Guest rooms are furnished in traditional American style and have work areas with wood desks. > 534 Broadway, 12866, tel. 518/584–4000, fax 518/584–7430, www.primehotelsandresorts.com. 235 rooms, 5 suites. Restaurant, room service, in-room data ports, some in-room hot tubs, some kitchenettes, some microwaves, some refrigerators, cable TV with movies, indoor pool, gym, sauna, pub, concierge, business services, car rental, no-smoking rooms. AE, D, DC, MC, V. CP. $–$$$

Saratoga Arms The Smith family greets you to this 1870 Second Empire brick hotel in the heart of downtown. Rooms may have white country-cottage or Victorian furnishings; some have fireplaces or clawfoot tubs. Printed fabrics outfit beds and windows, and every room has a CD player. Shower stalls contain a tile with a quote about local history, characters, or landmarks painted on it. The wraparound porch is roomy and has antique wicker chairs. At this writing, an expansion to nearly double the number of rooms is slated for completion by July 2004. > 495–497 Broadway, 12866, tel. 518/584–1775, fax 518/584–4064, www.saratoga-lodging.com. 16 rooms. Dining room, in-room data ports, some in-room hot tubs, cable TV, concierge, business services, meeting rooms; no kids under 12, no smoking. AE, D, DC, MC, V. BP. $$$–$$$$

Saratoga Motel Small rooms with knotty-pine paneling bring to mind rustic cabins at this small motel, which sits on more than 4 acres that encompass trees and ponds. The motel is about 3 mi west of the Saratoga tracks and 2 mi west of the heart of the city. Next door (434 Church St.) and under the same ownership is a four-room B&B in an 1860s farmhouse. > 440 Church St., 12866, tel. 518/584–0920, fax 518/584–7177, www.saratogamotel.com. 9 rooms, 2 efficiencies. Cable TV, some kitchenettes, refrigerators, some pets allowed. AE, D, MC, V. EP. ¢–$$

Union Gables Bed and Breakfast A sweeping front porch graces this turreted and gabled Queen Anne Victorian inn, along a row of equally impressive homes. Benches built into the wood paneling flank the foyer sitting area, and the dining room, dressed in purple, is a Victorian fantasy. A piano figures prominently in the living room. None of the guest rooms are cramped, and those on the second floor are particularly large. Pastels are coupled with busy florals in some rooms, while in others deep greens and blues set off paisleys or plaids. Hardwood floors gleam throughout. > 55 Union Ave., 12866, tel. 518/584–1558 or 800/398–1558, fax 518/583–0649, www.uniongables.com. 11 rooms, 1 suite. Dining room, refrigerators, cable TV, tennis court, gym, outdoor hot tub, bicycles, piano, pets; no smoking. AE, D, DC, MC, V. CP. **$$**

Westchester House Antique and reproduction furnishings fill lace-curtained rooms in this 1885 Victorian painted lady. The property, which contains gardens, is on a treed residential street within walking distance of downtown and the race track. A formal dining room is the setting for the full, cold breakfast, which includes baked goods and meat and cheese platters. The parlor contains a library and baby grand piano. > 102 Lincoln Ave., 12866, tel. 518/587–7613, www.westchesterhousebandb.com. 7 rooms. Dining room, some fans, in-room data ports, library, piano; no a/c in some rooms, no smoking. Closed Jan. and Feb. AE, D, DC, MC, V. BP. **$$$–$$$$**

WHAT'S NEARBY

The Mansion Inn Paper-bag inventor George West had this 23-room villa built in 1866 across from one of his mills, 7 mi west of Saratoga Springs. Today it serves as a luxurious B&B where special services may include being picked up at the train station by the inn's Bentley or having cocktails delivered to your room on a silver tray. Intricate moldings, mirrors, and mantels grace rooms with 14-foot ceilings and Victorian furnishings. Some rooms have four-poster beds; all have down comforters. In warm weather you may opt to have breakfast on the long porch, from which you may take in the mansion's gardens and ponds. > 801 Rte. 29, Rock City Falls 12863, tel. 518/885–1607 or 888/996–9977, fax 518/884–0364, www.themansionsaratoga.com. 7 rooms, 2 suites. Dining room, in-room data ports, some in-room hot tubs, cable TV, library, piano, Internet, some pets allowed (fee); no kids under 14, no smoking. AE, D, MC, V. BP. **$–$$**

Roosevelt Inn & Suites The landscaped, 16-acre complex, 2½ mi south of Saratoga Spa State Park, encompasses four buildings with rooms, two pools, and a spa. Rooms are spacious and fully carpeted; most have private balconies. Apartment-size suites are available. You may borrow tapes from the videotape library in the lobby. > 2961 U.S. 9, Ballston Spa, 12020, tel. 518/584–0980 or 800/524–9147, fax 518/581–8472, www.rooseveltsuites.com. 39 rooms, 13 suites. Restaurant, picnic area, in-room data ports, some in-room hot tubs, some kitchens, refrigerators, cable TV, in-room VCRs, 2 tennis courts, 2 pools (1 indoor), gym, hot tub, sauna, spa, lounge, business services, no-smoking rooms. AE, D, MC, V. CP. **$–$$**

CAMPING

Moreau Lake State Park The state campground, about 15 mi northeast of Saratoga Springs via U.S. 9, offers an escape from busy summertime streets—Saratoga's or New York's. Hiking trails, nature programs, and rowboat and canoe rentals are available. > 605 Old Saratoga Rd., Gansevoort 12831, tel. 518/793–0511, http://nysparks.state.ny.us. 148 tent sites. Flush toilets, drinking water, showers, picnic tables, playground, swimming (lake). Reservations 800/456–2267. AE, D, DC, MC, V. Closed Columbus Day–mid-May. ¢

WHERE TO EAT

Eartha's Restaurant Vintage liquor ads adorn the walls of this funky, small bistro in an old building painted purple. A hip crowd comes for the pasta and mesquite-grilled seafood. > 60 Court St., tel. 518/583–0602. Reservations essential. AE, D, DC, MC, V. $$–$$$

Esperanto The menu of this tiny basement eatery offers a smattering of inexpensive dishes from Thailand, Mexico, England, the Middle East, and Italy. There's counter service only and just a few tables. > 6½ Caroline St., tel. 518/587–4236. AE, D, DC, MC, V. ¢

43 Phila Bistro Old caricatures of patrons and Campari posters vie for space at this Saratoga hot spot known for innovative fare. Offerings might include pan-seared duck breast with lingonberry sauce or crab cakes with spicy coleslaw. The menu also lists prime steaks and ribs. > 43 Phila St., tel. 518/584–2720. AE, D, MC, V. Closed Sun. in Sept.–May. $$–$$$$

Hattie's Since 1938 this casual restaurant has been serving such Southern favorites as fried chicken, ribs, pork chops, and jambalaya. Meals include homemade biscuits and cornbread and a choice of sides, including macaroni-and-cheese and sweet potatoes. In nice weather you may eat on the courtyard patio. Inside, tables—in checkered cloths—crowd together; overhead fans and a banging screen door keep the air circulating. The place doesn't take reservations in July and August; you just show up and wait. > 45 Phila St., tel. 518/584–4790. AE, MC, V. Closed Mon. and Tues. in Sept.–June. No lunch. $–$$

Olde Bryan Inn Built in the late 1700s, this three-level tavern-restaurant retains Colonial-style fireplaces and exposed beams. Staff also have collected ghost stories of a woman sighted in period dress. The menu is broad, offering sandwiches as well as fresh seafood, chops, and pastas served with the popular homemade biscuits. > 123 Maple Ave., tel. 518/587–2990. No reservations. AE, D, DC, MC, V. $–$$

PJ's Bar-B-Q Seating at this seasonal local favorite just south of Spa State Park on U.S. 9 is either under a roof shared with the kitchen and order counter or at outdoor picnic tables; a small section has wait service. Barbecue chicken, ribs, and beef brisket are specialties. Try PJ's own loganberry soda. > 1 Kaydeross Ave. W, tel. 518/583–2445. No credit cards at counter; AE, MC, V for table service. Closed mid-Sept.–Easter. ¢–$$

Ravenous Savory and dessert crepes are the focus at this small eatery furnished with plain wooden tables and chairs. Side orders of Belgian-style *frites* (fries) come in paper cones sized for an individual or a table of diners, and may include several kinds of dipping sauce. > 21 Phila St., tel. 518/581–0560. No reservations. MC, V. Closed Mon. Closed Tues. in mid-Oct.–early Apr. No dinner Sun. ¢–$

Saratoga Stakes A life-size replica of the racehorse Man-O-War greets you as you enter this enormous steak house, which wagers that a steak dinner here will top the best you've ever had. In the dining room, rich, patterned fabrics break up expanses of dark, polished wood. The menu includes various Black Angus cuts and other meats, as well as chicken and seafood dishes; the kitchen prepares vegetarian (and vegan) meals upon request. > 86 Congress St., tel. 518/587–5637. AE, MC, V. $$–$$$$

Sargo's Restaurant and Lounge With high ceilings, clothed tables, and mahogany-stained paneling and trim, this restaurant in the Saratoga National Golf Club's Victorian-style clubhouse exudes quiet elegance. The food lives up to the decor. The menu might include roast chicken with artichoke hearts and cremini mushrooms in spring or Long Island duck prepared three ways in fall. Chefs create pasta dishes tableside on Wednesday nights; on Sunday, live jazz accompanies an international brunch buffet. A lounge with a granite-and-wood bar and an outdoor terrace are more-casual dining options. > 458 Union Ave., tel. 518/583–4653. AE, MC, V. No lunch Nov.–Mar. **$$$–$$$$**

Sperry's The 1930s art-deco design at this restaurant on a narrow side street includes a black-and-white tile floor and equestrian art; outside is a garden with herbs. Try the specialty, soft-shell crab (in season), or Maryland crab cakes, swordfish, or steaks. Reservations aren't accepted in August. > 30½ Caroline St., tel. 518/584–9618. AE, D, DC, MC, V. **$$–$$$**

Springwater Bistro The chef, who relies largely on locally sourced ingredients, changes the menu daily to reflect what's available from area farms. Carmelized-onion ravioli and spinach may accompany roast pork, for example. The bar area of this restaurant, which occupies a restored Victorian across from the track, serves tapas. and the kitchen prepares picnic baskets in summer. A tasting menu is available, if your entire table orders it ($52 per person). > 139 Union Ave., tel. 518/584–6440. AE, D, DC, MC, V. Closed Tues. in Sept.–June. No lunch in Sept.–June. **$$–$$$**

Sushi Thai Garden Restaurant A hostess dressed in a kimono is likely to greet you at this bright and airy restaurant furnished in light wood. A sushi bar serves up a large selection of sushi and sashimi combinations; entrées include Japanese teriyaki, tempura, and kutsu dishes as well as Thai curries and noodles. > 44–46 Phila St., tel. 518/580–0900. AE, D, MC, V. **$–$$**

The Wheat Fields You can see fettuccine, lasagna, and other pastas squeezing out of the pasta machine in the front window of this main-street restaurant. Traditional Italian dishes share menu space with more-creative fare. Smoked salmon, caviar, and scallions adorn angel-hair pasta in Alfredo sauce; the same sauce dresses breaded breast of chicken filled with asparagus mousse and served with tomato-tinted pasta. The menu includes selections for vegetarians and meat eaters. > 440 Broadway, tel. 518/587–0588. AE, D, MC, V. No lunch on weekdays. **$–$$**

WHAT'S NEARBY

Chez Sophie Bistro The second generation of owners (the original owners' son and daughter-in-law) has updated the classic French food served at this gleaming 1950s diner with an emphasis on ingredients from area farmers. But this is no casual eatery: inside are two refined dining rooms with cloth-covered tables and an abundance of artwork (by Joseph Parker, one of the original owners). The food is just as refined. Duck breast is glazed in green peppercorn–flecked apricot sauce; cassoulet is studded with bits of goose, pancetta, and lamb; and black sea bass is wrapped in parchment and steamed with herbs. A $25 three-course "pink plate special" dinner is available Tuesday through Thursday off-season. The restaurant is 4½ mi south of Saratoga Springs. > 2853 U.S. 9, Ballston Spa, tel. 518/583–3538. AE, DC, MC, V. Closed Sun. No lunch. **$$$**

ESSENTIALS

Getting Here

You can get to Saratoga Springs easily by train and bus, so you may want to skip driving, especially during the busy racing season, when parking is tight. Walking, cycling, or using public transportation (local bus or trolley) will get you to enough sights and activities around the city. The trolley shuttle runs from late June to early September, stopping at the major sights, but the local bus line operates all year. To explore the surrounding areas, however, you need a car.

BY BUS

Greyhound and Adirondack Trailways together provide service almost every hour from New York City's Port Authority to Saratoga Springs, with a 6 PM Friday departure tailor-made for weekenders. On average, the trip takes about four hours each way, even for buses that include a change in Albany. Return trips late Sunday afternoon and evening start at 4:15 and run through 9:30. The bus arrives and departs from the Saratoga Diner (133 S. Broadway), at the south end of downtown. Tickets for the two bus lines are interchangeable. A round trip costs $76.

LINES **Adirondack Trailways** > Tel. 800/858–8555, www.trailways.com. **Greyhound** > Tel. 800/231–2222, www.greyhound.com.

BY CAR

To get to Saratoga Springs by car from Manhattan, take the Palisades Interstate Parkway north to Exit 9, which links to the New York State Thruway (Interstate 87). Proceed north to Albany, where the thruway splits from Interstate 87 (and follows Interstate 90 instead), and continue northbound on Interstate 87 to exits 13N, 14, or 15. Try to avoid the Albany area between 4 and 6 PM on weekdays, when traffic to the northern suburbs can crawl. Saratoga Springs allows on-street parking and has a few free public lots, but finding parking downtown can be difficult during the racing season. Most lodgings have their own parking spaces. Note that Broadway and South Broadway are also U.S. 9 in town.

BY TRAIN

Two trains run daily between New York City's Penn Station and Saratoga Springs. They leave New York City early in the morning and late afternoon on weekdays. Return trains leave Saratoga Springs mid-afternoon and early evening on Sunday. The trip takes about 3½ hours and costs $86–$118 round-trip.

LINES **Amtrak** > Tel. 800/872–7245, www.amtrak.com.

STATIONS **Saratoga Springs** > Station La. and West Ave., Saratoga Springs, tel. 518/587–8354, www.amtrak.com.

Visitor Information

The Saratoga Visitor Center, in a former trolley station, shows a 15-minute video about the city. Brochures available include self-guided walking tours of residential neighborhoods.

CONTACTS **Saratoga Visitor Center** > 297 Broadway, Saratoga Springs 12866, tel. 518/587–3241, www.saratoga.org/visitorcenter.

Rhinebeck

90 mi north of New York City

10

By Gail Jaffe-Bennek

AT THE HEART OF RHINEBECK is a historic village with a dose of city sophistication. The influence of earlier times is present in the Victorian, Greek Revival, Colonial, and other architectural treasures scattered throughout the village. Some two dozen, including the early Dutch-style post office, are listed on the National Register of Historic Places. Meanwhile, up-to-the-minute shops, restaurants, and theaters keep bringing new life to the old churches, early educational institutions, and other repurposed buildings they occupy.

The venerable Beekman Arms has witnessed the comings and goings of many historical figures, including George Washington, Benedict Arnold, Alexander Hamilton, and Benjamin Harrison; Franklin Delano Roosevelt, who grew up about 12 mi downriver, visited the 1766 inn on several occasions. These days, from its central location at the corner of U.S. 9 and Route 308, "the Beek" seems to watch over the happenings in Rhinebeck's main commercial district, where indie boutiques, dignified shops, and funky cafés lure passersby.

A few miles to the west courses the Hudson River, its right bank lined north and south with magnificent estates that once belonged to Astors, Vanderbilts, Livingstons, and other prominent families. Many are open to the public, offering a window into a time of splendor long past as well as proximity to the mighty river. Stroll their grounds and gardens, or visit one of the state parks or reserves along the Hudson.

Rhinebeck is the cultural hub of the mid-Hudson Valley, and many of the Hudson River mansions host recreational and cultural events. In and around the village you can enjoy international films, chamber-music concerts, a local theater group, and an active performing-arts center. The Dutchess County Fairgrounds offers a full calendar of fairs, shows, and festivals, and the Old Rhinebeck Aerodrome adds a unique dimension to the countryside with its World War I biplanes soaring overhead. Arguably the most extraordinary cultural opportunities are to be experienced at the Fisher Center, in nearby Annandale-on-Hudson, home to the Bard Music Festival. But the Frank Gehry–designed center is a must-see even when nothing's on.

Springwood, FDR's formidable former home in the Hudson River village of Hyde Park, is well worth a stop. Hyde Park is also the home of the East Coast campus of the Culinary Institute of America (CIA). Rhinebeck—indeed much of Dutchess County, including nearby Tivoli and Red Hook—is blessed with outstanding restaurants, in part because so many CIA graduates decide to stay in the area after they've completed their training. Eateries here cover the bases, from the upscale to the casual, from the traditional to the contemporary. First-time visitors are often surprised by the high quality of the fare and the number of options.

The culinary institute itself has five restaurants, but only two are open on Saturday. One plan of action: leave the city midday Friday, tour the FDR estate and related sites, and then head to dinner at one of the CIA places before continuing on to your lodging in Rhinebeck. (Reserve a table as far ahead as possible and notify your lodging about your late arrival.)

In summer and during the fall foliage season, peak times to visit, the village swells with sidewalk and car traffic, and reservations—for restaurants and lodgings—are in high demand. But each season has its own pleasures. Far from boisterous any time of year, the village mellows more in winter. If you come without a car, choose an in-town inn or bed-and-breakfasts from which a short walk will get you to shops, eateries, and the movie theater.

WHAT TO SEE & DO

Center for Performing Arts at Rhinebeck A large red barn about 3½ mi east of the village center houses this busy community performing-arts space. Open year-round, the center hosts local, national, and international theater groups, dance troupes, and musicians. The ongoing series of Saturday-morning (11 AM) children's shows is popular. > 661 Rte. 308/E. Market St., tel. 845/876–3080, www.centerforperformingarts.org.

Old Rhinebeck Aerodrome All the vintage aircraft at this museum still fly; indeed, many are used during air shows, held on weekends from mid-June to mid-October (weather permitting). The collection includes a reproduction of Charles Lindbergh's *Spirit of St. Lewis* and fighter planes from World War I. For a thrill you can don a Snoopy-style cap and goggles and soar over the area in an open-cockpit biplane. Ride booths open at 10 on weekends of air shows, and the rides (fewer than 15 minutes long; $40 per person) book up quickly. Air shows start at 2. > 44 Stone Church Rd., tel. 845/752–3200, www.oldrhinebeck.org. $12 on air-show weekends, $6 otherwise. Mid-May–Oct., daily 10–5.

Rhinebeck Farmers' Market The freshest of the fresh, locally grown and produced vegetables, flowers, cheese, meats, honey, and baked goods are for sale at this Sunday market in the town's municipal parking lot. Special theme days are held, musicians perform, and samples are offered. The market is open rain or shine. > E. Market St., tel. 845/876–4778, www.rhinebeckfarmersmarket.com. Free. Late May–mid-Nov., Sun. 10–2.

Upstate Films Theater A cultural hub for everything about film, this small theater in the center of Rhinebeck shows documentaries, independent films, classics, and animation. Shows often sell out, so it's best to purchase tickets in advance. Talks and discussion groups are often held here. The theater is also a screening venue for the acclaimed Woodstock Film Festival, held in September. > 6415 Montgomery St./U.S. 9, tel. 845/876–2515 or 866/345–6688, www.upstatefilms.org. $6.50.

Wilderstein The grand, Queen Anne–style Victorian home with a dramatic five-story circular tower was owned by the Suckley family for more than 140 years. The last family member to occupy the estate was Margaret "Daisy" Suckley, a distant cousin of Franklin Delano Roosevelt; she assisted the president with his papers and was considered a close companion of his. The house, with main-floor interiors and stained-glass windows designed by J. B. Tiffany, is being restored in phases. Noted landscape architect Calvert Vaux designed the grounds, which have Hudson River views. > 330 Morton Rd., tel. 845/876–4818, www.wilderstein.org. $5. May–Oct., Thurs.–Sun. noon–4; Dec., weekends 1–4 (Victorian holiday house tours).

WHAT'S NEARBY

Center for Curatorial Studies The center, part of Bard College, is known for cutting-edge exhibits of contemporary art. Museum exhibitions take place in summer and fall; student shows are exhibited in spring. Artists Chuck Close, Joseph Kosuth, and Nam June Paik have participated in the center's public lectures and conferences, which focus on contemporary-art issues, including public policy. The center is on the south end of the 540-acre campus. > Bard College, Annandale Rd., west of Rte. 9G, Annandale-on-Hudson, tel. 845/758–7598, www.bard.edu/ccs. Free. Wed.–Sun. 1–5.

Mills-Norrie State Park Formed from Margaret Lewis Norrie State Park and Ogden Mills and Ruth Livingston Mills Memorial State Park, the park encompasses 1,000 scenic acres along the Hudson River, about 5 mi south of Rhinebeck. The grounds include 6 mi of hiking, biking, and horseback-riding trails; a marina; nature center; public golf course; and the **Staatsburg State Historic Site.** > Old Post Rd., off U.S. 9, Staatsburg, tel. 845/889–4646, http://nysparks.state.ny.us. Free.

Montgomery Place Amid 434 acres along the Hudson River north of Rhinebeck sits this 23-room mansion, once the Livingston family estate. Janet Livingston Montgomery, the widow of American Revolution hero General Richard Montgomery, commissioned the original house in the early 1800s. Built in the Federal style, the mansion was remodeled in the mid-19th century by noted American architect Andrew Jackson Davis, who applied a classical revival style. The well-maintained house is open for tours, but the grounds alone are worth seeing; they encompass orchards, flower gardens, and ancient trees, and offer plenty of picnic-perfect spots as well as views of the Hudson River and the Catskill Mountains. Special events include festivals, twilight walks, candlelight tours, and gardening workshops. > River Rd., off Rte. 9G, Annandale-on-Hudson, tel. 845/758–5461, www.hudsonvalley.org. $7 house and grounds, $4 grounds. Apr.–Oct., Wed.–Mon. 10–5; Nov., weekends 10–5, first half of Dec., weekends noon–5.

Olana State Historic Site In the 1870s, Hudson River School artist Frederic Church built this 37-room Moorish-style castle on a hilltop with panoramic valley and river vistas. Architect Calvert Vaux came up with the design of the house, to which the artist applied his own touches. The interior is an extravaganza of tile and stone, carved screens, Persian rugs, and paintings, including some by Church. The house, about 20 mi north of Rhinebeck, is open only for guided tours, which run about 45 minutes; reservations are urged. The grounds are open year-round. > Olana State Historic Site, Rte. 9G, Hudson, tel. 518/828–0135, www.olana.org. Tours $3; grounds free. House early Apr., May, and Oct., Wed.–Sun. 10–5; June–Sept., Wed.–Sun. 10–6; Nov., Wed.–Sun. 10–4; Dec., call for hrs. Grounds daily 8–sunset.

Poets' Walk Spectacular views of the Hudson River and the Catskill Mountains are your reward for trekking through the fields and wooded trails (2¼ mi) at this 120-acre park. Rustic cedar benches, foot bridges, and gazebos add to the park's charm and offer places to picnic and rest. The well-maintained paths are gravel in some places and dirt in others. > Rte. 103 ½ mi north of Kingston–Rhinecliff Bridge, Red Hook, tel. 845/473–4440 Ext. 270, www.scenichudson.org. Daily 9–dusk.

Richard B. Fisher Center for the Performing Arts at Bard College Noted architect Frank Gehry designed this extraordinary, 108,000-square-foot performing-arts center. Brushed stainless-steel panels, draped like massive ribbons over the roof and sides, reflect the light and colors of the sky as well as the hilly surroundings. The main **Sosnoff Theater** hosts world-class opera, dance, drama, and music performances throughout the year. The most notable performance series is the annual Bard Music Festival, held in August. The center is on the north end of the 540-acre campus.

Hyde Park Side Trip

ABOUT 12 MI SOUTH of Rhinebeck via U.S. 9 is the Hudson River village of Hyde Park. It dates to 1702, when an estate on this land was named for Edward Hyde, Lord Cornbury, then the provincial governor of New York. Hyde Park is most famous for being the boyhood home of Franklin Delano Roosevelt. It's also home to an impressive summer mansion built by one of the Vanderbilts, as well as to the renowned Culinary Institute of America.

Culinary Institute of America (CIA). The East Coast branch of the country's most respected cooking school is on the grounds of a former Jesuit seminary overlooking the Hudson River. Tours are available Monday and Thursday when school's in session. Five student-staffed restaurants are open to the public. The Craig Claiborne Bookstore stocks more than 1,300 cookbooks in addition to culinary equipment and specialty foods. One- and two-day workshops and lectures are offered on weekends. > 1946 Campus Dr., Hyde Park, tel. 845/452–9600, www.ciachef.edu. Tour $5. Tours Mon. 10 and 4, Thurs. 4; call for details.

Eleanor Roosevelt National Historic Site. An unpretentious cottage, **Val-Kill** was first a retreat and later the full-time residence for Eleanor Roosevelt. A biographical film entitled First Lady of The World is shown at the site. The property encompasses 180 acres of trails and gardens. It's also the location of Val-Kill Industries, Eleanor's attempt to prevent farm workers from relocating to the city for employment; reproductions of Early American furniture, pewter, and weavings were produced here. > Rte. 9G, Hyde Park, tel. 845/229–9115, www.nps.gov/elro. Tour $8. May.–Oct., daily 9–5; Nov.–Apr., Thurs.–Mon. 9–5.

Franklin D. Roosevelt National Historic Site. The birthplace and home of the county's 32nd president, the house, called **Springwood,** is just as it was when the Roosevelts lived here and contains family furnishings and keepsakes. On the grounds is a wonderful rose garden where Franklin and Eleanor are buried. At the **Franklin D. Roosevelt Library and Museum** (www.fdrlibrary.marist.edu.fdr), photographs, letters, speeches, and memorabilia document FDR's life. A multimedia exhibit examines World War II. The first of the presidential libraries, this building was designed by Roosevelt himself. The tour includes the home and the library and museum. > U.S. 9, Hyde Park, tel. 845/229–9115, www.nps.gov/hofr. Tour $14. Nov.–Apr., daily 9–5; May–Oct., daily 9–6.

Vanderbilt Mansion National Historic Site. The grand and imposing 1898 McKim, Mead, and White mansion, built for Cornelius Vanderbilt's grandson Fredrick, makes a striking contrast with its Roosevelt neighbor, Springwood. A fine example of life in the Gilded Age, the house is lavishly furnished and full of paintings. It conveys the wealth and privilege of one of the state's most prominent families. The grounds offer excellent views of the Hudson River and encompass lovely Italian gardens. > U.S. 9, Hyde Park, tel. 845/229–9115, www.nps.gov/vama. Tour $8, grounds free. Daily 9–5.

At the East Coast branch of the CIA, five restaurants are open to the public. Reservations are absolutely essential at four of them (reserve as far ahead as possible). Only the Escoffier Restaurant and American Bounty are open Saturday. None of the restaurants are open when classes are not in session.

American Bounty. Regional American fare is the specialty at this student-staffed restaurant on the East Coast campus of the CIA, and local and seasonal ingredients are emphasized. For instance, a salad with baked sheeps' milk cheese and candied walnuts gets a dressing with Hudson Valley apple cider. The restaurant is in venerable Roth Hall, once a Jesuit Seminary. > 1946 Campus Dr., Hyde Park, tel. 845/471–6608. Reservations essential. AE, D, MC, V. Closed Sun. and Mon., 3 wks in July, 2 wks in late Dec. $$–$$$$

Apple Pie Bakery Café. The CIA's most casual dining option showcases luscious desserts and breads made daily. However, the place isn't open on weekends. The light lunch menu lists soups, sandwiches, pizza, and salads. The atmosphere is relaxed, and prices are reasonable. The line can get quite long around noon but moves fairly quickly. > 1946 Campus Dr., Hyde Park, tel. 845/905–4500. Reservations not accepted. AE, D, MC, V. Closed weekends. ¢

Escoffier Restaurant. This elegant Culinary Institute restaurant presents modern interpretations of classic French dishes such as lobster salad, smoked salmon, and sautéed beef tenderloin. Other specialties include duck-liver terrine with mango chutney, seared sea scallops, and snails with basil cream sauce. > 1946 Campus Dr., Hyde Park, tel. 845/471–6608. Reservations essential. AE, D, MC, V. Closed Sun. and Mon., 3 wks in July, 2 wks in late Dec. $$–$$$

Ristorante Caterina de' Medici. The terraced Colavita Center for Italian Food and Wine is the setting for this complex of Italian dining areas, each with its own character. The ornately decorated main dining room has Venetian light fixtures and is the most formal; the Al Forno room has an open kitchen with a colorfully painted wood-fired oven. Antipasti choices are plentiful, followed by first and second courses. Panna cotta is a good dessert pick. > 1946 Campus Dr., Hyde Park, tel. 845/471–6608. Reservations essential. AE, D, MC, V. Closed weekends, 3 wks in July, 2 wks in late Dec. $–$$

St. Andrew's Café. Contemporary fare takes on Asian influences at this casual restaurant at the CIA—chicken-and-shrimp soup, warm spinach salad with wood-fired quail, and grilled tuna with soba noodles, for example. The wood-fired pizza-of-the-day is popular. > 1946 Campus Dr., Hyde Park, tel. 845/471–6608. Reservations essential. AE, D, MC, V. Closed weekends, 3 wks in July, 2 wks in late Dec. $$–$$$

> Annandale Rd., west of Rte. 9G, Annandale-on-Hudson, tel. 845/758–7900, www.bard.edu/fishercenter. Tour $5. Late Jan.–late Dec., tours daily at 11, 1, and 2.

Staatsburg State Historic Site The well-known architectural firm of McKim, Mead, and White was responsible for the beaux arts style of this grand 65-room mansion fronted with mammoth columns. Formerly known as Mills Mansion, the Hudson River estate, 5 mi south of Rhinebeck, was a family home of financier Ogden Mills and his wife, Ruth Livingston Mills, in the late 1800s to early 1900s. You may see the mansion's lavish interior by guided tour only. The estate, one of the most beautiful properties in the Hudson Valley, has hiking and cross-country-skiing trails, a huge hill for sledding in winter, and spectacular river views; state-park land surrounds it. > Old Post Rd., off U.S. 9, Staatsburg, tel. 845/889–8851, http://nysparks.state.ny.us. House tour $5, grounds free. Early Apr.–early Sept., Wed.–Sat. 10–5, Sun. noon–5; early Sept.–late Oct., Wed.–Sun. noon–5.

Sports

HIKING

Gentle hills, wooded trails, open pastures, and quiet country roads best describe the choices for hiking in the Rhinebeck area. Most anyone moderately fit can complete the hikes offered nearby.

Mills-Norrie State Park You can take an easy walk or an invigorating hike through the 6 mi of wooded trails here. The environmental center frequently offers guided walks. > Old Post Rd., off U.S. 9, Staatsburg, tel. 845/889–4646, http://nysparks.state.ny.us.

Staatsburg State Historic Site Numerous trails weave through the grounds of the magnificent Staatsburg estate, formerly called the Mills Mansion. A particularly scenic trail runs along the Hudson River as far as Mills-Norrie State Park and offers views of the Esopus Lighthouse as well as the Catskill Mountains. Be prepared to step over some tree roots; otherwise the hike, no more than a mile long, is easy, and the round-trip can be completed in little over an hour. In winter, trails accommodate cross-country skiers. > Old Post Rd., off U.S. 9, Staatsburg, tel. 845/889–8851.

Tivoli Bays A 1,720-acre nature reserve stretching for 2 mi along the east bank of the Hudson River has several short trails that wind through and around a freshwater tidal wetland. The bays, part of the Hudson River National Estuarine Research Reserve, are used for long-term field research and education, as well as for hunting in season. Tide charts are available at the research reserve's main office, at Bard College Field Station on Tivoli South Bay, as well as at the visitor center in Watts de Peyster Fireman's Hall (86 Broadway) in Tivoli. > Rte. 9G and Kidd La., about 10 mi north of Kingston–Rhinecliff Bridge, Tivoli, tel. 845/758–7010 reserve office, http://nerrs.noaa.gov/hudsonriver.

KAYAKING

The sport has been growing in popularity in the area, and on nice days colorful kayaks dot the Hudson River. The area has a number of excellent put-in spots, but no local rentals at this writing. The river can be challenging, and river traffic is heavy at times; personal flotation devices are a must. The *Daily Freeman* newspaper lists tide charts.

Mills-Norrie State Park Both large and small boats may be launched from the park's marina. Paddle south about ½ mi to reach a small island, which you can circle. For a more ambitious paddle, travel 3 mi upriver to the Esopus Lighthouse. Eagles have been spotted flying over the river in this area. > Old Post Rd. off U.S. 9, Staatsburgh, tel. 845/889–4646, http://nysparks.state.ny.us.

Rhinecliff Landing Both kayaks and larger boats on trailers can be launched from the Rhinecliff town landing, east of the railway station. To get here, follow Hutton Street toward the Hudson River. Across the river from the landing, a lighthouse sits at the mouth of the Roundout Creek. If you paddle up the creek about 1 mi, you can stop for lunch at any of Kingston's many creekside restaurants. If you head north from the landing, toward the Kingston–Rhinecliff Bridge, you may be lucky enough to spot a bald eagle.

Tivoli A popular put-in site for canoes and kayaks lies at the end of Route 78, off Route 9G, in Tivoli. Cross the railroad tracks to the small parking area. From here you can paddle across the river to the Saugerties Lighthouse or head south to explore Tivoli Bays. To reach the bays, travel along the river bank for about 1 mi and then pass under the railroad trestle. Follow the channels and you might see snapping turtles, beavers, blue herons, and an assortment of other wildlife and flora. Note that hunters use this area during duck season (usually in early October and most of November and December). Another entry point for the Tivoli Bays is from Kidd Lane, also off Route 9G. At this launch site you must carry your boat down— and, later, up—a steep hill.

Shopping

Clustered within a two-block radius from Rhinebeck's traffic light (by the Beekman Arms) are small shops, art galleries, and restaurants. Shopping covers everything from boutiques selling pricey designer clothes to an old-fashioned five-and-dime— you won't find any traditional malls or chain stores here. On the third weekend of May and August, the merchants hold a town-wide sidewalk sale, during which great deals can be found.

Beekman Arms Antique Market More than 30 antiques dealers sell their wares in a large, red barn behind the Beekman Arms. The space, a former livery stable, is clean and bright. The antiques mix is eclectic, with Americana, Victorian, country, and primitive pieces represented. The furniture has been spruced up and doesn't need work. Clinics, with appraisals and workshops, are occasionally held here. > 6387 Mill St., Rhinebeck, tel. 845/876–3477.

Hummingbird Jewelers Inspired by love of color and design, the owners of this exquisite jewelry shop give personal attention to every piece they carry. One-of-a-kind creations by local and international artisans are artfully displayed. An exceptional collection of designer wedding bands and engagement rings is showcased. > 20 W. Market St., Rhinebeck, tel. 845/876–4585. Closed Tues.; call for winter hrs.

Oblong Books and Music The well-stocked, all-purpose bookstore, one block north of the Beekman Arms, offers a good selection of novels, books about area places and local history, and works by local writers. It also sells CDs. The children's room, in the back, occasionally hosts kids' events. Author signings are on Friday at 7; on many Sunday afternoons the store accommodates music events. > Montgomery Row, 6420 Montgomery St., Rhinebeck, tel. 845/876–0500 or 800/625–6640.

SugarPlum Boutique "Life is chaotic, you might as well look good" is the motto of Diana Brind, owner and creative force behind this accessories boutique. (ChaosCosmetics is the name of her line of beauty products.) Her eye for the delicate is evident in the array of barrettes, scarves, hats, and personally designed silver jewelry here. > 71 E. Market St., Rhinebeck, tel. 845/876–6729.

Winter Sun/Summer Moon The ever-changing, exotically decorated display windows set the stage for these side-by-side stores. Luscious fabrics, bright colors, and rich textures give the shops the feel of a sophisticated bazaar. Comfortable, easy-to-wear, and elegant clothes, jewelry, and accessories are the signature of Winter Sun. Eileen Fisher, Flax, and Dansko are among the designers carried. Walk through to Summer Moon for natural personal-care products, yoga mats, and candles. > 10 E. Market St., Rhinebeck, tel. 845/876–2223 Winter Sun, 845/876–3555 Summer Moon.

Save the Date

MAY

Rhinebeck Antiques Fair One of the best known and loved antiques fairs in the country, the Rhinebeck Antiques Fair showcases more than 200 dealers at each of its three annual shows, held in four large exhibition halls. The fair interests both casual and serious collectors. Room-like settings set the stage for an eclectic selection of antiques from different periods. Delivery service is available. > Dutchess County Fairgrounds, U.S. 9, Rhinebeck, tel. 845/876–4001, 845/876–1989 in May, www.rhinebeckantiquesfair.com.

JUNE

Crafts at Rhinebeck More than 350 artists show their crafts at this prestigious juried event held near the third weekend in June (and again in October). An impressive array of handcrafted items including jewelry, blown glass, pottery, musical instruments, and wearable art is for sale. Most booths are manned by artists eager to discuss their work. The event is held in four buildings that tend to get crowded. > Dutchess County Fairgrounds, U.S. 9, Rhinebeck, tel. 845/876–4001, www.dutchessfair.com.

Hudson Valley Food and Wine Festival On the grounds of Montgomery Place in the beginning of June, New York State vineyards, stellar restaurants, and regional farms come together for a weekend of tastings, demonstrations, and lectures. Bring a blanket and enjoy a picnic on the mansion's spectacular grounds. > Montgomery Place, River Rd., off Rte. 9G, Annandale-on-Hudson, tel. 845/758–5461, www.hudsonvalley.org.

JULY

Rhinebeck Antiques Fair This fair, held in four large exhibition halls, brings more than 200 antiques dealers to Rhinebeck three times a year. > Dutchess County Fairgrounds, U.S. 9, Rhinebeck, tel. 845/876–4001, 845/876–1989 in July, www.rhinebeckantiquesfair.com.

JULY–AUGUST

Bard SummerScape The mix of events during Bard College's summer performing-arts festival, which runs from mid-July to mid-August, might blend orchestral and choral concerts, operas, dance performances, puppetry and other theater presentations, films, and panel discussions. Performances, which may include world or American premieres, are staged throughout the campus; the Richard B. Fisher Center for the Performing Arts is the main venue. > Bard College, Annandale Rd., west of Rte. 9G, Annandale-on-Hudson, tel. 845/758–7900, www.bard.edu/fishercenter.

AUGUST

Bard Music Festival Bard College's much-acclaimed festival is devoted to a single composer deemed worthy of a new look and is held over two consecutive weekends. The approach is multidisciplinary and includes lectures, demonstrations, art exhibits, and panel discussions, in addition to musical performances. The music is a heady blend of virtuoso performances and symphonic, chamber, and solo works; examples of works by contemporaries are used to put the composer in the larger context of his or her cultural milieu. > Bard College, Annandale Rd., west of Rte. 9G, Annandale-on-Hudson, tel. 845/758–7900, www.bard.edu.

Dutchess County Fair This favorite summer event is a cross between an old-fashioned country fair and a carnival. It's the second largest agricultural event in New York State: more than 1,600 animals—including rabbits, sheep, hogs, and horses—are judged for excellence. Pig racing, husband calling, and hay stacking are some of the diversions. > Dutchess County Fairgrounds, U.S. 9, Rhinebeck, tel. 845/876–4001, www.dutchessfair.com.

SEPTEMBER

Good Guys Classic Rod and Custom Car Show For a weekend every September, "traveling roadies," as they call themselves, can be seen driving their brightly decorated hot rods, muscle cars, and custom classics around Rhinebeck. It's quite a sight when 2,000 pre-1964 cars converge on the fairgrounds for this swap meet, exhibition, and sale. Food and old-time music are part of the fun. > Dutchess County Fairgrounds, U.S. 9, Rhinebeck, tel. 845/876–4001, www.good-guys.com.

Woodstock Film Festival Rhinebeck's Upstate Films theater hosts some of the screenings for this well-regarded film festival, usually held around the third week of the month. The festival includes an impressive selection of panel discussions and workshops, presented in Woodstock, Rhinebeck, and other area locations. > Upstate Films, 6415 Montgomery St./U.S. 9, tel. 845/679–4265 Woodstock Film Festival, 845/876–2515 Upstate Theater, woodstockfilmfestival.com.

OCTOBER

Crafts at Rhinebeck At this juried, indoor event, held also in June, 350-plus artists show their goods—everything from pottery to wearable art. > Dutchess County Fairgrounds, U.S. 9, Rhinebeck, tel. 845/876–4001, www.dutchessfair.com.

Harvest Fair at Montgomery Place One of the area's most magnificent mansions hosts this event on its equally magnificent grounds. The fair is traditionally held Columbus Day weekend, when the fall foliage is at its peak. The festivities include cider pressing, hay rides, music, sheepherding, weaving and wood-carving demos, and food concessions. > River Rd., off Rte. 9G, Annandale-on-Hudson, tel. 845/758–5461, www.hudsonvalley.org.

New York State Sheep and Wool Show Sheep, goats, llamas, and alpacas are on display and for auction on the third weekend in October. Demonstrations and workshops on topics such as spinning, rug braiding, felting, weaving, and knitting are part of the event. Yarns of all fibers are available for purchase. > Dutchess County Fairgrounds, U.S. 9, Rhinebeck, tel. 845/876–4001, www.sheepandwool.com.

Rhinebeck Antiques Fair This popular weekend antiques show, held indoors, makes its last appearance of the year in October. Miss this and you have to wait until next May to check out the offerings of the 200-plus dealers. > Dutchess County Fairgrounds, U.S. 9, Rhinebeck, tel. 845/876–4001, 845/876–1989 in Oct., www.rhinebeckantiquesfair.com.

WHERE TO STAY

Beekman Arms and Delamater Inn America's oldest operating inn, the Beekman Arms is a welcoming presence in the center of town. Beyond the massive doors of this pre-Revolutionary lodging are wide-plank floors, beamed ceilings, and a stone hearth. The original 1766 building has smallish though cheery and comfortable colonial-style rooms with modern baths. Contemporary motel-style rooms are available in a separate building behind the Beekman Arms. One block north on U.S. 9 is "the Beek's" sister, the Delamater Inn. It contains the Delamater House, an American Gothic masterpiece designed by Alexander Jackson Davis, and a hidden courtyard with six guest houses, perfect for family reunions or travel with friends. Many of the Delamater rooms have fireplaces. > 6387 Mill St., 12572, tel./fax 845/876–7077, www.beekmanarms.com. 61 rooms, 6 suites. Restaurant, some in-room data ports, some kitchenettes, some refrigerators, cable TV, bar, business services, meeting room, some pets allowed, no-smoking rooms; no a/c in some rooms. AE, D, DC, MC, V. EP Beekman Arms, CP Delamater Inn. $–$$$

Gables Bed and Breakfast Wicker, lace, pastels, and gables everywhere (17 in all) contribute to the sweetness of this light and airy pre–Civil War cottage surrounded with a white picket fence. Enjoy a quiet moment on one of the porches or a long soak in an original cast-iron tub. Terry robes and a goodies drawer stocked with commonly forgotten items and little treats make this B&B special. The suite, roomy enough for three and awash in rose-patterned wallpaper and fabric, is popular for "girlfriend get-aways." > 6358 Mill St., 12572, tel. 845/876–7577, www.gablesbnb.com. 2 rooms, 1 suite. Dining room; no room phones, no TV in some rooms, no kids under 12, no smoking. D, DC, MC, V. BP. $$–$$$

Olde Rhinebeck Inn On a quiet tree-lined street 3 mi from Rhinebeck center, Jonna Paolella caringly tends to her guests. She can tell you the fascinating history of this house, built by German Palatine settlers, and about George, the resident ghost who reportedly appears with some regularity in the Spirited Dove room. Much of the original detail in this circa-1745 inn has been beautifully preserved. The country decor mixes rustic pieces with some finer furnishings. > 340 Wurtemburg Rd., 12572, tel. 845/871–1745, fax 845/876–8809, www.rhinebeckinn.com. 2 rooms, 1 suite. Dining room, some in-room hot tubs, refrigerators, cable TV, pond, fishing, no-smoking rooms; no room phones. AE, MC, V. BP. $$$$

Sleeping Beauty B&B The late-19th-century Folk Victorian on a quiet side street has a twin design, with two adjacent sections that mirror each other. Innkeepers Christine and Doug Mosley occupy one half and guests stay in the other. Rooms have period toile, floral, and striped wallpapers and fabrics. One has a separate entrance and its own enclosed porch. Details such as fish-scale shingles, tiny stained-glass windows, pocket doors, dentil molding, and antique wall-hung sinks make it all the more interesting. > 28–30 Chestnut St., 12572, tel. 845/876–8986, www.sleepingbeautybandb.com. 4 rooms. Dining room, fans; no room phones, no room TVs, no kids under 10, no smoking. MC, V. BP. $$

Veranda House Bed & Breakfast If you like lace and antiques, this B&B in a circa-1845 Federal-style house is for you. Most rooms have canopy beds, crocheted bedspreads, lace curtains, and densely patterned wallpaper. Breakfast, which might include tomato-sausage tart, crepes, or orange pancakes, can be served on the stone patio, by the garden, weather permitting. A five-minute walk takes you to the village center or the Dutchess County Fairgrounds. > 6487 Montgomery St., 12572, tel./fax 845/876–4133, www.verandahouse.com. 5 rooms. Dining room, no-smoking rooms; no room TVs, no kids under 10. AE, MC, V. Closed Christmas wk. BP. $$

Village Inn of Rhinebeck A sign on the office door reads DON'T LET THE CATS OUT. But the few cats lounging inside don't look at all interested in escaping. The one-story motel-style lodging is close to the center of Rhinebeck, the train station, and Hyde Park, and is ideal for travelers who don't require more than the basics. Each room is spacious and carpeted and has two queen beds. Coffee and baked goods are available in the lobby each morning (where you might encounter the cats). > 6260 U.S. 9,

12572, tel. 845/876–7000, fax 845/876–4756. 16 rooms. Some refrigerators, some kitchenettes, cable TV, no-smoking rooms. D, MC, V. CP. ¢

Whistlewood Farm Bed & Breakfast You can't help but leave the city behind as you drive up the fence-lined road to this farm where thoroughbred horses graze. The main house is homey and rustic, with more-refined, contemporary-country guest rooms. You may sit on one of many decks and enjoy the display of wildflowers. In winter, the fieldstone fireplace is put to use. For more privacy, stay in the Carriage House, a converted barn with two suites. Breakfast, pancakes or egg dishes, is hearty, and home-baked pie and cake are readily available. After fueling up, explore one of the trails on the grounds. > 52 Pells Rd., off Rte. 308, 12572, tel. 845/876–6838, fax 845/876–5513, www.whistlewood.com. 3 rooms, 3 suites. Dining room, fans, some in-room hot tubs, some in-room VCRs, cross-country skiing, some pets allowed (fee), no-smoking rooms; no room phones, no TV in some rooms. AE. BP. **$$–$$$**

WHAT'S NEARBY

Belvedere Mansion The commanding neoclassical-style house sits on a hill with distant Hudson River and mountain views across a sometimes busy road. Trimmed with marble, crystal, silk, and damask, the main-house rooms are the most elegant lodgings on the property, which includes several other buildings. Most rooms in what's called the Hunt Lodge, in the woods behind the main house, are suites with fireplaces and private terraces. The more-modest Carriage House building—a motel-like strip—has small rooms, some with fireplaces, and king beds. Four teeny rooms ($) are available as well. > 10 Old Rte. 9, Staatsburg 12580, tel. 845/889–8000, fax 845/889–8811, www.belvederemansion.com. 30 rooms, 5 suites. Restaurant, picnic area, some fans, tennis court, pool, pond, volleyball, bar, no-smoking rooms; no room phones, no room TVs. AE, DC, MC, V. BP. **$$$–$$$$**

Grand Dutchess Bed & Breakfast Pass through the center of Red Hook and you can't help but notice this stately blue Victorian mansion. The owners are antiques collectors, so the house has the feel of a museum, especially in the common rooms. All but one of the bedrooms are corner rooms. The proprietors also own the more-relaxed Red Hook Inn. > 7571 Old Post Rd., Red Hook 12571, tel. 845/758–5818, fax 845/758–3143, www.granddutchess.com. 5 rooms, 2 with shared bath; 1 suite. Dining room, some in-room hot tubs; no room phones, no room TVs, no kids under 6, no smoking. AE, DC, MC, V. BP. **$**

Red Hook Inn Rooms in this 1840s inn with a wide front porch are mostly spacious and uncluttered; floral fabrics, some vintage, dress a couple of them. Breakfast is served in the restaurant, which offers contemporary American fare. The more formal Grand Dutchess Bed & Breakfast, two blocks away, shares owners with this inn. > 7460 S. Broadway, Red Hook 12571, tel. 845/758–8445, fax 845/758–3143, www.theredhookinn.com. 5 rooms, 1 suite. Restaurant, some in-room hot tubs, some cable TV, some in-room VCRs, bar, no room phones, no TV in some rooms, no smoking. AE, DC, MC, V. CP. **$$–$$$**

CAMPING

Mills-Norrie State Park The park, about 5 mi south of Rhinebeck, totals 1,000 scenic acres along the Hudson River and encompasses two adjoining state parks as well as the Staatsburg State Historic Site (home of the old Mills Mansion). The grounds include 6 mi of hiking trails as well as a marina, nature center, and an 18-hole public golf course. Cabins have two bedrooms and electricity (no heat). > Old Post Rd., off

U.S. 9, Staatsburg 12580, tel. 800/456–2267 reservations, http://nysparks.state.ny.us. 32 tent sites, 16 RV sites without hook-ups, 10 cabins. Flush toilets, dump station, drinking water, showers, grills, picnic tables, some electricity. Reservations essential. D, MC, V. Closed late Oct.–mid-May. ¢

WHERE TO EAT

Bread Alone The European-style bakery receives daily shipments of fresh bread from its main facility, in nearby Boiceville. The loaves, baked in wood-fired ovens and shaped by hand, come in varieties such as hearty whole-grain "health bread" and baguettes. Sensitive to gluten? Consider the spelt bread. The café, with six tables and a window bar, is a comfortable place for a light lunch. The cappuccino here is excellent. > 45 E. Market St., tel. 845/876–3108. ¢–$

Calico There's more to this little storefront patisserie-restaurant than meets the eye. Exquisite specialty cakes, tarts, and baked goods fill the pastry case. The lunch, dinner, and Sunday brunch fare is mostly American and includes a vegetarian option or two, such as napoleon of polenta layered with goat cheese, vegetables, and pesto. Bouillabaisse, brimming with shellfish in lobster broth, is a good deal. > 6384 Mill St., tel. 845/876–2749. AE, MC, V. Closed Mon. and Tues. No dinner Sun. $$

Cripple Creek Small touches add up to big-time pampering at this welcoming restaurant. Co-owner Patrick Hayes, a pianist who studied at the Juilliard School, treats diners to a selection of classical or soft contemporary tunes. Rose petals garnish tables and finger bowls. Dishes, elegantly presented, are American with Asian and European influences. Chanterelles and shaved Périgord black truffles adorn a rich lobster risotto; also decadent, and too good to pass up, is the warm chocolate-mousse cake. If you love what you have, ask and you shall be presented with a copy of the recipe. > 22 Garden St., tel. 845/876–4355. AE, DC, MC, V. Closed Tues. No lunch. $$–$$$

40 West The two-story restaurant, in a refurbished blacksmith shop set back from West Market Street in the center of town, serves excellent, creatively prepared and presented food in an unpretentious setting. The scrumptious choices include phyllo-wrapped goat cheese, a starter, and sweet-potato ravioli. Sitting at a table in the glassed-in mezzanine makes you feel like you're eating among the treetops. Live music is available some Friday and Saturday nights. > 40 W. Market St., tel. 845/876–2214. Reservations essential. MC, V. Closed Tues. and Wed. No lunch. $$–$$$

Garden Street Cafe The tiny café–juice bar occupies one end of the Rhinebeck Health Foods store. The kitchen uses the freshest local and organic ingredients, turning them into flavorful wraps, salads, sandwiches, and soups, such as the hearty Avocado Supreme (avocado and melted Havarti on multigrain bread) and Chili Works (vegetarian black-bean chili over brown rice). Daily specials are posted on a white board decorated with funky art by a staff member. To create a custom smoothie or juice drink, simply choose your ingredients. Take-out is popular. > 24 Garden St., tel. 845/876–2005. AE, MC, V. Closed Sun. No dinner. ¢–$

Gigi Trattoria A lively, sophisticated clientele crowds the bar, patio, and dining rooms of this popular Italian restaurant, once the showroom of a Chevrolet dealership. The food, billed as "Hudson Valley Mediterranean," includes artfully crafted salads, house-made pasta dishes, and hearty entrées. Baby greens provide a bed for roasted butternut squash, beets, and asparagus dressed with walnuts and crumbled goat cheese. Toppings for the Skizzas (flatbread pizzas) range from a sausage–broccoli rabe–mozzarella combo to a version with goat cheese, mozzarella, arugula, pears, and figs. The restaurant tends to be noisy, especially on weekends. Expect a wait, too.

> 6422 Montgomery St., tel. 845/876–1007. Reservations not accepted. AE, D, MC, V. Closed Mon. **$–$$$**

Le Petit Bistro You might walk by this small French restaurant in the center of Rhinebeck and not give it a second glance, but Le Petit Bistro has quite a following. On weekends, the crowd tends to be spirited. Chef Joseph Dalu is particular about ingredients, and uses local and organic when available; daily specials reflect his concept of "cooking with the season." The house pâté appetizer and English Dover sole are favorites on the regular menu. The dining room is warm, with worn pine floors and pale paneled walls. You may also order dinner at the bar. > 8 E. Market St., tel. 845/876–7400. AE, D, DC, MC, V. No lunch Tues.and Wed. **$$–$$$**

Osaka You can count on a cheerful greeting when you venture into this immaculate sushi bar and restaurant. The fish is super-fresh, the presentation artistic, and the sake assortment excellent. In addition to sushi, the menu covers teriyaki, tempura, and udon-noodle dishes. The place isn't large and it tends to fill up on weekends, but it is worth the wait. Nearby Tivoli is home to an Osaka branch. > 22 Garden St., tel. 845/876–7338. Reservations not accepted. AE, D, MC, V. Closed Tues. **$–$$$**

Terrapin An 1842 church contains two dining options within its soaring space: a bistro–bar, where reservations aren't taken, and a more-formal dining area. The bistro menu (**$–$$**) lists small plates, soups, stews, and a make-your-own sandwich board, as well as traditional entrées. Expect a lively crowd at the bar, especially on weekends. With white-cloth draped tables, the main dining area (**$$–$$$**) is quieter. The food veers from creative to comforting. A popular starter is baby-arugula salad with goat-cheese wontons. Three sauces—roasted-shallot hollandaise, mole verde, and ancho chile—accompany the salmon dish. Warm chocolate cake with a molten center is a winner. > 6426 Montgomery St., tel. 845/876–3330. Reservations essential for main dining room. AE, D, DC, MC, V. Closed Mon. **$–$$$**

Traphagen The venerable Beekman Arms, the oldest operating inn in the country, is home to this multiroom restaurant. With its warm and woody setting, the low-ceilinged Tap Room recalls the days when the inn was a true travelers' stop, back in the 1700s. The greenhouse room, a bright, 20th-century addition that's filled with plants and flowers, is a favorite for lunch and brunch. (The hearty Sunday brunch buffet is $22.) The food is solid American, fairly straightforward. For example, grilled Atlantic salmon, a specialty, comes with mashed potatoes and horseradish sauce. > 6387 Mill St., tel. 845/876–1766. AE, D, DC, MC, V. **$–$$$**

WHAT'S NEARBY

Milagros "A place with an identity crisis" is how owner Pamela Morin describes this 1892 church with a twist. It's a café, deli, bar, folk-art showcase, gallery, and convenience store under the same roof. Somehow it works. Locals, city folk, artists, and Bard College students come to shoot the breeze, drink coffee, and munch on wraps and salads. The quinoa wrap and BLT with chipotle mayonnaise are two favorites. Tables are large, great for spreading out papers. A patio beckons on nice days. > 73 Broadway, Tivoli, tel. 845/757–5300. MC, V. No dinner. ¢

Santa Fe Every year or two, owner David Weiss travels to Mexico in search of new culinary inspiration—and then he changes the menu. Luckily some of the most popular dishes are mainstays, such as the grilled-pork taco and the goat cheese–and–spinach enchilada. The frozen margaritas are made from scratch. People often eat here before checking out the latest showing at the Tivoli Artists' Co-op, a block away. > 52 Broadway, Tivoli, tel. 845/757–4100. AE, D, MC, V. Closed Mon. No lunch. **$–$$$**

ESSENTIALS

Getting Here

Driving allows you to detour onto scenic back roads and explore the spectacular Hudson River mansions. That said, if you stay in the village and plan to spend some time just relaxing in your room, you can find enough to do without a car. The Shortline bus stops in front of the Beekman Arms, in the village center. The bus trip take about three hours, however, compared with a drive of only about two hours. Alternatively, you can take Amtrak to the Rhinecliff station, about 3 mi from Rhinebeck. At the train station you can grab a taxi or call for one.

BY BUS

Shortline makes two trips daily, in the morning and around noon, from Manhattan's Port Authority to Rhinebeck, where it stops in front of the Beekman Arms Inn. The trip takes about three hours; tickets are $30 round-trip. Return trips to the city leave Rhinebeck midday and in the evening.

LINES **Coach USA Shortline** > Tel. 800/631–8405, www.shortlinebus.com.

BY CAR

The best way to see the area is to drive. Driving time from the city takes approximately two hours, depending on traffic. The New York State Thruway (Interstate 87) is usually the fastest way to get to Rhinebeck. To get to the thruway, take the Palisades Interstate Parkway north and proceed to Exit 9W. Take the thruway north to Exit 19 (Kingston). Immediately after the toll, bear right onto Route 28, which you take for ¼ mi to Route 209 north (a right exit). Continue to the Kingston–Rhinecliff Bridge. After crossing the bridge, turn right at the second traffic light, onto Route 9G. At the intersection of Route 9G and U.S. 9, turn right onto U.S. 9 south. Continue on this road for 2 mi into the heart of the village.

The more scenic route is via the Taconic State Parkway, reached via the Saw Mill River Parkway or the Sprain Brook Parkway.

Once on the Taconic, proceed north to the Red Hook–Pine Plains exit. Head west on Route 199 about 3 mi to a traffic light. Turn left onto Route 308 and proceed for about 7 mi to the village. Note that Route 308, as well as U.S. 9, take on different names in the village center. Route 308 is also called East Market and West Market streets; U.S. 9 is also Mill and Montgomery streets.

When driving, be on the lookout for deer—especially in the evenings and on the Taconic. You may also see deer between exits 17 and 18 of the thruway, as you head south.

Parking can get crowded in Rhinebeck on nice weekends. Most B&Bs and inns have free, off-street parking. A municipal parking lot is on East Market Street a block from the Beekman Arms.

BY TRAIN

Amtrak stops in Rhinecliff, 2½ mi from Rhinebeck; the trip takes about an hour and 40 minutes from New York City's Pennsylvania Station and costs $33 one-way during peak travel times. It's a good idea to reserve a ticket in advance, to assure a spot. You must make a reservation to bring a bike, for which there's an additional charge. Taxi service (845/876–2010) is available at the Rhinecliff station; you may need to call for a car.

LINES **Amtrak** > Tel. 800/872–7245, www.amtrak.com.

STATIONS **Rhinecliff** > Hutton and Charles Sts., Rhinecliff, no phone, www.amtrak.com.

Visitor Information

The Rhinebeck Chamber of Commerce has an information booth that's open Monday through Saturday 10–4. *AboutTown* (www.abouttownguide.com/dutchess), a free publication distributed in Rhinebeck, includes a calendar of events.

CONTACTS **Dutchess County Tourism** > 3 Neptune Rd., Suite M-17, Poughkeepsie 12601, tel. 845/463–4000 or 800/445–3131, www.dutchesstourism.com. **Rhinebeck Chamber of Commerce** > Information booth, 6372 Mill St., Rhinebeck 12572, tel. 845/876–4778, www.rhinebeckchamber.com.

Millbrook

90 mi north of New York City

11

By Diana Niles King

FOR MANY THIS DUTCHESS COUNTY VILLAGE midway between the Hudson River and Connecticut is just the right blend of town and country. Historic downtown streets, lined with shops and restaurants, sit amid rolling farms, country estates, and dense woodlands all laced with hiking and equestrian trails.

The area, settled in the 1700s, is largely agricultural. When you're face-to-face with a herd of Belted Galloways (so called because these cattle have a white-banded middle) grazing in a field by the road, it can be hard to believe that New York City is a little more than 1½ hours away by car. The locals—including supporters of the Dutchess Land Conservancy—take pride in preserving this environment and go to great lengths to protect working farms, open green space, and rural practices. Don't be surprised or impatient when you get stuck behind a tractor tooling down a narrow road; instead, take the opportunity to enjoy the slower pace of farm life while you can.

Where you don't see cows you're likely to see horses; meadows of them are round almost every bend outside the village, and the Millbrook Hunt is a longstanding tradition here. A horsey theme threads through the village, too, contributing to the old-money feel that pervades the area. Shops are filled with horse-inspired motifs and decorative accessories as well as riding accoutrements.

Old money certainly resides here, as does new wealth. Millbrook has long attracted the rich and famous, many of whom have eschewed the Hamptons to build luxurious weekend and summer homes here. Some have snapped up and renovated stately Greek Revival and Colonial mansions on vast estates. Exploring the winding back roads you can see the long, private drives that lead to these sprawling retreats. Or plan a visit for Columbus Day weekend, when many private farms are opened to the public for the one-day Dutchess Farm Country Tour. The region is also known for its wineries, with vineyards stretched along soft hills, and magnificent gardens, such as Innisfree, where views of natural features are framed for you.

Antiquing is the highlight of Millbrook shopping. More than 100 dealers are represented along Franklin Avenue, the small main street, where trees shade old two-story buildings housing enticing stores. Awnings and wooden benches grace shop fronts and flowerpots flank windows. When you're ready for an espresso, head east a couple of miles to Mabbettsville Market, where Land Rovers crowd the parking lot.

A few area lodgings definitely make you feel (and spend) like part of the moneyed set; others are comfortable but much more modest. In general, accommodations are mostly bed-and-breakfasts and inns; as there aren't many of them, summer and fall weekends tend to book up. Much less crowded are winter and early spring, when some places allow one-night weekend stays and lower their rates. Just remember that harsh weather this time of year can make getting around difficult.

WHAT TO SEE & DO

Innisfree Garden A unique contribution to garden design in America, Innisfree is based on Chinese-garden design and draws inspiration from ages-old Chinese paintings. The term "cup garden" is used to describe the concept; it refers to the way spaces frame, or "cup," features, such as striking rock formations or small pools. Cliffs, low hills, waterfalls, streams, and picnic spots surround the 40-acre lake at the center of the garden. A path takes you through Innisfree. > 362 Tyrrel Rd., tel. 845/677–8000, www.innisfreegarden.com. $3–$4. May–late Oct., Wed.–Fri. 10–4, weekends 11–5.

Institute of Ecosystem Studies The research center is part of the 2,000-acre **Mary Flagler Cary Arboretum,** which contains one of the largest perennial gardens in the Northeast, more than 1,000 species of plants, a fern glen, and miles of walking trails. Highlights include rose, butterfly, water, and hummingbird gardens. Other plant collections address such gardening issues as water conservation and deer resistance. The center also offers one-day courses about everything from Hudson Valley landscapes to rock-garden basics. > 181 Sharon Tpke., tel. 845/677–5359, www.ecostudies.org. Free. Oct.–Mar., Mon.–Sat. 9–4, Sun. 1–4; Apr.–Sept., Mon.–Sat. 9–6, Sun. 1–6.

Mary's Pub and Music Room On Saturday, and sometimes Friday, the pub hosts live music—rock, jazz, blues, folk, and classical acts. The music starts around 8:30 PM. > 1364 Franklin Ave., tel. 845/677–2282. Tues.–Fri. 4 PM–midnight, weekends 4 PM–1 AM.

Millbrook Winery At this 130-acre winery and vineyard, you may savor a chardonnay or cabernet franc against a backdrop of spectacular views. Summer-weekend programs combine lunch with film screenings and musical performances. A wine bar, in the winery's upstairs loft, is open on weekends and offers a selection of the vineyard's reds and whites. > 26 Wing Rd., tel. 845/677–8383 or 800/662–9463, www.millbrookwine.com. Tour free, tasting $4. Memorial Day–Labor Day, daily 11–6; rest of yr, daily noon–5.

Trevor Teaching Zoo Wallabies, chinchillas, emus, otters, parrots, snakes, and lemurs are among the more than 100 exotic and indigenous small mammals and birds that reside at this zoo on the grounds of the Millbrook School. Students, along with full-time and consulting staff, run the zoo and care for the animals as part of their curriculum at the college-preparatory school; their enthusiasm for their charges is infectious. > Millbrook School, Millbrook School Rd., off U.S. 44 about 5 mi east of Millbrook center, tel. 845/677–3704, www.millbrook.org. $4. Daily 8–5.

Wing's Castle The artist owners of this out-of-the-ordinary attraction constructed the multitowered stone castle using salvaged materials from old buildings. It's amusing to try and spot the exotic bits and pieces woven into the structure. The views take in the Catskills and the Millbrook Winery vineyard. > 717 Bangall Rd., off Rte. 57, tel. 845/677–9085. $7. June–Aug., Wed.–Sun. noon–4:30; Sept.–late Dec., weekends noon–4:30.

WHAT'S NEARBY

Absolute Auction Center You never know what or who you'll find at an auction here: the what varies from fabulous to flea market, whereas the who ranges from well-know New York City dealers to local farmers. Auctions are held most Saturdays. > 45 South Ave., Pleasant Valley, tel. 845/635–3169, www.absoluteauctionrealty.com.

Cascade Mountain Winery A Hudson Valley–wine pioneer, the now well-established winery produces a collection of reds and whites. A well-regarded chalet-style restaurant is on-site. > 835 Cascade Mountain Rd., Amenia, tel. 845/373–9021, www.cascademt.com. Tour free, tasting $5. Daily 10–5.

Clinton Vineyards and Winery Seyval blanc is the specialty of this family-run operation housed in an 1800s converted barn. The owner, when he's around and about, conducts tours himself, displaying wit, style, and a passion for wines and winemaking. > 212 Schultzville Rd., Clinton Corners, tel. 845/266–5372, www.clintonvineyards.com. Tour free, tasting $5. Fri.–Sun. 11–5, or by appointment.

Hudson Valley Raptor Center Meet eagles, owls, hawks, falcons, and vultures face-to-face at this center. Injured birds that have been rescued are brought here to recuperate. Many of the birds are released back into the wild after they've recovered. The center offers natural-history programs and flying demonstrations with the birds of prey. Fierce-looking creatures indeed, the birds are handled in such a manner as to be less frightening to small children. > 148 South Rd., Stanfordville, tel. 845/758–6957, www.ulster.net/~hvraptors. $7. Apr.–Oct., weekends 1–4, weekdays by appointment.

Wethersfield The late owner, philanthropist Chauncey Stillman, envisioned his property as a grand Edwardian estate and fully realized his dream. The Georgian-style brick mansion surveys formal gardens (complete with resident peacocks), fountains, a sculpture garden, and a dramatic view of the Catskills. The house has an important collection of paintings assembled by the owner. The stable block houses the carriage museum and a collection of coaching memorabilia. > 214 Pugsley Hill Rd., Amenia, tel. 845/373–8037. Free. Gardens June–Sept., Wed., Fri., and Sat. noon–5; house and stables June–Sept., by appointment.

Sports

HIKING

Stissing Mountain The Stissing Mountain Fire Tower crowns the summit (elevation 1,403 feet) of this mountain, an isolated Precambrian mound; clear-day views from the 90-foot-tall structure stretch from Albany to Bear Mountain and across the Catskills. You also may see eagles, hawks, and other birds in flight from the tower, which is reached via hiking trails accessed at the mountain base. The mountain is undeveloped, with no facilities. Trails, steep in parts, are treed all the way up and have intermittent markers. Parking is limited to a small dirt lot across the road from a trailhead. Trail maps are available from local businesses and Dutchess County Tourism. > Off Lake Rd., about 1½ mi off Rte. 82, Pine Plains, tel. 518/398–5247, 518/398–5673 Friends of Stissing Landmarks.

HORSEBACK RIDING

Millbrook is heaven for the horsey set. All manner of horse-related activity—polo, eventing, hunter pace (which has its roots in foxhunting)—takes place here. Bring your own horse to participate, or schedule a riding session. Otherwise, plan to attend the August horse trials or check the Mabbettsville Market's bulletin board for horse activities and events that might be fun to watch.

Cedar Crest Farm Equestrian Center The 70-acre boarding and instruction facility offers lessons in dressage, cross-country riding and jumping, and stadium jumping Tuesday through Sunday 8–4. Adult sessions start at $45 (group lesson) and climb to $75 (private lesson with senior staff member); most run 45 minutes. (Few horses here are suitable for small children.) The center requires you to wear a riding helmet with harness; shoes or boots (sneakers aren't allowed) must have a ¼- or ½-inch heel. > 2054 Rte. 83, Pine Plains, tel. 518/398–1034, www.equestcenter.com/cedarcrest.htm.

Western Riding Stables A western riding experience can include trail and moonlight rides and horseback pack trips. A 4-mi, 1- to 1½-hour introductory trail ride starts at $50; 9-mi moonlight rides are $100 and include dinner cooked over an open fire.

Lessons are held on the trail or in an arena; pony rides are available as well. > 228 Sawchuck Rd., Millerton, tel. 518/789–4848, www.westernridingstables.com. *EQUIPMENT* **Millbrook Tack Shop** > Franklin Ave., Millbrook, tel. 845/677–8225.

Shopping

Almost all the shopping possibilities in Millbrook are within a three-block stroll of each other on Franklin Avenue. Antiques are the big draw. The antiques dealers have different personalities and represent different price brackets; it makes sense to survey the scene by visiting them all quickly first, before plunking down your cash.

British Sporting Arms Hedges and trees shield this little shop, which is set back from the road and easy to overlook. It's worth seeking out for its country-squire inventory: hand-carved walking sticks, flasks, bird sculptures, and all manner of shooting-related items, including antique and modern long guns. Upstairs are leather outerwear and European tweed pieces, including one local favorite—a tweedy bonnet with a large, flat bow in back. > 3684 U.S. 44, Millbrook, tel. 845/677–5756. Closed Mon.

Jeannie Bean & Co. Just when you think you might be lost, you come upon this delightful little shop at a crossroads. A proper English tea shop, it has all sorts of specialty teas and tea-time trimmings and is open until 4 PM. Anglophile foodies can stock up on such hard-to-find items as Marmite. > 2411 Salt Point Tpke., Clinton Corners, tel. 845/266–3800.

Merritt Bookstore Can't find the book you want? The owner promises he can access any tome in print, and he means it. The store also sells offbeat greeting cards. > 57 Front St., Millbrook, tel. 845/677–5857.

Millbrook Antique Center For the best prices in town, come to this emporium with two floors of antiques and collectibles. A special Tiffany cabinet displays vintage Tiffany silver, objets d'art, and porcelain, all good values. > 3283 Franklin Ave., Millbrook, tel. 845/677–3921.

Millbrook Antique Mall With 38 dealers, this is the largest fine-antiques center for miles around. Almost every antiques category is represented: country furniture, botanical prints, porcelain, brass fireplace tools. The dealer collections create a series of nicely edited and presented boutique spaces. > 3301 Franklin Ave., Millbrook, tel. 845/677–9311, www.millbrookantiquesmall.com.

Ole Carousel Antique Centre The 9,000 square feet here are filled with every kind of antique and collectible. Specialist collections include tools, vintage clothing, coins, and toys. The Christmas suite instills a bit of yuletide spirit any time of year. > 6208 Rte. 82, Stanfordville, tel. 845/868–1586. Closed Tues.

Red School House The collections here are more edited and focused than at other shops in town. That's because this is the only single-dealer location in Millbrook. Specialties include 18th- and 19th-century furnishings, decorative arts, and European and American oil paintings. A two-story barn in Mabbettsville, east of Millbrook via U.S. 44, has additional collections that you can view by appointment. > 3300 Franklin Ave., Millbrook, tel. 845/677–9786. Closed Mon.–Wed.

Village Antique Center The dealers represented here are carefully chosen by the owner, and each collection is thoughtfully presented. The individual items are distinctive, with both personality and good provenance. > 3278 Franklin Ave., Millbrook, tel. 845/677–5160.

Yellow Church Antiques The beautifully restored 1850s church, with art-directed spiral-shape potted trees flanking double doors, suggests the bounty within. The fine (usually very expensive) antiques include English, American, and Continental furniture, and paintings and carpets from the 17th, 18th, and 19th centuries. The pieces are displayed in cohesive groupings that can inspire multiple acquisitions. > U.S. 44, Millbrook, tel. 845/677–6779. Closed Mon.–Thurs.

Save the Date

MAY–JUNE

Millbrook Antiques Show Sponsored by the Millbrook Rotary Club, the annual, three-day show is held in late spring (late May or early June) over a weekend on the grounds of the Dutchess Day School. The Friday preview party, admission $75, benefits a Rotary Club cause. Saturday and Sunday admission is $5. > Dutchess Day School, 415 Rte. 343, Millbrook, tel. 845/677–5247, www.showsfairsfestivals.com.

JUNE

Silver Ribbon House Tour The Dutchess County Historical Society sponsors this one-day event in mid-June, during which you can take a self-guided tour of historic homes and buildings in the Millbrook area. The tour usually includes Brick House Farm, Bullis Hall, Flagler Memorial Chapel, North Meadow Farm, Northeast House-Shekomeko, Samuel Huntting House, and Smithfield Presbyterian Church. > Dutchess County Historical Society, 459 Main St., Poughkeepsie, tel. 845/471–1630.

JULY

Millbrook Fire Department Carnival Food booths and nightly musical entertainment entertain kids of all ages at this three-day event (usually late in the month), but the highlight is the parade of firefighters and fire trucks. > Franklin Ave., Millbrook, tel. 845/677–3871.

AUGUST

Millbrook Horse Trials Eventing is an international (and Olympic) equestrian sport during which horse and rider compete over two to three days in dressage, cross-country, and show jumping. In the cross-country phase, competitors face a course of obstacles. The highest level of the sport, an advanced event, is held here over a Friday–Sunday period in mid-August; a training-beginner event is held the following weekend. Spectators are welcome; admission is free. > Bangall-Amenia Rd. opposite Coole Park Farm, Millbrook, tel. 845/677–3002, www.millbrookhorsetrials.com.

OCTOBER

Dutchess Farm Country Tour Private farms and estates open their doors to the public during this one-day event to benefit the nonprofit Dutchess Land Conservancy. Weaving, sheepherding, marksmanship, equestrian, and other demonstrations are held throughout the day (usually the Sunday of Columbus Day weekend); there's also an exhibit of local artwork. A special bike route weaves along horse trails and small farm roads and leads you to the various sites. > Dutchess Land Conservancy, tel. 845/677–3002, www.dutchessland.org.

Millbrook Antiques Show Sponsored by the Millbrook Rotary Club, the annual three-day, mid-month show is held over a weekend on the grounds of the Dutchess Day School. Admission to Friday's preview party is $75; Saturday and Sunday admission is $5. > Dutchess Day School, 415 Rte. 343, Millbrook, tel. 845/677–5247, www.showsfairsfestivals.com.

WHERE TO STAY

Antrim House The 2 acres on which this Victorian-style contemporary sits are secluded enough to appeal to wildlife, and on most mornings various critters (deer, wild turkeys) can be seen around the grounds. Inside, family heirlooms coexist with 1920s wicker. The largest room has a queen-size bed and a deck overlooking the lawn. In winter the glow of the constantly stoked fireplaces in the library and living/dining room creates a cozy respite from the cold. The highlight of a stay may well be the full Irish-style cooked breakfast; being of Irish descent, the owner knows how to do it up right. > 33 Deer Pond Rd., 12545, tel. 845/677–6265. 3 rooms. Dining room, fans; no a/c, no room phones, no room TVs, no smoking. No credit cards. BP. ¢–$

A Cat in Your Lap The simple 1840s farm house and adjacent 1890s barn sit pleasingly near a little stream and quiet woodlands. The two suites, in the barn, are filled with rustic antique furniture. Each has a fireplace and either a patio or a second-floor deck. The room in the house has a private entrance, accessed from the lawn, as well as its own patio. A cat does reside here. > 62 Old Rte. 82, 12545, tel. 845/677–3051, www.acatinyourlap.com. 1 room, 2 suites. Dining room, some pets allowed (fee); no room phones, no room TVs, no smoking. No credit cards. Closed Jan. BP. ¢–$$

Cottonwood Motel The design and decor of this roadside motel are standard issue: parking lot, vending machines in one corner, lobby in the other. What makes things interesting are the sights and sounds behind the motel. Each room has a little patio that looks out over acres of nature preserve. Local wildlife—deer, wild turkey, pheasant—roam right up to your doorstep. Towering cottonwoods frame your view across the stream to soft hills beyond. > 2639 U.S. 44, 12545, tel. 845/677–3283, fax 845/677–3577, www.cottonwoodmotel.com. 17 rooms, 1 suite, 1 cottage. Some in-room hot tubs, some refrigerators, cable TV, some pets allowed, no-smoking rooms. AE, MC, V. $–$$

Millbrook Country House The house, built in 1810, was remodeled in 1838 when classical detailing was all the rage (witness the majestic columns in the front hall). If the interior recalls 17th-century Italy, it's probably because most of the furniture came from the current owner's palazzo near Modena. Elegant marquetry tables grace the parlors (where you may come across the owners' three cats), and lush silk draperies dress many windows. Extensive gardens—perennial, herb, cutting, border—surround the house, which also has a sculpture garden displaying works by local artists. Afternoon tea and full breakfast are included; in warm-weather months, they're served on the lawn under the shade of an enormous maple tree. > 506 Sharon Tpke./Rte. 44A, 12545, tel./fax 845/677–9570, www.millbrookcountryhouse.com. 4 rooms. Dining room, bicycles, croquet; no kids under 10, no smoking. AE, MC. BP. $$$–$$$$

The Porter House Bed & Breakfast The original chestnut woodwork and wainscoting from this 1920 stone house are intact and restored. Their warm patina works well with the Victorian furniture that fills the sunny parlor. Bedrooms blend rustic pieces with more-refined furnishings; printed fabrics are limited to accents. The B&B is a block from the heart of Millbrook. > 17 Washington Ave., 12545, tel. 845/677–3057, www.porterhousebandb.com. 2 rooms, 3 suites. Dining room, fans; no room phones, no room TVs, no kids under 12, no smoking. CP. $–$$$

WHAT'S NEARBY

Bullis Hall The street-side facade of this once-derelict old building gives no hint about the surprises inside. The entrance, through a garden at the back, puts you in the front parlor. The owner's vision is of a small, European boutique hotel. Thick Turkish carpets are underfoot, and exquisite flowers adorn a mantle. Ice magically appears at cocktail time, and the self-serve bar is well stocked. If you wish to dine in, the in-house chef is happy to prepare a splendid meal. All of these to-the-manner-born touches come at a price and with certain expectations: tracksuit-and-sneakers travelers might not find this Relais & Châteaux property to be their cup of tea. > Hunns Lake Rd., Bangall 12506, tel. 845/868–1665, fax 845/868–1441, www.bullishall.com. 2 rooms, 3 suites. Restaurant, dining room, some in-room hot tubs, cable TV, croquet, wine bar, library, laundry service, concierge, Internet; no kids, no smoking. AE, MC, V. CP. **$$$$**

Calico Quail The B&B, about 5 mi from Millbrook, does double duty as additional display space for the overflow from the owners antiques business in the adjacent barn. If one of the country furnishings in the house strikes your fancy, ask about it; there's a good chance it's for sale. The location is convenient for exploring the countryside or—just as important for some—getting a cappuccino at the nearby Mabbettsville Market. > U.S. 44, Mabbettsville 12545, tel. 845/677–6016, www.calicoquail.com. 3 rooms, 2 with shared bath. Dining room, some fans, pond, no-smoking rooms; no room phones, no room TVs, no kids under 10. No credit cards. Closed Jan.–Mar. CP. **$**

Lakehouse Inn on Golden Pond Woods surround the lake at the center of the inn's 22 backcountry acres. Guest quarters are tucked into three buildings and have either water or woodland views. Each room has a whirlpool or soaking tub for two, a fireplace, and a deck; many beds have canopies and country quilts, and interior schemes swing from refined country to Victorian. > 419 Shelley Hill Rd., Stanfordville 12581, tel. 845/266–8093, fax 845/266–4051, www.lakehouseinn.com. 6 rooms, 1 suite. Fans, some in-room hot tubs, some minibars, some refrigerators, cable TV, some in-room VCRs, lake, boating, fishing; no kids under 16, no smoking. MC, V. BP. **$$$$**

Old Drovers Inn Cattle herders (aka drovers) bringing their stock to New York in the 18th century made a stopover at this inn, on 12 acres 15 mi southeast of Millbrook. Today the Relais & Châteaux property is one of the oldest continuously operating inns in the United States. Rooms are Victorian in style; three have fireplaces. Weekend rates include full breakfast and dinner (weekday rates are considerably lower and include only Continental breakfast). > 196 E. Duncan Rd., Dover Plains 12522, tel. 845/832–9311, fax 845/832–6356, www.olddroversinn.com. 4 suites. Closed first 3 wks in Jan. Restaurant, dining room, room service, fans, library, bicycles, mountain bikes, some pets allowed (fee); no room phones, no room TVs, no kids under 12, no smoking. DC, MC, V. MAP (CP weekdays). **$$$$**

Troutbeck Surrounded by elaborate landscaping and gardens, this resort on the bank of the Webatuck River encompasses 442 acres. The hotel, about 10 mi east of Millbrook, is exquisitely furnished with antiques. The library includes 12,000 books and videotapes. Rooms, some with fireplaces, have rich wood paneling and canopy beds. > Leedsville Rd., Amenia 12501, tel. 845/373–9681, fax 845/373–7080, www.troutbeck.com. 42 rooms, 6 suites. Restaurant, cable TV, in-room VCRs, 2 tennis courts, 2 pools (1 indoor), gym, spa, sauna, billiards, Ping-Pong, bar, library, business services, meeting rooms; no kids under 12, no smoking. AE, MC, V. CP. **$$$$**

WHERE TO EAT

Allyn's Restaurant and Café An 1834 church has successfully morphed into a Millbrook dining fixture. Locals treat Allyn's like a club and do much of their entertaining here; don't be surprised if you encounter most of the Millbrook Hunt having breakfast. The owner-chef is devoted to freshness and obtains all ingredients locally. The menu is huge and includes pan-roasted chicken, grilled duck breast, and seafood dishes. The wine list gives you more than 300 choices. Follow the lead of the locals: request a table on the lawn in warm weather and a table in the bar by the fireplace in winter. > 42–58 U.S. 44, tel. 845/677–5888. AE, D, DC, MC, V. Closed Tues. **$$–$$$**

Café Les Baux The jolly sunburst graphic on the café sign and the banks of colorful flowers on the front steps are *très* French country. Warm terra cotta–tone walls and vine-motif sconces continue the theme inside. The food is authentic French bistro fare, well prepared and presented. What a delight to find a really good *croque monsieur* (egg batter–dipped ham-and-cheese sandwich) and *moules* (mussels) or steak *frites* (with fries). Tarte tatin (an inverted apple tart), baked by the chef and served with a scoop of crème fraîche, is not to be missed. > 152 Church St., tel. 845/677–8166. AE, MC, V. Closed Tues. **$–$$$**

Dervin O'Brien's The pub-restaurant has a great long bar in the back, little tables and lace curtains in the front. House specials include barbecue chicken or ribs and grilled sirloin, but seafood and pasta dishes are also on the menu. The backroom bar is casual and has the requisite sports-tuned TV. > 156 Church St., tel. 845/677–5874. MC, V. **$–$$**

Marcello's With floral wallpaper, soft lighting, and paintings of Italian scenes, the main dining room of this Italian restaurant is fairly formal; the roomy bar area, down several steps, is *the* spot for an after-dinner Amaretto. Outside is a patio for more-casual dining. The signature chicken Marcello is topped with escarole, mozzarella, and bacon in white-wine sauce. *Zuppe di pesce* (fish soup), served for two, combines lobster, crab, clams, calamari, and shrimp in a thick, rich seafood stew; the portion is more than ample. Pasta dishes taste authentically Italian. > 18 Alden Pl., tel. 845/677–3080. AE, D, DC, MC, V. Closed Mon. No lunch. **$–$$**

Millbrook Café With a hunter-green awning over the entrance, walls covered with framed hunting prints, and wood paneling that recalls a stable, this restaurant plays up the horse-country theme. The food is billed as "authentic 19th-century cooking in a wood-fired oven." Everything is cooked in this oven; the open-plan kitchen invites you to watch. The house specialty, baked, stuffed Spanish onion, is a concoction of cheddar cheese and fresh vegetables that's worth trying. Entrées are served on sizzling cast-iron platters straight from the oven. > 3288 Franklin Ave., tel. 845/677–6956. AE, D, DC, MC, V. Closed Mon. No dinner Sun. **$–$$$**

Millbrook Diner Since 1929 a diner has sat on this spot. The current edition, a stainless-steel boxcar version, dates to '52. It's a great hangout for locals, who love how quickly that early-morning cup of coffee is served. Order hamburgers, french fries, BLTs, and other diner basics here. > 3266 Franklin Ave., tel. 845/677–5319. MC, V. **¢–$$**

TinHorn In warm weather you may watch the always-interesting doings in town while you have lunch or dinner on the restaurant's umbrella-sheltered front patio. The chef is a fanatic about using local, organic produce, and you can taste the difference. The Black Angus rib-eye steak, 21-day dry aged and from a local farm, is absolutely sublime in taste and texture. On many Mondays, three-course dinners are designed around an international theme—Spanish one week, perhaps French the next. The wine list is interesting and offers a good local selection. > 1129 Franklin Ave., tel. 845/677–5600. AE, MC, V. Closed Tues. and Wed. **$$–$$$**

WHAT'S NEARBY

Cascade Mountain Winery The chalet-style restaurant sits literally on top of Cascade Mountain's wine-making operation. The fermenting vats are incorporated into the front wooden deck, alongside umbrella-shaded tables. The kitchen often puts a creative spin on old standards: grilled chicken breast is stuffed with feta cheese and crab cakes come with an Asian-inspired mayonnaise. Pair a Cascade wine with your meal for the full experience. > 835 Cascade Mountain Rd., Amenia, tel. 845/373–9021. AE, MC, V. Closed Nov.–Mar. No lunch Tues. and Wed. No dinner Sun.–Fri. **$$–$$$**

Copperfield's A large oval bar dominates the front room and provides plenty of space for a drink before dinner. The adjacent dining room has a casual feel with a combination of wooden booths and cloth-draped tables. The menu is long and varied, ranging from Mexican and pasta dishes to burgers and sushi. Brunch is served Sunday; the bartender makes a great Bloody Mary to go along. The restaurant is about 3.8 miles west of Millbrook. > U.S. 44, Salt Point, tel. 845/677–8188. AE, MC, V. $–$$

Mabbettsville Market This café–deli–specialty foods market, about 2 mi east of Millbrook, is about the only place around where you can get excellent cappuccino. Eat at a table inside, or outside under the awning, or get goodies to go. The market serves hot breakfast and offers an array of salad and sandwich options for lunch as well as a case of prepared foods. > 3809 U.S. 44, Mabbettsville, tel. 845/677–5284. AE, MC, V. Closed Mon. No dinner. ¢–$

Old Drovers Inn In winter, the fireplace provides much of the light in the low-ceilinged Tap Room of this romantic inn 15 mi southeast of Millbrook. Old favorites such as rack of lamb and turkey hash blend with more-contemporary dishes, such as sesame-crusted tuna and marsala-braised Muscovy duck. The tavern menu includes hearty cheddar-cheese soup, offered here for more than 60 years and still a favorite. The wine list is extensive, and the drinks are legendary for their largesse. > 196 E. Duncan Rd., Dover Plains, tel. 845/832–9311. DC, MC, V. Closed Wed. No lunch Mon.–Thurs. $$$–$$$$

Quail Hollow Restaurant It's easy to drive right by this old farmhouse on the edge of an exit off the Taconic Parkway. Once inside with the antiques and art, you feel as if you're in a private house rather than a restaurant. The food is simple, unpretentious, well prepared, and nicely presented. Roast chicken is tender and moist, for example, and crab cakes come with an outstanding Dijon mustard sauce. The mixed green salad that accompanies entrées is tossed with ginger dressing. The list of wines by the glass is long and includes some good values. > 360 Hibernia Rd., Salt Point, tel. 845/266–8622. AE, MC, V. Closed Mon. and Tues. No lunch. $$–$$$

Stage Stop Decorative horsey items—horseshoes, bits of old tack, antique carriage parts, horse-show posters—adorn every available wall. One corner houses James Cagney memorabilia; the photos of the actor on his nearby farm as well as stills from his old films are fascinating. The main dining room has a huge salad bar with more than 60 items; abundant and reasonably priced, it can serve as dinner. The menu also has pasta, burgers, steaks, pork chops, chicken, and lobster tails. > 7 Stage Stop Way, Bangall, tel. 845/868–7343. AE, MC, V. No lunch Mon.–Sat. ¢–$$

ESSENTIALS

Getting Here

The best way to get to Millbrook is by car. Trains service the extended area (Poughkeepsie, Rhinecliff, and Dover Plains), but stations are a half hour or more from Millbrook by cab. Taxis are hard to come by and expensive, and there's no public transportation to get you around. Most lodging properties aren't right in Millbrook, so you also need a car to be able to visit sights and explore scenic backcountry roads. Some B&Bs and inns offer to meet guests at the train station; if you're interested in holing up for the weekend, inquire with individual properties about this option.

BY CAR

A car is absolutely recommended both to get to and around Millbrook. From Manhattan's West Side, take the West Side Highway north, which becomes the Saw Mill River Parkway, to the Taconic State Parkway.

From the East Side take the FDR Drive north to the Willis Avenue Bridge to Interstate 87 northbound. Take the exit for Route 100, which you follow to the Sprain Brook Parkway. The Sprain Brook turns into the Taconic north of White Plains.

Once on the Taconic, proceed to the Millbrook exit and take U.S. 44 east. The Taconic is particularly scenic, with good views of the Catskills to the west, but it's also narrow, with nearly nonexistent shoulders, and has patches of rough paving and poor drainage. Fog and rain can make this curvy road dangerous.

Traffic in Millbrook is usually thin, but you may get stuck behind a farm vehicle. Many of the most scenic driving routes include rough paved or dirt roads, and you must watch for deer, especially at night and on the Taconic.

BY TRAIN

Two train lines service the extended area, but the stations are at least a 30-minute car trip from Millbrook, and taxis are expensive. Amtrak stops in Rhinecliff; the train trip takes about an hour and 40 minutes from New York City's Pennsylvania Station and costs $29 one way during peak travel times. It's a good idea to reserve a ticket in advance, to assure a spot. You must make a reservation to bring a bike, and there's an additional charge. Metro-North trains are more frequent and less expensive. The trip from Grand Central Station to Dover Plains takes nearly two hours and costs $32.50 round-trip at peak times. The Metro-North train ride to Poughkeepsie can take as little as 1½ hours, but the ticket price is the same.

LINES **Amtrak** > Tel. 800/872–7245, www.amtrak.com. **Metro-North Railroad** > Tel. 212/532–4900 or 800/638–7646, http://mta.info/mnr.

STATIONS **Dover Plains** > Railroad Ave. at Main St., Dover Plains, no phone, http://mta.info/mnr. **Poughkeepsie** > 41 Main St., at U.S. 9 interchange, Poughkeepsie, no phone, http://mta.info/mnr. **Rhinecliff** > Hutton and Charles Sts., Rhinecliff, no phone, www.amtrak.com.

Visitor Information

Area restaurants, gas stations, and shops stock free brochures and pamphlets about local attractions. Allyn's Restaurant, designated a county Tourist Information Center, has a particularly abundant supply. The Hudson Valley Guide, a free booklet that's updated seasonally, is a good reference for farmer's markets, fairs, and other local events.

CONTACTS **Allyn's Restaurant and Café** > 42–58 U.S. 44, Millbrook, tel. 845/677–5888. **Dutchess County Tourism** > 3 Neptune Rd., Suite M-17, Poughkeepsie, 12601, tel. 845/463–4000 or 800/445–3131, www.dutchesstourism.com. **Hudson River Valley Travel & Tourism** > Box 284, Salt Point 12578, tel. 800/232–4782, www.travelhudsonvalley.org.

Cold Spring

55 mi north of New York City

12

By Wendy Kagan

MOUNTAIN TRAILS, KAYAKING WATERWAYS, Colonial facades, and antiques galore are among the riches of Cold Spring, New York, and its environs. The village edges one of the most dramatic bends of the Hudson River, and the region's true showpiece may well be its breath-stealing river-valley views. Cold Spring's waterfront beckons like an amphitheater with a round-the-clock, four-season show: the Hudson Highlands in full topographical regalia, from the deep-green folds of Crow's Nest to the granite dome of Storm King and beyond.

A handful of local sights bid discovery, but the chief pleasures of Cold Spring consist of its menagerie of shops and its proximity to green spaces and hiking trails. Main Street, a few steps from the Metro-North train stop, is the commercial heart of this well-preserved 19th-century village, with dozens of boutiques; a smattering of cafés and eateries, along with the requisite sidewalk tables in fair weather; and the occasional Colonial home. Antiques dealers tempt treasure seekers with retro furniture, vintage toys, Depression glass, and the like. Specialty shops hawk housewares, ethnic jewelry, and hand-painted ceramics, among other wares.

Hiking paths traverse local parks and peaks, many within walking distance of the village and train. You can choose among miniature, manageable climbs such as Little Stony Point; vertiginous, thrill-seeker cliffs like Breakneck Ridge; and something in between. Local outfitters rent kayaks and canoes for expeditions on the river or through marshes teeming with wildlife. After inland parks burst with mountain laurel and rhododendron in warm-weather months, winter's snowfall laces the rugged interior, and trails are groomed for cross-country skiing, skate-skiing, snowshoeing, and sledding.

You might not guess that this small, laid-back Putnam County village once bustled with an industry pivotal to the fate of the entire nation. When the West Point Foundry opened here in 1817, Cold Spring laid claim to the most innovative and productive ironworks in the United States. The facility turned out Civil War munitions as well as iron cast for the nation's first commissioned locomotive and steamboat. In 1884 the ironworkers' furnaces ceased blazing, and the foundry site succumbed to neglect and the hand of nature. Only one office building still stands in Foundry Cove; a small cache of artifacts and objects tells the foundry's story at the local museum.

One train stop south, sleepy Garrison takes full advantage of its riverside setting with a rambling waterfront park. Pleasure boats dock at the marina, and a gazebo and willow tree–shaded benches are front-row seats to the mighty Hudson River; across the shore loom the buildings of the United States Military Academy at West Point. At Garrison's Landing, as the waterfront area is known, a small clutch of art galleries, offices, and homes surrounds the old train station (now a community theater called the Philipstown Depot).

Beyond the Landing, restored homes and artful landscapes bespeak the region's rich aesthetic history. Boscobel showcases architecture and decorative arts from the early-

19th-century Federalist period, whereas Manitoga—the home, studio, and woodlands of industrial designer Russel Wright—fast-forwards into the mid-20th century. In summer the celebrated Hudson Valley Shakespeare Festival comes to town, gracing Boscobel with lively contemporary interpretations of the hallowed plays under an alfresco tent-theater. The Appalachian Trail passes through the region, crossing the Hudson River at Bear Mountain and meandering through Garrison's many acres of protected land.

For a touch of urban grit, arty cool, and coffeehouse grunge, head north of Cold Spring and into Dutchess County to Beacon, where a revitalization is under way. Dia:Beacon, an expansive contemporary-art museum in a former Nabisco printing plant, has put this small river city on the map. While Dia prepared its 2003 debut, artists and bargain seekers infiltrated the area, snatching up real estate that sold for a song; the renovated Colonials and Victorians already are fetching a prettier penny. Gentrification has progressed along the eastern end of Beacon's Main Street and continues its march toward the river, bringing funky clothing boutiques, java shops, galleries, and enough antiques dealers to give Cold Spring a run for its money.

WHAT TO SEE & DO

Chapel of Our Lady Greek Revival architecture finds expression in this 1833 chapel atop a bluff facing the Hudson River. Passing sailors have long taken pleasure in the landmark, originally built to support the spiritual lives of West Point Foundry workers. Initially a Catholic church, the nondenominational chapel now hosts ecumenical services, weddings, and other events. The chapel has no set open hours, but the facade is worth a look, and the columned porch is a great place for river gazing. > 45 Market St., tel. 845/265–5537.

Foundry Cove The ruins of a 19th-century iron foundry stand (barely) here amid a tangle of vines, a babbling brook, and 85 acres of preserved marshland and woodland. The original commercial hub of Cold Spring village, the West Point Foundry once buzzed with activity, as ironworkers manufactured Civil War cannons, cannon balls, and guns, as well as cast-iron facades for SoHo warehouses and even the nation's first domestically made locomotive. To get here from Main Street, turn south onto Kemble Avenue and take it to the end, proceed through the gate, turn left, and follow the path to the site. You can also follow the marked woodland trail to a waterfall at the site's edge. > Off Kemble Ave., south of Main St., no phone.

Putnam County Historical Society and Foundry School Museum Local historical memorabilia and changing exhibits fill this former 19th-century schoolhouse, once attended by children of West Point Foundry workers. A permanent installation and video chronicle the history of the foundry. Paintings, drawings, photographs, and other objects and artifacts round out the museum's collection. > 63 Chestnut St., tel. 845/265–4010, www.pchs-fsm.org. Suggested donation $5. Mar.–Dec., Tues.–Thurs. 10–4 and weekends 2–5.

Riverfront Bandstand and Dock The majesty of the Hudson Highlands surrounds this 100-by-100-foot dock, where you can promenade, fish, lounge, or simply behold the views of Bear Mountain, Crow's Nest, and Storm King. Free concerts bring musicians to the bandstand on Sunday evenings in July and August. > Lower Main St. at the Hudson River, no phone.

Stonecrop Gardens Sixty-three acres showcase the landscape design of Francis Cabot, founder of the Garden Conservancy. Display gardens span 12 of the acres, in settings ranging from rock cliffs and woodlands to placid pools and verdant lawns. Don't overlook the picture-perfect conservatory, where the winter garden includes trees and flowers native to South Africa, New Zealand, and Australia. > 81 Stonecrop La., off Rte. 301 between U.S. 9 and the Taconic State Parkway, tel. 845/265–2000, www.stonecrop.org. $3. By appointment only.

GARRISON

Boscobel Restoration High-style period furniture and collections of crystal, silver, and porcelain fill this restored 1808 mansion, now a museum of Federalist-period decorative arts. Built by States Morris Dyckman, a descendant of one of New Amsterdam's early Dutch families, the house originally stood in Montrose, some 15 mi south. It's open by tour only, but the grounds are reason enough to visit: the 30 sweeping acres give way to Hudson River views and encompass multiple gardens, an orangery, more than 140 varieties of roses, and a 1-mi woodland trail. > 1601 Rte. 9D, tel. 845/265–3638, www.boscobel.org. Tour $10. House Apr.–Nov., Wed.–Mon. 10–4:15 (last tour); Dec., Wed.–Mon. 10–3:15 (last tour). Grounds Apr.–Nov., Wed.–Mon. 9:30–dusk.

Constitution Marsh Audubon Center and Sanctuary An extensive boardwalk leads you deep into the reeds and rushes of this lush, wildlife-filled tidal marshland. In winter the boardwalk is a prime lookout spot for bald eagles. Tromp through the 200-acre sanctuary's bluffs and woodlands, or visit the Educational Center, where a 500-gallon aquarium offers an up-close look at fish, crabs, and other resident wildlife. > Indian Brook Rd. off Rte. 9D south, tel. 845/265–2601, http://ny.audubon.org/cmac.htm. Free. Trails daily 9–6, center Tues.–Sun. 9–5.

Garrison Art Center Exhibits by local artists working in a wide variety of media grace this gallery and educational center, housed in three 19th-century buildings by the waterfront. > 23 Garrison's Landing, tel. 845/424–3960, www.garrisonartcenter.org. Free. Daily noon–5.

Manitoga–The Russel Wright Design Center Nature and art blend seamlessly throughout the home, studio, and 75-acre grounds of mid-20th-century industrial designer Russel Wright. Boulders protrude through the ground floor of **Dragon Rock**, Wright's experimental home, which is built on a rock ledge and spans 11 levels; fist-size stones serve as door handles. Four miles of paths weave through a landscape that appears natural but is actually a studied design of native trees, rocks, mosses, and wildflowers. Daily 90-minute tours take in the buildings and woodlands (wear comfortable walking shoes), or you can take a self-guided tour of the grounds. > Rte. 9D 2½ mi north of Bear Mountain Bridge, tel. 845/424–3812, www.russelwrightcenter.org. Guided house-and-grounds tour $15, grounds $5 suggested donation. Grounds Apr.–Oct., daily dawn–dusk. Tours by appointment only.

WHAT'S NEARBY

Chthonic Clash Coffeehouse You can get a good cup of joe (or tea) and a muffin or other baked treat at this brick-walled neighborhood hot spot–hangout and then return in the evening to hear live music. Open-mike nights are held on the second and fourth Wednesday each month. > 418 Main St., Beacon, tel. 845/831–0359, www.chthonicclash.com. Events $3 and up. Mon.–Thurs. 6 AM–10 PM, Fri. 6 AM–midnight, Sat. 8 AM–midnight, Sun. 8 AM–6 PM.

Chuang Yen Monastery The largest indoor statue of Buddha in the Western Hemisphere resides here, standing 37 feet tall and surrounded by 10,000 Buddha figurines on a lotus terrace in Great Buddha Hall. The extensive grounds invite walking, with pathways leading to Seven Jewels Lake. The largest monastery in the eastern United States, Chuang Yen holds Sunday-morning English-language programs in Tai-Hsu Hall. Its vegetarian lunch ($5), at noon on weekends, may be the best deal in town. The monastery is in Kent, northeast of Cold Spring. > 2020 Rte. 301, Kent, tel. 845/225–1819, www.baus.org/baus. Free. Daily 9–5.

Dia:Beacon Works by some of the biggest names in modern art from the 1960s to today fill this former Nabisco printing plant on the banks of the Hudson River. The Dia Art Foundation's collection of mid-20th-century art finds a home here, along with works commissioned expressly for the museum. Highlights include Andy Warhol's *Shadows*, which includes several canvases, and works by minimalist icons Robert Ryman and Agnes Martin. Expansive spaces and luxuriant light make the nearly 300,000-square-foot building—on 34 acres with artistic landscaping—an experience in itself. > 3 Beekman St., Beacon, tel. 845/440–0100, www.diabeacon.org. $10. Mid-May–mid-Oct., Thurs.–Mon. 11–6; mid-Oct.–mid-May, Fri.–Mon. 11–4.

Madam Brett Homestead The oldest surviving home in Dutchess County, this white-clapboard dwelling housed seven generations of the Brett family from 1709 to 1954. During the Revolutionary War, the homestead was used to store military supplies, and George Washington and the Marquis de Lafayette attended a Christmas party here. Original furnishings include 18th- and 19th-century pieces; hand-hewn beams, hand-crafted shingles, and wide-board floors are among the architectural details. > 50 Van Nydeck Ave., Beacon, tel. 845/831–6533 or 845/896–6897. $4. Sept.–Dec., 1st Sun. each month 1–4, or by appointment.

Tours

Heritage Way Guided Walking Tours Each Sunday at 2 from mid-May to mid-November, the Putnam County Historical Society leads a 60- to 90-minute walking tour of Cold Spring village. It takes you past the village's oldest intact homes along Market and Main streets, as well as the spot where General George Washington drank from the spring for which the village is named. Reservations aren't required. A donation is suggested. > 72 Main St., Cold Spring, tel. 8845/265–4010 Putnam County Historical Society, www.pchs-fsm.org.

Sports

CROSS-COUNTRY SKIING

Fahnestock Winter Park Nearly 10-mi of groomed trails vein the meadows, woodlands, and snowed-over lake of this winter wonderland, part of Clarence Fahnestock Memorial State Park. Old pasture lanes weave through hemlock and hardwood groves, passing old stone walls and granite outcroppings. Come with your own gear or rent skis, boots, and poles on site ($15 a day). The park also rents skate skis and snowshoes, as well as inner tubes for use on the groomed sledding hill. Call ahead to check weather conditions, and for information about lessons and ski clinics. You can warm up with hot food and drinks in the park's lodge. > 12 Dennytown Rd., Cold Spring, tel. 845/225–3998, http://nysparks.state.ny.us. Trail pass $6. Daily 9–4:30.

GOLF

Garrison Golf & Country Club Top-of-the-world vistas of the Hudson Highlands enhance 18 holes of championship golf here. The river and valley views from the driving range are positively jaw-dropping. Greens fees range from $65 weekdays to $85 on weekends. Pick up refreshments at the snack bar next to the pro shop or from the circulating beverage cart. > 2015 U.S. 9, Garrison, tel. 845/424–3604, www.garrisongolfclub.com.

HIKING

Anthony's Nose A vigorous climb of about an hour leads you through an oak and hickory forest to the top of Anthony's Nose, a 900-foot mountain, for spectacular views of the Hudson Highlands and Bear Mountain across the Hudson River. The first ½ mi of the hike is part of the Appalachian Trail (at the trailhead you see traffic pullouts and an Appalachian Trail sign); at the fork in the trail halfway up, turn right on to the Hudson River Trail to reach the peak. > Rte. 9D immediately north of Bear Mountain Bridge.

Clarence Fahnestock Memorial State Park Hike past hemlock gorges and an old iron mine in this state park, which encompasses some 11,000 acres of protected land. More than 70 mi of trails, including a segment of the Appalachian Trail, wend through the wilderness here. **Canopus Lake** has picnic spots and a beach for swimming. Another lake and four ponds dot the landscape, with excellent bass, perch, pickerel, and trout fishing. The park office has trail maps. > Rte. 30 ½ mi west of the Taconic State Pkwy. (Cold Spring exit), Carmel, tel. 845/225–7207, http://nysparks.state.ny.us. Park free, beach area $7 per car. Park daily sunrise–sunset. Beach area Memorial Day–late June, weekends 9–7 (swimming 10–6); late June–Labor Day daily 9–7 (swimming 10–6).

Hudson Highlands State Park An easy walk from the Metro-North train station at Cold Spring, this park encompasses 5,800 acres of undeveloped land just north of town along the Hudson River. The trail to Bull Hill is the closest to the village. A moderately easy climb of about an hour through a forest offers successively grander views of Cold Spring and the river, culminating in a wide vista of the Hudson River Valley at the summit. Stop for a picnic at the rocky ledge overlooking the village halfway up and watch the trains trace the shore and, in summer, sailboats, freighters, and other riverboats ply the waterway. A more challenging hike is the aptly named Breakneck Ridge, whose trail climbs a cliff face over Route 9D halfway between Cold Spring and Beacon. The especially ambitious may want to climb the cliff face itself; if you prefer a more leisurely but still fairly strenuous climb, stick to the trail. Metro-North trains stop at the Breakneck Ridge trailhead on weekends. > Rte. 9D ½ mi north of Main St., Cold Spring, tel. 845/225–7207, http://nysparks.state.ny.us. Free. Daily sunrise–sunset.

Little Stony Point State Park Two trails—one to a sandy beach, another to a small peak with panoramic views—traverse this park, a short walk from the center of Cold Spring. Although swimming isn't officially permitted at the beach, hikers often dip their toes in the river on hot days. > Rte. 9D ½ mi north of Main St., Cold Spring, tel. 845/265–7815 Little Stony Point Citizens Association, www.hvgateway.com/stonypt.htm. Daily sunrise–sunset.

KAYAKING

The relatively calm waters of the river close to the Cold Spring and Garrison shorelines make kayaking in this area a serene, yet invigorating experience whether you're a novice or an experienced kayaker. Setting out from Garrison's Landing, you can head north to Cold Spring and Constitution Marsh, or enter the water at Cold Spring for quicker access to the marsh. Hudson Valley Outfitters, Outdoor Sports, and Pack & Paddle Adventures all rent kayaks and offer tours and individual instruction. Rentals are $30 to $70 a day. Tours to Constitution Marsh, Constitution Island, and other destinations are $40 to $100.

Constitution Marsh Removed from the river's currents, the marsh is one of the most peaceful places on the Hudson to dip your paddle. Wide canals let you steer amid the marsh plants and wildlife—but take care not to lose your sense of direction in this maze of waterways. To access the marsh, set out from the boat launch directly across the road from the parking lot of the Cold Spring train station. Once you're in the water, paddle downriver a short distance to the railroad bridge, and pass under it to enter the marsh. Keep in mind that because the Hudson is actually an estuary, tides affect the marsh. Avoid getting yourself grounded in the mud by leaving plenty of time to get back to the shore by low tide.

Garrison's Landing For a leisurely afternoon excursion, slip into the river from the boat launch at Garrison's Landing, near the Garrison train stop. Across the river loom the buildings of the United States Military Academy at West Point. Paddle up-river, past Constitution Island and Constitution Marsh, and land at Cold Spring. *RENTALS* **Hudson Valley Outfitters** > 63 Main St., Cold Spring, tel. 845/265–0221, www.hudsonvalleyoutfitters.com. **Outdoor Sports** > 141 Main St., Cold Spring, tel. 845/265–2048. **Pack & Paddle Adventures** > 14 Market St., Cold Spring, tel. 845/896–7225, www.packpaddleadventures.com.

Shopping

Back-to-back antiques and specialty shops flank Cold Spring's Main Street. Beacon's Main Street also has a few standouts.

Archipelago Browse amid hanging lanterns, funky glassware, wall tiles, and garden torches in this out-of-the-ordinary home-furnishings and gift shop. > 119 Main St., Cold Spring, tel. 845/265–3992.

Beacon Hill Antiques The selection at this eclectic shop includes period furniture, accessories, decorative items, and folk art. > 474 Main St., Beacon, tel. 845/831–4577. Closed Tues. and Wed.

Bijou Galleries, Ltd. More than 25 dealers of antiques, vintage clothes, jewelry, art, and collectibles hawk their wares in this jam-packed emporium. > 50 Main St., Cold Spring, tel. 845/265–4337.

The Country Goose British foodstuffs, tea cozies, and gift baskets are among the items at this shop. > 115 Main St., Cold Spring, tel. 845/265–2122.

Downtown Gallery The largest antiques center in the county, this 5,000-square-foot space teems with furniture from Victorian through modern periods, vintage textiles and clothes, and collectible toys. > 40 Main St., Cold Spring, tel. 845/265–2334.

Momminia You may try on a Zulu necklace, a jade pendant, or a string of Tahitian pearls at this avant-garde jewelry boutique. > 113 Main St., Cold Spring, tel. 845/265–2260.

Provincial Home Hand-painted ceramics from France, Spain, Italy, Poland, and Portugal are showcased amid antiques and other home furnishings. > 80 Main St., Cold Spring, tel. 845/265–5360, www.provincialhome.com.

Salmagundi Books Cold Spring is an independent-bookshop sort of town, and this village gem has a fine selection of Hudson Valley history and literature titles. > 66 Main St., Cold Spring, tel. 845/265–4058. Closed Mon.

20th Century Fox Antiques If art deco is your quarry, you're in luck at this showroom of lamps, furnishings, and decorative arts. > 466 Main St., Beacon, tel. 845/831–6059. Closed weekdays.

Save the Date

JUNE
Annual Beacon Sloop Club Strawberry Festival Bushels of fresh strawberries find their way into shortcakes, smoothies, and other goodies at this mid-June festival by the riverfront in Beacon. > Riverfront Park, Beacon, tel. 845/831–6962.

Cold Spring Antiques Show Some 60 dealers hawk their wares, from 19th-century furniture to antique tools and woodenware, at this twice-yearly event on the banks of the Hudson River. > Fair St., Cold Spring, tel. 800/470–4854, www.coldspringantiqueshow.com.

JUNE–AUGUST
Hudson Valley Shakespeare Festival Energetic and imaginative interpretations of Shakespeare's plays unfold under an open-air tent on Boscobel's sweeping grounds. The critically acclaimed company puts on two plays each summer, distilling the action and adding creative contemporary touches to rousing effect. > Boscobel Restoration, 1601 Rte. 9D, Garrison, tel. 845/265–9575, www.hvshakespeare.org.

AUGUST
Annual Fine Arts and Crafts Fair More than 90 craftspeople display works—from pottery, glassware, and jewelry to photography, metal works, and sculpture—in Garrison's riverfront park. The two-day juried event takes place in mid-August. > Garrison's Landing, Garrison, tel. 845/424–3960.

SEPTEMBER
Big Band Evening A 20-piece jazz orchestra brings big-band sound to the lawn at Boscobel in mid-September. Pack a picnic supper and savor one of the last evenings of summer. > Boscobel Restoration, 1601 Rte. 9D, Garrison, tel. 845/265–3638 Ext. 115, www.boscobel.org.

OCTOBER
Annual Beacon Sloop Club Pumpkin Festival Pumpkin pie, chili, and live music usher in the harvest season at this riverfront shindig in Beacon. > Riverfront Park, Beacon, tel. 845/831–6962.
Cold Spring Antiques Show A replay of the June event, amid an extravaganza of autumn color. > Fair St., Cold Spring, tel. 800/470–4854, www.coldspringantiqueshow.com.

WHERE TO STAY

Hudson House Inn A stunning riverfront setting and a wraparound porch distinguish this simple three-story clapboard inn built in 1832 to house steamboat passengers. Farmhouse antiques and French-country furnishings adorn the rooms, two of which have toile de Jouy wallpaper and bedspreads. Be sure to request a room with a private terrace looking out onto the Hudson River or quiet Main Street. Hiking trails, river sports, and antiques shops are a short walk away. > 2 Main St., 10516, tel. 845/265–9355, fax 845/265–4532, www.hudsonhouseinn.com. 11 rooms, 1 suite. Restaurant, cable TV, bar; no smoking. AE, DC, MC, V. BP (CP weekdays). $$–$$$
Pig Hill Inn An 1825 brick inn in the heart of the village re-creates a 19th-century country house. Guest rooms and lounges teem with antiques, from Chippendale to chinoiserie—and if you fall in love with that four-poster bed or mahogany armoire, you can buy it (price tags hang from nearly every furnishing). Most rooms have a wood-burning stove or a fireplace; one has a whirlpool tub. Breakfasts, served in the light-filled Victorian conservatory or on the garden patio, are ample. Sweet aromas also waft from the kitchen in early afternoon, when the innkeeper often bakes cookies or pound cakes to serve with tea. > 73 Main St., 10516, tel. 845/265–9247, fax 845/265–4614, www.pighillinn.com. 9 rooms, 4 with shared bath. Dining room, tea shop, some in-room hot tubs, lounge; no room phones, no room TVs, no smoking. AE, MC, V. BP. $$–$$$

Plumbush Inn The 19th-century Victorian inn, a short hop from the village, was once the home of a U.S.-born marquess. The rooms, commodious and serviceable, over-look the gardens. Vaulted ceilings and velvet furnishings bedeck the largest room, which is billed as a suite. An armchair-filled common parlor has a television and a pay phone. The landscaped grounds often host weddings on the weekends, and the restaurant serves Continental fare. > 1656 Rte. 9D, 10516, tel. 845/265–3904, fax 845/265–3997. 2 rooms, 1 suite. Restaurant, bar; no room phones, no room TVs, no smoking. AE, DC, MC, V. CP. Closed Mon.–Wed. **$$**

Riverview A popular village restaurant offers a couple of spacious and airy upstairs lodgings. Windows in the north-facing room—including one over the whirlpool tub for two—look out onto the Hudson River and Storm King. Extra-large bathrooms, shabby-chic armchairs, and other homey furnishings are inviting. > 45 Fair St., 10516, tel. 845/265–4778, fax 845/265–5596. 1 room, 1 suite. Restaurant, some in-room hot tubs, cable TV; no phone in 1 room, no smoking. No credit cards. EP. **$$**

GARRISON

Bird & Bottle Inn Step back in time at this 1761 buttercup-yellow, clapboard inn, once a well-known rest stop for stagecoaches along the postal road between New York and Albany. Flowers tumble from antique wagons out front, and the fragrance of wood smoke greets you at the door. Each room has a fireplace. It's worth the splurge for the Beverly Robinson suite, with its canopied bed, covered porch with wicker chairs, and sitting room with rough-hewn beams. Rates include a candlelit, four-course dinner for two. You can skip this and pocket a $75 credit, but then you'd be missing out on a sublime culinary experience. > 1123 Old Albany Post Rd., off U.S. 9, 10524, tel. 845/424–3000, fax 845/424–3283, www.birdbottle.com. 3 rooms, 1 suite. Restaurant, bar; no room phones, no room TVs, no kids under 12. AE, DC, MC, V. MAP. **$$$–$$$$**

CAMPING

Clarence Fahnestock Memorial State Park Choose from 80 campsites for an ideal jumping-off point to the park's hiking trails, beach, and other outdoor activities. Only the first 50 sites are wooded, so call to book these well in advance (reservations are essential for these). Each site includes a picnic table, grill, and fire ring. A wilderness-camping option ($1 per person per night) has bare-bones facilities—an outhouse, water source, and fire ring. The park doesn't have hook-ups or a dumping station. There's a convenience store at Canopus Beach. > Rte. 301 ½ mi west of the Taconic State Pkwy. (Cold Spring exit), Carmel 10512, tel. 800/456–2267 campsites, 845/265–7027 wilderness camping. 80 tent sites, 28 RV sites. Flush toilets, drinking water, showers, fire pits, grills, picnic tables, general store. Reservations essential for wilderness sites. No credit cards. Closed mid-Dec.–mid-Apr. **¢**

WHERE TO EAT

Brasserie Le Bouchon It's France-on-the-Hudson at this village hot spot with crim-son walls, lipstick-hued banquettes, and Edith Piaf on the stereo. Although purists might claim the fare is more bistro than brasserie, the extensive menu and wine lists give you many choices. Expertly executed classics range from croque monsieur to steak au poivre with cognac-and-cream dressing. The rum-infused crème brûlée and cloud-light profiteroles have gained a following. > 76 Main St., tel. 845/265–7676. AE, MC, V. Closed Tues. $–$$$

Café Maya Authentic Mexican fare and congenial service make up for the strip-mall setting of this tiny eatery. Homemade *mulato* sauce, a blend of four kinds of peppers, flavors the steak-filled house burrito; *mojo de ajo* (Mexican garlic sauce) envelops a dish of sautéed shrimp. The guacamole is served in the *molcajete* (stone bowl or mortar and pestle) in which it's made to order. > Perks Plaza, 3182 U.S. 9, tel. 845/265–4636. Reservations not accepted. AE, D, MC, V. BYOB. Closed Tues. $–$$

Cathryn's Dolcigno Tuscan Grill Swaths of sheer fabric and vibrant murals romance the interior of this rustic trattoria—a paean to northern Italian food and fresh herbs. Transplanted New Yorkers sip reds and whites from an extensive wine list. Sage-browned butter laces silky calves' liver, and an espresso demi-glace enlivens grilled hanger steak. Vegetarians choose from pasta dishes such as whole-wheat fusilli primavera. Sunday brunch, from noon to 3, is $20 prix fixe. > 91 Main St., tel. 845/265–5582. AE, D, MC, V. $–$$$

East Side Kitchen At this relaxed Main Street eatery, a stamping ground for local families, you can tuck into a chili-cheese dog with curly fries or a plate of barbecued ribs, or sample signature fare like tortilla-wrapped chicken with Jack cheese, spicy remoulade, and sweet-potato fries. Kids cozy up to the ice-cream counter, which turns out milkshakes and floats. Retro-hip 1950s decor, comfy banquettes, and oldies music set a feel-good tone. > 124 Main St., tel. 845/265–7223. AE, MC, V. Closed Mon. ¢–$$

Hudson House River Inn Watch sailboats drift by from the veranda tables at this riverfront restaurant, or dine by the window in the country-style River Room. A crust of red and blue tortillas gives crab cakes a new twist. Notable entrées include salmon filled with sun-dried-tomato pesto and arugula, and filet mignon wrapped in a crusty sleeve of pancetta. Sunday brunch is $23 prix fixe. > 2 Main St., tel. 845/265–9355. AE, DC, MC, V. Closed Tues. No lunch Wed. $$$–$$$$

Plumbush Inn Choose from several dining rooms at this Victorian inn: Two rooms, one dark with oak paneling and one abloom with rose wallpaper, have fireplaces, whereas the veranda and garden room look out at landscaped grounds. Chef Ans Benderer serves Continental fare with Swiss accents and makes the terrines and pâtés on site. Consider such starters as Swiss mushroom crepe or polenta torte, then move on to pecan-breasted chicken, pork medallions, or fresh trout. Reservations are essential on weekends. > 1656 Rte. 9D, tel. 845/265–3904. AE, MC, V. Closed Mon.–Wed. $$$$

Riverview Transcendent Hudson River views accompany "modern Continental" fare at this local favorite, where handblown sconces lend a golden glow to the dining room come evening. Wood-oven pizzas are praiseworthy, as are grilled rib-eye steak, fusilli Bolognese, and fish specials. Reservations are essential for the highly coveted terrace tables and on Wednesday nights, when special prices lure a spirited crowd. > 45 Fair St., tel. 845/265–4778. No credit cards. Closed Mon. $–$$

WHAT'S NEARBY

Bill Brown's Restaurant Local and organic produce—and herbs plucked from the kitchen garden—lend wholesome intensity to regional French and American fare that is creative but not fussy. The tavern menu includes lobster–and–wild mushroom risotto, dry-aged shell steak, and Nantucket Bay scallops. At Sunday brunch ($28 prix fixe), the buffet table groans under all the omelets, crepes, smoked fish, and scones. Large panel windows yield swoon-inducing valley views. (At this writing, lunch and dinner are being served on a tented patio—with heaters or fans, depending on the weather—while the restaurant is renovated. Call ahead.) > The Garrison, 2015 U.S. 9, Garrison, tel. 845/424–3604. AE, D, DC, MC, V. Closed Mon.–Wed. **$–$$$**

Bird & Bottle Inn Your four-course dinner is served by candlelight in the dining room of this 1761 inn. Chef Stephanie Hagquist uses as many local ingredients as possible to prepare her Hudson Valley cuisine. A signature crab-cakes appetizer comes with a foil of tomato remoulade. Rack of lamb is encrusted with horseradish and Dijon mustard, and duckling is dressed with wild-berry sauce. The four-course champagne Sunday brunch (from $20) has seatings at noon and 2. > 1123 Old Albany Post Rd., Garrison, tel. 845/424–3000. AE, DC, MC, V. Closed Mon. and Tues. No lunch. **$$$$**

The Piggy Bank Beacon's restaurant scene has yet to catch up with its vibrant arts arena, but this neighborhood mainstay dishes out slow-cooked Southern barbecue favorites. It's not Memphis, but the sweet-potato fries, hickory-smoked ribs, and barbecued pulled pork over tossed greens have won over the stomachs of some locals. The restaurant occupies a circa-1880 bank building where the vault now serves as wine cellar. The dining room, with glowing copper sconces and pink-brick walls, is open and airy but visually warm. > 448 Main St., Beacon, tel. 845/838–0028. AE, MC, V. **$–$$**

ESSENTIALS

Getting Here

The Cold Spring area is easy to reach by car or train; either way takes just over an hour. Traveling by car gives you the most flexibility in getting around once you arrive. You can reach most of the area's attractions on foot from the train stations at Garrison, Cold Spring, Breakneck Ridge, and Beacon, but don't count on Cold Spring's lone, extremely inconsistent, taxi service to take you anywhere else.

BY CAR

Although it may seem counterintuitive, the easiest way to reach Cold Spring and Garrison by car from Manhattan is to cross the Hudson River and travel most of the way on the western side, and then cross again at Bear Mountain to complete the trip. You encounter less traffic—and a less convoluted driving route—on the western side, with smooth sailing on all but the most crowded of weekends or holidays.

Take the Palisades Parkway north about 35 mi to its end, following the signs to Bear Mountain. At the end of the parkway, veer right onto U.S. 6. After about 3 mi you come to a traffic circle. Take the second exit from the circle to get on the Bear Mountain Bridge ($1 toll). Take the first left off the bridge onto Route 9D and proceed about 4½ mi to Garrison, or continue another 4 mi to reach Cold Spring.

It's almost impossible to find street parking in Cold Spring on weekends and holidays, but there is a free municipal parking lot on Fair Street. To reach it, drive west, toward the river, from 9D and turn right on Fair Street.

BY TRAIN

The Metro-North train to the area follows the Hudson River along the same line traveled by Cary Grant and Eva Marie Saint in the 1959 Hitchcock film *North By Northwest*. For many, the river views alone are worth the ticket price.

(Be sure to sit on the left side going to Cold Spring and on the right side back to the city.)

Hudson Line trains of the Metro-North Railroad depart at least hourly, every day including holidays, from Grand Central Terminal. The trip to Garrison takes about an hour and ten minutes; to Cold Spring it's about four minutes longer. Another eight minutes brings you to Beacon. In addition, there are two trains a day on weekends (and some holidays) to and from Breakneck Ridge. Trains depart promptly and can fill up on busy weekends, so be sure to arrive at least a few minutes early. Also, ticket lines can be long. You can buy your ticket on the train, but you'll pay an extra service charge. Bicycles are allowed only with a permit, which you can purchase for $5 (annual fee) in Grand Central.

LINES **Metro-North Railroad** > Tel. 212/532–4900 or 800/638–7646, http://mta.info/mnr.

STATIONS **Beacon** > Ferry Plaza and Beekman St., Beacon, no phone, http://mta.info/mnr. **Breakneck Ridge** > Rte. 9D ½ mi north of Breakneck Tunnel, Cold Spring, no phone, http://mta.info/mnr. **Cold Spring** > Market St., Cold Spring, no phone, http://mta.info/mnr. **Garrison** > Garrison's Landing, Garrison, no phone, http://mta.info/mnr.

Visitor Information

CONTACTS **Cold Spring/Garrison Area Chamber of Commerce** > Box 36, Cold Spring 10516, tel. 845/265–3200, www.hvgateway.com/chamber.htm. **Dutchess County Tourism** > 3 Neptune Rd., Suite M-17, Poughkeepsie 12601, tel. 845/463–4000 or 800/445–3131, www.dutchesstourism.com. **Putnam County Visitors Bureau** > 110 Old Rte. 6, Bldg. 3, Carmel 10512, tel. 800/470–4854, www.visitputnam.org.

Southampton

95 mi east of New York City

13

Revised by Amy Patton

ONE OF THE HAMLETS that make up the eastern end of Long Island's famed South Shore, Southampton is not only steeped in rich history but also in contemporary affluence. Pristine area beaches framed by sparkling Atlantic waters are a draw, but so are upscale shops, fine restaurants, polo matches and other horsey events, and antiques shows.

The village was settled in the 17th century by Puritans who had set sail from Lynn, Massachusetts, and landed at what is today known as Conscience Point. Southampton, which was formally incorporated in 1894, was named after the third Earl of Southampton, Henry Wriothesly, who was sympathetic to the early British settlers and was widely respected.

Southampton has several districts and buildings included on the National Register of Historic Places. Armed with maps obtained from the local chamber of commerce, you can take a walking tour that passes the Historical Museum and the Old Halsey Homestead, which claims to be the oldest frame house in the state.

The village is part of the much larger Town of Southampton, which spans from parts of Eastport to the west all the way out to Sagaponack, with its potato farms and seaside estates. A drive through the "estate section" takes you past graceful mansions surrounded by 20-foot privet hedges. Gin Lane, in particular, is worth a peek.

On a stroll up Jobs Lane you find places that carry gemstones, cashmere sweaters, antiques, and works of art—both collectible, from one of the galleries, and collected, in the Parrish Art Museum. The old town-hall building houses Saks Fifth Avenue, and there's also Hildreth's, billed as "America's oldest department store."

Rusticity and sophistication are often stitched together seamlessly in Southampton. Local baymen harvest clams and mussels and long-liners trail immense nets on Shinnecock Bay and the open ocean. The seafood they catch is just one of the things that makes the dining in the town's restaurants so fine. Regional wines are another.

The social scene starts to hum around Memorial Day. Throughout summer, showbiz types and Wall Street lions crowd trendy eateries and nightspots. The calendar is filled with exclusive sporting events, parties at gargantuan estates, and see-and-be-seen fund-raisers. The year-end holidays are also lively here. Festively decorated trees line the village streets and shops are adorned with ivy, bows, and twinkling lights.

WHAT TO SEE & DO

Cooper's Beach For a fee, you can stretch out on the sand of Southampton Village's beach, studying the sea in one direction and historic mansions in another. Facilities include lifeguards, rest rooms, outdoor showers, and a snack bar. > 268 Meadow La., tel. 631/283–0247, www.southamptonvillage.org. Memorial Day–Labor Day $25 week-days, $30 weekends. Lifeguards Memorial Day–Labor Day, daily 10–5.

Jet East At this seasonal superhip club, rich regulars regularly shell out hundreds of dollars to reserve weekend tables and bottles of champagne. Expect a wait at the velvet rope if you're not plugged in. > 1181 N. Sea Rd., tel. 631/283–0808. $20. Memorial Day–Labor Day, Thurs.–Sun.; call for hrs.

Long Island University, Southampton College In summer the campus hums with such musical events as Pianofest in the Hamptons and the All for the Sea fund-raising concert, which draws the likes of Jimmy Buffett and Paul Simon here in July. Throughout the season several organizations sponsor plays, art shows, readings, workshops, and other activities for adults and children. > 239 Montauk Hwy., tel. 631/283–4000, www.southampton.liu.edu.

Lynch's Links The 18-hole miniature-golf course is open daily from Memorial Day to Labor Day and then on weekends until Columbus Day. > 375 David Whites La., tel. 631/283–0049. $8.

Old Halsey House This 1648 saltbox was built by town founder Thomas Halsey. English General William Erskine had his headquarters here during the American Revolution. Today it's a museum that includes furniture from the 17th and 18th centuries and a 16th-century "breeches" bible that has an interesting take on what Adam and Eve actually wore after the Fall. > 189 S. Main St., tel. 631/283–2494. $3. Mid-Apr.–mid-Sept., Tues.–Sun. 11–5.

Parrish Art Museum Its founder, Samuel Longstreth Parrish, built the museum in 1898 as repository for his Italian Renaissance art. Through the years the museum has also developed a strong collection of American paintings, including works by renowned Long Island artists. Traveling exhibits have ranged from pieces by sculptor August Saint-Gaudens to photographs of the civil rights movement by Herbert Randall. The gardens are filled with reproductions of sculpture from the museum's permanent collection. There's a full calendar of lectures, workshops, concerts, and children's programs. Juried art exhibitions hang on the walls during the year. > 25 Jobs La., tel. 631/283–2118. $5 suggested donation. Mon.–Sat. 11–5, Sun. 1–5.

Southampton Historical Museum The museum encompasses seven historic structures, including an 1843 whaling captain's home, a country store, an old-fashioned apothecary, a pre–Revolutionary War barn, and a blacksmith shop. Montauk and Shinnecock Indian artifacts are also on display. > 17 Meeting House La., tel. 631/283–2494. $3. Mid-June–Sept., Tues.–Sat. 11–5, Sun. 1–5.

WHAT'S NEARBY

Ponquogue Beach This beach, a 15-minute drive west of Southampton Village and at the end of Ponquogue Bridge, is open from June 28 through September 15. Out-of-towners and others without a permit must pay $15 to park. There are lifeguards, changing and shower facilities, and a snack bar. > Dune Rd., Hampton Bays, tel. 631/728–8585, www.town.southampton.ny.us. Late June–mid-Sept., $15 (nonresidents). Daily sunrise–sunset.

Sports

HIKING

Quogue Wildlife Refuge About 30 minutes west of Southampton Village, you can bird-watch, hike along a self-guided trail, visit a complex where injured animals are rehabilitated, or take a class on field ecology or wildlife photography. The refuge also has children's programs. > 3 Old Country Rd., Quogue, tel. 631/653–4771, www.quoguerefuge.com. Free. Daily dawn–dusk.

WINDSURFING

The area's many protected waterways, including Cold Spring Pond and Peconic Bay, are popular with windsurfers and kiteboarders. You can rent gear or bring your own. If you rent, experts will assess your ability, steer you to an appropriate spot, and haul the equipment there and back. Instruction is also available; the cost for two hours on the water runs about $40 with rentals, $85 for a full day.

EQUIPMENT **Windsurfing Hampton, Inc.** > 1688 North Hwy./Rte. 27, tel. 631/283–9463, www.w-surf.com.

Shopping

Ann Madonia Antiques You might find a French daybed with carved classical urns; a Venetian headboard; or a Second Empire bed with mother-of-pearl accents. This shop is absolutely packed with 18th- and 19th-century-American and -European furniture and decorative items. Many pieces are right from Hamptons-area estates. > 36 Jobs La., tel. 631/283–1878. Closed Oct.–late May, except by appointment.

Bookhampton It's an independent bookstore with an autonomous spirit and chain-store selection and pricing (hardcovers are always 20% off). There's plenty of contemporary fiction and nonfiction as well as a wide variety of classical literature, cookbooks, and children's books. The store also carries many titles on the Hamptons. > 91 Main St., tel. 631/283–0270.

Chrysalis Gallery The space is in a corner building that dates to the 1920s; out back there's a sculpture garden. The fine art for sale and on display may include oil and acrylic paintings, pastels, and bronze pieces. > 2 Main St., tel. 631/287–1883.

The Fudge Co. The scent of homemade fudge wafts into the street in front of this cheery establishment. Storefront displays of colorful, scrumptious confections—including many novelty items—delight kids as well as grownups. > 67 Main St., tel. 631/283–8108. Closed Christmas–Easter.

Hildreth's To say that it's a Hamptons institution is an understatement. This home furnishings store has been in business—on this spot and owned by the same family—since 1842. It would be almost disrespectful to visit Southampton and not stop in. Besides, it's fun to shop for 21st-century carpets, lamps, furniture, linens, and table settings amid 19th-century architectural details. There are other outlets in Southampton, East Hampton, and Bridgehampton, but this one is the original. > 51 Main St., tel. 631/283–2300, www.hildreths.com.

Mecox Gardens It's all about steeply pitched gables, cascading ivy, and tasteful topiary at this posh shop selling pieces for indoor and outdoor spaces. Look for antique, reproduction, and contemporary furniture; unusual garden ornaments; and intriguing accessories. This is the flagship store; there are branches in East Hampton, Manhattan, and Palm Beach, Florida. > 257 Rte. 39A, tel. 631/287–5015, www.mecoxgardens.com.

Ralph Lauren Polo Country Store A whitewashed interior with flea-market furnishings forms the perfect backdrop for the casual but upscale men's and women's resort wear and accessories. > 41 Jobs La., tel. 631/287–6953. Closed Tues. and Wed. Oct.–late Mar.

Rose Jewelers This family-owned shop sells gems, crystal, estate jewelry, and watches by Rolex, TAG Heuer, and Baume & Mercier. > 57 Main St., tel. 631/283–5757.

Saks Fifth Avenue Southampton's former town hall makes an intimate outpost for this venerable department store. It's all about designer stuff here: resort wear by

Donna Karan and Calvin Klein, bags by Burberry and Prada, cosmetics and skin-care products by Chanel and Kiehl's. > 1 Hampton Rd., tel. 631/283–3500.

Stevenson's Toys and Games This old-fashioned toy shop stocks Madame Alexander dolls, Playmobiles, stuffed animals, art-and-crafts supplies, and puzzles for the diminutive set. > 68 Jobs La., tel. 631/283–2111.

Tate's Bake Shop Tate's is famous for its sinfully yummy chocolate-chip cookies. The aromatic shop also sells freshly baked, pies, scones, muffins, and specialty cakes. > 43 N. Sea Rd., tel. 631/283–9830.

Save the Date

JUNE
Southampton Antiques Classic Five bucks gets you into this annual antiques extravaganza on the grounds of the Elks Club. It's held the last weekend of the month. > 605 Rte. 39, tel. 631/261–4590, www.flamingoshows.com.

JUNE–JULY
Bridgehampton Polo On midsummer Saturday afternoons, pack a picnic and head to Two Trees Farm in Bridgehampton for some Hamptons-style tailgating. The polo spectacle includes swinging mallets, players and their mounts, and well-heeled patrons on the sidelines under the VIP tent. Be sure to brush up on the lingo so you know a "made pony" from a "pony goal." General admission is $20 per carload. > Hayground Rd., Bridgehampton, tel. 631/537–3881, www.bhpolo.com.

JUNE–AUGUST
Pianofest in the Hamptons A summer music festival that showcases young pianists from around the world, who must audition for coveted spots in this concert series and study program. Performances are held weekly at Southampton College and at East Hampton's Guild Hall. Tickets are $10 at the door. > Southampton College, 239 Montauk Hwy., Southampton, tel. 631/329–9115, www.pianofest.org; Guild Hall, 158 Main St., Easthampton.

JULY–AUGUST
Concerts in Agawam Park On Wednesday evenings in July and August, you can grab a blanket, pack a picnic, and enjoy rock 'n' roll, classical music, or jazz at free outdoor concerts in Agawam Park. Shows begin at 6:45. > Jobs La., tel. 631/287–4377 Southampton Cultural Center.

AUGUST
Hampton Classic Horse Show Late in August, the Hampton Classic show grounds in Bridgehampton, about 10 minutes east of Southampton, hosts one of North America's most prestigious equestrian shows. Participants from around the globe compete in several events that challenge their hunter and jumper skills. Huge cash prizes are put up by Calvin Klein, David Yurman jewelers, and other deep-pocketed entities. > Snake Hollow Rd., Bridgehampton, tel. 631/537–3177, www.hamptonclassic.com.

Hamptons Shakespeare Festival For two weeks each August, professional actors perform outdoors in Agawam Park. Plays are free but a donation of $15 is suggested per family or carload. Actors also host Camp Shakespeare, a series of one-day workshops for kids. > Jobs La., Southampton, tel. 631/267–0105, www.hamptons-shakespeare.org.

AUGUST–SEPTEMBER
Shinnecock Indian Pow Wow Traditional Native American–tribal dances, craft sales, and ceremonies take place Labor Day weekend on the Shinnecock Reservation. > Old Montauk Hwy., Southampton, tel. 631/287–2460.

WHERE TO STAY

The Atlantic On the outside it looks like just another raised ranch circa 1975. Inside, though, rooms are up to date with sleek, contemporary maple furniture, stainless-steel headboards, lamps, and other details. Plump white duvets, soft sheets, and Aveda bath goodies are among the comforts. The grounds are well manicured, and the pool seems to stretch on for an eternity. > 1655 Rte. 39, 11968, tel. 631/283–6100, fax 631/283–6102, www.hrhresorts.com. 62 rooms, 5 suites. In-room data ports, some in-room hot tubs, some kitchenettes, minibars, cable TV, in-room VCRs, tennis court, pool, gym, business services, some pets allowed (fee); no smoking. AE, MC, V. CP. **$$–$$$**

The Bentley Each large suite overlooks the Peconic Bay and has a patio or a deck. Richly hued paint effects, accent pieces, and contemporary Italian furniture either complement or tastefully contrast with the overall palette of beiges and creams. Breakfast bars face kitchenettes equipped with microwaves, coffeemakers, and java from Starbuck's. In the bathroom, it's all about Aveda products. The $4\frac{1}{2}$-acre property has a kidney-shape pool with a large sundeck. > 161 Hill Station Rd., 11968, tel. 631/283–0908, fax 631/283–6102, www.hrhresorts.com. 39 suites. Picnic area, in-room data ports, kitchenettes, minibars, microwaves, cable TV, in-room VCRs, tennis court, pool, laundry facilities, business services, some pets allowed (fee); no smoking. AE, D, DC, MC, V. Closed Labor Day–Memorial Day. CP. **$$$–$$$$**

The Capri Outside clapboards, shingles, and creatively used bits of canvas all recall classic seaside properties. Inside, the fluffy white duvets and pillows do, too. But all the other interior details seem to be about mid-20th-century modern, from the custom headboards to the bold, linear paint effects. All rooms face the pool in the central courtyard. The hotel is 3 mi from the beach and $\frac{1}{2}$ mi from Southampton Village. > 281 Rte. 39A, 11968, tel. 631/283–4220, fax 631/283–6102, www.hrhresorts.com. 27 rooms, 4 suites. Restaurant, in-room data ports, minibars, some refrigerators, cable TV, pool, business services, some pets allowed (fee); no smoking. AE, D, MC, V. Closed Labor Day–Memorial Day. CP. **$$–$$$$**

Enclave Inn Not all motels have to be about '50s kitsch. Rooms in this one have chunky, country-style furniture and accessories that work well with highly polished wood floors, floral drapes, crisp white window sheers, and lacy white bed linens. The hotel and its tree-filled grounds are just minutes from the Hampton Jitney stop and a few miles from area beaches. > 450 Rte. 39, 11968, tel. 631/537–2900, fax 631/537–5436, www.enclaveinn.com. 11 rooms. Fans, refrigerators, cable TV, pool, Internet, business services, meeting room; no smoking. AE, MC, V. CP May–Oct. **$$–$$$$**

Evergreen on Pine Tall, carefully groomed hedges front a house with a pretty porch and flower-filled window boxes on each sill. The five guest rooms are singular: a suite has a sitting area and Laura Ashley bedding; one room has an ornamental fireplace and a brass bed, another has a French-lace canopy bed. You can walk to the beach, which is less than a mile away. > 89 Pine St., 11968, tel. 631/283–0564 or 877/824–6600, www.evergreenonpine.com. 5 rooms. Dining room, in-room data ports, cable TV, Internet; no kids under age 12, no smoking. AE, DC, MC, V. CP. **$$$–$$$$**

Mainstay Inn Every bedroom in this shingle-covered neo-Colonial has antique cast-iron beds and country pine furniture. Each also seems to be filled with yard upon yard of fabric: generous floral table covers and drapes, white duvets, and quilted spreads.

Whether the gardens were inspired by the guest room fabrics or the fabrics were chosen to mirror the gardens is hard to know. Southampton's main street is a 15-minute walk away, and the public beach is a mile away. > 579 Hill St., 11968, tel. 631/283–4375, fax 631/614–6300, www.themainstay.com. 8 rooms, 5 with bath; 1 suite. Dining room, some fans, cable TV, pool, business services; no a/c in some rooms, no TV in some rooms, no smoking. AE, DC, MC, V. CP. $$–$$$$

1708 House It's truly a Colonial, from the wide clapboards outside to the wood beams within. Antiques, Asian rugs, and rich fabrics fill this bed-and-breakfast in the heart of Southampton Village. Public areas include an informal card room, a more formal dining room, and an even more formal parlor. Guest quarters in the house and in the separate two-bedroom cottages have four-poster beds. Some rooms are elegantly rustic; others are simply elegant. All are true to the age and style of the house. > 126 Main St., 11968, tel. 631/287–1708, fax 631/287–3593, www.1708house.com. 6 rooms, 3 suites, 3 cottages. Dining room, some kitchens, cable TV; no kids under 12, no smoking. AE, MC, V. BP. $$$–$$$$

Southampton Inn The interior of this modern inn is dressed in refined contemporary-country furniture and fittings. Beds have down comforters and lots of pillows. Adirondack chairs are scattered throughout the expansive, formally landscaped grounds, and there's a patio courtyard and a pool. There's plenty of on-site parking and shuttle service to the beach. Great shopping, dining, and sightseeing are steps away. > 91 Hill St., 11968, tel. 631/283–6500 or 800/832–6500, fax 631/283–6559, www.southamptoninn.com. 90 rooms. Restaurant, in-room data ports, refrigerators, cable TV, tennis court, pool, badminton, billiards, croquet, shuffleboard, volleyball, bar, library, video game room, business services, meeting rooms, some pets allowed (fee), no-smoking rooms. AE, D, DC, MC, V. CP weekends. $$$–$$$$

Southampton Village Latch Inn A collective of local artists owns and runs this hotel. The interior design reflects their tastes: Burmese puppets, New Guinea masks, African artifacts, and Tibetan rugs are among the furnishings. Some rooms and duplexes have balconies and decks. The inn is on 5 acres in Southampton Village and just over a mile from the beach. > 101 Hill St., 11968, tel. 631/283–2160 or 800/545–2824, fax 631/283–3236, www.villagelatch.com. 43 rooms, 18 suites, 6 duplexes. Dining room, some refrigerators, cable TV with movies, tennis court, pool, bicycles, business services, some pets allowed (fee); no smoking. AE, D, DC, MC, V. CP. $$$$

WHAT'S NEARBY

Arlington Shores You might see a gorgeous Hamptons sunset from the common balcony at this condominium resort on Shinnecock Bay 10 mi west of Southampton. Standard condos have a queen-size bed, kitchen, and oak floors. Stay for a week, a month, a season, or even a year. A shuttle to the train or bus stops is provided. > 40 Penny La., Hampton Bays 11946, tel. 631/723–6000, fax 631/723–4517, www.arlingtonshores.com. 28 condos. Picnic area, kitchens, cable TV, tennis court, pool, volleyball. AE, MC, V. CP. $$–$$$$

Bayview House Guest quarters here are in seaside villas or the main house, which dates from 1902; all rooms are beautifully appointed and have private bathrooms. You can cycle the neighborhood or cross the Ponquogue Bridge to the ocean beaches just minutes away. A covered veranda overlooks Shinnecock Bay. Seasonal and short-term accommodations are available. > 32 Lighthouse Rd., Hampton Bays 11946, tel.

631/728–1200, fax 631/728–3197, www.bayviewhouse.com. 4 rooms, 9 villas. Restaurant, some refrigerators, cable TV, no-smoking rooms. AE, MC, V. EP. **$$$$**

Inn at Quogue This tranquil complex in the center of Quogue Village consists of a house from the 18th century, another from the 19th century right across the road, and various private cottages. Although all the rooms were done under the supervision of Ralph Lauren designers, each room is different. You can relax on the beach, which is just minutes away, or get a massage, an exfoliating scrub, or a paraffin-wax treatment. The restaurant here is stellar. > 47 and 52 Quogue St., Quogue 11946, tel. 631/653–6560, fax 631/723–4517, www.innatquogue.com. 67 rooms, 2 cottages. Restaurant, dining room, some kitchens, some microwaves, cable TV, pool, spa, bicycles, volleyball, bar, some pets allowed (fee). AE, MC, V. EP. **$$$–$$$$**

CAMPING

Shinnecock East County Park This beach park has 100 RV campsites (no tents are allowed) on either the Atlantic or on the inlet to Shinnecock Bay. If you're not a resident of Suffolk County, call to check rules about staying here. > Dune Rd., Southampton 11968, tel. 631/852–8899 or 631/852–8290, www.co.suffolk.ny.us. 100 sites. Dump station, drinking water, public telephone, swimming (ocean). Reservations not accepted. MC, V. **¢**

WHERE TO EAT

Armand's You can dine on fabulous pasta by the light of candles and, on chilly nights, the fireplace at this relaxed spot. The shrimp scampi is a good choice, and so are the garlic knots. Monday is brick-oven-pizza night. > 1271 Noyac Rd., tel. 631/283–9742. MC, V. No lunch weekdays. **$$–$$$**

Barrister's Simple but good American fare is the rule here, as are friendly service and a general conviviality. Try for a table at the front for an entertaining view of Main Street. There are daily specials as well as a steady menu of burgers, seafood entrées, and pasta dishes; salads rise above the usual. The bar draws locals for after-work drinks. > 36 Main St., tel. 631/283–6206. Reservations not accepted. AE, D, DC, MC, V. **$–$$$**

basilico The upscale patrons who favor this restaurant in Southampton Village come for the brick-oven pizzas and the Tuscan-tinged entrées. The pasta is homemade, and the portions are large. In the evening, the interior's wood trim and terra-cotta tiles seem to glow in the candlelight. Weekend lunches are leisurely events. > 10 Windmill La., tel. 631/283–7987. AE, D, DC, MC, V. **$$–$$$$**

Belle's East This fancy outpost of Belle's Cafe in Westhampton Beach serves such New Orleans–style dishes as barbecued shrimp alongside more standard American fare. If possible, opt for a table on the patio, which is open in the spring and fall as well as in the summer thanks to the use of heaters. Inside, the lounge has live music—often Latin or reggae—six nights a week and a late-night menu of barbecue items on weekends. There's also a buffet brunch on Sunday. > 256 Elm St., tel. 631/204–0300. AE, MC, V. Closed Tues. **$$–$$$$**

Coast Grill Super-fresh fish dishes are the mainstay at this unpretentious eatery with pretty views of Wooley Pond. Sesame noodles accompany pepper-crusted tuna, and lime-papaya puree dresses grilled swordfish. Steak, lamb, and buffalo filet mignon also get raves. > 1109 Noyac Rd., tel. 631/283–2277. AE, MC, V. Closed Mon.–Thurs. Oct.–May. No lunch. **$$$$**

Driver's Seat Casual fare is the rule here. The dining room, whose huge stone fireplace is often ablaze in winter, hums with diners eager to order one of the daily seafood specials or such stick-to-your-ribs dishes as pot roast, meat loaf and mashed potatoes, burgers, and homemade soups. The bar business is brisk, too. > 62 Jobs La., tel. 631/283–6606. AE, MC, V. **$–$$$**

George Martin The new American takes on steak and seafood, the regional specialties, the stellar desserts, and the generous portions earn this restaurant high marks. Try the herb-roasted free-range chicken or the signature steak, a dry-aged, prime New York sirloin. There's also a $20 prix-fixe menu daily. > 56 Nugent St./Main St., tel. 631/204–8700. AE, MC, V. No lunch. **$$–$$$$**

Golden Pear Place your order at the counter of this chic café and then sit at one of 12 tables to be served while watching Southampton's scene from the large windows. For breakfast, try the scrambled eggs on a croissant with a side of fruit. For lunch good choices include the chili, the vegetable lasagna, or one of the interesting combo sandwiches. The coffee is delicious at any time of the day. > 97–99 Main St., tel. 631/283–8900. AE, MC, V. No dinner. **$–$$**

John Duck Jr. The restaurant, in a converted farmhouse on a terraced hill, has been a family business for more than a century. It has five dining rooms, one of which is a glassed-in porch. Local produce is key, as are seafood and steak dishes. The roast Long Island duckling is a good bet. Sunday brunch is available, as is a children's menu. > 15 Prospect St., tel. 631/283–0311. AE, D, DC, MC, V. Closed Mon. **$$–$$$**

La Parmigiana Everyone seems to love this family-style place for its "red-sauce" Italian menu, its huge portions, and its reasonable prices. Spaghetti *celestino* (with tomato-cream sauce) and prosciutto with tomato and basil are favorites. Be prepared for a wait on summer weekends. > 44–48 Hampton Rd., tel. 631/283–8030. AE, MC, V. Closed Mon. **$–$$**

Le Chef It's a warm, welcoming, busy little bistro that serves, appropriately, mainly French food. Standouts include rack of lamb and lobster with a tomato-cognac cream sauce. All meals are prix fixe. > 75 Jobs La., tel. 631/283–8581. AE, MC, V. **$$$**

Lobster Inn This crowded, family-friendly, seafood restaurant was once a marina and boat shop. It's still nautical and rustic—the perfect place to dine on Manhattan clam chowder, lobster, and mussels. There's also a salad bar. > 162 Inlet Rd., tel. 631/283–1525. Reservations not accepted. AE, D, DC, MC, V. Closed Dec.–mid-Feb. **$$$–$$$$**

Meson Ole Tuck into a reasonably priced meal of chicken fajitas, rice and beans, or spicy seafood tacos. Wash it all down with a pitcher of margaritas. > 1746 North Hwy., tel. 631/283–8574. Reservations not accepted. AE, D, DC, MC, V. **$–$$**

Mt. Fuji You can dine in a Japanese-style booth with your shoes off, or keep them on while you sit at the restful central sushi bar, perhaps with a plate of California rolls and miso soup. The fare includes sukiyaki and tempura dishes as well as such classic sushi and sashimi as sweet-water shrimp, fluke, and sea urchin. The service is very attentive. > 1678 North Hwy., tel. 631/287–1700. AE, DC, MC, V. **$–$$**

Red Bar Brasserie It's a romantic, 1930s roadhouse, whose wonderful casement windows are lined with candle sconces. Grilled salmon with local corn or grilled tuna with steamed baby bok choy are good choices. The social scene is lively here on summer nights. > 210 Hampton Rd., tel. 631/283–0704. AE, MC, V. Closed Tues. No lunch. **$$$–$$$$**

Savanna's The building, which is just steps from the train depot, was originally the Southampton Village Hall. Its dining room has wainscoting, ceiling fans, and lots of candlelight. You can also eat on the patio, though tables there are hard to snag. Wood-oven-roasted Long Island duckling, miso-glazed monkfish with soba noodles, and spinach fettuccine with beef tenderloin are all noteworthy. The banana pie is sublime. There's brunch on weekends. > 268 Elm St., tel. 631/283–0202. AE, D, DC, MC, V. Closed Mon. and Tues. Oct.–Apr. No lunch weekdays. **$$–$$$$**

75 Main The interior of this old clapboard building in the middle of town is light and airy. Dishes have international (mostly Asian) twists and may include duck-and-vegetable spring rolls with tamarind barbecue sauce and jicama slaw or grilled Nova Scotia salmon served over Beluga lentils with Swiss chard and red-onion marmalade. There's a weekend brunch as well as a menu for kids. The bar gets busy after 11 PM on Friday and Saturday thanks to a DJ and a crowd that likes to dance. > 75 Main St., tel. 631/283–7575. AE, MC, V. **$$–$$$**

Sip 'n Soda This retro luncheonette serves breakfast, lunch, and dinner seven days a week. The menu is full of the usual casual fare: burgers, sandwiches, omelets, salads, and ice cream. > 40 Hampton Rd., tel. 631/283–9752. Reservations not accepted. No credit cards. **¢**

Southampton Publick House This family-friendly restaurant's microbrews and flavored ales go well with its burgers, clam fritters, beer-battered shrimp, crab cakes, steak sandwiches, and pastas. This is a great place to grab an Oyster Stout or a Scottish ale and take in a televised sporting event on a Sunday afternoon. > 40 Bowden Sq., tel. 631/283–2800. Reservations not accepted. AE, MC, V. **$$–$$$**

WHAT'S NEARBY

Almond Classic Parisian bistro–style food is the norm at this cozy spot about eight minutes north of Southampton Village. The flounder on a bed of spinach served in its own tureen is sublime, as is the striped bass Provençal. Surprisingly fair prices and friendly service add to Almond's appeal. > 1970 Montauk Hwy., Bridgehampton, tel. 631/537–8885. AE, MC, V. **$$**

Mirko's Shrimp and pork dishes—as well as the chef's sauces—are considered the specialties of this quiet, intimate restaurant. Calamari may come pan seared with a sauce of lemon, garlic, and sherry. You can dine inside or out on the terrace. > Water Mill Sq., Water Mill, tel. 631/726–4444. Reservations essential. AE, DC, MC, V. **$$–$$$$**

Oakland's Restaurant and Marina Unmatched marina views and an open-air bar attract crowds in summer. Although offerings and preparations vary, the emphasis is on shrimp, lobster, and local fish. > 365 Dune Rd., Hampton Bays, tel. 631/728–6900. Reservations not accepted. AE, DC, MC, V. **$$–$$$$**

Q, a Thai Bistro Inventive Thai cuisine and nightly Asian-fusion specials are the draws at this Noyac spot. A stylish cocktail lounge and a patio encourage you to linger here. > 129 Noyac Rd., North Sea, tel. 631/204–0007. Reservations essential. AE, MC, V. Closed Tues. and Dec.–Mar. No lunch. **$$–$$$$**

Restaurant at the Inn at Quogue The dining room of this romantic dining spot has a hint of the antebellum South about it. The chef is known for such innovative dishes as sour apple and Gorgonzola salad, seared ahi tuna, and tangy lemon-lobster risotto. > 47–52 Quogue St., Quogue, tel. 631/653–6560. Reservations essential. AE, D, MC, V. **$$–$$$$**

ESSENTIALS

Getting Here

The best way to explore the Southampton area is by car. A few of the Southampton lodging properties are about a mile or so away from the beach, so you might be able to get a lot out of your stay here even without car. The village itself is walkable, with many shops and restaurants clustered together. Travel by train allows you to skip traffic troubles, but you more than likely will need to call a cab after you arrive in Southampton. Buses are another option, but you won't avoid Long Island traffic with this mode of transport.

BY BUS

Two major bus lines serve the Hamptons all year, dropping off in Southampton as well as Westhampton, Hampton Bays, East Quogue, Quogue, and other points east. The Hampton Jitney, a coach line that travels from Manhattan's East Side to the Hamptons, has reclining seats, a bathroom, and free beverages. It leaves from four points between 40th and 86th streets; on the return it drops off mostly on the East Side but some routes stop on the Upper West Side if requested. Depending on the season, six to nine trips are made daily, taking 2½ to 3 hours. The one-way peak fare is $27. Reservations are required. Bringing a bike costs an extra $10.

The Hampton Luxury Liner also provides service from the city to the Hamptons. These buses have 21 leather reclining seats, carpeting, upholstery, and a bathroom, and offer drinks and snacks. They depart from five points between 40th and 86th streets on the East Side. The trip to Southampton takes 2½ to 3 hours and costs $37 one-way at peak times. Reservations are required. *LINES* **Hampton Jitney** > Tel. 631/283–4600 or 800/936–0440, www.hamptonjitney.com. **Hampton Luxury Liner** > Tel. 631/537–5800, www.hamptonluxuryliner.com.

BY CAR

Driving time ranges from two hours in ideal conditions to three hours or more in traffic. Heavy traffic is mostly unavoidable if you leave the city on Friday afternoon or evening or if you return on Sunday afternoon or evening. Long Island has several west–east routes: the Long Island Expressway (I–495), the Southern State Parkway, and the Northern State Parkway. Depending on traffic, you may want to use more than one of these. The LIE is the most straightforward way to go. Taking the Queens-Midtown Tunnel out of Manhattan puts you right on the expressway. If you drive with at least one other person, you can travel in the high-occupancy-vehicle (HOV) lane.

Take the LIE to Exit 70 (Manorville) and head south to Route 27, on which you proceed eastward. (If Exit 70 looks backed up, take Exit 71 to Route 24 through Flanders instead and pick up Route 27 in Hampton Bays.) The road narrows to two lanes in Southampton. Take North Sea Road south to the village center.

Rates at most lodgings in the area include parking. When you're driving elsewhere, read village parking signs carefully—some spaces allow parking only for one or two hours.

BY TRAIN

Long Island Rail Road trains leave for Southampton at least four times a day from Pennsylvania Station in Manhattan and the Flatbush Avenue Station in

Brooklyn. Trains require transfer at Jamaica Station, in Queens. The trip takes about 2½ hours; the fare is $19 one-way during peak travel times. Bicycles are allowed with a permit ($5 annual fee); applications are available on the LIRR Web site. In summer the LIRR offers Hamptons Reserve service (aka "the Cannonball"); these express trains leave from Penn Station and have reserved seats and bar and snack service. The fare is $28 one-way during peak travel times.

LINES **Long Island Rail Road** > Tel. 718/217–5477 or 631/231–5477, www.lirr.org.
STATIONS **Southampton** > N. Sea Rd. and Prospect St., 1 mi north of Montauk Hwy., no phone, www.lirr.org.

Visitor Information

Hamptonstravelguide.com is a comprehensive Web site administered by the chambers of commerce from all of the East End's towns.

CONTACTS **Southampton Chamber of Commerce** > 72 Main St., Southampton 11968, tel. 631/283–0402, www.southamptonchamber.com.

Montauk

120 mi east of New York City

14

Revised by Ann Hammerle

A LONG STRETCH OF ROAD SEPARATES MONTAUK, on Long Island's eastern tip, from the Hamptons, and as you roll into the small seaside village you notice immediately that here is a place apart in other respects as well. Surrounded by water on three sides, Montauk is known for its distinct natural beauty. In summer the fragrance of warm honeysuckle and wild beach roses blends with the ocean air. The spectacular undeveloped beaches and parks attract surfers and hikers, and the waters are superb for fishing.

Route 27, the main artery across the South Fork, is the quickest way to Montauk; for a more scenic ride, veer onto the hilly Old Montauk Highway, where each rise in the road affords a glimpse of the Atlantic Ocean and is promptly followed by a sharp dip (known locally as a "tummy-taker").

Continue east past the village center and you arrive at land's end, where the Montauk Lighthouse, commissioned by President George Washington in 1792 and the oldest operating lighthouse in the state, perches on a rocky bluff overlooking the sea. It's here, in the 724-acre Montauk Point State Park, surrounded by ocean and craggy coastline, that you find the finest surf casting, naturalist-led seal walks, the informative Montauk Point Lighthouse Museum, and a myriad of places to relax and contemplate the view.

More than 50 hotels, inns, and guest houses, along with many top-notch restaurants and a sprinkling of shops, are concentrated in two distinct sections of Montauk—the village center, including Old Montauk Highway, and the harbor area, reached by following either West Lake Drive or Edgemere Street to the end. Most lodgings and eateries here are family-friendly, and you can leave your heels and neckties at home.

The harbor is home to the local fishing fleet as well as to dozens of party, charter, and whale-watching boats, available daily for hire. Take a stroll around the docks between 4 and 5 in the afternoon and you see fishing boats arriving with their catch of the day—some of it bound for local restaurants.

Between the harbor area and the village center is Montauk Downs State Park, with one of the top public golf courses in the country. The park is off West Lake Drive, from which you have breathtaking views of Lake Montauk to the east and Gardiner's Island to the northwest.

Just west of Montauk is Amagansett. Its name is a Native American word meaning "place of good water," and from its earliest beginnings, Amagansett's tranquil setting was perfectly suited to fishing and offshore whaling. If you choose to stay at a lodging property here and have a car, you can easily make forays into Montauk as well as East Hampton, a few miles west.

WHAT TO SEE & DO

Deep Hollow Ranch Deep Hollow claims to be the oldest working cattle ranch in the country. The sunset beach rides are unforgettable, as are the trail rides through Theodore Roosevelt County Park, just across the road. Pony rides and a petting zoo keep little ones occupied. English and Western riding lessons, outdoor barbecue dinners and bonfires, wagon tours, and historical re-enactments are among the special things to do and see here. > Montauk Hwy. across from Theodore Roosevelt County Park, tel. 631/668–2744, fax 631/668–3902, www.deephollowranch.com. Free. June–early Sept., daily 9–6; early Sept.–May, daily 9–5.

Fort Pond Bay Park Sitting at the western end of Fort Pond Bay, near Rocky Point, this spot is perfect for picnics and beachcombing, but not suitable for swimming. Comb the shore for shells or walk to the end of the sturdy pier and do some fishing. There are shorefront trails that tie into the Hither Woods trail system, a parking lot (follow Navy Road to the end) and portable bathrooms. A resident permit is required for parking. > End of Navy Rd., off 2nd House Rd. Free. Daily dawn–dusk.

Gin Beach On Block Island Sound, this beach east of the jetty has calm water and sparkling clean sand—perfect for families with little ones. You can watch the boats go in and out of the harbor all day. There are public rest rooms, a snack trailer, and outdoor showers. A resident permit is required for parking. > End of East Lake Dr., off Montauk Hwy., tel. 631/324–2417. Free. Daily, dawn–dusk. Lifeguards on duty late May–June 20, weekends 9–6; June 21–early Sept., daily 9–6; early Sept.–late Sept., weekends 9–6.

Hither Hills State Park This 1,755-acre park, with rolling moors and forests of pitch pine and scrub oak, encompasses a campground, picnic areas, a playground, general store, miles of ocean beach, and hiking and bicycling trails. An unusual natural phenomenon in the park is known as the Walking Dunes, named so because strong northwest winds cause the 80-foot dunes to travel 3 or more feet per year. The $\frac{3}{4}$-mi loop through cranberry bogs, beaches, and pine forests submerged in sand is not too far for little feet to travel, and most people find the natural lore of the area fascinating. Pick up the descriptive brochure, which includes trail maps, at the park office or the chamber of commerce before you set out. > Old Montauk Hwy., tel. 631/668–2554, 800/456–2267 camping reservations, http://nysparks.state.ny.us. $8 per vehicle late May–early Sept., free early Sept.–late May. Daily dawn–dusk.

Kirk Park Beach This sandy, clean, protected ocean beach has a picnic area across the street; public rest rooms are in the parking lot. > Montauk Hwy. near IGA supermarket, tel. 631/324–2417. $10 per vehicle. Daily, dawn–dusk. Lifeguards on duty late May–June 20, weekends 9–6; June 21–early Sept., daily 9–6; early Sept.–late Sept., weekends 9–6.

Montauk Downs State Park An 18-hole Robert Trent Jones–designed championship-length golf course is the main draw at this park. The park also has six well-maintained Har-Tru tennis courts ($16 per hour on weekends), a locker room, showers, a pro shop, a snack bar, a restaurant, a children's pool, and a large, sparkling recreational pool surrounded by comfortable lounge chairs. > 50 S. Fairview Ave., tel. 631/668–3781, http://nysparks.state.ny.us. Free, pool $3.50. Daily dawn–dusk.

Montauk Point State Park About 6 mi east of the village, the 724 acres of rocky shoreline, grassy dunes, and bayberry-covered moors surrounding Montauk's lighthouse have been so well protected that you might feel as if you're standing at an undiscovered frontier of pounding surf and pristine land. Frequently, a wild riptide (this is not a swimming beach) sets up perfect conditions for exciting surf casting. If you love fishing, this is one of the best spots in Montauk to try your luck at catching the "big one." A fishing permit isn't necessary. Other activities include hiking (get a trail map from the info booth), bird-watching, and beachcombing. Every weekend from early December to late April, weather permitting, naturalists lead two- to three–hour **Guided Seal Walks** (tel. 631/668–5000) in Montauk Point State Park. Hikers are guided to the haul-out sites along the north beach to observe seals and winter birds, and to learn about marine geology. Tours are $5; call for tour times.

The **Montauk Lighthouse** (tel. 631/668–2544, www.montauklighthouse.com), the oldest lighthouse still in operation in the state and a well-known Long Island landmark, is perched solidly on a bluff in Montauk Point State Park. President George Washington signed an order to build the lighthouse in 1792. Climb the 137 iron steps to the top for spectacular views of the Atlantic Ocean and, to the northeast, Block Island, or take a moment to ponder the touching memorial to local fisherman who were lost at sea. The museum, in the former light keeper's quarters, displays a wealth of photos and artifacts. > East end of Rte. 27, tel. 631/668–3781, http://nysparks.state.ny.us. $6 per vehicle. Daily dawn–dusk. Lighthouse Mar.–late May and mid-Oct.–Nov., weekends 10:30–4:30; late May–early Sept., daily 10:30–6; early Sept.–mid-Oct., weekdays 10:30–4:30, weekends 10:30–5.

Puff and Putt Family Fun Center On a narrow strip of land between Montauk Highway and sparkling Fort Pond, this complex encompasses a miniature-golf course, video-game room, and boat-rental center. Boats for hire include Sunfish, pedal boats, canoes, rowboats, and kayaks. The waters of Fort Pond are usually quite calm, and sightings of local waterfowl are common. > Montauk Hwy. across from IGA supermarket, tel. 631/668–4473. Miniature golf $5, boat rentals $13–$22. July–Aug., daily; Sept.–June, weekends. Hrs vary; call ahead.

Second House Museum The second house built in Montauk, this 1700s farmhouse holds a collection of early photos and artifacts that depict the era when it was surrounded by pastures, sheep, and cattle. Now enveloped by gorgeous lawns, rose gardens and hydrangeas, it is the site of daily tours and two well-attended summer craft fairs. > Montauk Hwy. at 2nd House Rd., tel. 631/668–5340. $2. Memorial Day–Columbus Day, Thurs.–Tues. 10–4.

Shadmoor State Park With 99 acres of steep bluffs, sand beach, rare plants, and hiking trails, this gem of a park is a quiet place to walk, think, and take in the view. Parking is at the entrance, just east of Montauk center on Montauk Highway (look for the sign). > Montauk Hwy. east of Montauk center, tel. 631/324–2417. Free. Daily dawn–dusk.

Theodore Roosevelt County Park Miles of hiking and horseback-riding trails vein this 1,126-acre park, which also includes an exhibit about the Spanish–American War. At the close of the war in Cuba, Teddy Roosevelt and his band of Roughriders and 28,000 soldiers came to this site for a long season of rest and recovery after their ordeal. The museum is a memorial to their courage and tenacity. The gift shop sells related books and souvenirs. In July and August, the annual Hamptons Shakespeare Festival takes place in the park. Fishing, outer-beach camping (self-contained trailers only), picnicking, and bird-watching. > Off Montauk Hwy. 3 mi east of Montauk Village, tel. 631/852–7878. Free. Daily dawn–dusk; museum and gift shop, daily 10–5.

AMAGANSETT

Atlantic Avenue Beach Swimming and looking for seashells are popular pastimes at this public beach. It's convenient to the center of Amagansett, and there are food concessions right on the sand, making it possible to stay all day. A lifeguard is on duty daily 10–5. An East Hampton parking permit is required on weekends and holidays but during the week you can pay to park without a permit. > South end of Atlantic Ave. off Bluff Rd., tel. 631/324–2417. $10 per vehicle weekdays; parking permit required weekends and holidays. Memorial Day–Labor Day.

Miss Amelia's Cottage and Roy Lester Carriage Museum Built in 1725 and full of beautifully preserved Colonial antiques—including a collection of rare Dominy furniture—the museum contains artifacts and exhibits illustrating Amagansett life from the Colonial period through the 20th century. On summer weekends, pony rides are given on the museum lawn from 10 to 2, and twice during the season there are huge antiques sales full of local treasures. In barn to the rear of the property is the Roy Lester Carriage Museum, which displays locally made horse-drawn carriages. > Main St., tel. 631/267–3020. $2, pony rides $5. Late May–early Sept., Fri.–Sun. 10–4.

Stephen Talkhouse You can hear live music, including many well-known acts, nearly every summer night and most off-season weekend nights, at this little house. With two bars, a small stage, and a dance floor, it's usually a laid-back scene but can get packed on the weekends. Cover charges start at around $20. > 161 Main St., tel. 631/267–3117. Doors open 1 hr prior to showtime. Box office May–Sept., 11–5 on show days; Oct.–Apr., call ahead.

Tours

Montauk Trolley This old-fashioned trolley traverses the sights of Montauk—the village, the lighthouse, the harbor, and several parks. The 90-min tours ($15) are given Memorial Day to Columbus Day, with five round-trips daily. The friendly tour director answers questions and gives interesting observations. Same-day ticket holders are allowed all-day boarding privileges (15 stops), which makes this a great way to get around. Pick up a map and schedule at the chamber of commerce or at any of several businesses in town. Tours begin at the chamber of commerce. > Main St. across from village green, Montauk, tel. 631/668–6868, www.montaukchamber.com.

White Swan Harbor Cruises You can take an hour-long guided tour of Montauk Harbor in the shade of a white-canopied boat. Marine-life tours are given daily at 9 AM, and sunset cruises take place each evening. Cruises are $12. > Gosman's Dock, Montauk Harbor, Montauk, tel. 631/668–7878. Memorial Day–Labor Day; guided tours every hr.

Sports

FISHING

Excellent surf casting (at Montauk Point or along the ocean beaches) and inshore or offshore trips on party and charter boats make Montauk one of the premier fishing destinations on the East Coast. A trip to the chamber of commerce or to the Harbor area (off West Lake Drive) yields the information you need to choose from the many fishing options.

Breakaway This 42-foot Downeaster can take up to six people inshore fishing for striped bass and fluke, or offshore for tuna and shark. Make reservations several months in advance for summer trips. > Montauk Harbor, Montauk, tel. 631/668–2914.

Lazy Bones Half-day fishing for up to 40 people take place on this popular party boat. Sailing spring, summer, and fall, you can catch flounder, fluke, striped bass, and bluefish, according to season. Book as far in advance as possible for summer trips, although on occassion, same-day bookings are available. > Montauk Harbor, Montauk, tel. 631/668–5671.

Oh Brother Choose from deep-sea fishing or a half-day inshore haul for bass and bluefish. Families are welcome. Summer trips fill up fast; make reservations as far in advance as possible. > Montauk Harbor, Montauk, tel. 631/668–2707.

Viking Fleet Enjoy half- or full-day offshore or night-fishing trips aboard Viking party boats. Reserve as early as possible for summer excursions. > Montauk Harbor, Montauk, tel. 631/668–5700, www.vikingfleet.com.

EQUIPMENT **Freddie's Bait and Tackle** > S. Edgemere Ave. south of the Plaza, Montauk, tel. 631/668–5520, www.freddiesofmontauk.com. **Johnny's Tackle Shop** > Montauk Hwy., Montauk, tel. 631/668–2940. **Star Island Yacht Club** > Star Island Rd., Montauk, tel. 631/668–5052, www.starislandyc.com.

GOLF

Montauk Downs State Park The park's 18-hole par-72 golf course, designed by Robert Trent Jones, is one of the top public courses in the nation. Club and cart rentals, instruction, a driving range, a putting green, and a restaurant are available. Call at least one week in advance during summer months to reserve tee times. The Downs is off West Lake Drive, near the harbor. > 50 S. Fairview Ave., Montauk, tel. 631/668–5000, 631/668–1234 reservations. Greens fee $30 weekdays, $36 weekends for NY residents; $60 weekdays, $72 weekends nonresidents.

HIKING

Hither Hills State Park Miles of hiking trails meander through this peaceful, beautiful park. On the western edge of the park you can wander the Walking Dunes trail, a ¾-mi loop through some of the most interesting local ecology around. At the eastern edge, the trails connect to Fort Pond Bay Park. Pick up a map at the campground office before you go. > Old Montauk Hwy., Montauk, tel. 631/668–2554. $8 per vehicle late May–early Sept., free early Sept.–late May. Daily dawn–dusk.

Montauk Point State Park This 724-acre preserve with miles of trails surrounds Montauk Lighthouse. The northern paths lead you through the woods or along the rocky beach to the seal haul-out sites, whereas the southern paths lead through the moors and along the bluffs for spectacular ocean views. > Montauk Point, at end of Rte. 27 E, Montauk, tel. 631/668–3781, http://nysparks.state.ny.us. $7 per vehicle. Daily dawn–dusk.

SURFING

The Air and Speed Board Shop is the place to reserve group or private lessons.

Ditch Plains This is the place to be if you want to surf in Montauk. It's an insider's spot, but the locals welcome newcomers who have a modicum of surfing etiquette. Grab a wrap sandwich or an iced coffee at Lily's Ditch Witch wagon and enjoy the waves, the beach, the sun, and the scene. You need a town parking permit or temporary beach sticker to park here. Take Montauk Highway through town, make a right on Ditch Plains Road, and follow it to the beach. > Ditch Plains Rd. Beach free, parking permit required.

EQUIPMENT **Air and Speed Board Shop** > 7 The Plaza, Montauk, tel. 631/668–0356. **Plaza Sports** > 716 Main St., Montauk, tel. 631/668–9300.

Shopping

Downtown Montauk has an eclectic mix of shops that sell books, clothing, jewelry, antiques, home furnishings, and gifts. At a similar but more limited grouping of shops in the harbor area, you can find Irish knits, pricier clothing shops, and a great toy store.

At Home en Provence European-style home accessories, quilts, clothing, jewelry, and linens are available here. > 625 Tuthill Rd., Fort Pond Bay, tel. 631/668–4808. Closed Mon.–Wed. Nov.–Apr.

The Book Shoppe Small, charming, and friendly, this shop has a good selection of books in all categories, including new releases. > The Plaza South, tel. 631/668–4599. Closed Tues. Nov.–Apr.

Captain Kid Toys Fabulous toys, colorful trinkets, and artistic and educational kits fill this harborside shop. > Gosman's Dock, Montauk Harbor, tel. 631/668–4482. Closed weekdays Sept.–May.

Irish Country Loft Stunning Irish knits, children's kilts, and collectible Mosse Pottery and linens abound at this captivating shop. > Gosman's Dock, Montauk Harbor, tel. 631/668–4964. Closed Dec.–Apr.

Seagrass Cove You can find handmade one-of-a-kind jewelry here, along with antique furniture and other unusual items. > Edgemere Rd., tel. 631/668–8886. Closed Tues. and Wed. Nov.–Apr.

Strawberry Fields Flowers and Gifts Walk into this shop and your senses are filled with the fragrance of flowers and spice and a riot of color. Flowers, baskets, plants, unusual gifts, candles, and wrought-iron wall hangings are just the beginning. > Main St., tel. 631/668–6279.

Willow Beautifully designed and crafted handmade quilts, as well as outfits for American Girl dolls, are made here. The assortment of unusual gifts include garden ornaments, linens, stationery, and candles. > 41 The Plaza, tel. 631/668–0772. Closed Tues.–Wed. in Nov.–Apr.

Save the Date

JUNE

Blessing of the Fleet Witness the blessing of the local fishing fleet and take a trip out on one of the boats at this annual, multidenominational ceremony. Or just join crowd on the docks for daylong festivities. > Montauk Harbor, Montauk, tel. 631/668–2428, www.montaukchamber.com.

AUGUST

Hamptons Shakespeare Festival Held in late summer under the stars, this annual festival presents one of the Bard's plays, performed by a professional company in the open-air theater. Some seating is available, but feel free to bring a blanket and picnic and watch from the lawn. > Theodore Roosevelt County Park, off Montauk Hwy. 3 mi east of Montauk Village, tel. 631/852–7878.

OCTOBER

Montauk Chamber of Commerce Annual Fall Festival A clam chowder cook-off, a clam-shucking contest, hay and pony rides, Long Island wine tastings, pumpkin decorating, kids' art contests, music, and a boat raffle draw crowds to this popular autumn festival. > Montauk Hwy., Montauk, tel. 631/668–2428, www.montaukchamber.com.

WHERE TO STAY

Beachcomber Resort The four two-story buildings that make up this airy, modern resort overlook the ocean and are right across from the beach. Studio and apartment-style suites are clean and comfortable, with contemporary furnishings.

Complimentary beach stickers are provided. > 727 Old Montauk Hwy., 11954, tel. 631/668–2894, fax 631/668–3154, www.beachcomber-montauk.com. 88 suites. Kitchenettes, cable TV, in-room VCRs, tennis court, pool, sauna, beach, laundry facilities, business services, no-smoking rooms. Closed Nov.–Mar. AE, D, DC, MC, V. $$$$

Burcliffe by the Sea Peace and quiet are the hallmarks of this beautifully landscaped property only 1 mi from town and right across from the beach. The small inn has studio efficiencies with alcove bedrooms and one- and two-bedroom cottages; some have ocean views and three have fireplaces. Beach permits are provided. > 397 Old Montauk Hwy., 11954, tel. 631/668–2880, www.montauklife.com. 4 efficiencies, 3 cottages. Picnic area, kitchenettes, cable TV, beach, some pets allowed, no-smoking rooms. MC, V. $$–$$$$

Culloden House Motel A three-minute walk from famous Gosman's Dock and the Harbor area, the modern accommodations here are sparkling clean, reasonable, and include two handicapped-accessible units. Barbecues are on-site, and beach passes are available. > 540 W. Lake Dr., 11954, tel. 631/668–9293, fax 631/668–3228, www.montauklife.com. 29 rooms. Some kitchenettes, refrigerators, cable TV, no-smoking rooms. AE, MC, V. Closed late Oct.–mid-May. $–$$

Gurney's Inn Resort and Spa Long popular for its fabulous location on a bluff overlooking 1,000 feet of private ocean beach, Gurney's has become even more famous in recent years for its European-style spa. The large, luxurious rooms and suites all have ocean views. > 290 Old Montauk Hwy., 11954, tel. 631/668–2345, fax 631/668–3576, www.gurneys-inn.com. 100 rooms, 4 suites, 5 cottages. 2 restaurants, room service, refrigerators, cable TV, pool, gym, health club, hair salon, hot tub, sauna, spa, steam room, beach, bar, business services, no-smoking rooms. AE, D, DC, MC, V. MAP. $$$$

Hartman's Briney Breezes Motel This two-story motel is steps from the dunes and the beach, just across the two-lane Old Montauk Highway. Bright, clean, one- and two-room suites all have full kitchens and ocean views. You can walk the seaside path to town and restaurants. Beach passes are provided. > 693 Old Montauk Hwy., 11954, tel. 631/668–2290, fax 631/668–2987, www.brineybreezes.com. 18 studios, 64 1-bdrm suites. Kitchens, microwaves, refrigerators, cable TV, pool, no-smoking rooms. MC, V. Closed mid-Nov.–early Mar. $$$$

Montauk Manor The sprawling, family-friendly "American castle" has views of the bay and myriad amenities. The Tudor-style Manor, built in 1927 as a luxury resort, today is a condominium, so each unit is decorated differently. Most units are bright and have contemporary furnishings; some have loft bedrooms with skylights, patios, or balconies. Jitneys take to you to the beaches, and beach passes are available. > 236 Edgemere St., 11954, tel. 631/668–4400, fax 631/668–3535, www.montaukmanor.com. 18 studios, 81 suites. Restaurant, picnic area, cable TV, putting green, 3 tennis courts, 2 pools (1 indoor) pool, gym, hot tub, sauna, basketball, boccie, shuffleboard, squash, meeting rooms, no-smoking rooms. AE, D, DC, MC, V. $$$$

Montauk Yacht Club, Resort and Marina The plush resort on Star Island, in Montauk Harbor, has its own mini replica of the Montauk Lighthouse as well as a 232-slip marina. Rooms, contemporary and bright, have floor-to-ceiling windows and private terraces. The waterfront villas contain 23 oversize rooms. > 32 Star Island Rd., 11954, tel. 631/668–3100, 800/832–4200 in NY, fax 631/668–6181, www.montaukyachtclub.com. 107 rooms. 2 restaurants, room service, in-room data ports, cable TV, 3 tennis courts, 3 pools (1 indoor), health club, spa, boating, marina, 2 bars, business services, no-smoking rooms. AE, DC, MC, V. Closed mid-Dec.–early Mar. $$–$$$$

Ocean Resort Inn Hanging baskets of flowers and picnic tables on the deck invite you to relax and enjoy the surroundings at this in-town two-story inn, a half-block from the ocean. Some rooms have whirlpool baths and more than one bathroom; all are well-maintained and clean. Complimentary beach permits are given. > 95 S. Embassy St., 11954, tel. 631/668–2300, fax 631/668–4075, www.oceanresortinn.com. 17 rooms. Picnic area, some in-room hot tubs, microwaves, refrigerators, cable TV, no-smoking rooms. AE, MC, V. Closed Nov.–early Mar. **$$–$$$**

Panoramic View Tucked into a treed hillside that rises directly from the beach, this hotel complex has landscaped lawns and flower gardens. Rooms have picture windows, to frame the ocean views, and are wood-paneled and fully carpeted. The beach houses have wood floors, a fireplace, a porch and patio, and two bathrooms. > 272 Old Montauk Hwy., 11954, tel. 631/668–3000, fax 631/668–7870, www.panoramicview.com. 101 rooms, 14 suites, 3 beach houses. In-room data ports, kitchenettes, refrigerators, cable TV, pool, gym, beach, laundry facilities, business services, no-smoking rooms; no kids under 10. Closed mid-Nov.–mid-Apr. No credit cards. **$$$–$$$$**

Sunrise Guest House Small and romantic, this country home by the sea has an old-fashioned porch with rockers overlooking the ocean. Tables are garnished with wildflowers, and there's an outdoor hot tub. The common living-dining area has a fireplace. Rooms have hardwood floors and are done in soft vintage-floral prints. > 681 Old Montauk Hwy., 11954, tel. 631/668–7286, www.sunrisebnb.com. 4 rooms. Dining room, cable TV, outdoor hot tub; no kids under 12, no smoking. MC, V. CP. **$$**

Surf Club A cluster of low, gray-shingled buildings with one- and two-bedroom duplex apartments sits on 8½ beachfront acres within walking distance of the village. Each unit has a large, private terrace. The apartments are spacious and fully carpeted and have contemporary furnishings. > Surfside Ave. and S. Essex St. (Box 1174, 11954), tel. 631/668–3800, www.duneresorts.com. 92 apartments. Kitchenettes, cable TV, some in-room VCRs, tennis court, pool, sauna, beach, no-smoking rooms. MC, V. Closed mid-Nov.–mid-Apr. **$$$$**

Wavecrest Resort This modern complex was built on a rise, so that each room has an ocean view from its private terrace. Rooms are carpeted and have wood furniture. The resort is popular with couples and families because of its beach access and proximity to Hither Hills State Park. > Old Montauk Hwy. (Box 952, 11954), tel. 631/668–2141, fax 631/668–2337, www.wavecrestonocean.com. 65 rooms. Picnic area, kitchenettes, cable TV, in-room VCRs, indoor pool, beach, no-smoking rooms. AE, D, MC, V. Closed mid-Nov.–mid-Apr. **$$$$**

AMAGANSETT

Mill Garth Country Inn This two-story antiques-filled bed-and-breakfast is a mile from the beach and within walking distance of Amagansett restaurants and shops. Suites in the main house have living rooms and kitchenettes, and additional lodging is available in charming separate cottages. There's a lovely terrace, and guests receive complimentary beach-parking passes. > 23 Windmill La., 11930, tel. 631/267–3757. 2 rooms, 4 suites, 5 cottages. Picnic area, kitchenettes; no phones in some rooms, no TV in some rooms, no smoking. MC, V. **$$–$$$$**

Sea Crest on the Ocean Many of the one- and two-bedroom units at this family-friendly resort have direct beach access. Accommodations, furnished in neutral tones, are bright and airy and have dinette sets. The two-bedroom units are especially large. Barbecue pits allow you to grill on the dunes. > 2166 Montauk Hwy., 11930, tel. 631/267–3159, fax 631/267–6840, www.duneresorts.com. 6 studios, 70 suites. Picnic area, some kitchens, some kitchenettes, cable TV, 2 tennis courts, pool, beach, basketball, shuffleboard, laundry facilities, business services, no-smoking rooms. D, MC, V. **$$$$**

White Sands Resort Hotel The beach is steps away from this peaceful seaside hotel nestled between open ocean and gorgeous flower gardens. Uncluttered, simple rooms have private decks and lounge chairs; all have views of the ocean. > 28 Shore Rd., 11930, tel. 631/267–3350, fax 631/267–2728, www.whitesands-resort.com. 20 rooms. Fans, some kitchens, refrigerators, cable TV, beach; no smoking. MC, V. Closed mid-Oct.–mid-Apr. **$$–$$$$**

CAMPING

Hither Hills State Park The campsites in this popular park are just off a gorgeous, protected beach. They book up quickly, sometimes nearly a year in advance. The campground has a softball field and daily planned activities for the kids. The park has basketball, volleyball, tetherball, sportfishing, and hiking and biking trails. > Old Montauk Hwy., Montauk 11937, tel. 631/668–2554 or 800/456–2267. 165 sites. Flush toilets, dump station, laundry facilities, showers, fire grates, picnic tables, public telephone, general store, playground. Reservations essential, www.reserveamerica.com. MC, V. Closed mid-Nov.–mid-Apr. ¢

WHERE TO EAT

Dave's Grill Unpretentious yet stylish, Dave's is at the Montauk fishing docks next to Salivar's. Indoor seating is in a small, candlelit room or around a cozy adjoining bar; outdoor seating is on a deck next to the harbor. Come for succulent steaks and contemporary dishes prepared with fresh local seafood. This is a popular spot with locals, and there's always a wait for a table. > 468 W. Lake Dr., tel. 631/668–9190. Reservations not accepted. MC, V. Closed Nov.–Apr. No lunch. **$$–$$$**

The Dock Seafaring-related antiques festoon the rustic wood walls and ceiling of Montauk's favorite dockside restaurant. Great nachos, burgers, fish sandwiches, specials, and a cozy, local bar scene are hallmarks here. > Montauk Harbor near the town dock, tel. 631/668–9778. Reservations not accepted. No credit cards. Closed Dec.–Mar. **$–$$**

East by Northeast Sophisticated and soothing, this restaurant has an earth-toned, Asian decor. Entrées are served family-style, meant to be shared. Try the crisp duck tacos or the seared sesame tuna as you settle back into comfortable chairs or banquettes and watch the sun set over Fort Pond. The service is attentive, the bar cosmopolitan. > 51 Edgemere Rd., tel. 631/668–2872. Reservations essential. AE, MC, V. **$–$$$**

Gianni's The best brick-oven pizza and focaccia sandwiches in Montauk are served here. Try the special salads; margherita pizza, with basil and garlic; grandma pizza, a square, thin-crust pizza with fresh mozzarella, plum tomato sauce, and basil; or Sicilian pizza, with caramelized onions and sausage. There's no seating here; only takeout and delivery. > 54 S. Erie Ave., tel. 631/668–8888. No credit cards. ¢–**$$**

Harvest on Fort Pond The glass-enclosed dining room of this restaurant affords stunning views of sunsets on Fort Pond. There's family-style service—entrées are huge and serve at least two. Try the calamari salad and the sizzling whole red snapper. You can dine outside in the herb garden in summer. > 11 S. Emory St., tel. 631/668–5574. Reservations essential. AE, MC, V. **$$–$$$**

Inlet Cafe at Gosman's Dock The view from the waterside tables and sushi bar is so mesmerizing that you may forget to bite into the sushi or succulent local lobster on your plate. There are four Gosman's eating establishments on the dock; this one serves up fresh seafood right off the boat. > Gosman's Dock, Montauk Harbor, tel. 631/668–2549. Reservations not accepted. AE, MC, V. Closed mid-Oct.–mid-May. $–$$$

John's Pancake House Omelets and delicious pancakes are served all day at this bustling Main Street restaurant, along with hearty homemade soups and chowders, thick burgers and shakes, spicy chicken-salad wraps, and fried ice cream. Come at off-hours especially on weekends, because there's always a line. Breakfast service begins at 6:15. > Main St., tel. 631/668–2383. Reservations not accepted. No credit cards. No dinner. ¢–$

Joni's Rejuvenating fresh-squeezed juices and smoothies, daily special breakfasts and lunches, exotic wraps—such as the Zen Rabbit, with mixed greens, avocado, goat cheese, tomato, onion, and calamata olives on a spinach tortilla—salads, and good coffee are available at this casual place. Eat at the outdoor picnic tables or bring your meal to the beach or hotel. > 9 S. Edison St., tel. 631/668–3663. Reservations not accepted. MC, V. ¢–$

Salivar's This dockside eatery has classic diner food with a lot of local flavor. You can have breakfast with local fishermen at 4 AM, grab a bite of lunch while you watch the boats sail in and out of the harbor, or stop by in the evening for an ice-cold beer under the watchful eye of the biggest great white shark ever caught. > 470 W. Lake Dr., tel. 631/668–2555. Reservations not accepted. No credit cards. No dinner Nov.–Apr. $–$$

Shagwong Tavern The specials at this local hangout next to Herb's Market change daily, but are straightforward, well-prepared dishes such as cedar-planked salmon, beer-battered fish-and-chips, and chicken saltimbocca. The bar scene makes the wait for a table on weekends bearable. > 774 Main St., tel. 631/668–3050. Reservations not accepted. AE, D, DC, MC, V. $$–$$$

Topside at Gosman's Dock Watch from your table on the upper deck as the boats sail in and out of the harbor during sunset—not a sight you'll soon forget. The cocktails are excellent, the fresh seafood and pasta are well prepared. > Gosman's Dock, Montauk Harbor, tel. 631/668–2549. Reservations not accepted. AE, MC, V. Closed mid-Oct.–mid-May. $–$$$

AMAGANSETT

Lobster Roll This local institution (affectionately known as "Lunch"), along the no-man's land between Amagansett and Montauk, is the proverbial shanty by the sea. Its booths and outdoor picnic tables are filled with people coming and going from the beach. They come for the fresh lobster rolls, fish-and-chips, puffers (blowfish), and mouthwatering grilled tuna and swordfish. > 1980 Montauk Hwy., tel. 631/267–3740. MC, V. Closed Nov.–Apr. $–$$$

Napeague Stretch You might feel as if you are standing on the deck of a fabulous yacht inside this sleek restaurant with gleaming wooden floors and teak and white-canvas accents. The three-sided bar serves infused cocktails such as fresh strawberry margaritas and pineapple-rum punch. Everything about this restaurant is fresh, from the baby-spinach salad and the sesame-crusted tuna to the exquisite lobster salad, bouillabaisse, and fabulous steaks. Attentive service and an outdoor terrace with stunning northeast views round out your experience. > 2095 Montauk Hwy., tel. 631/267–6980. AE, MC, V. Closed Nov.–Mar. $–$$$

ESSENTIALS

Getting Here

Bus, train, or car are all easy and quick ways to get to Montauk if you travel outside of peak travel times. Once you have arrived, the best way to get around is by car, but walking (if you're staying in town), bicycling, and taking cabs or the trolley in summer are options. Local cab fares are reasonable.

BY BUS

Two major bus lines serve Montauk and other Hamptons points all year. The Hampton Jitney, a coach line that travels from Manhattan's East Side to the Hamptons, has reclining seats, a bathroom, and free beverages. It leaves several times daily from four points between 40th and 86th streets; on the return it drops off mostly on the East Side (some routes stop on the Upper West Side if requested). The trip takes about 3½ hours. The one-way peak fare is $27. Reservations are required. Bringing a bike costs an extra $10.

The Hampton Luxury Liner provides service from the city to Amagansett—you have to travel the last 10 mi to Montauk by cab or train. These buses have 21 leather reclining seats, carpeting, upholstery, and a bathroom, and offer drinks and snacks. They depart several times a day from five points between 40th and 86th streets on the East Side. The trip takes about 3½ hours and costs $37 one-way at peak times. Reservations are required.

LINES **Hampton Jitney** > Tel. 631/283–4600 or 800/936–0440, www.hamptonjitney.com. **Hampton Luxury Liner** > Tel. 631/537–5800, www.hamptonluxuryliner.com.

BY CAR

Traveling by car to Montauk is the quickest way to get there and gives you the freedom to explore the area, especially if you want to head to the lighthouse or other destinations outside the village. The Long Island Expressway (I–495) is the most straightforward way to go. The Queens-Midtown Tunnel puts you right on the LIE from Manhattan. If you have at least two people in the vehicle, you can travel in the high-occupancy-vehicle (HOV) lane. (If LIE traffic is bad, you may also want to consider using the Southern State or the Northern State parkways.) Take the LIE to Exit 70 (Manorville) and head south to Route 27 east, which you follow into Montauk. If Exit 70 looks backed up, take Exit 71 to Route 24 through Flanders and pick up Route 27 in Hampton Bays.

The 2½-hour trip can turn into 3 or 4 hours in heavy traffic, so avoid leaving the city on Friday afternoon or returning late Sunday afternoon or evening.

Most beaches require a town-parking sticker on your car (to the tune of $200 for nonresidents). Nearly all lodging places furnish guests with complimentary beach-parking passes, which are good at all beaches. Options, besides walking, bicycling, or taking a cab to the beach, include parking for a fee at Kirk Park Beach or Hither Hills State Park.

BY TRAIN

Long Island Rail Road trains leave for Montauk at least four times a day from Pennsylvania Station in Manhattan and the Flatbush Avenue Station in Brooklyn. All trains have transfers at Jamaica Station, in Queens. The trip takes about 3½ hours; the fare is $19 one-way during peak travel times. Bicycles are allowed with a permit ($5 annual fee); applications are available on the LIRR

Web site. In summer the LIRR offers Hamptons Reserve service (aka "the Cannonball"), express trains with reserved seats and bar and snack service.

The Montauk train station is less than a mile from town. Local cabs are usually waiting to take you to your destination.
LINES **Long Island Rail Road** > Tel. 718/217–5477 or 631/231–5477, www.lirr.org.
STATIONS **Montauk** > Edgemere St. and Firestone La., 1 mi north of Montauk Hwy., no phone, www.lirr.org.

Visitor Information

CONTACTS **Montauk Chamber of Commerce** > Main St. (Box 5029, Montauk 11954), tel. 631/668–2428, www.montaukchamber.com.

Sag Harbor & Shelter Island

Sag Harbor is about 100 mi east of New York City

15

By Heather Buchanan

ON THE NORTH COAST of Long Island's South Fork, Sag Harbor has a strong maritime flavor that largely stems from its history as a whaling port. The first white settlers arrived in the late 1600s, learned a thing or two about whaling from the resident Native Americans, and started sending out whaleboats in the mid-1700s. By the time the industry hit its peak, in the mid-1800s, Sag Harbor had become one of the world's busiest ports.

Sag Harbor's centuries'-old Main Street leads to the wharf where tall ships from around the world would arrive. Today, impressive sailboats and powerboats line the marina and bay.

Thanks to careful preservation, much of Sag Harbor's 18th- and 19th-century architecture remains intact, including Greek Revival houses once owned by whaling captains. Also abundant are early-colonists' homes as well as Victorian houses that were built for wealthy industrialists. The Sag Harbor Whaling Museum, itself in a spectacular mansion that had been built for a prominent shipowner, provides a glimpse back to the earlier era.

The village has long attracted the literary set (John Steinbeck and James Fenimore Cooper lived or wrote here at one point). Today many writers and artists make Sag Harbor their home, including E.L. Doctorow and Joe Pintauro, and the village is culturally blessed. Numerous galleries display paintings, sculpture, photography, and original glass creations. Local bookstores host frequent readings, the Bay Street Theater presents classic and original plays, and the Sag Harbor Cinema screens movies from around the world.

The sheer beauty of the sea and the quality of light on Long Island's East End attract nature enthusiasts as well as artists. Havens Beach and Long Beach are both pleasant, open stretches of sand on the bay, and the pristine ocean beaches of the Hamptons are a short drive away.

Summer is the high season here, and the village's bistros and inns book up. Make reservations far in advance, or consider a visit in autumn or spring, when the crowds thin. In winter, snow-blanketed lanes and frozen ponds can be a part of a wonderful break, and Main Street is festooned with lights and pine garlands in anticipation of the holidays.

Just a couple miles north of Sag Harbor, Shelter Island lies between Long Island's north and south forks. Reachable only by boat (there's regular ferry service), the 11½-square-mi island offers at least a partial escape from the summer traffic and crowd snarls of the Hamptons. Quiet country lanes wind through the island's rolling land, nearly a third of which has been set aside as a nature preserve that's a bird-watcher's delight.

Taking advantage of its hilltop elevation, Shelter Island Heights is the island's center of activity. Its Queen Anne, Victorian, and Colonial Revival houses, stores, and inns show off embellished porches, scalloped shingles, and carved friezes. This relaxed place becomes even mellower in the off-season, when many restaurants and other businesses reduce their hours or close for extended periods. If you're planning an off-season visit, call ahead to see what's open.

WHAT TO SEE & DO

SAG HARBOR

Bay Street Theater The regional theater presents new plays on their way to Broadway as well as time-honored classics. Bay Street also mounts holiday shows, comedy and music performances, and children's programs. > Bay St. at Long Wharf, tel. 631/725–9500, www.baystreet.org.

Cigar Bar It's not just the cigars that are smoking at this late-night hot spot, an intimate space where locals and out-of-towners gather to drink to the strains of lounge music. During the day, before things get hopping, the place serves as an Internet café. > 2 Main St., tel. 631/725–2575, www.hamptonscigarbar.com. Daily 11 AM–4 AM.

Custom House Henry Packer Dering, the port's first U.S. custom master, lived in this beautifully appointed 1789 Federal home that doubled as customhouse and now serves as a museum. Historical documents and period furnishings are on display. > Garden and Main Sts., tel. 631/725–0250, www.splia.org. $3. July and Aug., daily, 10–5; Sept.–June, weekends 10–5.

First Presbyterian/Old Whaler's Church Majestic by day and mysterious by night, the 1844 Egyptian Revival church has a simple but grand design. Its original steeple soared 180-feet but was destroyed by hurricane in the 1930s. The church cemetery contains many empty graves for sailors who perished at sea. > 44 Union St., tel. 631/725–0894. Tours by appointment.

Foster Memorial Beach The slightly rocky bay beach, also known as Long Beach, runs along Noyac Bay a couple of miles west of Sag Harbor and is a great spot from which to watch sunsets. The beach has a snack truck, lifeguard, and rest rooms. You need a nonresident daily permit, sold at the beach, for parking. > Long Beach Rd., tel. 631/283–6011. Parking permit $15 (Memorial Day–Labor Day).

Havens Beach A walk or bike ride from the village center, this long sandy stretch of bay beach has calm waters for swimming, a swing set and playing field, and public rest rooms. Obtain a parking permit at the Sag Harbor municipal hall, at 55 Main Street. > Off Bay St. near Hempstead St., tel. 631/725–0222. Parking permit $10 (Memorial Day–Labor Day).

Morton National Wildlife Refuge The 187-acre refuge, on a small peninsula that juts into Little Peconic and Noyac bays a few miles west of Sag Harbor, encompasses beaches and woody bluffs inhabited by terns, osprey, and wading birds as well as deer. Hiking trails vein the area. > Noyac Rd., Noyac, tel. 631/286–0485. $4 per car. Daily 1/2 hr before sunrise–1/2 hr after sunset.

Sag Harbor Fire Department Museum Sag Harbor, which saw four severe blazes in the 1800s, established the first volunteer fire department in New York State. The museum, housed in an 1833 building that served as fire-company quarters as well as town hall, displays an 1890 hand-pulled hose cart, a 1920s fire chief's vehicle, model fire trucks, and other old firefighting equipment. > Sage and Church Sts., tel. 631/725–0779. $1. July 4–Labor Day, daily 11–4.

Sag Harbor Whaling Museum Noted 19th-century architect Minard Lafever designed this striking 1845 Greek Revival mansion for shipowner Benjamin Huntting and his family. Museum displays include scrimshaw pieces, a boat collection, period furnishings, and model ships. > 200 Main St., tel. 631/725–0770, www.sagharborwhalingmuseum.org. $3. Mid-May–Sept., Mon.–Sat. 10–5, Sun. 1–5; Oct.–Dec., weekends noon–4.

SHELTER ISLAND

Crescent Beach The bay beach, a long sandy strip across the street from the trendy Sunset Beach restaurant, faces northeast and is especially popular at sunset. It has picnic tables and rest rooms. Island lodging properties have parking permits for guests; otherwise, contact the town clerk to get one. > Shore Rd. off W. Neck Rd., tel. 631/749–1166. Weekly parking permit $25 (mid-June–Labor Day).

Havens House The home of First Colonial Congress member William Havens, listed on the National Register of Historic Places, was built in 1743. The Shelter Island Historical Society maintains a museum here—seven rooms with period furnishings and a toy collection. > 16 S. Ferry Rd., tel. 631/749–0025. $2 donation, www.shelterislandhistsoc.org. Mid-May–mid-Sept., Fri.–Sun. 1–5.

Mashomack Nature Preserve Marked hiking trails of 1½ to 11 mi lace the preserve's 2,000-plus acres of beech and oak forest, meadows, tidal wetlands, beach, and freshwater ponds. A large population of ospreys nests here, along with many other bird species. The preserve also is home to harbor seals, turtles, and foxes. At the visitor center, ask for directions to the gazebo, which has a water view and is only a short walk from the center. The Nature Conservancy, which owns the preserve, also runs tours and educational programs here. > 79 S. Ferry Rd., tel. 631/749–1001, www.nature.org. $2.50 donation. July and Aug., daily 9–5; Sept. and Apr.–June, Wed.–Mon., 9–5; Oct.–Mar., Wed.–Mon. 9–4.

Wades Beach the shallow, sandy beach, on the island's south side, has picnic tables, rest rooms, and a life guard. Locals comb the beach's salt-marsh area for clams and crab. Island lodging properties have parking permits for guests, or contact the town clerk for one. > Heron La., off Shorewood Rd., tel. 631/749–1166. $25 weekly parking permit (mid-June–Labor Day).

Whale's Tale The 18-hole, lighted minigolf course has an ice-cream stand and outdoor terrace for taking a break after the game. > 3 Ram Island Rd., tel. 631/749–1839, www.onisland.com/whalestale. $6.50. Memorial Day–Labor Day, daily 10 AM–11 PM; Apr.–late May and early Sept.–mid-Oct., weekends 10 AM–11 PM.

Sports

BOATING & KAYAKING

With numerous deep-water harbors, Sag Harbor and Shelter Island attract sailors from all over the world. Everything from kayaks to luxury yachts are in the protected bays that lead out to Long Island Sound. At the Sag Harbor Sailing School, a sailboat rental runs from $225 for a half day to $275 for a full day, excluding the captain's fee. Two-day introductory sailing courses are offered on weekends; tuition is about $450. More-advanced courses also are available.

The waters around Shelter Island are perfect for kayaking. If you set out on a kayak you have the option of exploring on your own or taking a guided tour. The Mashomack Nature Preserve, rich with bird life and other animals, is a favorite kayaking destination. A solo kayak from Shelter Island Kayak Tours rents for about $26 for two hours; tours are $45.

RENTALS & LESSONS **Sag Harbor Sailing School** > Hidden Cove Marina, Noyac Rd., Sag Harbor, tel. 631/725–5100, www.sagharborsailing.com. **Shelter Island Kayak Tours** > Rte. 114 at Duval Rd., Shelter Island, tel. 631/749–1990, www.kayaksi.com.

FISHING

Fluke, flounder, striped bass, and skate are some of what you might catch in the in these parts. Guides and full- and half-day captained charters are available; a half day for two anglers is about $325.

OUTFITTERS **Jack's Marine & Tackle Shop** > Bridge St. at Rte. 114, Shelter Island, tel. 631/749–0114. **Light Tackle Challenge** > 91 W. Neck Rd., Shelter Island, tel. 631/749–1906, http://reel-time.com/guides/captjimhull.

GOLF

Sag Harbor State Golf Course The dense woods of Barcelona Neck surround this 9-hole, 2,660-yard public course. Greens fees are $12–$18, and tees are on a first-come, first-served basis. The course is open all year, weather permitting, and has a clubhouse. > Golf Club Rd., off Rte. 114, Sag Harbor, tel. 631/725–2503, http://nysparks.state.ny.us.

Shelter Island Country Club The well-maintained 2,510-yard public golf course has 9 holes with small greens on slightly rolling grass. It's open from April to late October. Greens fees are $15–$18. > 26 Sunnyside Ave., Shelter Island Heights, tel. 631/749–0416.

Shopping

Shelter Island is home to only a few shops. Sag Harbor's shopping district, which spills over from Main Street onto some small side streets, has everything from books and clothes to antiques and housewares—enough to occupy you for at least a couple of hours. Although most stores are open on weekends, open hours and days change with the month and season. Call ahead if you're making a special trip.

Beach Bungalow Decorator details abound in this stylish home-furnishings store. Vintage and new rugs, pillows, lamp shades, and nautical prints are part of the mix. > 26 Main St., Sag Harbor, tel. 631/725–4292.

Black Cat Books Browse for favorites in this discriminating used-book store. > 78 Main St., Sag Harbor, tel. 631/725–8654.

BookHampton The gleaming wood shelves here are filled with contemporary and classic fiction and nonfiction, with a large section of books of local interest. > 20 Main St., Sag Harbor, tel. 631/725–8425.

Canio's Books The oldest bookshop in Sag Harbor, Canio's carries new and used poetry, literary fiction, art, nature, and history books as well as cookbooks. Readings and other events are regularly scheduled. > 290 Main St., Sag Harbor, tel. 631/725–4926.

Carriage House Only the finest fabrics in the highest thread counts grace the shelves of this boutique. A great place for a hostess gift or a treat for yourself, this store stocks bed and table linens, hand towels, soaps, candles, and even a smattering of fine lingerie. > 42 Main St., Sag Harbor, tel. 631/725–8004.

Christy's Art and Design Inside this Victorian house, you may buy antiques as small as a vintage vase on up through enormous fireplaces and columns. Modern tableware is also for sale here, and everything is from Europe. > 3 Madison St., Sag Harbor, tel. 631/725–7000.

Flashbacks Indonesian crafts, penny candy, candles, and a large selection of casual women's clothes and shoes populate this chic store. > 69B Main St., Sag Harbor, tel. 631/725–9683.

Megna Hot Glass Studio A working glassblowing studio, Megna sells handmade doorknobs, lighting, sculptures, and art glass. You can watch the work in process here. > 11 Bridge St., Sag Harbor, tel. 631/725–1131.

Metaphysical Books and Tools The shop carries New Age and self-help books as well as "magical" stones and CDs of mystical music. A tarot-card reader makes occasional visits. > 83 Main St., Sag Harbor, tel. 631/725–9393.

Paradise Books The two floors here are filled with classics, best-sellers, and children's books. In back is the New Paradise Café. > 126 Main St., Sag Harbor, tel. 631/725–1114.

Punch At this source for preppy children's clothes, you can find everything from hand-knit sweaters and brightly colored galoshes to baby bikinis. It's a great place to find a gift for a baby or toddler. > 80 Main St., Sag Harbor, tel. 631/725–2741.

Romany Kramoris Gallery This mix of international artwork, music, and books makes for good browsing. Items include Brazilian CDs and Indonesian jewelry. > 41 Main St., Sag Harbor, tel. 631/725–2499.

Simpatico The brightly painted shoe boutique carries a name-brand selection of sandals, dress shoes, boots, and sneakers for men and women. You can match your pairs with the purses and wallets on display. > 82 Main St., Sag Harbor, tel. 631/725–2210.

Save the Date

MAY

Flounder Fest Experienced and amateur fishing enthusiasts compete to catch the largest flounder in Sag Harbor Bay. Fish are weighed on the dock, and the awards at the Corner Bar turn into a real party. > Sag Harbor, tel. 631/725–0011, www.sagharborchamber.com.

JUNE

Shelter Island Annual 10K Run Runners from around the world—more than 1,000 of them—participate in this race and the festivities that follow. The run, organized primarily to benefit the Special Olympics, is usually held on an early-June Saturday and starts in front of the Shelter Island School. > Tel. 631/749–0399, www.shelter-island.org.

AUGUST

Arts and Crafts Fair Local artisans offer their wares during this juried two-day event, usually in the middle of the month. > Long Wharf, Sag Harbor, tel. 631/725–0011, www.sagharborchamber.com.

Art Show and Craft Fair The one-day art-and-crafts sale is held toward the end of the month and includes high-quality items and fine art. > Shelter Island School, Rte. 114, Shelter Island, tel. 631/749–0399, www.shelter-island.org.

SEPTEMBER

HarborFest Each year, Sag Harbor celebrates its maritime and whaling history over a Friday through Sunday period in mid-September. Whaleboat races, period-costume contests, walking tours, a clambake, an auction, a parade, and live music performances are among the doings. Long Wharf and Main and Bay streets are the primary event areas. > Sag Harbor, tel. 631/725–0011, www.sagharborchamber.com.

OCTOBER

Fall Harvest Festival Hayrides, pumpkin carving, and pie contests are part of this festival, held at the Havens House on the Sunday of Columbus Day weekend. > 16 S. Ferry Rd., Shelter Island, tel. 631/749–0025, www.shelterislandhistsoc.org.

WHERE TO STAY

Many of the inns in the area don't staff their front desks round-the-clock, so it's a good idea to let the place you've chosen know when you plan to arrive.

SAG HARBOR

The American Hotel Victorian elegance defines this hotel dating to 1846. The three-story brick facade and white-pillared porch look out on Main Street, in the center of town. Guest rooms have turn-of-the-20th-century antiques and a spacious bathroom with fine Italian towels and bathrobes. > 25 Main St., 11963, tel. 631/725–3535, fax 631/725–3573, www.theamericanhotel.com. 8 rooms. Restaurant, in-room hot tubs, minibars, lounge, piano bar, no-smoking rooms; no room TVs. AE, D, DC, MC, V. CP. **$$$$**

Baron's Cove Inn The largest hotel in the area, Baron's Cove is a short walk to the village center and is across the street from a marina. The casual, comfortable rooms, well suited for families, vary in size from a standard room, which can accommodate three, to a loft, which sleeps six. Rooms in back look out over the parking lot and tennis court; those in front have views of the pool and bay. > 31 W. Water St., 11963, tel. 631/725–2100, fax 631/725–2144, www.baronscove.com. 66 rooms. Microwaves, refrigerators, cable TV, tennis court, pool, business services, meeting room, no-smoking rooms. AE, MC, V. **$$$$**

Sag Harbor Inn The two-story hotel is across from the marina and within walking distance of Main Street. Each room is simple but spacious, with a sitting area and modern pine furniture. French doors open onto patios and balconies, which look over the water in front rooms and the pool in back rooms. The breakfast room and promenade deck take advantage of their harbor views. > W. Water St., 11963, tel. 631/725–2949, fax 631/725–5009, www.sagharborinn.com. 42 rooms. Dining room, cable TV, pool, meeting rooms, no-smoking rooms. AE, MC, V. CP. **$$$$**

SHELTER ISLAND

Belle Crest Inn & Aimee's Cottage Built in the 1920s, the cozy inn, decorated with period antiques and personal artifacts, remains family-owned and -operated. Oriental rugs, a piano, and family photos grace the front parlor. Bedrooms have floral wallpaper, canopy beds, and lace curtains. The cottage out back has a kitchenette and its own patio. Breakfast is served on the front or back porch, both of which are filled with an eclectic mix of wicker furniture. The town dock and historic district are a short walk away. > 163 N. Ferry Rd., Shelter Island Heights 11965, tel. 631/749–2041. 7 rooms, 2 with shared bath; 1 cottage. Dining room, some kitchenettes, cable TV, piano, Internet, some pets allowed, no-smoking rooms; no room phones. MC, V. Closed mid-Oct.–early May. BP. **$$$**

Chequit Inn The 1872 Victorian inn sits in the center of activity in the Heights. The main building, which houses the restaurant and bar, has a tree-shaded patio and a sitting room. Guest rooms, furnished sparingly with country antiques and reproductions, are bright and comfortable. In summer two adjunct buildings, the Cedar House and Summer Cottage, also accommodate overnighters; front rooms and those near the doors may get some street and foot-traffic noise. Guests here may also use the facilities at the Ram's Head, a sister property. > 23 Grand Ave., Shelter Island Heights 11965, tel. 631/749–0018, fax 631/749–0183, www.shelterislandinns.com. 35 rooms. Restaurant, dining room, room service, fans, billiards, bar; no TV in some rooms, no smoking. AE, MC, V. CP. **$–$$$**

Dering Harbor Inn With spectacular views of Dering Harbor, this co-op complex offers motel studios, which are by the road, as well as one- and two-bedroom units. The two-bedroom waterfront suites have a fireplace and private deck. The marina dock is a few steps away. > 13 Winthrop Rd., Shelter Island Heights 11965, tel. 631/749–0900, www.deringharborinn.com. 4 rooms, 21 suites. Restaurant, picnic area, some kitchenettes, some microwaves, some refrigerators, cable TV, some in-room VCRs, 2 tennis courts, saltwater pool, marina, volleyball, bar, laundry facilities, no-smoking rooms. AE, D, MC, V. Mid-Oct.–mid-May. EP. $$$–$$$$

Olde Country Inn Privacy and romance are yours at this Victorian inn on a country lane. Rooms are named after their color schemes ("Rose Room," "Emerald Room"), which are subdued, and include antique furnishings. You can relax in the library, which has a fireplace, or sip a drink on the wraparound porch. The full country breakfast is served in the garden in the summer. > 11 Stearns Point Rd., Shelter Island Heights 11965, tel. 631/749–1633, www.oldecountryinn.com. 9 rooms, 4 suites, 1 cottage. Restaurant, fans, some in-room hot tubs, bar, library; no room phones, no room TVs, no kids under 14, no smoking. AE, MC, V. BP. $$–$$$$

Pridwin The rambling, old-timey, family-friendly resort is on Crescent Beach. In summer meals may be served on the deck, and there's outdoor dancing at night. Rooms, some with water views, are simple but comfortable; some of the cottages have fireplaces. > Shore Rd., Shelter Island 11964, tel. 631/749–0476 or 800/273–2497, fax 631/749–2071, www.pridwin.com. 40 rooms, 8 cottages. Restaurant, some kitchens, some microwaves, some refrigerators, cable TV, 3 tennis courts, pool, beach, dock, boating, fishing, bicycles, billiards, Ping-Pong, shuffleboard, bar, laundry facilities, no-smoking rooms. AE, D, MC, V. Closed Nov.–Apr. BP. $$$

Ram's Head Inn At this 1929 Colonial-style inn, Adirondack chairs are scattered across lawns sloping down to Coecles Harbor. The secluded spot at the end of Ram Island has a small beach for swimming (bring insect repellant) or sailing as well as a tennis court and a gazebo. The restaurant has outdoor seating in warm weather. Rooms, furnished a simple country style, are bright; they often book up months ahead of time. Suites have two bedrooms. > Ram Island Dr., Shelter Island 11965, tel. 631/749–0811, fax 631/749–0059, www.shelterislandinns.com. 13 rooms, 9 with bath; 4 suites. Restaurant, bar, tennis court, gym, sauna, beach, boating, playground; no room TVs, no smoking. AE, MC, V. Closed Nov.–Mar. CP. $–$$$$

Sunset Beach An international crowd has flocked to this trendy hotel ever since celebrity hotelier Andre Balazs (of L.A.'s Chateau Marmont and SoHo's Mercer) opened it in the late1990s. Each retro-style guest room has a sun deck that looks out over the parking lot to the water. The outdoor restaurant is a big draw. > 35 Shore Rd., Shelter Island 11965, tel. 631/749–2001, www.sunsetbeachli.com. 20 rooms. Restaurant, picnic area, some kitchenettes, cable TV, beach, bar, business services, some pets allowed (fee), no-smoking rooms. AE, D, MC, V. Closed Oct.–Apr. CP. $$$$

WHERE TO EAT

Many area restaurants change their schedules depending on the season. It's especially important to call ahead when planning to visit in the off-season.

SAG HARBOR

The American Hotel The restaurant and bar inhabit four intimate rooms, including a front room with a piano and a bar room with a fireplace. Antique furniture is used throughout. The fare is largely French but encompasses other cuisines, so you might find sushi and sashimi, or grilled local seafood mixed with cilantro-spiked Asian noodles, on the menu. The wine list runs 85 pages. The bar and lounge attract a sophisticated crowd. > 25 Main St., tel. 631/725–3535. No lunch weekdays. AE, MC, V. $$$–$$$$

Beacon On the second floor of a yacht club, this hidden gem offers exceptional food with a terrific view. The emphasis here is on local fish, chicken, or pasta prepared with savory sauces, including Thai-peanut and mustard-cream versions. Separate menus are devoted to martinis and margaritas. The owner attends to details, part of the reason for the friendly, efficient service. > 8 W. Water St., tel. 631/725–7088. Closed mid-Oct.–May.; and Tues. and Wed. June–mid-Oct. No lunch. AE, MC, V. $$–$$$

B. Smith's The world's finest yachts sit at your feet when you're on the deck of B. Smith's, on Long Wharf. The restaurant attracts crowds on sunny days and steamy nights. Seafood preparations and a raw-bar menu are mixed with a dose of Southern cooking. Be prepared for slower service when things get busy here. > 1 Bay St., tel. 631/725–5858. Closed mid-Oct.–Memorial Day. AE, D, MC, V. $$–$$$

Conca D'oro A casual pizza parlor in front serves slices to go, whereas the Italian restaurant in back can seat the whole gang for platters of antipasto, spaghetti and meatballs, and carafes of Chianti. Large portions, down-home cooking, and reasonable prices make this a good choice for families. > Main St. near Washington St., tel. 631/725–3167. Reservations not accepted. AE, MC, V. $–$$

Corner Bar For true local flavor, head for this harbor hangout. Open when everything else has closed for the night, it's ideal for a late-night snack—the burger is one of the best in town. Bands play some weekends. > 1 Main St., tel. 631/725–9760. No reservations. AE, MC, V. $–$$

Dockside Bar & Grill The first warm day of the season, locals flock to the umbrella-shaded patio tables of this casual spot next to the American Legion Hall. Have a bowl of steamers and watch the boats head into the marina. Inside are two simple dining rooms and a small bar. Traditional seafood favorites, such as seared scallops and fried oysters, share the menu with paella and chicken potpie. > 26 Bay St., tel. 631/725–7100. Reservations not accepted. AE, MC, V. $–$$

Estia's Little Kitchen A mile outside Sag Harbor center, this roadside restaurant serves good breakfasts as well as fresh American dishes for lunch and dinner. > 1615 Bridgehampton–Sag Harbor Tpke., tel. 631/725–1045. Reservations not accepted. AE, MC, V. Closed Mon. and Tues. $–$$$

Il Capuccino Chianti bottles hang from the ceiling over tables draped in red-and-white-checked cloths. Consistently good cooking and service make the three rooms of this Italian family eatery a year-round favorite. The garlic bread and the ravioli, made in-house, are the must-haves. > 30 Madison St., tel. 631/725–2747. Reservations not accepted. AE, DC, MC, V. No lunch. $$–$$$

Jeff & Eddy's Seafood With leather booths, white-tiled walls, and vintage photographs, this lively seafood joint resembles an old-fashioned chowder house. It's known for fresh local fish, simple preparations, and extensive raw bar, and there's often a wait; a beeper system lets you enjoy a drink at the long zinc bar or a stroll around town. Standouts include fish-and-chips, cornmeal-crusted oysters, and barbecued baby-back ribs. The on-premises fish market means you can also get something to go or place a special seafood order. > 62 Main St., tel. 631/725–0055. Reservations not accepted. AE, MC, V. $$–$$$$

La Superica From the fresh lime juice in the margaritas to the fresh tuna in the tacos, the Mexican offerings here are well prepared and tasty. Traditional burritos and quesadillas are large, with many options for vegetarians. Next to the wharf, this casual eatery attracts sailors. At the large bar in back you can watch the sun set while sipping a tequila sunrise. > Main St. at Long Island Ave., tel. 631/725–3388. Reservations not accepted. AE, MC, V. No lunch. $–$$$

Magnolia At this storefront restaurant, generous portions and gracious service satisfy the upscale crowd in search of Southern cooking—fried chicken, popcorn shrimp, jambalaya. The bar is popular, too. > 29 Main St., tel. 631/725–0101. AE, MC, V. No lunch. $$–$$$

New Paradise Café You may browse the bookstore in front before walking to the restaurant in back for a cappuccino or a meal. A copper bar with tall café tables leads to a main dining room with original artwork on the walls. A covered patio is used in summer. The diverse dinner menu ranges from couscous to Tuscan-style pot roast. Sunday brunch is available all year. > 126 Main St., tel. 631/725–6080. AE, MC, V. $–$$$

Sen An attractive, black-clad staff serves sushi and other Japanese dishes to the hip crowd that frequents this place. Sashimi and rolls of all varieties are available; vegetable, noodle, and fresh-fish dishes help fill out the menu, which includes an extensive sake list. You may encounter a wait, but the beeper system lets you be mobile. > 23 Main St., tel. 631/725–1774. Reservations not accepted. AE, MC, V. Closed Tues. No lunch Sun.–Thurs. $–$$$

SHELTER ISLAND

Chequit Inn The inn's restaurant is the epicenter of activity in Shelter Island Heights. In warm weather, crowds swarm the tree-covered patio, where lighter fare is served. The formal dining room, which feels like a country club, has a more extensive menu that ranges from curried chicken breast to mustard-coated rack of lamb. Sunday brunch is a casual affair. The pub hosts live music on some weekends. > 23 Grand Ave. Shelter Island Heights, tel. 631/749–0018. AE, MC, V. No lunch Mon.–Thurs. $$–$$$$

The Dory At this relaxed spot, seafood dishes are served on a scenic deck along Chase Creek. Daily specials round out a regular menu that includes fish-and-chips and chowder. In the off-season locals gather in the pub and dining room for a beer and a game of pool. > Bridge St., Shelter Island Heights, tel. 631/749–8871. AE. Closed Feb. $–$$

Olde Country Inn The small inn's intimate French restaurant serves dinner in cozy rooms or outside on the wraparound porch in summer. The menu includes simple country French favorites, like steamed mussels in cream sauce and rack of lamb with ratatouille. > 11 Stearns Point Rd., Shelter Island Heights, tel. 631/749–1633. AE, MC, V. No lunch. $$–$$$

Planet Bliss You can't miss this brightly painted, funky restaurant in a converted Victorian. The menu of healthful but delicious fare includes everything from rice-and-bean dishes to fruit smoothies and fine wine. Weekend brunch on the porch and patio is busy. > 23 N. Ferry Rd., Shelter Island, tel. 631/749–0053. AE, MC, V. Closed Mon.–Thurs. Oct.–May. $–$$$

Ram's Head Inn Dine on the porch or patio of this 1929 Colonial-style inn for a view of sloping lawn leading down to Coecles Harbor. The seasonal cuisine here is as outstanding as the view. Sauces, such as the aged-sherry syrup that accompanies quail, set this restaurant apart, as does the attentive and knowledgeable service. Jazz musicians play during Sunday brunch, served late May to late October. > 108 Ram Island Dr., Shelter Island, tel. 631/749–0811. Reservations essential. AE, MC, V. Closed late Oct.–late May; closed Tues. and Wed. late May–mid-June. $$$–$$$$

Sunset Beach This beachfront restaurant provides the best sunset and people watching around. You can stick your toes in the sand during cocktail hour or dine on the open-air deck under Japanese lanterns. French bistro dishes, such as *moules frites* (mussels and fries) and fried calamari, are the things to get here, but choose an American finale and go for the chocolate sundae. Service can be slow in season, but you can stay all night, enjoying the world music that plays until the wee hours. > 35 Shore Rd., Shelter Island, tel. 631/749–2001. Reservations essential. AE, MC, V. Closed late Oct.–mid-May; Mon.–Wed. mid-May–July and Labor Day–late Oct. $$–$$$$

Tom's Coffee Shoppe An old-fashioned soda shop with stools at the counter and a few plastic tables outside, Tom's offers breakfast and lunch menus with items such as grilled-cheese sandwiches and lobster rolls. > S. Ferry Rd. next to fire station, Shelter Island, tel. 631/749–2655. No reservations. No credit cards. No dinner. ¢–$

Vine Street Cafe Husband-and-wife team Terry and Lisa Harwood create casual but sophisticated dishes, and their staff provides exceptional service. Daily specials such as bouillabaisse and crispy duck confit augment the limited menu, which lists staples such as steak frites and miso-glazed salmon. The simple interior employs beige walls, exposed beams, and a wooden bar. In warm weather you may dine alfresco under tiki lights. Save room for dessert. > 41 S. Ferry Rd., Shelter Island, tel. 631/749–3210. Reservations essential. AE, MC, V. Closed Tues. and Wed. $$–$$$

ESSENTIALS

Getting Here

Sag Harbor is compact enough that you don't need a car if you plan to just stay in the village center. Shelter Island, however, is more sprawling. Taxi service is limited, so having your own vehicle, especially if you want to explore the rest of the Hamptons, is a good idea. The drive to eastern Long Island is usually traffic-ridden, however.

Taking a train is a way to avoid traffic, especially if you're traveling to Shelter Island via Greenport, but it may involve a transfer. The Long Island Rail Road doesn't stop in Sag Harbor.

Buses from Manhattan are more expensive than trains and are subject to the same traffic delays cars face, but they're a comfortable option. Buses stop in Sag Harbor and Greenport, have a bathroom, and offer onboard snacks and beverages.

BY BUS

The Hampton Jitney, a coach line that travels from Manhattan's East Side to the Hamptons, has reclining seats, a bathroom, and free beverages. It leaves from four points between 40th and 86th streets; on the return it drops off mostly on the East Side but some routes stop on the Upper West Side if requested. In Sag Harbor, the jitney drops off in front of the American Hotel on Main Street. Buses heading back to Manhattan pick up passengers in front of the Sag Harbor Cinema, also on Main Street. Depending on the season, six to nine trips are made daily; each taking 2½ to 3½ hours. The one-way peak fare is $27. Reservations are required. Bringing a bike costs an extra $10.

The Hampton Luxury Liner also provides service from the city to the Hamptons. These buses have 21 leather reclining seats, carpeting, upholstery, and a bathroom, and offer drinks and snacks. They depart from five points between 40th and 86th streets on the East Side. The trip to Bridgehampton, from where you need to take a seven-minute taxi ride to Sag Harbor, takes about 2½ to 3½ hours and costs $37 one-way at peak times. Reservations are required.

Only Sunrise Coach Lines serves the North Fork, offering direct daily service from Manhattan and Queens to Riverhead, Mattituck, Cutchogue, Southold, and Greenport, for $16 one-way during peak-travel times. The trip to Greenport takes about 2½ hours. Sunrise picks up at 44th Street and 3rd Avenue, on Manhattan's East Side; on the return trip it drops off at limited 3rd Avenue bus stops from 37th Street to 79th Street. Seats must be reserved in advance. *LINES* **Hampton Jitney** > Tel. 631/283–4600 or 800/936–0440, www.hamptonjitney.com. **Hampton Luxury Liner** > Tel. 631/537–5800, www.hamptonluxuryliner.com. **Sunrise Coach Lines** > Tel. 631/477–1200 or 800/527–7709, www.sunrisecoach.com.

BY CAR

Driving time ranges from 2 hours, in ideal conditions, to 3½ hours or more in traffic. Heavy traffic is mostly unavoidable if you leave the city on Friday afternoon or evening or if you return on Sunday afternoon or evening. You face less traffic if you leave the city around noon (or earlier) Friday, or wait until after 8 PM to get going. Long Island has several west–east routes: the Long Island Expressway (I–495), the Southern State Parkway, and the Northern State Parkway. Depending on traffic, you may want to use more than one of these. The LIE is probably the most straightforward way to get to either the North or South Fork; if you drive with at least one other person, you can travel in the high-occupancy-vehicle (HOV) lane.

The main road on the South Fork, Route 27 is also known as Sunrise Highway and merges with Montauk Highway (Route 27A) in Southampton. Route 25 is the main road on the North Fork and leads to Greenport.

For Sag Harbor (and the South Ferry to Shelter Island), take the LIE to Exit 70 (Manorville) and head south to Route 27, on which you proceed eastward. (If Exit 70 looks backed up, take Exit 71 to Route 24 through Flanders instead and pick up Route 27 in Hampton Bays.) Once on Route 27, continue east to Bridgehampton and then turn north onto Route 79, which leads into Sag Harbor; from Sag Harbor, Route 114 (also known as South Ferry Road here), leads north to the ferry for Shelter Island.

Getting to Shelter Island via Greenport can often be the less-crowded way to go. Take the LIE's Exit 72 (the next-to-last exit east) to Route 25 northeast and proceed to Greenport.

Rates at most lodgings in the area include parking. When you're driving elsewhere, read village parking signs carefully—some spaces allow parking only for one or two hours.

BY FERRY

The two ferry lines are the only way to reach Shelter Island. Both the North Ferry and the South Ferry are prone to backups on summer weekends, in both directions. To avoid the Sunday morning and afternoon backups to get off Shelter Island, consider getting an early start or even taking the car over to Greenport or Sag Harbor the night before.

The South Ferry leaves from the end of Route 114 (South Ferry Road) in Sag Harbor about every 10 to 12 minutes. It runs 6 AM–11:45 PM daily from January to early spring. From early spring to mid-June, and from September to December, Friday and Saturday hours are extended until 1:45 AM. In July and August it runs 6 AM–1:45 AM daily. The fare (cash only) is $7 one-way for a car and driver. Pedestrians and additional car passengers cost $1 each way.

The North Ferry is the best way to get to the Chequit Inn and other places in Shelter Island Heights. It leaves from Greenport, off Route 25, about every 20 minutes. From Memorial Day to Labor Day the ferry runs 6 AM–12:45 AM Friday and Saturday; every other day of the year it runs 6 AM–11:45 PM. The fare is $8 one-way for a car and driver. Pedestrians and additional car passengers cost $1 each way.

LINES **South Ferry Inc.** > Tel. 631/749–1200, www.southferry.com. **North Ferry Company** > Tel. 631/749–0139, www.northferry.com.

BY TRAIN

LIRR trains leave throughout the day from Manhattan's Pennsylvania Station for Long Island's East End.

The nearest stop to Sag Harbor is Bridgehampton (on the Montauk line), a trip that takes about 2 hours and 40 minutes and usually requires transfer at Jamaica Station. The fare is $19 one-way during peak-travel times. In summer the LIRR offers Hamptons Reserve service (aka "the Cannonball"), express trains to the Hamptons (from Penn Station) that make their first stop in Westhampton. The fare is $28 one-way during peak-travel times. The express trains have reserved seats and bar and snack service. From the Bridgehampton train station, you have to call a taxi for the seven-minute ride to Sag Harbor.

To get to Shelter Island, take the Greenport line all the way to Greenport, near the tip of the North Fork. The train stops next to the North Ferry. Trains to Greenport depart at least twice daily from Penn Station; the trip takes about 2 hours and 40 minutes, sometimes with a transfer in Ronkonkoma or Jamaica, and costs $19 one-way at peak times.

To bring a bicycle, you must obtain a permit in advance ($5 annual fee). Permit applications are available via the LIRR Web site.

LINES **Long Island Rail Road** > Tel. 718/217–5477 or 631/231–5477, www.lirr.org. *STATIONS* **Bridgehampton** > Halsey and Butler La., no phone, www.lirr.org. **Greenport** > Wiggins and 4th Sts. at ferry dock, no phone, www.lirr.org.

Visitor Information

The Sag Harbor Chamber of Commerce maintains an information booth at the Windmill on Long Wharf, at the end of Main Street. It's open daily 10–4 from Memorial Day to Labor Day and weekends 10–4 during the rest of May and September.

CONTACTS **Sag Harbor Chamber of Commerce** > Box 2810, Sag Harbor 11963, tel. 631/725–0011, www.sagharborchamber.com. **Sag Harbor Town Hall** > Main St., Sag Harbor, tel. 631/725–0222, www.sagharborvillage.com. **Shelter Island Chamber of Commerce** > 47 W. Neck Rd., Shelter Island 11964, tel. 631/749–0399, www.shelter-island.org. **Shelter Island Town Hall** > 38 N. Ferry Rd., Shelter Island, tel. 631/749–0015, www.shelterislandtown.us.

The North Fork

Riverhead is 90 mi east of New York City

16

By Lisa S. Kahn

THE NORTH FORK IS ONE OF THOSE MIRACLES of Mother Nature. It was formed many eons ago by a glacier that crept down from the north, leaving behind a moraine of rich, hospitable soil. Stretching from Riverhead in the west to Orient Point at its easternmost tip, this sedate sister of the South Fork forms the upper finger of what looks like a sideways peace sign.

The peace-sign shape of this stretch of Long Island reflects the sense of serenity you feel after you take the last exit of the Long Island Expressway (LIE) and begin cruising east on Route 58. Riverhead, like most other places on the North Fork, began as a farming village. Although agriculture remains a key factor in its economy, the town's main industry today is shopping and tourism. The sprawling Tanger outlet mall annually draws thousands of bargain hunters and tour groups, and has spawned the growth of several major shopping centers along Route 58.

But it's not long before Route 58 yields to the distinctly rural Route 25, in Aquebogue. It is here that the air seems to change and harried urban dwellers breathe their first sigh of relief. Tidy woodframe farmhouses and fancier Victorians are followed by acres of green, once chiefly potato farms, that now hold row after row of meticulously tended grape vines.

The New England–style hamlets of the western North Fork, particularly Jamesport, Mattituck, and Southold, are peppered with unpretentious restaurants and interesting stores that seem transported from another era. Antiques shops beckon here and there. Clean, uncrowded beaches lie to the south on Great Peconic Bay and to the north on the Long Island Sound.

Farther east is Greenport. "Greenport is the real thing" is the sincere catchphrase adopted by the town leaders of this folksy, faintly honky-tonk fishing village. Since the late 1600s, Greenport's saga—which includes a brisk rum-running business during Prohibition—has depended on the sea. The deep waters of Long Island Sound still summon home tall ships reminiscent of the whaling boats that once harbored in its safe waters, and the view from the wharf can awaken the swashbuckler in just about anyone. The shorefront area encompasses many points of interest as well as small gift shops and modest eateries. Ferries leave from here for Shelter Island, not far to the south. Orient Point, at the eastern tip of the North Fork, is a charming 18th-century seaside village. Surrounded by water to the north and south, it, like nearby neighbor East Marion, is a photographer's dream.

You can effortlessly fill a weekend on the North Fork with winery tours and tastings, lobster dinners, beachcombing, and trinket hunting. During the growing season, roadside nurseries and farm stands explode with vivid blooms and bins piled high with fresh-picked produce. But what you're likely to remember most when you get home is the quiet. It's less the absence of noise than the sound of life lived more slowly.

WHAT TO SEE & DO

CUTCHOGUE

Cutchogue Village Green and Old Burial Ground Five old buildings, maintained by the Cutchogue–New Suffolk Historical Council, inhabit the village green. The 1649 Old House is one of the oldest frame houses in the country. Also here are the 1840 Old School House and the 1890 Red Barn, both filled with period furnishings. To see the interiors, you must take the tour, which lasts one hour. > Main Rd. at Case La., tel. 631/734–7122. Free. Late June–Labor Day, Sun. and Mon. 1–4.

Fort Corchaug/Downs Farm Preserve You may walk along peaceful woodland trails filled with native flora and fauna at this National Historic Landmark and important archaeological site. The fort that was here dated back to at least the early 1600s. At the visitor center, a volunteer can explain exhibits about the native Corchaug Indians and early Colonial settlers. > Main Rd., tel. 631/734–5630, http://southoldtown.north-fork.net. Free. Daily dawn–dusk.

GREENPORT

East End Seaport and Maritime Museum A former Long Island Rail Road passenger terminal contains exhibits about lighthouses, ships, East End shipbuilding, and yacht racing. > 3rd St. at ferry dock, tel. 631/477–2100, www.eastendseaport.org. $2. Late May, weekends 11–5; June–Sept., Wed.–Mon. 11–5.

Mitchell Park Carousel The 1920s carousel, housed in a round, gleaming glass structure that allows year-round enjoyment, is the highlight of Greenport's waterfront renovation. > Front St., no phone. $1. Weekends 10–6.

Railroad Museum of Long Island The museum, in an 1892 Greenport freight station, exhibits a Reading Railroad track car, a 1907 snow plow, and a 1925 LIRR caboose. > 440 4th St., tel. 631/727–7920, www.rmli.org. $3. Memorial Day–Columbus Day, weekends 11–4.

Stirling Historical Society Maritime exhibits emphasize whaling and oyster industries; displayed are whaling tools and oil lamps, as well as a collection of artifacts, furniture, and tools from the 1800s. > Main and Adams Sts., tel. 631/477–1719. Donations suggested. July–Sept., weekends 1–4.

ORIENT

Orient Beach State Park The park occupies a tendril of land that extends southward from Orient Point and stretches west, surrounded by Gardiner's Bay on its south side and Orient Harbor and Long Beach Bay on it's north side. The beach nestles beside a waterfront forest. In addition to swimming (from late June to early September), you may fish, picnic, hike, and bike here. > South of Rte. 25, tel. 631/323–2440, http://nysparks.state.ny.us. Parking $7, Memorial Day–Labor Day. Daily sunrise–sunset.

Oysterponds Historical Society A collection of old buildings, including the 19th-century Village House and the 18th-century Orange Webb House, depict the maritime and rural past of Orient and East Marion. Antique furniture, art, and scrimshaw fill the buildings. > Village La., tel. 631/323–2480. $3. June–Sept., Thurs. and weekends 2–5.

RIVERHEAD

Atlantis Marine World Indoor exhibits, such as a natural rock-scape pool and a sandshark lagoon, offer a compelling glimpse of regional marine life. Kids love the frisky resident sea lions. The aquarium even has a submarine-simulator ride. > 431 E. Main St., Riverhead, tel. 631/208–9200, www.atlantismarineworld.com. $13.50. Daily 10–5.

South Jamesport Beach On Peconic Bay, this 3,000-foot-long beach has shallow-water areas for children. Lifeguards are on duty weekends from mid-May through June and daily in July to early September. > Off Peconic Bay Blvd., Jamesport, tel. 631/727–5744. Nonresident parking $25.

Peconic River Herb Farm The working farm on 13 riverfront acres west of Riverhead grows more than 700 varieties of plants, including herbs, heirloom vegetables, beautiful shrubs, and roses. Wander through the trail gardens or visit (in season) the farm's market. Garden-related workshops and other events are offered off-season. > 2749 River Rd., Calverton, tel. 631/369–0058, www.prherbfarm.com. Free. Apr.–June, daily 9–5; July–Oct., daily 9–4.

Riverhead Raceway From April through September, this stock-car track with a figure-eight course hosts NASCAR events, spectator drag racing, and demolition derbies. In season, early-evening races are scheduled for each Saturday and one Sunday a month; gates open at 3. > Rte. 58 ½ mi east of the LIE, Riverhead, tel. 631/842–7223, www.riverheadraceway.com. $18–$30. Apr.–Sept.

Splish Splash At this 96-acre water park, you may ride an inner tube down the 1,300-foot-long Lazy River, passing waterfalls, geysers, and wave pools. Other attractions include Monsoon Lagoon, Mammoth River Ride, and Kiddie Cove. The park has three pools, a beach area, and two restaurants. > 2549 Splish Splash Dr., Riverhead, tel. 631/727–3600, www.splishsplashlongisland.com. $24. Memorial Day–Labor Day, daily 10–6.

Tanger Outlet Stores Coach, Nike, DKNY, and Pottery Barn are among the more than 170 brand-name factory stores at this outlet complex. > 1770 W. Main St., at Rte. 25, Riverhead, tel. 631/369–2732 or 800/407–4894, www.tangeroutlet.com. Jan.–Mar., Sun.–Fri. 10–7, Sat. 9–9; Apr.–Dec., Mon.–Sat. 9–9, Sun. 10–8.

SOUTHOLD & PECONIC

Custer Institute Taking advantage of some of the darkest night skies on Long Island, this observatory is a prime viewing spot for astronomy buffs and star-deprived urbanites. Atop the barnlike structure is a motorized dome with a telescope you can use to track the heavenly view. > Main Bayview Rd., Southold, tel. 631/765–2626, www.custerobservatory.org. Free. Sat. after dusk–midnight.

Historic Museums of Southold The complex encompasses a dozen buildings, including the **Ann Currie-Bell Home,** which has antique dolls and toys, costume collections, and period rooms; the **Thomas Moore House,** a mid-18th-century carriage house and blacksmith shop; and the circa-1821 **Old Bay View School,** which now looks as it did in 1914; and a buttery and an ice house. > Main Rd. and Maple La., Southold, tel. 631/765–5500, www.southoldhistoricalsociety.org. Donation suggested. July and Aug., Wed. and weekends 1–4.

Horton Point Lighthouse and Nautical Museum The 58-foot-tall lighthouse, operated by the Southold Historical Society, was built in 1847. Together with the adjoining lighthouse keeper's home, it resembles a church. The museum, in the keeper's residence, displays sea captains' journals, sea chests, paintings, and maps. The 8-acre park surrounding the lighthouse includes public barbecue grills. > Lighthouse Rd., Southold, tel. 631/765–5500 or 631/765–3262, www.longislandlighthouses.com. $2 suggested donation. Memorial Day–Columbus Day, weekends 11:30–4.

Punkinville USA At this mini-zoo, kids can feed and pet farm and other animals as well as hop on a pony. > 26085 Rte. 48, Peconic, tel. 631/734–5530. $5. Thurs.–Sun. 10–5.

The North Fork Wine Trail

WHEN LOUISA AND ALEX *Hargrave planted their first grape vines at their eponymous vineyard in 1973, they also planted the seeds of a new North Fork industry. Little more than a quarter-century later, the area's burgeoning wine industry is attracting ever-more attention. (The Hargraves sold the winery in 1999 and the place was renamed Castello di Borghese Vineyard.)*

Chardonnay and merlot together account for more than 60% of the varietals grown on Long Island; cabernet franc, cabernet sauvignon, sauvignon blanc, chenin blanc, malbec, pinot blanc, pinot gris, pinot noir, Riesling, and viognier are among the others planted here. Land devoted to vineyards on the East End exceeds 3,000 acres.

From Aquebogue to Greenport, 20-plus wineries and vineyards—the majority on or close to routes 25 or 48—are open to the public for tastings and, at some, tours; most host special events as well. To follow the North Fork Wine Trail, take the last LIE exit (73) and follow it to Route 25 (via Route 58), where green "Wine Trail" road signs guide you to the wineries. Before making a special trip or taking a detour to visit a winery or vineyard, call to confirm hours. At the **Tasting Room** *(2885 Peconic La., Peconic, tel. 631/765-6404), open Wednesday through Monday 11–6, you may try (and buy) wines from small North Fork producers not open to the public.*

Bedell Cellars > 36225 Main Rd., Cutchogue, tel. 631/734-7537, www.bedellcellars.com. Tasting and tour free. Tastings daily 11–5, tours weekends at 3 and by appointment; Corey Creek Tasting Room, Main Rd. east of Peconic La., Southold, tel. 631/765-4168, www.bedellcellars.com. Tasting free. May–Dec., daily 11–5; Jan.–Apr., Wed.–Mon. 11–5.

Castello di Borghese Vineyard > Rte. 48 at Alvah's La., Cutchogue, tel. 631/734-5111, www.castellodiborghese.com. Tasting $3, tour free. Jan.–Mar., Thurs.–Mon. 11–5; Apr.–Dec., weekdays 11–5, weekends 11–6.

Galluccio Family Estates > 24385 Main Rd., Cutchogue, tel. 631/734-7089, www.galluciofamilywineries.com. Tasting fees vary, tour $25. Tastings weekdays 11–5, weekends 11–6; tours May–Sept., by appointment.

Lenz Winery > Main Rd. west of Peconic La., Peconic, tel. 631/734-6010, www.lenzwine.com. Tasting fees vary, tour free. Tastings daily 10–6, tours by appointment.

Lieb Family Cellars > 35 Cox Neck Rd., Mattituck, tel. 631/734-1100, www.liebcellars.com. Tasting $3, tour free. Daily 11–6.

Macari Vineyards & Winery > 150 Bergen Ave., south side of Sound Ave., Mattituck, tel. 631/298-0100, www.macariwines.com. Tasting fees vary, tour $10. Tastings daily 11–5, tours by appointment.

Osprey's Dominion Vineyards > 44075 Main Rd., Peconic, tel. 631/765-6188, www.ospreysdominion.com. Tasting fees vary, tour free. Daily 11–5.

Palmer Vineyards > Sound Ave. off Osborne Ave., Aquebogue, tel. 631/722-9463, www.palmervineyards.com. Tasting fees vary, tour free. Daily 11–6.

Paumanok Vineyards > 1074 Main Rd., Aquebogue, tel. 631/722-8800, www.paumanok.com. Tasting fees vary, tour free. Tastings daily 11–5, tours by appointment.

Pellegrini Vineyards > 23005 Main Rd., Cutchogue, tel. 631/734-4111, www.pellegrinivineyards.com. Tasting fees vary, tour free. Daily 11–5.

Pindar Vineyards > Main Rd. between Bridge La. and Peconic La., Peconic, tel. 631/734-6200, www.pindar.net. Tasting and tour free. Daily 11–6.

Raphael > 39390 Main Rd., Peconic, tel. 631/765-1100, www.raphaelwine.com. Tasting $8, tour $10. Daily noon–5.

Southold Indian Museum At this museum focused on natural history and archaeology, permanent exhibits record the cultural evolution of Native Americans. A large collection of Algonquin pottery is among the highlights, and most of the artifacts and handiworks here are relics of local tribes. > 1080 Bayview Rd., Southold, tel. 631/765-5577, www.southoldindianmuseum.org. $1 suggested donation. July and Aug., weekends 1:30–4:30; Sept.–June, Sun. 1:30–4:30.

Tours

Atlantis Explorer Environmental Boat Tours During the two-hour boat tours ($17) down the Peconic River, naturalists explain the geological history of the Peconic Estuary system and discuss local flora and fauna. There's also a shoreline walking tour. The tours, run by the Cornell Cooperative Extension Marine Program, are offered twice daily April through September. Call to make a reservation. > 431 E. Main St., Riverhead, tel. 631/208-9200, www.atlantismarineworld.com.

Mary E From April through October, you may take a 2½-hour tour around Long Island Sound aboard this 1906 schooner for $20–$25. > Preston's Dock, Main St., Greenport, tel. 631/477-8966, http://themarye.netfirms.com.

Sports

CANOEING & KAYAKING

Paddling is an ideal way to experience the North Fork's waterways at low tide. You may be surprised by the wide assortment of birds and plants you encounter along the Peconic River on a two-hour trip from Calverton to Riverhead. For sea kayaking, Hallock's Bay in Orient is a favorite spot. Eagle's Neck Paddling Company and Sound View Scuba, both in Southold, offer guided kayak tours. Matt-A-Mar Marina in Mattituck also runs canoe and kayak tours. Eagle's Neck Paddling Company and Matt-A-Mar also rent craft.

RENTALS & GUIDES **Eagle's Neck Paddling Company** > 49295 Main Rd., Southold, tel. 631/323-2660, www.eaglesneck.com. **Matt-A-Mar Marina** > 2255 Wickham Ave., Mattituck, tel. 631/298-4739, www.mattamar.com. **Sound View Scuba** > 46770 Rte. 48, Southold, tel. 631/765-9515, www.soundviewscuba.com.

FISHING

Hooking the big one is not an impossible dream on the North Fork. Bait-and-tackle shops usually can tell you what's running, or you can check out the weekly fishing report in the *Suffolk Times*. Seasonal freshwater licenses in the towns of Riverhead and Southold cost $14 for New York State residents, $35 for nonresidents; they're available at town hall and local sporting-goods stores. Shellfish permits are restricted to residents in the town of Riverhead. In the town of Southold, part-time residents may purchase a shellfish permit for $10.

Island Star Lines The 65-foot open fishing boat, *Island Star,* can provide rods and bait, if you need them. You can go out from May through November and bring the kids. > Railroad Dock, 3rd St., Greenport, tel. 631/696-0936, http://islandstarfishing.com.

Peconic Star II The 90-foot, 150-passenger cruiser regularly offers fishing trips from May through December. Full-day rates are $49 per person ($29 for a child) and include bait and a rod and reel. > Railroad Dock, 3rd St., Greenport, tel. 631/289-6899, www.peconicstar.com.

GOLF

Island's End Golf & Country Club The semiprivate golf club has a well-maintained 18-hole, 6,639-yard course with great views. One hole overlooks Long Island Sound. High-season greens fees are $48 on weekends (June through October). > Rte. 25, Greenport, tel. 631/477–0777, www.islandsendgolf.com.

Save the Date

JUNE

Strawberry Festival & Country Fair Along with strawberry shortcake, the popular summer festival includes a crafts fair, amusement rides, and fireworks. The festival is held over three days in the middle of the month. > Strawberry Fields, Rte. 48, Mattituck, tel. 631/298–5757, www.northfork.org.

JULY

Riverhead Blues Festival The annual five-day event held along the Peconic River features more than 50 acts on four stages, plus crafts and food vendors and carnival rides. > Tel. 631/727–0048, www.riverheadblues.com.

Riverhead River Festival & Boat Show Centered on the Peconic River waterfront, off Peconic Avenue, this one-day event encompasses activities and demonstrations on and off the water, including kayak and road races, skydiving exhibitions, puppet shows, and treasure hunts for kids. > Tel. 631/744–5951, www.riverheadli.com.

AUGUST

Fruits of the Region Festival The Castello di Borghese Vineyard hosts two days of East End arts, crafts, food, and other pleasures. > Rte. 48 at Alvah's La., Cutchogue, tel. 631/734–5111, www.castellodiborghese.com.

SEPTEMBER

Annual North Fork Jazz Festival Pianists Bill Charlap and Ahmad Jamal and trumpeter Clark Terry are among the great jazz musicians who have performed at this one-night event, held in the auditorium of Southold High School. > Oaklawn Ave., Southold, tel. 631/734–7696 Arts in Southold Town.

Greenport Maritime Festival For two days, Greenport closes down its main drags for this festival, which includes a chowder contest, regatta, parade, food vendors, and activities for children. > Tel. 631/477–0004, www.eastendseaport.org.

OCTOBER

Harvest Fair The bounty of autumn is celebrated with prepared foods, a farmer's market, crafts vendors, and kids' activities. > Village green, Cutchogue, tel. 631/734–2335, www.northfork.org.

Riverhead Country Fair Most of downtown Riverhead is taken over by this fair that includes a carnival with food and crafts booths, folk musicians, pony and boat rides, and contests for everything from the best jams and jellies to the largest pumpkin. > Tel. 631/727–1215 or 631/727–7600, www.riverheadli.com.

DECEMBER

Holiday House Tour The Friends of the Mattituck–Laurel Library sponsor this annual, self-guided tour of private Mattituck homes decorated for the holiday season. Tickets include light refreshments served at the library and are $20 in advance or $24 on tour day. > Tel. 631/298–4134, www.northfork.org.

WHERE TO STAY

CUTCHOGUE

Santorini Hotel Location is everything at this motel-style complex, which sits amid 17 acres with a 500-foot-long beach on Long Island Sound. Rooms are spare and simple. > 3800 Duck Pond Rd., 11935, tel. 631/734–6370, www.santorinibeach.com. 45 rooms. Restaurant, some room phones, cable TV, pool, wading pool, beach, basketball, some pets allowed, no-smoking rooms. AE, D, MC, V. CP. $$$–$$$$

EAST MARION

Blue Dolphin Resort This neat and welcoming resort makes it easy to vacation with the whole family, including the dog. There's even a dog run on the premises. Rooms are simple and bright. > 7850 Main Rd., 11939, tel. 631/477–0907, www.bluedolphinmotel.net. 29 studios. Café, picnic area, kitchenettes, refrigerators, cable TV, pool, video game room, lounge, playground, laundry facilities, some pets allowed (fee), no-smoking rooms. AE, MC, V. $$–$$$

Quintessentials Bed & Breakfast Innkeeper Sylvia Daley imbues her antiques-filled home with warm hospitality. Fresh flowers, Caribbean colors, chocolates, and maximum pampering await in this gingerbread Victorian set amid feng shui gardens. The spa offers such extras as massage, reflexology, facials, and body wraps. Sylvia's homemade corned-beef hash and fried plantains are a breakfast specialty. > 8985 Main Rd., 11939, tel. 631/477–9400 or 877/259–0939, www.quintessentialsinc.com. 6 rooms. Dining room, fans, in-room data ports, some in-room hot tubs, cable TV, in-room VCRs, spa, library, Internet; no smoking. AE, MC, V. CP. $$$$

GREENPORT

The Greenporter Hotel & Spa A 1950s motel, a block from the waterfront, has been converted into this sleek, minimalist lodging with a cool green interior scheme. A full spa is in the works for sometime in 2004. In the meantime, you may schedule in-room spa treatments, from shiatsu to body polishes and reflexology. > 326 Front St., 11944, tel. 631/477–0066, fax 631/477–2317, www.thegreenporter.com. 15 rooms. Restaurant, in-room data ports, cable TV, pool, hot tub, massage, bar, some pets allowed (fee), no-smoking rooms. AE, MC, V. EP. $$$–$$$$

Shady Lady Inn The Victorian-style inn, decorated to the hilt with furnishings and objets d'art from the owner's collections, offers an over-the-top, frilly rendezvous. Rooms have 14-foot ceilings, a fireplace, marble bathroom, feather bed, and massive antique headboard and armoire. Both the formal Scarlet Room and more casual Pine Lounge serve sophisticated Continental cuisine. > 305 North Rd., 11944, tel. 631/477–4500, www.shadyladyinn.com. 6 rooms, 2 suites. Restaurant, cable TV, lounge, Internet; no kids under 18, no smoking. AE, D, DC, MC, V. CP. $$$$

Sound View Inn Each room in this complex of modern motel-style buildings has a deck overlooking the 1,400-foot-long private beach. Interiors are bright, with contemporary wood furniture in light tones and pale wood paneling. > 57185 North Rd., 11944, tel. 631/477–1910, fax 631/477–9436, www.soundviewinn.com. 49 rooms, 31 suites. Restaurant, some in-room data ports, some kitchenettes, refrigerators, cable TV, 4 tennis courts, pool, sauna, beach, bar, no-smoking rooms. AE, D, DC, MC, V. EP. $$

The Victorian Lady The delightful in-town bed-and-breakfast has a sizable front porch where you can sit while savoring a confection from the fudge factory across the street. The rooms, each named after a flower, are furnished with antiques and Victorian-period pieces. The Lilac Room is the most flowery of the three. A resident dog shares common rooms with guests. > 151 Bay Ave., 11944, tel. 631/477–1837, www.victorianladybnb.com. 3 rooms. Dining room, fans, cable TV, library; no smoking. MC, V. BP. $$–$$$

Watson's by the Bay Built in 1873, this three-story Victorian home sits on a quiet cul-de-sac two blocks from the village, overlooking the Peconic Bay and Shelter Island. Rooms have period antiques and bay views. The wraparound porch is a great place to relax while sipping some local wine. > 104 Bay Ave., 11944, tel. 631/477–0426, fax 631/477–8441, www.greenport.com/watsons. 3 rooms. Dining room, fans, cable TV, pool; no kids, no smoking. Closed Labor Day–Memorial Day. No credit cards. CP. $–$$$

RIVERHEAD

Best Western East End The chain property, next to the Tanger outlet center (just off the LIE) and 1 mi from Splish Splash and the Riverhead Raceway, earns high marks for comfort and convenience. > 1830 Rte. 25, Riverhead 11901, tel. 631/369–2200, fax 631/369–1202, www.bestwestern.com. 100 rooms. Restaurant, room service, in-room data ports, cable TV with movies, pool, gym, laundry facilities, business services, meeting rooms, car rental, some pets allowed, no-smoking rooms. AE, D, DC, MC, V. CP. $$–$$$$

Budget Host Inn This motel-style budget option is on 6 acres 6 mi from the Splish Splash water park. The grounds include a play and picnic areas. Rooms are carpeted and colorful. > 30 E. Moriches Rd., Riverhead 11901, tel. 631/727–6200, fax 631/727–6466, www.budgethost.com. 68 rooms. Restaurant, coffee shop, picnic area, some kitchenettes, cable TV, pool, lounge, playground, business services, meeting rooms, no-smoking rooms. AE, D, DC, MC, V. EP. ¢–$$

Motel on the Bay All rooms at this motel overlook Peconic Bay and its sandy beach. Some units have full kitchens. The two-room suites and waterfront apartments, furnished in a contemporary style, are especially roomy. > Front St., South Jamesport, 11970, tel. 631/722–3458, fax 631/722–5166, www.northforkmotels.com. 7 studios, 10 suites. Some kitchens, some kitchenettes, refrigerators, cable TV, beach, no-smoking rooms. AE, D, MC, V. EP. $$–$$$

Red Barn Bed & Breakfast At this lovingly restored 1877 farmhouse, you can relax in a hammock, sip lemonade on the porch, and star-gaze through the owner's telescope. Rooms are tidy and uncluttered. Breakfast features free-range local eggs, homemade scones, and desserts such as strawberry-rhubarb cobbler. > 733 Herricks La., Jamesport 11947, tel./fax 631/722–3695, www.redbarnbandb.com. 3 rooms. Dining room, croquet, horseshoes, some pets allowed; no room TVs, no smoking. MC, V. BP. $$–$$$$

WHERE TO EAT

GREENPORT

Chowder Pot Pub The views of Peconic Bay at this casual seafood spot are best at sunset. You may eat outside when the weather's nice. The places hosts live music on weekends. > 104 3rd St., tel. 631/477–1345. AE, MC, V. Closed Jan.–Mar.; Mon.–Wed. Apr.–June and Labor Day–Dec. $$–$$$

Claudio's Clam Bar/Claudio's Restaurant/Crabby Jerry's These three restaurants share a 2½-acre waterfront property. The Clam Bar, right on the dock, serves salads, hot dogs, fried clams, mussels, and soft-shell crab. Claudio's is known for seafood, porterhouse steaks, and lobsters; the bar dates to the late 1800s. Crabby Jerry's offers self-service with picnic tables on the Main Street Dock. > 111 Main St., tel. 631/477–0627. MC, V. Closed Dec.–mid-Apr. $$

The Frisky Oyster Celebrity sightings are not uncommon at this sophisticated retro-modern seafood restaurant, a departure from Greenport's largely pub-grub dining scene. Hamptons types come for the lively bar scene and contemporary fare, such as goat cheese–and–leek tart and grilled swordfish with couscous and orange vinaigrette. > 27 Front St., tel. 631/477–4265. AE, D, DC, MC, V. No lunch. $$–$$$

Michael's Part of this breezy, relaxed restaurant is a diner from 1937; an enclosed deck and patio have alfresco tables. The casual contemporary fare ranges from roasted-vegetable quesadillas with homemade salsa to top sirloin; a raw bar is available on weekends. For dessert, consider fresh raspberry-peach crisp or carrot cake. Kids get their own list of dishes. > 212 Front St., tel. 631/477–9577. Closed Tues. and Wed. AE, DC, MC, V. $–$$

MATTITUCK

Old Mill Inn Tables at this old gristmill, which dates to 1821, overlook the inlet. You may eat on the outdoor patio in warm weather and hear live music on weekends. Popular dishes include lobster specials and broiled rack of lamb. A children's menu is available. > 5775 W. Mill Rd., tel. 631/298–8080. AE, MC, V. Closed Mon. $$–$$$

Touch of Venice Every table provides a waterfront view at this Italian restaurant. The stuffed-artichoke appetizer is a popular choice, as are the inventive pasta dishes, steak dinners, and lobster preparations. In the warm-weather months you may eat on the patio. A kids' menu is offered, and sometimes the place has live music. > Matt-A-Mar Marina, 2255 Wickham Ave., tel. 631/298–5851. AE, D, MC, V. Closed Mon.; Tues. and no lunch in Nov.–Mar.; Wed. in Jan.–Mar. $–$$

ORIENT

Hellenic Snack Bar Heavenly homemade lemonade—well known on the North Fork—and authentic Greek appetizers and main courses are the draws at this East Marion restaurant. The outdoor patio is covered and has a huge rotisserie for barbecuing lamb. > 5145 Main Rd., East Marion, tel. 631/477–0138. AE, D, DC, MC, V. ¢–$$

Orient by the Sea The casual marina restaurant overlooks Gardiner's Bay. Dishes include a broiled-seafood combo of lobster tail, stuffed flounder, shrimps, and scallops, as well as steaks and chicken and pasta options. Outdoor dining is on the deck. A children's menu is available. > Main Rd., Orient, tel. 631/323–2424. D, DC, MC, V. Closed Nov.–Apr. $$–$$$

RIVERHEAD

Digger O'Dells In addition to such pub standards as shepherd's pie, fish-and-chips, and corned beef and cabbage, the menu here includes prime rib, steaks, and pasta and chicken dishes. The pub-restaurant hosts live music on Friday and Saturday. A children's menu is available. > 58 W. Main St., Riverhead, tel. 631/369–3200. AE, D, DC, MC, V. $–$$

Jamesport Country Kitchen The food outshines the decor at this eatery, which looks like a simple, wood-shingled country store. The menu is contemporary, and dishes feature local ingredients such as fresh seafood and Long Island duck. The wine list also has a local focus. > Main Rd., Jamesport, tel. 631/722–3537. AE, DC, MC, V. $–$$

Meetinghouse Creek Inn The seafood at this waterside restaurant 4 mi east of River-head are a big draw, but the kitchen also turns out good steaks and pasta dishes. A patio offers open-air dining. A pianist plays here Friday and Saturday. A children's menu is available, as is Sunday brunch. > 177 Meeting House Creek Rd., Aquebogue, tel. 631/722–4220. AE, D, MC, V. Closed Tues. Labor Day–late May. $–$$
Modern Snack Bar At this unpretentious family-owned café beloved by locals and out-of-towners alike, you can savor sauerbraten with potato dumplings, delectable lobster salad, and home-baked strawberry-rhubarb and lemon-meringue pies. > 628 Main Rd., Aquebogue, tel. 631/722–3655. No reservations. AE, D, MC, V. Closed Mon. and Dec.–Mar. $–$$

ESSENTIALS

Getting Here

Getting to the North Fork by bus or train from New York City is fairly simple, and taking the train is a way to avoid traffic; the question of how to get around without a car once you arrive is the tricky part. A local taxi might suffice to get you from your accommodation to the restaurants. However, the area's charm lies in its lazy country roads dotted with farm stands and wineries—best sampled via car and on your own schedule.

BY BUS
Sunrise Coach Lines serves the North Fork, offering direct daily service from Manhattan and Queens to Riverhead, Mattituck, Cutchogue, Southold, and Greenport, for $16 one-way during peak travel times. The trip to Greenport takes about 2½ hours. Sunrise picks up at 44th Street and 3rd Avenue, on Manhattan's East Side; on the return trip it drops off at limited 3rd Avenue bus stops from 37th Street to 79th Street. Seats must be reserved.
LINES **Sunrise Coach Lines** > Tel. 631/477–1200 or 800/527–7709, www.sunrisecoach.com.

BY CAR
Driving time ranges from two hours, in ideal conditions, to three hours or more in traffic. Heavy traffic is mostly unavoidable if you leave the city on Friday afternoon or evening or if you return late Sunday afternoon or evening. You face less traffic if you leave the city around noon (or earlier) Friday, or wait until after 8 PM to get going. The best way to get to the North Fork is the LIE (I–495), which you take to the last exit (73), in Riverhead. From here, the road becomes Route 58 until Aquebogue, where it changes to Route 25, also known as Main Road, and continues to Greenport. In Greenport it turns northward and then continues east with the North Fork's other west-east route, the North Road (also known as Sound Avenue, Route 48, and Truck Route 25, depending on where you are).

BY TRAIN
The LIRR runs four daily trains to the North Fork on weekdays and two daily on weekends. Trains depart from Manhattan's Pennsylvania Station and make stops in Ronkonkoma, Riverhead, Mattituck, Southold, and Greenport. Travel time is just under three hours; the one-way peak fare is $19. To bring a bicycle, you must obtain a permit in advance; the $5 permit is good for one year. Permit applications are available via the LIRR Web site.

LINES **Long Island Rail Road** > Tel. 718/217–5477 or 631/231–5477, www.lirr.org. *STATIONS* **Greenport** > Wiggins and 4th Sts., at ferry dock, no phone, www.lirr.org. **Mattituck** > Love La. and Pike St., north of Rte. 25, no phone, www.lirr.org. **Riverhead** > Osborne Ave. and Railroad St., north of W. Main St./Rte. 25, no phone, www.lirr.org. **Southold** > Youngs Ave. and Traveler St., north of Main Rd./Rte. 25, no phone, www.lirr.org.

Visitor Information

The North Fork Promotion Council runs a tourist-information booth in Greenport that's open Friday through Monday from April through October.
CONTACTS **Greenport-Southold Chamber of Commerce** > Box 1415, Southold 11971, tel. 631/765–3161, www.greenportsouthold.org. **Long Island Wine Council** > Tel. 631/369–5887, www.liwines.com. **North Fork Promotion Council** > Box 1865, Southold 11971, tel. 631/298–5757, www.northfork.org; Tourist Information Booth, Main Rd. near Chapel La., Greenport. **Riverhead Chamber of Commerce** > 524 E. Main St., Box 291, Riverhead 11901, tel. 631/727–7600, www.riverheadchamber.com. **Riverhead Tourist Information Booth** > Tanger Outlet Stores, 1770 W. Main St., at Rte. 25, Riverhead, tel. 631/727–0048.

The Litchfield Hills

New Milford is 75 mi northeast of New York City; Salisbury is 110 mi north of New York City

17

Revised by Jane E. Zarem

FOOTHILLS TO THE BERKSHIRE MOUNTAINS, the Litchfield Hills encompass some of the most spectacular and unspoiled scenery in Connecticut. Grand inns and charming bed-and-breakfasts are plentiful, as are sophisticated eateries. Forested trails—including a 51-mi section of the Appalachian Trail—traverse several state parks; the Housatonic and the Farmington rivers attract anglers and canoeing enthusiasts; and the state's three largest natural lakes, Bantam, Waramaug, and Twin, reside here. Picturesque town greens and stately homes anchor Litchfield and New Milford, and Kent, New Preston, and Woodbury draw avid antiquers. Washington and Salisbury provide a glimpse into New England village life that hasn't changed significantly for two centuries.

Two highways, I–84 and Route 8, form the southern and eastern boundaries of the region. When driving to the Litchfield Hills from New York City, New Milford is the usual gateway and a good starting point. The town also was the starting point for Roger Sherman, who, in 1743, opened his cobbler shop at the intersection of Main and Church streets. Sherman later signed the Declaration of Independence and helped draft the Articles of Confederation and the U.S. Constitution. New Milford is now large and busy, but interesting shops, galleries, and restaurants surround its town green, one of the longest in New England.

From New Milford, U.S. 7 continues north to Kent, the Cornwalls, Lakeville, and Salisbury before crossing into Massachusetts. Kent, home to a prep school of the same name, has the area's greatest concentration of art galleries—most of them on U.S. 7, which serves as the main street. Kent's art tradition began with the founding of the Kent Art Association in 1923 by a group of "runaway" New York artists.

North of Kent are the Cornwalls, a peaceful area primarily known for its vistas of woods and mountains and its historic covered bridges, which span the Housatonic River. About half the charming town of Sharon, west of the Cornwalls and bordering New York State, is forested. Many of Sharon's fewer than 3,000 residents are part-time New Yorkers for whom the weekend commute is absolutely worth it.

In Lakeville, about 7 mi north of Sharon, you can usually spot an original Colonial home by looking for the grapevine design cut into the frieze above the front door—the trademark of the builder of the village's first homes. Lakeville gets its name from Lake Wononscopomuc. Most of its shoreline is private property, but you glimpse the waters as you drive along U.S. 44 or Route 41.

Were it not for the obsolescence of its ironworks, Salisbury, the center of which is mi northeast of Lakeville, might today be the largest city in Connecticut. Iron was discovered here in 1732, and for the next century the slopes of Salisbury's Mt. Riga produced the finest iron in America. The introduction of the Bessemer process of steel manufacturing from molten pig iron—adapted to U.S. steelmaking needs by Lakeville native Alexander Holley in 1864—reduced the demand for iron products. Most signs of cinder heaps and slag dumps are long gone, replaced by grand summer homes, gardens, and inns, and today Salisbury settles for having both the state's highest mountain, Bear Mountain (2,355 feet), and its highest point, on the shoulder of Mt. Frissel (2,380 feet)—whose peak is actually in Massachusetts. There's a spot on Mt. Frissel where, if the urge strikes you (as it does many), you can stretch your limbs across the Connecticut, Massachusetts, and New York borders all at once.

Off the beaten track is Norfolk, in the northeast corner of the Litchfield Hills. Enormous homesteads still exist in Norfolk, where the fountain in the striking village green was designed by Augustus Saint-Gaudens and executed by Stanford White.

An alternative and equally scenic route into the Litchfield Hills from New Milford is U.S. 202, which you can take northeast to Litchfield, passing through New Preston and detouring a few miles to Washington on the way. The tiny village center of New Preston, perched above a 40-foot waterfall on the Aspetuck River, is merely a crossroads, but several antiques shops stand cheek by jowl here. Just north of the village on Route 45 is Lake Waramaug, the second-largest natural lake in the state. It was named for Chief Waramaug, one of the most revered figures in Connecticut's Native American history. A drive or bicycle trip around the 8-mi perimeter of the lake takes you past lovely homes and some noteworthy inns.

Washington was settled in 1734 and, in 1779, became one of the first towns in the new United States to be named for George Washington. The Gunnery prep school, with its stone walls and gardens, mingles with other classic Colonial buildings and churches in Washington, one of the best-preserved Colonial villages in Connecticut.

Litchfield has an impressive village green and broad, elm-shaded streets lined with stately Colonial and Greek Revival homes. Harriet Beecher Stowe, author of *Uncle Tom's Cabin,* and her brother, abolitionist preacher Henry Ward Beecher, were born and raised in Litchfield, and many famous Americans earned their law degrees at the Litchfield Law School. About 8 mi south is Bethlehem, an obvious focus at Christmastime; another 10 mi south, in the southeast corner of the Litchfield Hills, is Woodbury, the state's antiques capital, with more antiques shops than all the other villages in the region combined.

The Litchfield Hills are a four-season destination. Fishing, walks in the woods, exploring museums and gardens, river canoeing and kayaking, and lake swimming are tops in the warmer months, whereas cross-country and downhill skiing and toasty inn rooms with fireplaces provide winter temptations. The fall foliage is magnificent, one reason autumn is the region's busiest season. If this is when you hope to visit, reserve your room months in advance.

WHAT TO SEE & DO

KENT & CORNWALL

Bachelier-Cardonsky Gallery One of the area's foremost galleries, run by Jacques Kaplan, exhibits works by local artists and American contemporary masters such as Alexander Calder, Carol Anthony, and Jackson Pollock. > 10 N. Main St., 2nd fl., Kent, tel. 860/927-3129. Mid-Apr.–Dec., Fri.–Sun. 11–5, and by appointment.

Bull's Bridge Since 1760 several bridges have connected the two banks of the Housatonic River at this site; the 110-foot-long covered bridge you see today, built in 1842, replaced them. Isaac Bull built the first bridge, which wasn't covered, to transport iron ore and charcoal across the river; the first covered bridge was built by Jacob Bull in 1811. > Bull's Bridge Rd. west of U.S. 7, Bull's Bridge.

Cornwall Bridge The barn-red, one-lane covered bridge is in West Cornwall, several miles up U.S. 7 from the village called Cornwall Bridge. Built in 1837 of native oak, it incorporates strut techniques later copied by bridge builders around the country. The bridge links the towns of Cornwall and Sharon and, along with nearby Bull's Bridge, is one of three covered bridges remaining in Connecticut and one of two still open to automobile traffic. > Rte. 128 off U.S. 7, West Cornwall.

Housatonic Meadows State Park The 450-acre park includes a 2-mi stretch of the Housatonic River that fly-fishing enthusiasts consider to be among the best places in New England to test their skill. You can camp along the shores of the river, hike, picnic, and canoe here. > U.S. 7 about 2 mi north of Rte. 4, Sharon, tel. 860/927-3238, www.dep.state.ct.us/rec. Free. Daily 8–sunset.

Kent Falls State Park Connecticut's most impressive waterfall is in this 295-acre park. You can hike along a path adjacent to the 200-foot cascade to view it at all levels. A lush hemlock grove above the falls has a picnic area. > U.S. 7 about 7 mi north of village, Kent, tel. 860/927-3238, www.dep.state.ct.us/rec. Parking $7 CT resident, $10 nonresident. Daily 8–sunset.

Macedonia Brook State Park The 2,300 acres of this park include streams, hiking and cross-country-skiing trails, and rustic campsites. You can see the remains of a Kent Iron Co. forge at the park's south end, near the park entrance. > 159 Macedonia Brook Rd., Kent, tel. 860/927-3238, www.dep.state.ct.us/rec. Free. Daily 8–sunset.

Mohawk Mountain State Park The park encompasses more than 2,900 acres that include craggy hills and a black spruce bog. The view from the top of 1,683-foot Mohawk Mountain is breathtaking, especially during fall foliage season; the hike up is 2½ mi. A privately owned downhill-ski area, called Mohawk Mountain, is within the park boundaries. > Rte. 4 about 4 mi west of Goshen, Cornwall, tel. 860/424-3200, www.dep.state.ct.us/rec. Free. Daily 8 AM–sunset.

Paris–New York–Kent Gallery This respected gallery exhibits well-established 20th-century artists as well as contemporary international and American artists. Outdoor sculpture exhibitions are sometimes held. > Kent Station Sq., U.S. 7, Kent, tel. 860/927-4152. Free. Mid-Apr.–Dec., Fri.–Sun. 11–5, and by appointment.

Sharon Audubon Center With 11 mi of trails, this 1,200-acre bird sanctuary is one of the best places to hike in the area. The center also includes an exhibit space, gift shop, and picnic area. > 325 Cornwall Bridge Rd./Rte. 4, Sharon, tel. 860/364-0520, www.audubon.org/local/sanctuary/sharon. $3. Exhibit space Tues.–Sat. 9–5, Sun. 1–5. Trails daily, dawn–dusk.

Sloane-Stanley Museum Hardware-store buffs and vintage-tool aficionados adore this unusual museum. Artist and author Eric Sloane (1905–85) was fascinated by early-American woodworking tools, and his collection ranges from the 17th to the 19th centuries. The museum, a re-creation of Sloane's last studio, also encompasses the ruins of Kent Iron Furnace (1826–92). (Wednesday hours are tentative; call ahead if you plan to visit midweek.) > U.S. 7 1 mi north of Rte. 341, Kent, tel. 860/927-3849 or 860/566-3005, www.chc.state.ct.us/sloanestanleymuseum.htm. $4. Mid-May–Oct., Wed.–Sun. 10–4.

LAKEVILLE & LIME ROCK

Holley-Williams House Museum It won't cost you anything to wander around the gardens, which include a maze, an ice house, and, of all things, a seven-hole outhouse. The museum, in an ironmaster's 1808 classical revival homestead, chronicles

18th- and 19th-century life and contains family furnishings, Colonial-era portraits, and a Holley Manufacturing Co. pocketknife exhibit. "From Corsets to Freedom," an exhibit set in the 1870s, demonstrates the debate between women's rights and "women's sphere" in the home. Admission to the Holley-Williams House includes the on-site **Salisbury Cannon Museum,** where hands-on exhibits and activities account for the contribution of area residents and the local iron industry to the American Revolution. > U.S. 44, Lakeville, tel. 860/435–2878, www.salisburyassociation.org/hhm. Museum $3, grounds free. Mid-June–mid-Oct., weekends noon–5 or by appointment.

White Hollow Farm Corn Maze Finding the way through the maze in this 11-acre corn-field is great family fun. There's a hay ride, lots of farm animals, and homemade cookies and drinks. Plus, you can buy end-of-season sweet corn and Halloween pumpkins. > U.S. 7 and Rte. 112, Lime Rock, tel. 860/435–0382, www.cornmazewhitehollowfarm.com. $7. Late Aug.–Oct., weekends 10–6.

LITCHFIELD

Haight Vineyard Despite the area's fluctuating climate, Connecticut's first estab-lished winery flourishes. Wines here include chardonnay, seyval blanc, riesling, and merlot, as well as some light blushes and interesting blends. You can stop in for vine-yard walks, a guided winery tour (hourly), and complimentary tastings. > 29 Chestnut Hill Rd./Rte. 118, 1 mi east of Litchfield center,, tel. 860/567–4045, www.haightvineyards.com. Free. Mon.–Sat. 10:30–5, Sun. noon–5.

Litchfield History Museum Galleries at this museum are well organized and display decorative arts, paintings, and antique furnishings that effectively serve as records of the village's history and evolution. The extensive reference library has information about the village's historic buildings, including the Sheldon Tavern (where George Washington slept on several occasions) and the Litchfield Female Academy, where, in the late 1700s, forward-thinking Sarah Pierce taught girls not just sewing and deport-ment but also mathematics and history. > 7 South St., at Rtes. 63 and 118, tel. 860/567–4501, www.litchfieldhistoricalsociety.org. $5 (includes Tapping Reeve House and Litchfield Law School). Mid-Apr.–late Nov., Tues.–Sat. 11–5, Sun. 1–5.

Mount Tom State Park Connecticut's first state park was named for the small moun-tain (really a big hill) that it surrounds. Canoes, kayaks, and other boats without mo-tors are allowed in Mount Tom Pond, which is stocked with trout and other freshwater fish; there's also a small beach for swimming. A mile-long trail leads up Mount Tom (1,325 feet) to a stone tower, where the panoramic view is outstanding. > U.S. 202 3½ mi west of Bantam, tel. 860/868–2592, www.dep.state.ct.us/rec. Park-ing $7 CT residents, $10 nonresidents. Daily 8–dusk.

Tapping Reeve House and Litchfield Law School In 1773, Judge Tapping Reeve en-rolled his first student, Aaron Burr, in what was to become the first law school in the country. Before that students studied the law as apprentices, not in formal classes. This site is dedicated to Reeve's remarkable achievement and to the notable students who passed through its halls: Oliver Wolcott Jr., John C. Calhoun, Horace Mann, three U.S. Supreme Court justices, and 15 governors, not to mention innumerable senators, congressmen, and ambassadors. The museum has interactive multimedia exhibits, an excellent introductory film, and beautifully restored facilities. > 82 South St., tel. 860/567–4501, www.litchfieldhistoricalsociety.org. $5 (includes Litchfield His-tory Museum). Mid-Apr.–late Nov., Tues.–Sat. 11–5, Sun. 1–5.

Topsmead State Forest The forest's chief attractions are the 1929 English Tudor-style "cottage" of Miss Edith Chase, heiress to a brass fortune from nearby Water-bury, and its beautiful gardens and lawns. Also on the 511-acre property are picnic grounds and trails for hiking and cross-country skiing. The house, designed by architect Richard Henry Dana Jr. and completely furnished in Elizabethan antiques, is open for guided tours June through October. > Buell Rd. off E. Litchfield Rd., tel. 860/567–5694, www.dep.state.ct.us/rec. Free. Forest daily 8–dusk; house tours June–Oct., 2nd and 4th weekends each month, noon–5.

White Flower Farm A stroll through the nursery's landscaped grounds is always a pleasure, and gardeners find many ideas to bring home. This is the home base of the renowned garden mail-order operation. > Rte. 63 3 mi south of village center, tel. 860/567–8789, www.whiteflowerfarm.com. Free. Apr.–Oct., daily 9–5:30.

White Memorial Conservation Center Connecticut's largest nature center and wildlife sanctuary encompasses 4,000 acres with fishing areas, bird-watching platforms, two self-guided nature trails, several boardwalks, and 35 mi of hiking, cross-country-skiing, and horseback-riding trails. The grounds are always open; you may even come to stargaze, if you wish. The conservation center houses a natural-history museum, the best in the state and a must-see for lovers of the outdoors. > Off U.S. 202, 2 mi west of village center, Litchfield, tel. 860/567–0857, www.whitememorialcc.org. Grounds free, museum $4. Museum Mon.–Sat. 9–5, Sun. noon–5.

NEW PRESTON & WASHINGTON

Gunn Historical Museum and Library A 1781 house on Washington's green is occupied by a museum with changing exhibits that relate local history via period furnishings, decorative arts, and antique clothing. The 1908 library includes the Connecticut Reference Room, which contains state, local, and genealogical books. > 5 Wykeham Rd., at Rte. 47, Washington, tel. 860/868–7756 museum, 860/868–7586 library, www.biblio.org/gunn. Free. Museum Thurs.–Sat. 10–4, Sun. noon–4. Library Mon. and Fri. 9:30–5, Tues. and Thurs. 9:30–8, and Sat. 9:30–3.

Hopkins Vineyard The vineyard overlooks Lake Waramaug, and the winery produces more than 13 varieties of wine, from sparkling to dessert. A weathered red barn contains a gift shop and a tasting room, and the property has a picnic area. The wine bar serves a fine cheese-and-pâté board. > 25 Hopkins Rd., New Preston, tel. 860/868–7954, www.hopkinsvineyard.com. Free. Jan. and Feb., Fri.–Sat. 10–5, Sun. 11–5; Mar. and Apr., Wed.–Sat. 10–5, Sun. 11–5; May–Dec., Mon.–Sat. 10–5, Sun. 11–5.

Institute for American Indian Studies The center has a thoughtfully arranged collection of permanent exhibits and displays that detail the history of the Northeastern Woodland Native Americans. Highlights include a replicated longhouse and nature trails. Two Native American art galleries have changing shows. > 38 Curtis Rd., off Rte. 199, Washington, tel. 860/868–0518, www.birdstone.org. $4. Mon.–Sat. 10–5, Sun. noon–5.

Lake Waramaug State Park At the northwest tip of 680-acre Lake Waramaug, the second-largest natural lake in Connecticut, sits this idyllic 75-acre park with a shaded picnic area, sandy beach, and lakeside campground. Biking around the lake (about 8 mi) is a favorite activity. > 30 Lake Waramaug Rd., New Preston, tel. 860/868–2592, www.dep.state.ct.us/rec. Parking $7 CT residents, $10 nonresidents. Daily 8–dusk.

WOODBURY & BETHLEHEM

Abbey of Regina Laudis The 40 cloistered Benedictine nuns who live at the abbey became celebrities when they released their first *Women in Chant* CD. The nuns, who sing Gregorian chants at their daily prayers, also make and sell fine handicrafts, honey, cheese, herbs, and beauty products, among other goods. An 18th-century Neapolitan crèche with 80 hand-painted baroque porcelain figures is on view from

Easter to December here. > 273 Flanders Rd., Bethlehem, tel. 203/266–7637,
www.abbeyofreginalaudis.com. Mon., Tues., and Thurs.–Sun., 10–noon and 1:30–4.
Glebe House Museum The large, antiques-filled gambrel roof Colonial (c. 1750), one of
the most authentically preserved houses in the state, is where Dr. Samuel Seabury was
elected America's first Episcopal bishop in 1783. (*Glebe* is an archaic term for a minis-
ter's farmhouse.) Renowned British horticulturist Gertrude Jekyll designed the garden.
> Hollow Rd., off Rte. 317, Woodbury, tel. 203/263–2855, www.theglebehouse.org. $5.
Apr.–Oct., Wed.–Sun. 1–4; Nov., weekends 1–4.

Sports

AUTO RACING

Lime Rock Park Formula One, stock-, and vintage-car races, as well as Sports Car
Club of America events, are held at this renowned venue. The main events happen on
Memorial Day, July 4, and Labor Day weekends. The free-form track surrounds a
large, shady infield, where spectators set up their lawn chairs, have a picnic, and
enjoy great close-up views of the races. Admission prices depend on the race, the day
(no Sunday races), and whether tickets are purchased in advance. > Rte. 112 west of
U.S. 7, Lime Rock, tel. 860/435–5000 or 800/722–3577, www.limerock.com. $5–$35.
Mar.–Oct.; days and times vary.

Skip Barber Racing School Racing pro Skip Barber offers day-long and weekend
(and longer) safe-driving lessons as well as car-racing classes. The school is part of
Lime Rock Park. > Rte. 112, Lakeville, tel. 860/435–1300 or 800/221–1131,
www.skipbarber.com.

BOATING & RAFTING

Canoeing or kayaking on the Housatonic River, specifically the 10-mi stretch between
Falls Village and Housatonic Meadows State Park, and the Farmington River between
Riverton and New Hartford is spectacular from April to October; the balance of flat
water and Class I, II, III, and IV rapids on both rivers is good. Bull's Bridge Gorge is
terrific for white-water rafting when the water is high in spring. For those who just
want to paddle around a lake, Lake Waramaug State Park in New Preston and Mount
Tom State Park in Litchfield are good options.
OUTFITTERS **Clarke Outdoors** > 163 U.S. 7, West Cornwall, tel. 860/672–6365,
www.clarkeoutdoors.com. **Main Stream Canoe and Kayaks** > 170 Main St./U.S. 44,
New Hartford, tel. 860/693–6791, www.mainstreamcanoe.com. **Riverrunning Expeditions** > 85 Main St., Falls Village, tel. 860/824–5579.

FISHING

Anglers can catch trout, bass, and other freshwater fish in the rivers, lakes, ponds,
and streams in the Litchfield Hills. The early-season trout fishing at Macedonia Brook
State Park in Kent is superb, and fly fishermen consider the 2-mi stretch of the
Housatonic River that is within Housatonic Meadows State Park, in Sharon, to be
among the best places in New England to test their skills. The Housatonic River also
has a 9-mi catch-and-release trout management area from Sharon to Cornwall. Fishing licenses are required for anyone 16 years of age or older.
OUTFITTERS **Housatonic Meadows Fly Shop** > 13 U.S. 7, Cornwall Bridge, tel.
860/672–46064, www.flyfishct.com. **Housatonic River Outfitters** > 24 Kent Rd.,
Cornwall Bridge, tel. 860/672–1010, www.dryflies.com.

HIKING

Many of the area state parks and forest—Housatonic Meadows in Sharon, Macedonia Brook and Kent Falls in Kent, Mount Tom in Litchfield, and Lake Waramaug in
New Preston, to name a few—have hiking trails that lead to the summit of a hill and

a great panoramic view. The Sharon Audubon Center in Sharon and White Memorial Conservation Center in Litchfield also have extensive trails that the public is invited to use. Meanwhile, the southbound Appalachian Trail enters Connecticut in Salisbury, at the northwest corner of Litchfield County, and runs parallel to U.S. 7 and the Housatonic River from just south of Falls Village to Bull's Bridge, where it then veers westward into New York State. The trail's longest river walk is an almost 8-mi hike that you can start on Route 341 near Kent and follow to Cornwall Bridge. The elevation range of the Connecticut portion of the Appalachian Trail is 260 to 2,316 feet, and the best time to hike it is between May and October.

Sharon Audubon Center The 1,200-acre sanctuary, open daily from dawn to dusk, has 11 mi of hiking trails that are open to the public. > 325 Cornwall Bridge Rd./ Rte.4, Sharon, tel. 860/364–0520, www.audubon.org/local/sanctuary/sharon. $3.

White Memorial Conservation Center This 4,000-acre wildlife sanctuary has 35 mi of old carriage roads and trails open to the public for hiking daily. There is no charge to hike the trails; trail maps may be purchased at the museum store for $2.50. > Off U.S. 202, 2 mi west of village center, Litchfield, tel. 860/567–0857, www.whitememorialcc.org.

SKIING & SNOWBOARDING

The Litchfield Hills region has three downhill-skiing areas: one in Cornwall, one in New Hartford, one in Woodbury. They're modest compared with ski areas farther north, but they do have snowmaking capabilities, are closer to home, and usually aren't crowded. Snowboarders have access to all three. The vast amount of open land in the area is good news for cross-country skiers when snow falls. Trails at White Memorial Conservation Center in Litchfield and Macedonia Brook State Park in Kent are extensive. Limited cross-country skiing is available on hiking trails in Housatonic Meadows in Sharon and Topsmead forest in Litchfield as well as in other state parks.

Macedonia Brook State Park The 2,300-acre park has 13 mi of blazed trails that are ideal for cross-country skiing. > 159 Macedonia Brook Rd., Kent, tel. 860/927–3238, www.dep.state.ct.us/rec.

Mohawk Mountain The 23 downhill trails here, with a maximum vertical drop of 650 feet, include plenty of intermediate terrain as well as a few trails for beginners and a few steeper sections toward the top of the mountain. A small section is devoted to snowboarders. Trails are serviced by one triple lift and four doubles; 14 trails are lit for night skiing. The base lodge has snacks and a retail shop. > 46 Great Hollow Rd., off Rte. 4, Cornwall, tel. 860/672–6100, 800/895–5222, 800/672–6100, www.mohawkmtn.com.

Ski Sundown The longest of the 15 downhill trails here is the 1-mi Tom's Treat, with a vertical drop of 625 feet. Most trails are designed for intermediate skiers, while 20% are rated "most difficult" and one-third are "easy." The ski area has 100% snowmaking ability, three triple lifts, and one double lift. The lodge has a cafeteria and lounge, as well as a ski school and rental facilities. Trails are open for night skiing and snowboarding. > Ratlum Rd. off U.S. 44 and Rte. 219, New Hartford, tel. 800/379–7669, www.skisundown.com.

White Memorial Conservation Center Crisscrossing the wildlife sanctuary are 35 mi of old carriage roads and trails open to cross-country skiers. There's no charge to use the trails; the museum store here has trail maps for sale for $2.50. > Off U.S. 202, 2 mi west of village center, Litchfield, tel. 860/567–0857, www.whitememorialcc.org.

Woodbury Ski Park The park has a dozen downhill trails on 100 skiable acres, with a vertical drop of 300 feet. The number of trails is divided equally among beginner, intermediate, and difficult categories. A specially designed 1/2-mi-long snowboarding trail has jumps and moguls to challenge beginners and experts. The trails are serviced by one chair lift, a rope tow, and a T-bar. About 9 mi of the 15 mi of cross-country-ski trails here are groomed. Snowmaking equipment is used, and trails are lit for night skiing (cross-country and downhill) and snowboarding. Snow tubing and sledding are among the other activities here. Instruction is available. You may rent equipment in the lodge, which also has a snack bar. > 785 Washington Rd./Rte. 47, Woodbury, tel. 203/263–2203, www.woodburyskiarea.com.

RENTALS **Backcountry Outfitters** > 8 Old Barn Rd., Kent, tel. 860/927–3377 or 888/549–3377, www.bcoutfitters.com. **Wilderness Shop** > 85 West St., Litchfield, tel. 860/567–5905.

TUBING

Farmington River Tubing Festooned with a life jacket and sitting in an oversize inner tube specially designed for the task, you float downriver for 2½ mi through both flat water and white-water rapids. You must be at least 10 years old, 4 feet 5 inches or taller, and able to swim to go tubing here. Lifeguards are posted at the second (and swifter) set of rapids; you're on your own otherwise. River tubing is available Memorial Day through Labor Day. A shuttle bus returns you to the starting point. > Satan's Kingdom State Recreation Area, U.S. 44, New Hartford, tel. 860/693–6465, www.farmingtonrivertubing.com.

Shopping

Dealers and individual collectors alike come to the Litchfield Hills from miles around to scour its many antiques shops. Although Litchfield and New Preston have their fair share, Woodbury is unquestionably the antiques center of the region. In addition to antique furniture and decorative accessories, local art galleries and craft studios, bookshops, specialty-food shops, and a few factory outlets lure shoppers.

KENT & CORNWALL

Barbara Farnsworth, Bookseller Although it's open only on Saturday, this vast shop is filled to the brim with 40,000 used, out-of-print, and rare books in all fields; horticulture and the decorative trades are specialties. > 407 Rte. 128, West Cornwall, tel. 860/672–3099. Closed Sun.–Fri.

Belgique Patisserie & Chocolatier Inside this Victorian carriage house, temptation comes in the form of the most delectable European pastries and Belgian chocolates. > 1 Bridge St., Kent, tel. 860/927–3681. Closed Tues. and Wed.

Cornwall Bridge Pottery Stoneware plates, pitchers, casseroles, flower and garden pots, lamps, and more are created in the workshop on Route 128 in Cornwall Bridge, 5 mi south of the store. > Rte. 128, West Cornwall, tel. 860/672–6545. Closed Tues. and Wed.

John Steele Book Shop The shop has a collection of more than 20,000 old and recent second-hand books, both hardcover and paperback, along with maps, prints, and postcards. > 15 South St., Litchfield, tel. 860/567–0748. Closed Mon. and Tues.

Pauline's Place Fine antique jewelry is the specialty: Georgian, Victorian, art nouveau, Edwardian, art deco, retro, and contemporary. The shop also offers consultations, appraisals, and repairs. > 79 N. Main St., Kent, tel. 860/927–4475. Closed Tues.–Fri.

LITCHFIELD & BANTAM

Bantam Bread Company Whether you're stocking a picnic basket, on the way home, or just hungry, be sure to stop for a loaf or two of healthful bread baked solely with organic stone-ground flour, seeds, and grains. > 853 Bantam Rd./U.S. 202, Bantam, tel. 860/567–2737. Closed Mon.

Black Swan Antiques Specialties include 17th- and 19th-century English and Continental furniture and accessories, along with items from local estates. > 710 Bantam St., Bantam, tel. 860/567–4429. Closed Mon.–Wed.

P. S. Gallery Paintings, prints, and sculptures by area artists are showcased here. > 41 West St., Litchfield, tel. 860/567–1059. Closed Mon.–Thurs. in Jan.–Apr.

NEW PRESTON

Ile de France The shop specializes in French antiques, including walnut armoires and chestnut farm tables; kitchen and wine-related items; and decorative accessories such as wrought-iron chandeliers. > 267 New Milford Tpke./U.S. 202, Marbledale, tel. 860/868–4321. Closed Tues. and Wed.

J. Seitz & Co. The 5,000-square-foot emporium stocks everything from stylish home furnishings to men's and women's fashions and gift items galore. Leather bucket chairs, casual Mitchell Gold–make sofas, Lulu Guinness handbags, Petit Bateau T-shirts, blown-glass lanterns, and Hartford linen shirts for him are part of the mix here. > 9 E. Shore Rd./Rte. 45, New Preston, tel. 860/868–0119.

The Silo at Hunt Hill Farm Objéts of cookery, crafts, and an array of goodies and sauces fill this silo and barn about 10 mi southwest of Washington. Skitch Henderson, founder and director of the New York Pops Orchestra, and his wife, Ruth, own and operate this bazaar, where culinary luminaries offer a variety of cooking classes between April and December. > 44 Upland Rd., New Milford, tel. 860/355–0300. Closed Tues.

NORFOLK & RIVERTON

Hitchcock Factory Store Two levels of home furnishings include the famous Hitchcock chairs, accessories, and area rugs. The lower level has clearance items and seconds. > Rte. 20, Riverton, tel. 860/379–4826.

Norfolk Artisans Guild Unusual, whimsical, and practical gift items made by local artisans are displayed in the shop. Items change frequently as different guest artisans are featured. > U.S. 44, Norfolk, tel. 860/542–5487. Closed Mon.–Thurs. in Jan.–Mar., Mon. and Tues. in Apr.–Nov.

SALISBURY

Harney & Sons Fine Teas John Harney travels throughout Asia collecting teas and offers more than 100 single varieties or custom blends, along with elegant accessories. The tasting room may help you to decide which you like best. > 11 Brook St., off U.S. 44, tel. 860/435–5051 or 888/427–6398.

Johnnycake Books Some 3,000 rare and collectible titles on a variety of subjects are housed in a pretty 19th-century cottage. > 12 Academy St., tel. 860/435–6677. Closed Tues. and Wed.

Lauray of Salisbury If unusual indoor plants are your interest, this is the greenhouse for you. Lauray specializes in orchids, cacti, succulents, and begonias. > 432 Undermountain Rd./Rte. 4, tel. 860/435–2263. By appointment only.

Salisbury Antiques Center One of the largest shops in the area has formal English and American furniture, country furnishings, paintings, silver, and small decorative items. > 45 Library St., tel. 860/435–0424. Closed Mon.–Thurs.

WOODBURY

Country Loft Antiques On display in a converted barn and silo are 18th- and 19th-century furniture, faience, art objects, and accessories from the French countryside. > 557 Main St. S, tel. 203/266–4500.

Mill House Antiques The shop specializes in formal and country English and French furniture and has a large collection of Welsh dressers. > 1068 Main St. N, tel. 203/263–3446. Closed Tues.

Monique Shay Antiques The country antiques here come from Canada and include a large selection of painted and natural pine tables, armoires, cupboards, and chairs. > 920 Main St. S, tel. 203/263–3186.

Wayne Pratt Antiques American furniture from the 18th and 19th centuries is featured, with emphasis on original condition, along with hand-crafted reproductions. > 346 Main St. S, tel. 203/263–5676.

Woodbury Pewter Factory Outlet Pewter tankards, Revere bowls, and some 5,000 other Early American–pewter reproductions and accessory items are sold at discount prices here. > 860 Main St. S, tel. 800/648–2014.

Save the Date

MAY

Lime Rock Park Grand Prix The largest sports-car race in North America features top drivers from the International Motorsports Association and the Sports Car Club of America. It takes place Memorial Day weekend at Lime Rock Park. > Rte. 112 west of U.S. 7, Lime Rock, tel. 860/435–5000 or 800/722–3577, www.limerock.com.

JUNE–AUGUST

Norfolk Chamber Music Festival The Yale Summer School of Music presents a series of performances and workshops with various artists and ensembles at a 70-acre estate across from the Norfolk village green. > Ellen Battell Stoeckel Estate, Rte. 272 at U.S. 44, Norfolk, tel. 860/542–3004 June–Aug., 203/432–1966 Sept.–May, www.yale.edu/norfolk.

JUNE–SEPTEMBER

Music Mountain Summer Music Festival From mid-June to mid-September, the festival, held in Gordon Hall, presents chamber-music concerts on Sunday afternoons and some Saturday evenings and jazz concerts on Saturday nights. > Music Mountain, U.S. 7 and Rte. 112, Falls Village, tel. 860/824–7126, www.musicmountain.org.

JULY

Litchfield Open House Tour A self-guided tour of the village's historic homes and gardens, both private and public, takes place annually, on the second Saturday of the month. > Tel. 860/567–9423 Connecticut Junior Republic.

JULY–AUGUST

TriArts at the Sharon Playhouse TriArts presents three plays during the summer theater season, as well as some special events and a Saturday-morning young-audience series. > 49 Amenia Rd., Sharon, tel. 860/364–7469 or 860/435–6414, www.triarts.net.

AUGUST

Litchfield Jazz Festival On the first weekend in August, a long list of jazz greats performs at the Goshen Fairgrounds. > Rte. 63 about 5 mi north of Litchfield, Goshen, tel. 860/567–4162, www.litchfieldjazzfest.com.

SEPTEMBER

Goshen Fair One of the state's premier agricultural fairs since the 1930s is held at the Goshen Fairgrounds, about 5 mi north of Litchfield, each Labor Day weekend. Flower, crafts, produce, and farm animals are judged. Also here: horse shows, tractor and oxen pulls, live music, magicians, food concessions, and carnival rides. > Rte. 63, Goshen, tel. 860/491–3655, www.goshenfair.org.

Harvest Festival New England artisans gather to demonstrate, display, and sell their handicrafts at this old-fashioned two-day festival at Haight Vineyard. Wine is a theme; you can see grape stomps and tour the winery as well as drink some of the goods. > 29 Chestnut Hill Rd./Rte. 118, 1 mi east of Litchfield center, Litchfield, tel. 860/567–4045, www.haightvineyards.com.

Vintage Car Festival Over Labor Day weekend, more than 200 cars from before 1941 to the early 1970s race at Lime Rock Park. You don't have to be a racing enthusiast to enjoy this event. > Rte. 112 west of U.S. 7, Lime Rock, tel. 860/435–5000 or 800/722–3577, www.limerock.com.

DECEMBER

Bethlehem Christmas Town Festival On the first full weekend in December, the little town of Bethlehem erupts with Christmas celebrations: a tree-lighting ceremony, Santa's arrival, musical performances, candlelight processions, ornament-making workshops, food, and more. You can mail your holiday cards from the Bethlehem post office, where the postmaster marks them with a special cachet. > Main St., Bethlehem, tel. 203/266–5557, www.ci.bethlehem.ct.us.

WHERE TO STAY

KENT & CORNWALL

The Cornwall Inn The 1871 inn on scenic U.S. 7 is convenient for anyone wanting to explore the Appalachian Trail, a portion of which abuts the inn's 3-acre property, or canoe or kayak on the Housatonic River, 300 yards from the front door. The main building has six rooms. An adjacent lodge has eight slightly more rustic rooms. All rooms have feather beds and down comforters and are uncluttered. > 270 Kent Rd./U.S. 7, Cornwall Bridge 06754, tel. 860/672–6884 or 800/786–6884, fax 860/672–0352, www.cornwallinn.com. 14 rooms, 2 with shared bath. Restaurant, in-room data ports, cable TV, putting green, pool, croquet, hiking, horseshoes, bar, no-smoking rooms. AE, D, MC, V. CP. **$$–$$$**

Fife 'n Drum In the center of town, this inn–restaurant–gift shop has been owned and operated by the same family since 1973. One guest room is one the ground floor, but the others are on the second floor. A pleasing assortment of antiques, reproductions, and flowery decorative accessories outfits rooms, some of which have four-poster beds. > 53 N. Main St./U.S. 7, Kent 06757, tel. 860/927–3509, fax 860/927–4595, www.fifendrum.com. 8 rooms. Restaurant, fans, cable TV, bar, shop; no smoking. AE, MC, V. EP. **$–$$**

Hilltop Haven Bed & Breakfast Built as a summer home by owner-innkeeper Everett Van Dorn's parents in the 1930s, Hilltop Haven sits on 63 wooded acres at the edge of a bluff 800 feet above the Housatonic River. You may relax in various sitting rooms, on the wraparound porch, or in the library, which has a grand fireplace and windows on three sides. Each of the two bedrooms is furnished with antiques and either a brass or sleigh bed made up with lace-trimmed pillowcases. Chef Victoria Marks prepares a full country breakfast, presented on fine china. Note that the B&B has a resident cat. > 175 Dibble Hill Rd., West Cornwall 06796, tel. 860/672–6871, www.hilltopbb.com. 2 rooms. Dining room, hiking, Internet; no room phones, no room TVs, no kids under 14, no smoking. No credit cards. BP. **$$**

The Huckleberry Inn While the wide-plank floors, hand-hewn beams, elegant fireplaces, and other architectural details original to the 18th-century building have been preserved, the innkeepers have added luxury bathrooms and sophisticated decor. With a fireplace, king canopy bed, two-person whirlpool tub, and heated marble bathroom floor, the Honeybee room is all romance. The Dragonfly, which has a mahogany sleigh bed and a deep whirlpool tub, is more tailored; the unexpected touch is a crystal chandelier in the bathroom. Ladybug is pure country charm, with antique quilts and handwoven rugs. The cottage has a fireplace, kitchen, and dining area. > 219 Kent Rd., Warren 06754, tel. 860/868–1947 or 866/868–1947, fax 860/868–6014, www.thehuckleberryinn.com. 3 rooms, 1 cottage. Dining room, fans, some in-room hot tubs, in-room VCRs, massage; no room phones, no smoking. AE, D, MC, V. BP. $$$–$$$$

The Inn at Kent Falls The main building of this inn near Kent Falls State Park dates to around 1738. Of the six guest rooms, the Lake Suite is a romantics' favorite; the bedroom and bathroom each have a fireplace (illuminated with candles rather than firewood), and there's a clawfoot tub. The Meadow Room has a brass bed and soaking tub. All rooms have views of the 2½-acre grounds. Breakfast is served in the dining room, on the screened-in porch, or in your room. > 107 Kent-Cornwall Rd., Kent 06757, tel. 860/927–3197, www.theinnatkentfalls.com. 3 rooms, 3 suites. Dining room, in-room data ports, cable TV, pool, Internet; no kids under 12, no smoking. AE, MC, V. CP. $$–$$$$

LAKEVILLE

Inn at Iron Masters Although the inn's architecture is "motel-style," English-country gardens and several gazebos grace the grounds, and rooms have spacious sitting areas with comfortable chairs. In nippy weather a fireplace warms the Hearth Room, one of the common spaces. > 229 Main St./U.S. 44, Lakeville 06039, tel. 860/435–9844, fax 860/435–2254, www.innatironmasters.com. 28 rooms. Restaurant, cable TV, pool, bar, shop, some pets allowed, no-smoking rooms. AE, D, DC, MC, V. CP. $–$$

Interlaken Inn The large, family-appropriate resort is also a conference center and business-retreat venue. The 30-acre property in the Berkshire foothills is near Music Mountain and the Lime Rock racetrack, and guests benefit from preferred tee times at five nearby golf courses (one of which adjoins the resort). There are canoes and rowboats to use on Lake Wononscopomuc. Rooms are in several buildings around the property, including the main lodge, an English Tudor–style house, and a Victorian-style building with a wraparound porch. Townhouse buildings (former condos) include suites with fireplaces. > 74 Interlaken Rd., Lakeville 06039, tel. 860/435–9878, fax 860/435–2980, www.interlakeninn.com. 73 rooms, 7 suites. Restaurant, room service, some in-room hot tubs, some kitchens, some microwaves, some refrigerators, cable TV, some in-room VCRs, golf privileges, 2 tennis courts, pool, lake, gym, sauna, boating, fishing, billiards, bar, recreation room, laundry facilities, laundry service, business services, meeting rooms, some pets allowed (fee), no-smoking rooms. AE, MC, V. EP. $$–$$$

Wake Robin Inn The inn's main building, a classical revival–style structure with a two-story, columned entry porch, was built in 1896 and originally served as a girls' school. Sharing the 12-acre hilltop site with it today is a 15-room motel-like building with direct room access. Rooms have period furnishings, and some have fireplaces. An on-site Irish pub serves good food. Lake swimming, boating, and fishing are moments away, and bikes can be rented in nearby Salisbury. The Lime Rock auto-race park is a five-minute drive away. > 104 Sharon Rd./Rte. 41, Lakeville 06039, tel. 860/435–2515, fax 860/435–6523, www.wakerobininn.com. 34 rooms, 4 suites. Cable TV, badminton, croquet, volleyball, pub, meeting room, some pets allowed (fee); no smoking. AE, MC, V. EP. $$–$$$

White Hart Inn The expansive front porch of this rambling 19th-century country inn overlooks Salisbury's village green. The interior scheme relies on Thomasville mahogany furniture (some rooms have Lane pine pieces) and bolts of sprigged Waverly fabrics. > Village green, Rte. 41, Salisbury 06068, tel. 860/435–0030 or 800/832–0041, fax 860/435–0040, www.whitehartinn.com. 26 rooms. 2 restaurants, refrigerators, cable TV, bar, laundry service, business services, meeting rooms, some pets allowed (fee); no smoking. AE, DC, MC, V. EP. **$–$$$**

LITCHFIELD

The Litchfield Inn The Colonial-style inn is less than a mile west of Litchfield's town green. Period accents adorn the modern rooms, eight of which are themed; in the "Irish Room," for example, the four-poster bed is draped in green floral chintz. Trees surround the landscaped grounds, and the inn is close to hiking trails and shopping. > U.S. 202 about 1½ mi west of Rte. 63, 06759, tel. 860/567–4503 or 800/499–3444, fax 860/567–5358, www.litchfieldinnct.com. 32 rooms. Restaurant, room service, in-room data ports, cable TV, bar, laundry service, business services, no-smoking rooms. AE, DC, MC, V. EP. **$$–$$$**

Tollgate Hill Inn The inn includes a 1745 tavern, where Colonial style rules, and a newer building with 10 spacious, cheerier rooms. Innkeeper Alicia Pecora wants you to feel like you're staying at the country house of a thoughtful friend. Many guest rooms have decks; suites have fireplaces and canopy beds. The inn is about 2½ mi north of Litchfield's green. > 571 Torrington Rd./U.S. 202, 06759, tel. 860/567–1233 or 866/567–1233, fax 860/567–1230, www.tollgatehillinn.com. 20 rooms, 4 suites. Restaurant, in-room data ports, some refrigerators, cable TV, some in-room VCRs, Internet, some pets allowed (fee); no smoking. AE, MC, V. CP. **$$**

NEW PRESTON & WASHINGTON

Apple Blossom Country Inn The B&B, in a classic 1842 New England–Colonial home, is 3 mi from Lake Waramaug and 2 mi from Mount Tom Pond—a great location for swimming, canoeing, boating, fishing, biking, and hiking. Rooms are airy, with braided rugs, wide-plank floors, country quilts, and numerous antiques. Two rooms have a fireplace. > 137 Litchfield Tpke., New Preston 06777, tel. 860/868–9954, www.appleblossominn.com. 2 rooms, 1 suite. Dining room, fans; no room phones, no room TVs, no smoking. AE, D, DC, MC, V. CP. **¢–$$**

The Birches Inn The turn-of-the-20th-century, Adirondack-style inn overlooking Lake Waramaug is something of an institution in the area. The five rooms in the main building contain antiques and country furnishings; two rooms have lake views and three have a deck. The Lake House, next to the lake, has two rooms with private decks. Birch House, with two rooms and a suite, overlooks the grounds from its hilltop position. > 233 W. Shore Rd., New Preston 06777, tel. 860/868–1735 or 800/525–3466, fax 860/868–1815, www.thebirchesinn.com. 8 rooms, 1 suite. Restaurant, some in-room hot tubs, some refrigerators, cable TV, lake, boating, bicycles, hiking, bar; no kids under 10, no smoking. AE, MC, V. CP. **$$$–$$$$**

The Boulders Inn A grand 1895 Dutch Colonial mansion, a carriage house, and four hillside cottages hold rooms at this elegant country inn on Lake Waramaug. Most rooms have a lake view, and those in the carriage house and cottages have fireplaces (with plenty of logs outside the door) and deep soaking or whirlpool tubs. The palette, in creams, tans, and browns, is serene, and patterns are used solely as accents. Down duvets, profuse pillows, and pashmina shawls bedeck beds. Complimentary afternoon tea is served on the porch or in front of an impressive stone fireplace in the lounge. The restaurant is a standout. > E. Shore Rd./Rte. 45, New Preston 06777, tel. 860/868–0541 or 800/455–1565, fax 860/868–1925, www.bouldersinn.com. 18 rooms, 2 suites. Restaurant, fans, some in-room hot tubs, lake, gym, massage, boating, bicycles, hiking, bar; no a/c, no room TVs, no kids under 12, no smoking. AE, MC, V. BP. $$$$

The Homestead Inn Life is casual at the Homestead, which overlooks the town green from a high hilltop. Innkeeper Bill Greenman is always game for a leisurely chat, and breakfast is served in a cheery living room with a fireplace. In the main house, built in 1853 as a private residence and opened as an inn in 1928, rooms are decorated with antique furniture as well as reproductions and are awash in floral fabrics. Rooms in the Treadwell House, next door, have less personality. > 5 Elm St., New Milford 06776, tel. 860/354–4080, fax 860/354–7046, www.homesteadct.com. 14 rooms, 1 suite. Dining room, cable TV, Internet, some pets allowed; no smoking. AE, D, DC, MC, V. CP. $–$$$

The Hopkins Inn Most rooms at this grand 1847 Victorian, one of the best bargains in the Litchfield Hills, have Lake Waramaug views. White bedspreads, simple antiques, and subdued floral wallpapers prevail in the rooms, which are bright and airy. The aromas of the restaurant's outstanding Austrian dishes are joined in winter by the smell of burning firewood. > 22 Hopkins Rd., New Preston 06777, tel. 860/868–7295, fax 860/868–7464, www.thehopkinsinn.com. 11 rooms, 2 with shared bath; 2 apartments. Restaurant, some kitchens, lake, beach, bar; no a/c, no room phones, no TV in some rooms, no smoking. AE, D, MC, V. EP. ¢–$

The Mayflower Inn The 28 acres of manicured grounds, rippling streams, rambling stone walls, beautiful gardens, a maze, and hiking trails are the perfect setting for this inn, a grand three-story, clapboard-and-shingle structure with two additional buildings. Rooms are furnished with canopy beds, fine antiques, and 18th- and 19th-century art. Florals and ruffles are tempered with neutral solids. Some rooms have fireplaces, and the Frette bed linens are sublime. Marble bathrooms have mahogany wainscoting, brass and Limoges fittings, and deep tubs. The most expensive suites here are twice the regular-room rates, but the Mayflower usually books up far in advance nevertheless. > 118 Woodbury Rd./Rte. 47, Washington 06793, tel. 860/868–9466, fax 860/868–1497, www.mayflowerinn.com. 17 rooms, 8 suites. Restaurant, in-room data ports, minibars, cable TV with movies, tennis court, pool, fitness classes, health club, massage, sauna, steam room, croquet, hiking, bar, library, laundry services, business services, meeting room; no children under 12, no smoking. AE, MC, V. EP. $$$$

NORFOLK & RIVERTON

Manor House Bed and Breakfast Among this 1898 Victorian Tudor's remarkable appointments are 20 stained-glass windows designed by Louis Comfort Tiffany. The mansion was built by Charles Spofford, architect of London's subway system and son of Abraham Lincoln's Librarian of Congress. All rooms overlook the expansive grounds and gardens and have period antiques. Notable are the vast Spofford Room, which has windows on three sides, a king canopy bed, a fireplace, and a balcony, and the Morgan Room, which has a private wood-paneled elevator. > 69 Maple Ave., Norfolk 06058, tel./fax 860/542–5690, www.manorhouse-norfolk.com. 11 rooms. Dining room, room service, some in-room hot tubs, meeting room; no room TVs, no kids under 12, no smoking. AE, MC, V. BP. $$–$$$$

The Old Riverton Inn Originally a stagecoach stop between Hartford and Albany, this inn overlooking a branch of the Farmington River has been accommodating guests since 1796. Rooms (excluding the suite) are small and rather ordinary, even though most of the furniture is from the nearby Hitchcock factory, but warm hospitality makes up for this. > Box 6, Rte. 20, Riverton 06065, tel. 860/379–8678 or

800/378–1796, fax 860/379–1006, www.rivertoninn.com. 11 rooms, 1 suite. Restaurant, cable TV, bar; no a/c, no room phones, no smoking. AE, D, MC, V. BP. ¢–$$

WOODBURY

Longwood, A Country Inn The traditional white-clapboard, Federal-style, New England home was built in 1789. Furniture in the guest rooms includes 18th- and early-19th-century antiques or reproductions; two rooms have working fireplaces, and some have whirlpool tubs in the bathrooms. The restaurant, managed separately, serves lunch and dinner. Golf, tennis, hiking, skiing, and swimming are all within a few minutes drive of the inn. > 1204 Main St. S, Woodbury 06798, tel. 203/266–0800, www.longwoodcountryinn.com. 4 rooms, 1 suite. Restaurant, some in-room hot tubs, cable TV, meeting room; no kids under 10, no smoking. AE, D, MC, V. BP. $$–$$$

CAMPING

Hemlock Hill Camp Resort A peaceful, rural setting with three ponds offers camping by the day, week, or month. > Hemlock Hill Rd., Litchfield 06759, tel. 860/567–2267, www.hemlockhillcamp.com. 125 sites. Flush toilets, full hook-ups, drinking water, showers, picnic tables, snack bar, general store, playground, 2 pools. Reservations essential. No credit cards. Closed late-Oct.–Apr. ¢

Housatonic Meadows State Park Rustic sites are available for camping, with a 14-day maximum limit. There are no lodges, shelters, firewood, laundry units, or electrical hook-ups, but the park does have hiking trails, and boating and fishing are nearby. > U.S. 7 about 2 mi north of Rte. 4, Sharon 06754, tel. 860/376–0313, www.dep.state.ct.us/rec. 95 sites. Flush toilets, dump station, drinking water, showers. Reservations essential. No credit cards. Closed Oct.–mid-Apr. ¢

Lake Waramaug State Park Rustic sites are available for camping, with a 14-day limit. Hiking trails lace the park, and there's boating and fishing on the lake. > 30 Lake Waramaug Rd., New Preston 06777, tel. 860/868–0220, www.dep.state.ct.us/rec. 78 sites. Flush toilets, dump station, drinking water, showers, snack bar, swimming (lake). Reservations essential. No credit cards. Closed Oct.–mid-May. ¢

Lone Oak Campsites The full-service RV facility is on 150 wooded acres. In addition to the store and deli and propane-filling station, there's free cable TV, a nightclub for adults, a recreation hall for kids, and plenty of planned activities for everyone. > 360 Norfolk Rd., East Canaan 06024, tel. 860/824–7051 or 800/422–2267, fax 860/824–1585, www.loneoakcampsites.com. 500 RV sites. Full hook-ups, laundry facilities, general store, playground, 2 pools, swimming (lake). Reservations essential. D, MC, V. Closed mid-Oct.–mid-Apr. ¢

Macedonia Brook State Park Campsites here are rustic, with almost no facilities. Boating, fishing, and hiking opportunities are available. > 159 Macedonia Brook Rd., Kent 06757, tel. 860/927–4100, www.dep.state.ct.us/rec. 80 sites. Pit toilets, snack bar. No credit cards. Closed Oct.–mid-Apr. ¢

WHERE TO EAT

KENT & CORNWALL

The Cornwall Inn The restaurant of this 19th-century inn has two cheery dining rooms and offers casual country dining. Entrées might include steak au poivre (with peppercorn-cognac sauce) or fresh-seafood preparations. The tavern room, with its big fireplace, is a good place for a pre-dinner drink on chilly nights. > 270 Kent Rd./U.S. 7, Cornwall Bridge, tel. 860/672–6884. AE, D, MC, V. **$$–$$$**

Fife 'n Drum The venerable institution—restaurant, inn, and gift shop—in the heart of town serves a blend of French, Italian, and American dishes in either of two dining rooms. In the main dining room, which is romantic and candlelit, you might opt for Caesar salad mixed at table, chateaubriand for two, or one of the seasonal specials. The Taproom is perfect for brunch, lunch, or a casual dinner of, say, six-cheese ravioli or shrimp-and-scallop brochette. There's piano music nightly in the Taproom. > 53 N. Main St./U.S. 7, Kent, tel. 860/927–3509. AE, MC, V. **$$–$$$**

Stroble Baking Company Locals and students from nearby boarding schools frequent this tiny, friendly café that serves baked goods, homemade soups, sandwiches, salads, and desserts. For a quick lunch or breakfast on the run, this is the place. > 14 N. Main St., Kent, tel. 860/927–4073. AE, DC, MC, V. No dinner. **¢–$**

LITCHFIELD

Village Restaurant The folks who run this storefront eatery in an 1890s town house serve inexpensive pub grub in one room and updated New England cuisine in the other. Whether you order the classic burger, homemade ravioli, or salmon crab cakes, you get plenty of good food. > 25 West St., tel. 860/567–8307. AE, MC, V. **$–$$**

West Street Grill On the village green, this sophisticated restaurant is *the* place to see and be seen, both for patrons and for the state's up-and-coming chefs, many of whom get their start here. Imaginative grilled fish, steak, poultry, and lamb dishes are served with fresh vegetables and pasta or risotto. The side of fried onions—thin strands of delectably sweet onions with just enough crunch—is fantastic. The homemade ice creams and sorbets are also worth every calorie. > 43 West St., tel. 860/567–3885. Reservations essential. AE, MC, V. **$$–$$$$**

NEW PRESTON & WASHINGTON

The Birches Inn Executive chef Frederic Faveau presides over the restaurant of this handsome inn overlooking Lake Waramaug. Innovative French and Asian touches are applied to style new American cuisine. Recommended dishes include roasted garlic–goat cheese flan, seared Atlantic salmon fillet, and twin grilled lamb chops. Porch dining is available when the weather permits. > 233 W. Shore Rd., New Preston, tel. 860/868–1735. Reservations essential. AE, MC, V. Closed Tues. in May–Dec. Closed Mon.–Wed. in Jan.–Apr. No lunch. **$$–$$$**

The Boulders Inn In a dining room of this grand turn-of-the-20th-century inn, three sides of windows face the sunset and pretty Lake Waramaug. For a true taste sensation, try halibut fillet wrapped in steamed savoy cabbage and served with shiitake mushrooms and arugula-quinoa pilaf. The terrace is used for open-air dining in the warmer months. > E. Shore Rd./Rte. 45, New Preston, tel. 860/868–0541. Reservations essential. AE, MC, V. Closed Tues. in June–Oct. Closed Mon.–Wed. in Nov.–May. No lunch. **$$–$$$**

G.W. Tavern Traditional New England dishes coexist with contemporary American fare and creative specials in this rustic tavern named for George . . . well, you know who. A mural depicts the surrounding countryside; the vaulted ceiling exposes hand-hewn beams. On the menu are homey favorites such as fish-and-chips, meat loaf, chicken potpie, hamburgers, steaks, and chops. > 20 Bee Brook Rd., Washington Depot, tel. 860/868–6633. AE, MC, V. **$–$$$**

The Hopkins Inn The restaurant at this hilltop Victorian inn presents an extensive menu emphasizing contemporary Austrian specialties—reminders of the innkeeper's native country. Trout comes from the tank in the foyer and is prepared several ways; veal appears as Wiener schnitzel, piccata, and other dishes. There are at least 15 appetizers and nearly as many dessert options. > 22 Hopkins Rd., New Preston, tel. 860/868–7295. AE, MC, V. Closed Mon. and Jan.–Mar. $$–$$$$

The Mayflower Inn Before sitting down to eat in the Mayflower, one of Connecticut's most striking inns, have a drink in the sophisticated bar, in the clubby library, or on the wicker-filled porch. The dining room overlooks a garden, and fresh orchids grace the tables. Dishes are imaginative and elegant at dinner, from starters of house-smoked salmon or game sausage to main dishes such as sliced duck breast with duck confit spring rolls. At lunch, on the terrace when the weather permits, fresh salads, club sandwiches, and tasty burgers are served. > 118 Woodbury Rd./Rte. 47, Washington, tel. 860/868–9466. Reservations essential. AE, MC, V. $$–$$$

Oliva Owner-chef Riad Aamar focuses on North African and Mediterranean dishes—all of which seem to add interesting combos of nuts, fruit, and aromatic spices to meats and fish. Pizzas, with toppings such as Gorgonzola, Portobello mushrooms, and caramelized onions, serve as a shared appetizer or filling entrée. > Rte. 45, New Preston, tel. 860/868–1787. AE, MC, V. BYOB. Closed Mon. and Tues. No lunch Wed.–Fri. $–$$$

NORFOLK

The Pub Bottles of trendy beers line the shelves of this down-to-earth restaurant on the ground floor of a redbrick Victorian-era building near the village green. Pub fare coexists on the menu with strip steak and lamb burgers. > U.S. 44, Norfolk, tel. 860/542–5716. AE, MC, V. Closed Mon. ¢–$$

SALISBURY & CANAAN

The Boathouse at Lakeville You know you're in prep-school country here: crew oars from nearby Kent, Hotchkiss, and Berkshire accent the dining room, and canoes hang from the ceiling. The bistro-style restaurant caters to all tastes—from sushi lovers to carnivores. > 349 Main St., Lakeville, tel. 860/435–2111. AE, MC, V. $$–$$$

The Cannery, An American Bistro The teal-and-chartreuse walls of this storefront American bistro may seem a little startling, but they work. All is crisp and neat, the service chatty but refined. Pan-roasted monkfish and grilled rack of lamb are among the popular dishes. > 85 Main St./U.S. 44, Canaan, tel. 860/824–7333. AE, MC, V. No lunch. Closed Tues. $$–$$$

Chaiwalla Tea House Enjoy "afternoon tea" all day long. Owner Mary O'Brien imports and blends fine teas from China and India; you may pair them with homemade soup, open-faced sandwiches, scones, crumpets, home-baked pies and cakes, or ice cream. > One Main St., Salisbury, tel. 860/435–9758. AE, MC, V. Closed Mon. and Tues. No dinner. ¢–$

Collin's Diner There's no denying that this 1942 diner, inspired by the jazzy railroad dining cars of the 1920s and '30s, is a classic. Locals count on Collin's for American diner fare, but the specials are the biggest draw—on Friday, baked stuffed shrimp is often served; on Saturday its a meaty 2-inch cut of prime rib. The diner closes at 3 PM (1 PM on Wednesday); call for extended summer hours. > U.S. 44, Canaan, tel. 860/824–7040. No credit cards. No dinner. ¢–$

West Main This spot is known for its eclectic blend of innovative American fare and Asian and Middle Eastern influences. Asian grilled tuna and seared shrimp with noodles are among the most popular dishes. You can dine on the deck outside.

Take-out, delivery, and a prix-fixe menu are available. > 8 Holley St., Lakeville, tel. 860/435–1450. AE, MC, V. Closed Tues. $–$$$

White Hart Inn Tap Room The historic tavern within the White Hart Inn has an antique bar, wide-plank wood floors, and candlelit tables. Spicy shrimp, artichoke and tomato on olive bread, and beef tournedos with Brie and potatoes are among the top choices. The adjacent enclosed patio, the Garden Room, serves the same menu. > Village green, Rte. 41, Salisbury, tel. 860/435–0030. AE, DC, MC, V. $$–$$$

WOODBURY

Carol Peck's Good News Café Whether at lunch or dinner, you don't want to miss a chance to sample Carol Peck's "American Fusion" cooking. The extensive and broad menu has more than a dozen entrées that run the gamut from wok-seared gulf shrimp with vegetables to pasta with asparagus, pecans, and Gorgonzola. Peck's knack of combining morsels you might never consider putting together ("adult" macaroni and cheese, for example, gets lobster chunks and truffle oil) results in some amazing dishes. The vegetarian fare is just as good. > 694 Main St./U.S. 6, tel. 203/266–4663. AE, MC, V. Closed Tues. $$–$$$

ESSENTIALS

Getting Here

Although there is scheduled bus service into the Litchfield Hills, you need a car to get around the area. There is virtually no public transportation within the region.

BY BUS

Bonanza Bus Lines operates scheduled daily bus service between New York City's Port Authority and New Milford, Kent, Southbury (in the southern part of the region), and Canaan (in the far north). Of these, Kent is the only village where shops, restaurants, lodgings are all within a comfortable walking distance, and New Milford has two hotels and several restaurants within walking distance—but you'll have to be content staying put.

LINES **Bonanza Bus Lines** > Tel. 800/556–3815, www.bonanzabus.com.

BY CAR

The most direct route by car from New York City to the Litchfield Hills is to take the Hutchinson River Parkway north to I–684 north and proceed to I–84 east in Brewster. Take I–84 east to Danbury, Connecticut, and turn north onto U.S. 7 to New Milford. Travel time between New York and New Milford is about two hours, depending on traffic.

From New Milford, U.S. 7 becomes increasingly more scenic as it continues through Kent, Cornwall Bridge, West Cornwall, and Canaan before crossing the Massachusetts border. Sharon is west of U.S. 7 via Route 4 from Cornwall Bridge; from Sharon Route 41 north takes you to Lakeville and Salisbury. From Salisbury, U.S. 44 heads east through Canaan and Norfolk to Winsted and New Hartford. Riverton is north of Winsted via Route 8.

Alternatively, you can turn off U.S. 7 at New Milford and onto U.S. 202, a scenic road that leads to New Preston, the Washington area, and Litchfield. Woodbury is east of New Milford via routes 67 and 317; Bethlehem is north of Woodbury via U.S. 6 and Route 61. You can also reach Woodbury and Bethlehem more directly (a less scenic route) by taking I–84 east beyond Danbury to the Southbury exit (U.S. 6 north).

Visitor Information

The Litchfield Hills Visitors Bureau offers a free 36-page brochure, "Touring by Car, Foot, Boat & Bike," that outlines two dozen self-guided driving, hiking, boating, and biking tours in the region.

CONTACTS **Litchfield Hills Visitors Bureau** > Box 968, Litchfield 06759, tel. 860/567–4506, www.litchfieldhills.com.

The Mystic Coast

About 125 mi northeast of New York City

18

By Patricia Earnest

TIES TO THE SEA and to the area's native American origins run deep here. Masts, sails, and glimpses of water peek from behind trees and houses, and Indian place-names pepper the region. Indeed, the name Mystic is said to come from an Algonquin word, *mis-si-tuk* ("little river running to the sea"). You can still see Colonial-era homes and wander around Old Mystic graveyards that are filled with the names—and perhaps a ghost or two—of early-day settlers.

Present-day Mystic lies a couple of miles south, where the Mystic River enters the Long Island Sound, protected from the weather by nearby Fishers Island. This maritime village is a fine place for a weekend jaunt; the trip can be made in about 2½ hours if traffic is on your side. Good accommodations, from chain hotels and bed-and-breakfasts to yacht staterooms, abound. Some have ocean views; some are within walking distance of shopping and attractions. As you might expect, dining options are plentiful as well, from the completely casual seaside fish-in-a-basket joints to fancy dining rooms. And most attractions are kid- and family-friendly.

The village of Mystic has imaginatively recaptured the seafaring spirit of the 18th and 19th centuries. Some of the nation's fastest clipper ships were built here in the mid-19th century, and the busy river and harbor still echo from those earlier days. Downtown you find a varied collection of boutiques, galleries, bookshops, restaurants, and ice-cream parlors, all within a few blocks of the river. A unique Bascule drawbridge, which raises at a quarter past each hour during summer daylight hours, connects the two banks of the river in the middle of the village. (Mystic village is somewhat unusual—and confusing—in that its west-bank side is part of the town of Groton and the east-bank side belongs to the town of Stonington.) Mystic Seaport is the country's largest maritime-history museum; Mystic Aquarium & Institute for Exploration is a major draw. But there are also beaches and parks and plenty of places for bird-watching, sailing, kayaking, fishing, and horseback riding. Cruises leave from the seaport area.

The historic center of Stonington pokes into Fishers Island Sound. Less commercial than Mystic, it still has a working fishing fleet. Its narrow streets brim with white-spire churches, elegant Colonial houses, and village greens, as well as galleries, restaurants, and gift and antiques shops. The area also has a few wineries.

Often called the submarine capital of the world, Groton is home to a naval submarine base (referred to as the New London Naval Submarine Base) and the Electric Boat Division of General Dynamics, designer and manufacturer of nuclear submarines. The major draw is the USS *Nautilus,* the world's first nuclear-powered submarine and a National Historic Landmark.

A short drive north of Mystic are Connecticut's two much-visited casinos: the Mohegan Sun, which is run by the Mohegan Indians (also known as the Wolf People), and the Mashantucket Pequot Tribal Nation's Foxwoods Resort Casino.

WHAT TO SEE & DO

MYSTIC & OLD MYSTIC

B. F. Clyde's Cider Mill This spot has the only steam-powered cider mill in the United States. Sweet cider is pressed fresh daily from September to late December, with special demonstrations on weekends at 11, 1, and 3. The sixth generation of the Clyde family is still making cider the way the original B. F. Clyde did in the late 1800s. You can buy hard cider, apple wines, jams, jellies, local honey, maple syrup, fudge pies, apples, breads, and more. Fresh johnnycake meal is ground on the premises in a 1920 grist mill. > 129 N. Stonington Rd., off Rte. 184, Old Mystic, tel. 860/536–3354. July–Dec., daily 9–5.

Denison Homestead Museum Mystic's oldest house, on 200 acres of woodlands and meadows, was owned and occupied by the Denison family from 1717 to 1941. The homestead is furnished entirely with family heirlooms spanning two centuries. On the tour you learn the history of six generations of Denisons. The grounds include more than 8 mi of mapped nature trails. > 120 Pequotsepos Rd., Mystic, tel. 860/536–9248, www.denisonsociety.org. $4. Mid-May–mid-Oct., Thurs.–Mon. 11–4.

Denison Pequotsepos Nature Center More than 150 species of birds have been spotted at this 200-acre nature preserve. The 7 mi of trails cut through woodlands, wetlands, and meadows (including some ideal for cross-country skiing in winter). Also on site are wildflower, bird, and butterfly gardens, and a natural-history museum with native-wildlife exhibits and a gift shop. Educational programs focus on environmental awareness. A wonderful exhibit lets you experience the sounds of a nighttime marsh. > 109 Pequotsepos Rd., Mystic, tel. 860/536–1216, www.dpnc.org. $4. Mon.–Sat. 10–4, Sun. 10–4; trails daily dawn–dusk.

Galleries & Studios of the Mystic Art Association Founded in 1913, the Mystic Art Association was home to the original Mystic Art Colony. Today the buildings spill down to the river and harbor, and air-conditioned galleries feature changing exhibits and ongoing classes. Classes are held for children on Saturday. Pick up a folder for a walking tour that takes you by the original houses of the Mystic colony artists. > 9 Water St., Mystic, tel. 860/536–7601, www.mystic-art.org. $2. Daily 11–5.

Mystic Aquarium & Institute for Exploration With more than 3,500 specimens and 34 exhibits of sea life—including an Alaskan coast section, where beluga whales and seals patrol the chilly waters—the aquarium is a major regional draw. At the Roger Tory Peterson Penguin Exhibit you can get a close-up look at African black-footed penguins above and below water. The Aquatic Animal Study Center, a research and critical-care facility, aims to advance the veterinary care of wild populations of whales, dolphins, and other aquatic life and to provide information that can be used to help preserve these populations. > 55 Coogan Blvd., Mystic, tel. 860/572–5955, www.mysticaquarium.org. $16. July–early Sept., Sun.–Thurs. 9–7, Fri. and Sat. 9–6; early Sept.–Nov. and Feb.–June, daily 9–6; Dec. and Jan., weekdays 10–5, weekends 9–6.

Mystic Seaport The world's largest marine museum encompasses 17 acres of indoor and outdoor exhibits focusing on the area's rich maritime heritage. In the narrow streets and historic homes and buildings (some moved here from other sites), craftspeople give demonstrations of open-hearth cooking, weaving, and other skills of yesteryear. You may enjoy sing-along sea chanteys and visit the museum's more than 480 vessels, including the *Charles W. Morgan,* the last remaining wooden whaling ship afloat, and the 1882 training ship *Joseph Conrad.* Among the other attractions here are dozens of spectacular ship's figureheads, the world's largest collection of maritime art, cruises on 19th-century vessels, thousands of manuscripts and maps, and a period tavern. The museum can be crowded in summer and early fall. In December a costumed interpreter doing his 19th-century errands leads tours by lantern light. These evening dramas sell out fast. > 75 Greenmanville Ave., Mystic, tel. 860/572–0711, 888/732–7678 tickets, www.mysticseaport.org. $17. Apr.–Oct., daily 9–5; Nov.–Mar., daily 10–4.

Williams Beach Park The beach here is just 300 feet long but it is sheltered and inviting for families. The Mystic Community Center includes an indoor pool, baseball fields, volleyball and tennis courts, picnic facilities, and a playground. > Mystic Community Center, off Harry Austin Dr., Mystic, tel. 860/536–3575. Free. Mid-June–Labor Day, daily 10–dusk.

GROTON

Bluff Point Coastal Reserve The rocky bluff for which this park is named is a 1½-mi hike from the parking lot. A mile-long stretch of sand and tidal salt marsh overlooks Mumford Cove, the Poquonnock River, and the Long Island Sound. Facilities are limited, but horseback riding, biking, snorkeling, hiking, and swimming are encouraged. > Depot Rd., Groton, tel. 860/445–1729, http://dep.state.ct.us. Free. Daily 8–dusk.

Fort Griswold Battlefield State Park The park contains the remnants of a Revolutionary War fort. Historic displays at the museum mark the site of the massacre of American defenders by Benedict Arnold's British troops in 1781. Climb to the top of the Groton monument for a sweeping view of the shoreline. > Monument St. and Park Ave., Groton, tel. 860/445–1729, http://dep.state.ct.us. Free. Park daily 8 AM–dusk; museum and monument Memorial Day–Labor Day, daily 10–5.

Submarine Force Museum The world's first nuclear-powered submarine, the *Nautilus*, launched from Groton in 1954 and is now permanently berthed here. You're welcome to climb aboard and imagine yourself as a crew member during the boat's trip under the North Pole more than 40 years ago. The adjacent museum, outside the entrance to the submarine base, charts submarine history with memorabilia, artifacts, and displays, including working periscopes and controls. > Crystal Lake Rd., Groton, tel. 860/694–3174 or 800/343–0079, www.ussnautilus.org. Free. Mid-May–Oct., Wed.–Mon. 9–5, Tues. 1–5; Nov.–mid-May, Wed.–Mon. 9–4.

STONINGTON

Captain Nathaniel B. Palmer House This house was the Victorian home of the man who discovered Antarctica in 1820. Exhibits focus on both his career and family life and include a scale model of Palmer's ship, *The Hero*. > 40 Palmer St., Stonington, tel. 860/535–8445, www.stoningtonhistory.org. $4. May–Nov., Tues.–Sun. 10–4 (last tour at 3) or by appointment.

Old Lighthouse Museum Six rooms of exhibits depict life in the coastal town circa 1649. The lighthouse itself dates to 1823, but it was moved to higher ground 17 years later. Be sure to check out the cannon from the British ship *Nimrod*—complete with original cannon balls, powder, and wadding—which was rescued from Buzzards Bay off nearby Cape Cod. > 7 Water St., Stonington, tel. 860/535–1440, www.stoningtonhistory.org. $4. July and Aug., daily 10–5; May, June, Sept., and Oct., Tues.–Sun. 10–5; or by appointment.

Jonathan Edwards Winery In the quaint town of North Stonington, this winery handcrafts premium Napa Valley–style wines from carefully selected vineyards. Tours are offered, and there is a gift shop. > 74 Chester Main Rd., North Stonington, tel. 860/535–0202, www.jedwardswinery.com. Wed.–Sun. 11–5; tours 1–3.

Connecticut's Casinos

A DRIVE OF 15 TO 30 MINUTES north of Mystic gets you to Mohegan Sun, run by the Mohegan Indians, and Foxwoods Resort Casino, operated by the Mashantucket Pequot Tribal Nation.

Foxwoods Resort Casino. *On the Mashantucket Pequot Indian Reservation near Ledyard, Foxwoods is the world's largest gambling operation, encompassing several casinos. With 6,500-plus slot machines, 350 table games, blackjack, roulette, craps, poker, Caribbean stud, pai gow, baccarat, keno, a 3,200-seat high-stakes bingo hall, and theater, the skylighted compound draws more than 40,000 visitors daily. Two dozen restaurants offer every kind of food imaginable. Entertainment includes traveling Broadway shows and major concerts. This massive complex includes three accommodations options. The casino is about 8 mi north of Mystic via Route 27. > Rte. 2, Mashantucket, tel. 860/312–3000 or 800/752–9244, www.foxwoods.com.*

Mohegan Sun. *The Mohegan Indians operate this huge, imaginatively thought-out casino complex designed by David Rockwell (his group's lengthy project list includes New York City's Nobu and Vong restaurants). Majestic murals pay homage to the 13 lost tribes of Connecticut, and 29 dining options delight the senses. The Casino of the Sky has slots, table games, and special no-smoking areas in a three-story crystal mountain. The Casino of the Earth pays tribute to the culture and traditions of the Mohegan Tribe. Both offer excellent entertainment and overnight accommodations. The resort holds more than 300,000 square feet of gaming space, including 6,000 slot machines, more than 200 gaming tables, a bingo area, and a theater. The resort is about 14 mi from Mystic in Uncasville, which is west of Ledyard and north of New London. To reach the casino from Mystic, take I–95 south to I–395 north, Exit 79A east. > 1 Mohegan Sun Blvd., off I–395, Uncasville, tel. 888/226–7711, www.mohegansun.com.*

Stonington Vineyards The small winery grows premium grapes, including chardonnay and hybrid French varieties. You can take a tour to learn about wine-making, browse through the works of local artists in the small gallery, or picnic on the grounds. Taste and purchase wines in the tasting room–gift shop. > 523 Taugwonk Rd., Stonington, tel. 860/535–1222 or 800/421–9463, www.stoningtonvineyards.com. Daily 11–5; tours daily at 2.

WHAT'S NEARBY

Lyman Allyn Art Museum The collection of more than 15,000 contemporary, modern, and early-American works at this museum is impressive. "American Stories," an ongoing exhibition, showcases a broad spectrum of American art from the 1640s to 1950. > 625 Williams St., New London, tel. 860/443–2545, http://lymanallyn.conncoll.edu. $5. Tues.–Sat. 10–5, Sun. 1–5.

Mashantucket Pequot Museum & Research Center A large complex 1 mi from the Foxwoods Resort Casino explores the history and culture of northeastern woodland tribes in general and the Pequots in particular with exquisitely researched detail. Highlights include re-creations of a glacial crevasse, a caribou hunt from 11,000 years ago, and a 17th-century fort. Perhaps most remarkable is a sprawling "immersion environment"—a 16th-century village with life-size figures and real smells and sounds—in which you use audio devices to hear detailed information about the sights. Allow three to five hours to see everything. The research center, open to scholars and schoolchildren free of charge, contains thousands of books and arti-

facts. > 110 Pequot Trail, Mashantucket, tel. 800/411–9671, www.pequotmuseum.org.
$15. Daily 9–5.

Ocean Beach Park The 40-acre park has a white-sand beach, ½-mi-long boardwalk,
50-meter pool, carousel, 18-hole miniature golf course, full-service bar, video game
room, gift shop, and snack stands. A popular summer concert series runs from May
through August, and other events are held throughout the year. > 1225 Ocean Ave.,
New London, tel. 860/447–3031 or 800/510–7263. Memorial Day–Labor Day $9 per
vehicle weekdays, $13 per vehicle weekends; rest of yr free. Weekdays 9–sunset, week-
ends 8–sunset.

Science Center of Eastern Connecticut A hands-on science-and-technology
experience for young and old, the museum has more than 100 activity stations, a
Science Explorers' Hall, and light and sound rooms. Classes, lectures, and demonstrations for all ages are regularly scheduled. You can also enjoy the gardens,
trails, and the science store. > 33 Gallows La., New London, tel. 860/442–0391,
www.science-epicenter.org. $6. Tues.–Sat. 10–6, Sun. 1–5.

Tours

Mystic Whaler In addition to lobster-dinner cruises and day sails, the ship has
a series of one- to four-night cruises calling at such ports as Newport, Block
Island, and even Martha's Vineyard. > 15 Holmes St., Mystic, tel. 800/697–8420,
www.mysticwhaler.com. One-day cruises $75–$90, multiday cruises $250–$360.
May–Oct.

Project Oceanology The 55-foot *Enviro-Lab* leaves from the Avery Point Campus
of the University of Connecticut on a 2½-hour hands-on, oceanographic cruise to
New London's Ledge Lighthouse, where you can walk up to the top of the tower.
Winter cruises are seal-watching trips. > 1084 Shennecossett Rd., Groton, tel.
800/364–8472, www.oceanology.org. $19. Mid-June–Aug., daily 1–4. Seal Watch week-
ends Feb. and Mar.; call for details.

Voyager Cruises Cruises of Fishers Island Sound are offered on a replica of a 19th-
century Chesapeake Packet schooner, the *Argia*, which has polished brass fittings and
a varnished mahogany interior. Half- and full-day sails are available. > 73 Steamboat
Wharf, Mystic, tel. 860/536–0416, www.voyagermystic.com. $34–$36. May–Oct.

Yachting Services of Mystic You ride on a quiet Duffy electric boat as you tour Mystic Harbor and learn about the rich maritime heritage of the area in a small-group atmosphere. > 31 Water St., Mystic, tel. 860/536–9980. $20–$25. Mid-May–mid-Sept.,
weekdays 1–5, weekends 10–5.

Sports

FISHING

Hel-Cat II Striped bass and blues are the catch of the day on a 144-foot party-fishing
boat, which operates regularly scheduled trips year-round. In winter and spring it's
cod, pollock, mackerel, blackfish, and sea bass you're after. > 181 Thames St., Groton,
tel. 860/535–2066 or 860/445–5991, www.helcat.com. $30–$48.

GOLF

Foxwoods Golf & Country Club The 6,004-yard, par-70 championship course at
Boulder Hills also has a driving range, practice green, halfway house, and PGA-
staffed pro shop. Greens fees are $41 on weekdays, $53 on weekends, including a
cart. The semiprivate course is in Rhode Island, about 30 mi northseast of Stonington. > 87 Kingstown Rd., Richmond, RI, tel. 401/539–4653.

Pequot Golf Club The club's 18-hole, par-70 public course is known for its rolling terrain and well-kept lawns cut out of the scenic Connecticut woods. Jack Nicklaus set the "official" course record of 65 in 1966. Green fees range from $18 for 9 holes during the week to $31 for 18 holes on a weekend morning. > 127 Wheeler Rd., Stonington, tel. 860/535–1898, www.pequotgolf.com.

Shopping

Finer Line Gallery The gallery specializes in nautical and other prints. > 48 W. Main St., Mystic, tel. 860/536–8339.
Monk's Walk At the junction of U.S. 1 and Rte. 27 as you approach Mystic village, Monk's Walk specializes in young people's books but also has a selection of local titles. Owner Lyn Sandow is one of only a handful of book binders left in the state. > 5 Roosevelt Ave., Mystic, tel. 860/572–0003.
Mystic Antiques Co. Antiques, collectibles, and gifts fill this 10,000-square-foot store. It's a short walk from downtown Mystic and the Mystic River Park. > 40 Washington St., Mystic, tel. 860/536–4819. Closed Mon.
Olde Mistick Village Styled as a re-creation of what a Colonial American village might have looked like, the shopping center has 60 shops, restaurants, and a movie theater. Strolling musicians, dancers, and storytellers provide free entertainment. At Christmastime the village is transformed into a winter wonderland, with more than 4,000 luminarias lining the walkways in the Festival of Lights. > Coogan Blvd. and Rte. 27, Mystic, tel. 860/536–1641.
Tradewinds Gallery The gallery represents some New England artists but specializes in antique maps and prints and marine art. > 42 W. Main St., Mystic, tel. 860/536–0119.

Save the Date

APRIL

Connecticut Storytelling Festival You can listen to some of the country's top taletellers at this annual festival presented by the Connecticut Storytelling Center, based at Connecticut College in New London. Workshops are also part of the event, held the last weekend in April. > Connecticut College, 270 Mohegan Ave., New London, tel. 860/439–2764, www.connstorycenter.org.

LATE MAY–EARLY JUNE

Lobsterfest A good old-fashioned lobster bake takes place Memorial Day weekend at Mystic Seaport. > Mystic Seaport, off Rte. 27, Mystic, tel. 860/572–5315, www.mysticseaport.org.

JUNE

Sea Music Festival The theme is definitely nautical at this three-day event packed with live music performances. It's usually held in mid-June. > Mystic Seaport, off Rte. 27, Mystic, tel. 860/572–5315, www.mysticseaport.org.
Yale-Harvard Regatta The Thames River is the scene of this venerable boat race, which dates back to the mid-1800s and is the oldest intercollegiate sporting event in the United States. The annual event is held on a Saturday afternoon early in the month. > New London, www.yale.edu/rowing.

JULY

Antique and Classic Boat Rendezvous Pre-1950s wooden sailboats and motorboats gather at Mystic Seaport and for a parade on the Mystic River the third weekend in July. > Mystic Seaport, off Rte. 27, Mystic, tel. 860/572–5315, www.mysticseaport.org.

Blessing of the Fleet A celebration of Stonington's commercial fishing fleet the last weekend in July includes a parade and clam-and-lobster bake. The event stems from a Portuguese tradition. > Stonington Harbor, tel. 860/444–2206.

Melville Marathon You can't say they don't know how to throw a party at Mystic Seaport. Melville and *Moby Dick* enthusiasts gather at the seaport on the last weekend of July for this 24-hour reading of the novel in celebration of the author's birthday. > Mystic Seaport, off Rte. 27, Mystic, tel. 888/973–7678, www.mysticseaport.org.

AUGUST

Mystic Outdoor Art Festival Some 300 artists take part in a juried outdoor show on the second weekend in August. Food, live music, and children's activities are part of the event, which also includes more than 50 crafts exhibitors. > Downtown, Mystic, tel. 860/572–9578.

SEPTEMBER

Ledyard Fair The annual weekend-long town fair, held the first weekend in September, started in 1945. It has everything from a garden-tractor pull to a pie-eating contest. Many activities, including a Little Miss Ledyard Fair contest and a pet show, are aimed at the kids. Ledyard is a few miles northwest of Old Mystic. > Box 9, Ledyard 06339, tel. 860/464–9122.

OCTOBER

Chowderfest Whether you like your chowder clear or creamy, with clams or with corn, you'll find it at this annual Mystic Seaport festival each Columbus Day weekend. > Mystic Seaport, off Rte. 27, Mystic, tel. 860/572–5315, www.mysticseaport.org.

WHERE TO STAY

MYSTIC & OLD MYSTIC

Brigadoon Bed & Breakfast Two acres of landscaped grounds with stone walls, fruit trees, and an outdoor eating area surround the 1750s farmhouse, which is a little more than a mile from town. Rooms in this traditional Scottish-style B&B have king or queen beds, and most have fireplaces. Afternoon tea and evening beverages are served daily. > 180 Cow Hill Rd., 06355, tel. 860/536–3033, fax 860/536–1628, www.brigadoonofmystic.com. 8 rooms. Cable TV; no smoking. AE, MC, V. BP. $–$$$

Comfort Inn This chain hotel is less than 1 mi from Mystic's aquarium and seaport and offers shuttle service to Foxwoods Resort Casino. > 48 Whitehall Ave., 06355, tel. 860/572–8531, fax 860/572–9358, www.choicehotels.com. 120 rooms. Cable TV, gym, laundry service, business services. AE, D, DC, MC, V. CP. ¢–$$

Days Inn The Mystic trolley stops in front of this hotel, which is less than 1 mi from Mystic's aquarium and seaport. Another shuttle takes you to the Foxwoods casino. > 55 Whitehall Ave., 06355, tel. 860/572–0574, fax 860/572–1164, www.whghotels.com. 121 rooms, 2 suites. Restaurant, room service, some in-room hot tubs, cable TV, pool, playground, laundry service, laundry facilities, business services. AE, D, DC, MC, V. EP. ¢–$$

Hilton Mystic The four-story hotel is across from Mystic Aquarium and close to the seaport, as well as to Mystic's shops and restaurants. Rooms have either two double beds or a king-size bed, and a few can connect for family and group use. The hotel offers free transportation to the Foxwoods casino on weekends. > 20 Coogan Blvd., 06355, tel. 860/572–0731, fax 860/572–0328, www.hilton.com. 183 rooms. Restaurant, room service, in-room data ports, some minibars, cable TV, indoor pool, gym, bar, playground, laundry service, business services. AE, D, MC, V. CP. $–$$$

House of 1833 The grand white-clapboard Greek Revival house, a wonderful architectural specimen, sits on 3 acres. The common rooms, including a formal parlor with a Belgian marble fireplace and a music room with a baby grand piano and 19th-century chandelier, are large. Floral fabrics and wallpapers are used extensively in the guest rooms, which have both antiques and reproductions; some have canopy beds and fireplaces. At breakfast you're treated to live piano music. > 72 N. Stonington Rd., 06355, tel. 860/536–6325 or 800/367–1833, www.houseof1833.com. 5 rooms. Pool, tennis court, bicycles; no room phones, no room TVs. MC, V. BP. $$$–$$$$

Howard Johnson–Mystic The two-story, inn-style motel was built in 1965. Spacious and comfortably furnished, rooms have been updated to look as contemporary as those of residential-hotel counterparts. Mystic's aquarium and seaport are within walking distance; a Bickford's restaurant is on the property and a Friendly's is next door. > 179 Greenmanville Ave., 06355, tel. 860/536–2654 or 800/406–1411, fax 860/536–1950, www.hojo.com. 77 rooms. Restaurant, in-room data ports, microwaves, refrigerators, cable TV, indoor pool, bar. AE, D, DC, MC, V. EP. $–$$

Inn at Mystic The highlight of this complex, which sprawls over 15 hilltop acres and overlooks picturesque Pequotsepos Cove, is the five-bedroom Georgian Colonial mansion. Almost as impressive are the rambling four-bedroom gatehouse (where Lauren Bacall and Humphrey Bogart honeymooned) and the unusually attractive motor lodge. The convivial, sun-filled Flood Tide restaurant is a popular Sunday brunch spot. > U.S. 1 and Rte. 27, 06355, tel. 860/536–9604 or 800/237–2415, fax 860/572–1635, www.innatmystic.com. 67 rooms. Restaurant, tennis court, pool, dock, boating. AE, D, DC, MC, V. EP. $$$–$$$$

The Old Mystic Inn Built in 1784, when Mystic was noted for whaling, fishing, and shipbuilding, the inn was once a shop specializing in antique books and maps. Today all its rooms, some with working fireplaces and whirlpool tubs, are named after authors. Each is a welcoming and comfortable mix of antiques and owner-innkeeper Michael Cardillo's personal touches. > 52 Main St., 06372, tel. 860/572–9422, fax 860/572–9954, www.oldmysticinn.com. 8 rooms. Dining room; no room phones, no room TVs. AE, MC, V. BP. $$–$$$

Residence Inn Mystic The three-story all-suites hotel is ½ mi from the Mystic Aquarium and Olde Mistick Village and 1 mi from the Mystic Seaport. Rooms have sleek, contemporary furniture in neutral colors. All rooms have kitchens, making this a good choice for families who want to avoid restaurant meals. > 40 Whitehall Ave., 06355, tel. 860/536–5150 or 800/331–3131, fax 860/572–4724, www.residenceinn.com. 128 suites. In-room data ports, in-room safe, kitchens, cable TV with movies, indoor pool, gym, hot tub, laundry facilities, laundry service, business services, meeting room, some pets allowed (fee). AE, MC, V. CP. $–$$$

Steamboat Inn The rooms at this inn overlooking the Mystic River in the downtown area are named after famous Mystic schooners, but it's hardly a creaky old establishment—many of the rooms look as though they've been arranged for a *House Beautiful* cover. Six have wood-burning fireplaces, all have whirlpool baths, and most have dramatic river views. Despite the inn's busy downtown location (within earshot of the eerie hoot of the Bascule Drawbridge and the chatter of tourists), the rooms are the most luxurious and romantic in town. Staterooms in the inn's classic yacht, moored alongside the inn on the Mystic River, are also available for overnights. > 73 Steamboat Wharf, off W. Main St., 06355, tel. 860/536–8300, fax 860/536–9528, www.steamboatinnmystic.com. 10 rooms. In-room data ports, cable TV; no smoking. AE, D, MC, V. CP. $$$$

Whaler's Inn and Motor Court A perfect blend of chain motel and a country inn, this complex with public rooms that contain lovely antiques is one block from the

Mystic River and downtown. The motel-style guest rooms exude a Victorian ambience, with quilts and reproduction four-poster beds. The restaurant, Bravo Bravo, serves nouvelle Italian food. > 20 E. Main St., 06355, tel. 860/536–1506 or 800/243–2588, fax 860/572–1250, www.whalersinnmystic.com. 41 rooms. Restaurant, café, in-room data ports, cable TV, business services, meeting room. AE, MC, V. CP. $$–$$$

GROTON

Clarion Inn The comfortable, family-oriented hotel has a good selection of amenities and puts you about 11 mi from the Foxwoods casino and fewer than 5 mi from the beaches. The two suites have a living room with pull-out couch, so they're especially good options for families. Weekday rates include Continental breakfast. > 156 Kings Hwy., 06340, tel. 860/446–0660, fax 860/445–4082, www.choicehotels.com. 69 rooms, 2 suites. Restaurant, room service, cable TV, indoor pool, gym, hair salon, hot tub, bar, video game room, laundry facilities, business services, some pets allowed (fee), no-smoking rooms. AE, D, MC, V. EP. ¢–$$$

Mystic Marriott Hotel & Spa The full-service six-story hotel, within Mystic Executive Park, has Georgian-style architecture and modern guest rooms. Among the elegant details are rich fabrics and gleaming wood furnishings. An Elizabeth Arden Red Door Spa is attached. > 625 North Rd./Rte. 117, 06340, tel. 860/446–2600 or 800/228–9290, fax 860/446–2696, www.marriott.com. 285 rooms, 6 suites. Restaurant, coffee shop, in-room data ports, some in-room hot tubs, cable TV, pool, health club, spa, lounge, business services, meeting rooms, no-smoking rooms. AE, D, DC, MC, V. EP. $$$–$$$$

Quality Inn The pleasant budget alternative is near the U.S. submarine base, golf course, and beach. Shuttle service to Mohegan Sun is available. > 404 Bridge St., 06340, tel. 860/445–8141, www.choicehotels.com. 110 rooms. Restaurant, in-room data ports, cable TV, pool, wading pool, gym, bar, laundry facilities, business services, no-smoking rooms. AE, D, DC, MC, V. CP. $–$$

STONINGTON

Antiques & Accommodations The British influence is evident in the Georgian formality of this Victorian country home, built about 1861. Exquisite furniture and accessories decorate the rooms. An 1820 house has similarly furnished suites. Aromatic candles and fresh flowers create an inviting atmosphere. Some rooms have fireplaces. Breakfast is a grand four-course affair served by candlelight on fine china, sterling silver, and crystal. > 32 Main St., North Stonington 06359, tel. 860/535–1736 or 800/554–7829, www.antiquesandaccommodations.com. 7 rooms, 1 suites. Some in-room hot tubs. MC, V. BP. $$$–$$$$

The Inn at Stonington The views of Stonington Harbor and Fishers Island Sound are spectacular from this waterfront inn in the heart of Stonington Village. Each room is individually decorated; all have fireplaces, and most have whirlpool baths. Kayaks and bicycles are available for use. The inn also has a 400-foot deep-water pier if you are arriving by boat. Public rooms include a top-floor sitting room overlooking Stonington Harbor, an intimate bar with adjoining breakfast room, and a cozy living room. > 60 Water St., Stonington 06378, tel. 860/535–2000, fax 860/535–8193, www.innatstonington.com. 18 rooms. In-room data ports, some in-room hot tubs, gym, dock, boating, bicycles; no kids under 16, no smoking. AE, MC, V. CP. $$$–$$$$

Randall's Ordinary On 250 wooded acres 2 mi northeast of Stonington are two historic buildings containing guest quarters. The rooms in the 17th-century John Randall House are simple, but all units have modern baths with whirlpool tubs and showers. The 1819 barn houses irregular-shaped guest rooms, all with authentic early-Colonial appointments. Three rooms have stone patios. The restaurant serves a Colonial-style prix-fixe menu, cooked in an open hearth. > Rte. 2, Box 243, North Stonington 06359, tel. 860/599–4540, fax 860/599–3308, www.randallsordinary.com. 14 rooms, 1 suite. Restaurant, in-room hot tubs, cable TV, meeting room; no smoking. AE, MC, V. EP. $$–$$$$

WHAT'S NEARBY

Foxwoods Resort The resort is huge and has three lodging options. The most luxurious of these is the 25-story Grand Pequot Tower; the oldest is the Great Cedar Hotel; there's also the three-story Two Trees Inn, which is more intimate and is the best choice for families with children. Some rooms combine to form two-bedroom apartments. Many rooms and all suites have separate sitting areas; some have dining tables. Shuttle buses transport you to the casino and Pequot museum. > Rte. 2, Mashantucket 06338, tel. 860/312–3000 or 800/752–9244, fax 860/312–3113, www.foxwoods.com. 1,380 rooms and suites. 24 restaurants, food court, some room service, in-room data ports, refrigerators, cable TV with movies, 3 indoor pools, 2 gyms, spa, bar, casino, video game room, shops, business services, meeting rooms, no-smoking rooms. AE, D, DC, MC, V. EP. $$–$$$$

Mohegan Sun Hotel The sophisticated design and decor pay tribute to Native American traditions and lore; the four seasons, earth and sky, timber and water, and the wolf and the turtle are among the themes used to represent Mohegan culture. In addition to the casinos, the hotel has a spa with 13 private therapy rooms, more than 30 shops and boutiques, a 10,000-seat sports arena, a 350-seat live-music venue, and a cabaret theater. Guest rooms are large (450 square feet) and have fine bedding, king or queen beds, marble baths, and state-of-the-art entertainment centers. > 1 Mohegan Sun Blvd., off I–395, Uncasville 06382, tel. 860/862–7100, www.mohegansun.com. 1,200 rooms, 175 suites. 29 restaurants, 2 food courts, some kitchenettes, in-room data ports, indoor pool, health club, spa, 3 bars, 2 pubs, sports bar, cabaret, casino, dance club, lounge, shops, children's programs (ages 6 wks–12 yrs), business services, meeting rooms, no-smoking rooms. AE, D, DC, MC, V. EP. $$$$

WHERE TO EAT

MYSTIC & OLD MYSTIC

Abbott's Lobster in the Rough If you want some of the state's best lobsters, mussels, crabs, or clams on the half shell, slip down to this unassuming seaside lobster shack in sleepy Noank, a few miles southwest of Mystic. Most seating is outdoors or on the dock, where the views are magnificent. > 117 Pearl St., Noank, tel. 860/536–7719. AE, MC, V. Closed Columbus Day–1st Fri. in May; closed weekdays Labor Day–Columbus Day. $–$$$

Bravo Bravo This bistro in Whaler's Inn overlooks the main street in downtown Mystic. Fettuccine with grilled scallops, roasted apples, sun-dried tomatoes, and Gorgonzola-cream sauce is a good example of the Italian dishes served here. > Whaler's Inn, 20 E. Main St., Mystic, tel. 860/536–1506. AE, MC, V. $$–$$$

Go Fish In this town by the sea, it's only right to dine on seafood, and this sophisticated restaurant captures all the tastes—and colors—of the ocean. The black-granite sushi bar, with its myriad tiny, briny morsels, is worth the trip in itself. The signature bouillabaisse blends aioli, fennel toast, and saffron-scented broth; lobster ravioli in a light cream sauce is a must. The menu also lists options for vegetarians and carnivores. > Olde Mistick Village, Coogan Blvd., I–95 Exit 90, Mystic, tel. 860/536–2662. AE, MC, V. **$–$$$**

Mystic Pizza It's hard to say who benefited more from the success of the 1988 sleeper film *Mystic Pizza*: then-budding actress Julia Roberts or the pizza parlor on which the film is based (though no scenes were filmed here). This joint, which is often teeming with customers in summer, serves other dishes but is best known for its pizza, garlic bread, and grinders. > 56 W. Main St., Mystic, tel. 860/536–3700 or 860/536–3737. D, MC, V. **¢–$$**

Seamen's Inne Traditional New England fare, including steak and seafood, is on the menu at this restaurant overlooking Mystic Seaport. Try the clambake dinners, lobster, Portuguese fisherman's stew, or prime rib. A Colonial style, with wood furniture and a fireplace, distinguishes the dining room. A children's menu is available. > 75 Greenmanville Ave., Mystic, tel. 860/572–5303. AE, D, MC, V. **$$–$$$**

STONINGTON

Boom A candlelit restaurant with bay windows on all sides gives you a view of the boatyard and Stonington Harbor. The seafood comes from the Patty Jo Fishing Company, a local fishery. Consider a starter of lightly battered, cornmeal-crusted oysters before moving on to filet mignon with cognac-peppercorn sauce and Gorgonzola polenta or native flounder with lump crab-meat sauce and tomato orzo. A children's menu is available. > 194 Water St., Stonington, tel. 860/535–2588. AE, MC, V. **$–$$**

One South Cafe The dishes cover everything from One South scampi, jumbo shrimp in a roasted-garlic sauce with pasta, to traditional *caldeirada*, Portuguese fish stew with shrimp, scallops, fish, and other shellfish in a savory tomato sauce over cappellini. This international restaurant is great for families and those looking for fairly light fare. > 201 N. Main St., Stonington, tel. 860/535–0418. Closed Mon. AE, D, MC, V. **$$–$$$**

Randall's Ordinary The waitstaff at this 17th-century inn about 8 mi northeast of Stonington village wear Colonial garb as they serve traditional New England fare—such as Yankee pot roast, chicken potpie, and steak—that's prepared over an open hearth. All three dining rooms have antique tables and chairs and are lit by candles. The dinner menu is prix fixe. > Rte. 2, North Stonington, tel. 860/599–4540. AE, MC, V. **$$$$**

Water Street Cafe The menu at this tiny place emphasizes entrées with an Asian influence. You can get such delicacies as tuna tartare with shiitake mushrooms, wasabi, and pickled ginger, or warm duck salad with sesame-orange dressing. The list of daily specials is relatively extensive compared to the regular menu and usually includes an interesting dish or two as well as seafood and steak offerings. > 142 Water St., Stonington, tel. 860/535–2122. No lunch Tues. AE, D, DC, MC, V. **$–$$**

ESSENTIALS

Getting Here

The village sits about 2 mi south of I–95, so getting here by car is relatively straightforward. Amtrak stops in Mystic, and several hotels will pick up guests at the train station, but getting around by car is the easiest way to enjoy the sights and get the most from your visit.

BY CAR

From New York City, the quickest route by car is to take I–95 north to Exit 90. Take Route 27 south and you quickly come up on Mystic Seaport, on your right. The trip usually takes about 2½ hours, but traffic on I–95 can be heavy on weekends, especially in summer and fall. Leaving midday on Friday is a good idea.

BY TRAIN

Amtrak leaves for Mystic from New York's Penn Station three to five times a day. The trip takes just over 2½ hours. The train stops right in Mystic, whose station was used as a model for the Lionel train sets; however, the station isn't staffed, so be sure to ask all your questions before leaving New York City. The station is also the Mystic Depot Welcome Center, so you can step off the train and immediately be helped by information agents.

LINES **Amtrak** > Tel. 800/872–7245, www.amtrak.com.

STATIONS **Mystic Train Station** > 2 Roosevelt Ave., Mystic, tel. 860/572–1102.

Visitor Information

INFORMATION **Mystic Chamber of Commerce** > 28 Cottrell St., Mystic (Box 143, 06355), tel. 860/572–9578, fax 860/572–9273, www.mysticchamber.com. **Mystic & Shoreline Visitor Information Center** > Bldg. D., Olde Mistick Village, Mystic, tel. 860/536–1641, www.mysticinfo.com. **North Stonington Welcome Center** > I–395, North Stonington, tel. 860/887–1647. **Southeastern Connecticut Tourism District** > 470 Bank St., New London (Box 89, 06320), tel. 860/444–2206 or 800/863–6569, fax 860/442–4257, www.mysticmore.com.

19

Revised by Jane E. Zarem

FROM THE 19TH CENTURY until fairly recently, Block Island was a popular, if slightly funky, summer destination for middle-class Rhode Island and Connecticut families who maintained vacation homes on the island. It also drew fun-loving daytrippers and yachtsmen, who usually didn't stray too far from the ferry landing, where a convivial beach-and-bar scene was (and still is) guaranteed all summer long. In the 1990s, however, land prices surged as vacationers accustomed to spending summer getaways on Cape Cod or eastern Long Island built homes here. But forward-thinking locals anticipated this level of interest and, since 1967, have been setting aside open space to preserve the island's moorlike character.

Block Island has two harbors. Approaching by sea from Galilee/Point Judith, in New London (Connecticut), you see Old Harbor, the island's only true village, and its stunning group of Victorian hotels. Most of the island's inns, shops, and restaurants are here, and it's a short walk or taxi ride from the ferry landing to any hotel. A high-speed ferry from Galilee and a seasonal ferry from Montauk (New York) head for New Harbor in the Great Salt Pond. The southeast shore of Great Salt Pond has two hotels, four casual dockside restaurants, a few nightspots, and yacht services—some 2,000 private boats might be moored here on a busy summer weekend.

Most of the 850 year-round residents make a living by accommodating visitors and newcomers, and Block Island is an exceptionally friendly destination. To meet travelers' increasingly sophisticated demands, the island's modest accommodations have been remarkably refurbished over the past few years. Turn-of-the-20th-century Victorian inns, such as the Atlantic Inn and Spring House, are totally revamped, and some of the larger summer homes have been turned into delightful bed-and-breakfasts. Many people still come to Block Island for an extended stay—several weeks, a month, or the whole summer—but weekenders also account for a large segment of visitors. Restaurant fare also has reached exceptional levels of quality—even though you can dine nearly anywhere in shorts and a T-shirt. Such is the island's laid-back charm.

Walking paths crisscross the island, which has fairly flat country roads that make bicycling a pleasure. A large variety of birds is seen in and around the coastal brushlands and marshes, and the stunning glacial wash-out basin called Rodman's Hollow has great hiking trails. Fishing is another attraction. Block Island is renowned for its striped bass, and its freshwater ponds hold record-size largemouth bass. Offshore, tuna, shark, and bluefish are commonly hooked. But swordfish has historically been the mainstay of Block Island fishermen (you're bound to find swordfish steak on restaurant menus).

By July and August and certainly into September, the chilly Atlantic waters finally warm to tolerable levels, making swimming, snorkeling, and surfing enjoyable. The clarity and color of the water along Crescent Beach can be dazzling—one reason the island is affectionately referred to as the Bermuda of the North.

The period between May and Columbus Day is the island's busiest—when the population soars to about 15,000. At other times of the year, most restaurants, inns, stores, and visitor services close down. If you plan to overnight in summer, make reservations well in advance; for weekends in July and August, March is not too early.

WHAT TO SEE & DO

Block Island Historical Cemetery On West Side Road ½ mi west of New Harbor, this well-maintained cemetery has held the remains of island residents since the 1700s. You can spot the names of long-standing Block Island families (Ball, Rose, Champlin) and take in fine views of the Great Salt Pond, North Light, and, on clear days, the distant mainland.

Block Island Historical Society Many original pieces of furniture and historical artifacts furnish the society's headquarters, an 1850 mansard-roof farmhouse that's well worth a visit. Exhibits display the island's farming and maritime pasts. > Old Town Rd., tel. 401/466–2481. $3. July and Aug., daily 10–5; Sept.–June, weekends or by appointment.

Capt. Nick's Rock & Roll Bar This is *the* happenin' place, with two huge bars inside and a patio bar outside. There's live music on weekends—reggae and rhythm and blues—as well as Disco Night on Monday and Open Mike Night on Wednesday. In mid-June, the Block Island Music Festival is held here. > Ocean Ave., Old Harbor, tel. 401/466–5670.

Crescent Beach Just north of Old Harbor, this broad, 2½-mi-long strand faces east onto Block Island Sound between Old Harbor and Jerry's Point. Crescent Beach is divided into a series of magnificent beaches. **Fred Benson Town Beach,** 1 mi north of Old Harbor, is a family beach. It has a pavilion with rest rooms, showers, and lockers; parking is free and plentiful, and there's a bike rack. Lifeguards patrol the beach 8–4 daily. The concession stand serves snacks and lunch. You can rent boogie boards, beach chairs, beach umbrellas, body boards, and kayaks. Young summer workers swim, surf, hang out, and play volleyball at **Scotch Beach,** 1½ mi north of Fred Benson Town Beach. Down a dirt road (Mansion Road) at the north end of Crescent Beach, **Mansion Beach** has deep, white sand and is easily one of New England's most beautiful beaches. > Free. Daily 9–6.

Empire Theatre Believe it or not, tiny Block Island has a movie theater that, all summer long, shows first-run movies nightly—sometimes a double feature—and matinées on rainy days. As in old times, a live piano performance precedes the showing of the film. Children's Fairy Tale Theatre entertains young ones three mornings each week in midsummer. > Water St., Old Harbor, tel. 401/466–2555.

Manisses Animal Farm The owners of the 1661 Inn and Hotel Manisses have a collection of exotic animals—llamas, emus, sheep, goats, donkeys, swans, and ducks—who happily coexist in a 3½-acre meadow near the hotel and are a hit with kids. > 1 Spring St., tel. 401/466–2063. Free. Daily dawn–dusk.

Mohegan Bluffs The 200-foot cliffs along the Mohegan Trail, which crosses the south coast of the island, are so named for an Indian battle in which the local Manisses pinned down an attacking band of Mohegans at the base of the cliffs. From Payne Overlook, just west of the Southeast Lighthouse, Montauk Point, New York, which is 20 mi away, is visible on clear days. An extraordinarily steep but safe wooden stairway (with handrails) leads down to the beach below; climbing back up can be challenging, however. Beware of the undertow if you choose to swim here. > Mohegan Trail.

New Harbor Three docks, two hotels, and four restaurants are huddled in the southeast corner of the Great Salt Pond. The harbor itself was created in 1897 when the breachway, the seasonal opening through the sand barrier separating Great Salt Pond from the ocean, was permanently opened. The resultant Boat Basin now shelters as many as 2,000 boats on busy weekends, hosts sail races and fishing tournaments, and is the landing point for two ferries: one from Montauk on New York's Long Island and the high-speed ferry from Point Judith, Rhode Island.

North Light At Sandy Point, the northern tip of Block Island, is this imposing structure that was constructed in 1867 of Connecticut granite. It is the fourth lighthouse in this location. The first one washed away in a storm; the second was too far from the point and caused more harm than good; and the third was also done in by the sea. The **Block Island National Wildlife Refuge,** which surrounds the lighthouse, is an important nesting site for many birds, including rare migrating species and the endangered piping plover. A small maritime interpretive center now inhabits the base of North Light. > Corn Neck Rd., tel. 401/466–3200. $2. July and Aug., daily 10–4; Sept. and Oct., weekends 10–4.

Rodman's Hollow When this unique valley, a fine example of a glacial outwash basin, was eyed by developers in the 1960s, it spurred the formation of the Block Island Conservancy. The group today has succeeded in preserving nearly 40% of the island, and Rodman's Hollow remains wild and beautiful—home-sweet-home to white-tailed deer, hawks, and the endangered meadow vole. Winding paths lead down to the ocean, where you may hike along the coastline, enjoy the beaches, and take a swim if the water is calm. > Cooneymus Rd., tel. 401/466–2129, www.asri.org. Free. Daily dawn–dusk.

Settler's Rock On the spit of land between Sachem Pond and Cow Beach, at the northern end of the island, this stone monument lists the family names of the 16 European settlers who first came to Block Island and marks the spot where they landed in 1661. Finding no natural harbor, the settlers waded ashore; the cows swam into a little beach nearby, hence the name Cow Beach. Hiking 1 mi along the beach brings you to North Light. > Corn Neck Rd., Sandy Point.

Southeast Light The massive redbrick lighthouse sits high above the sea on Mohegan Bluffs. In a feat of engineering, the entire structure was moved back from the eroding cliffs in 1993, after a grassroots initiative demanded that the 1875 beacon be saved. It is now a National Historic Landmark, with a small museum inside and a docent to answer questions. > Mohegan Trail, tel. 401/466–5009. Free, tour $5 donation. Late May–late June and early Sept.–mid.-Oct., weekends 10–4; late June–early Sept., daily 10–4.

Sports

BICYCLING

The best way to explore Block Island is by bicycle (about $15 a day to rent) or moped (about $40). The state roadways and most town roads are paved and mostly flat, with only gentle hills. (Mopeds aren't allowed on dirt roads, however.) The Chamber of Commerce, at the Old Harbor Ferry Landing, gives out a free Bike & Tour Guide, outlining five island circuits with a map. Bicyclists and moped operators are asked to ride single file, stay to the right side of the road, and wear a helmet (required, along with eye protection, for moped operators). The fragile Greenway Trails are off limits to bicycles and mopeds.

RENTALS **Island Bike & Moped** > Weldon's Way, Old Harbor, tel. 401/466–2700. **Moped Man** > Water St. across from Ferry Landing, Old Harbor, tel. 401/466–544. **Old Harbor Bike Shop** > Adjacent to Ferry Landing, Old Harbor, tel. 401/466–2029.

KAYAKING

Block Island has 365 ponds, but the best place for kayaking is along the shoreline of the Great Salt Pond.

RENTALS **Oceans and Ponds** > 217 Ocean Ave., New Harbor, tel. 401/466–5131.

FISHING

Block Island Fishworks Half- or full-day fishing charters or guided beach fishing trips (surf casting or fly fishing) include all the gear and tackle—and no experience is necessary. > Ocean Ave., New Harbor, tel. 401/466–5392 or 401/742–3992, www.bifishworks.com.

Oceans and Ponds In addition to arranging sportfishing charters, the outfitter can set you up with fishing guides for light-tackle angling. > 217 Ocean Ave., New Harbor, tel. 401/466–5131.

HIKING

Block Island has approximately 25 mi of well-maintained hiking trails. The two major trails are Clay Head, which passes Clay Head Swamp and follows 150-foot-high oceanside cliffs; and the Greenway, which meanders through natural areas all across the island. Some of the best hikes, though, are along the island's 17 mi of beaches. You can hike around the entire island in about eight hours.

The Nature Conservancy The conservancy has a free trail map of the Greenway. It also conducts nature walks, which are listed in the *Block Island Times.* > Ocean Ave. near Payne's Dock, New Harbor, tel. 401/466–2129, www.nature.org.

SAILING

The offshore breezes around Block Island are perfect for sailing. Passion for Sailing offers cruises, while Sail Block Island rents 15- to 30-foot sailboats and offers private or group lessons. Novices like the calm area adjacent to New Harbor, on the protected Great Salt Pond, while accomplished sailors sail outside the channel.

Passion for Sailing The whole family can enjoy a two-hour cruise aboard *Ruling Passion,* a 45-foot trimaran. Trips leave at 11 and 2 each day from late May through Labor Day; a champagne sunset cruise is offered daily from late May until mid-October. Board the boat at Block Island Boat Basin in New Harbor. > Oceans and Ponds, 217 Ocean Ave., New Harbor, tel. 401/466–5131.

RENTALS **Sail Block Island** > Smuggler's Cove Marina, New Harbor, tel. 401/466–7938.

Save the Date

JUNE

Annual Block Island Music Festival For six nights in mid-June, nearly 50 bands play live music for free on three stages. There's also a free barbecue, but you must be at least 21 years old to attend. > Capt. Nick's, Ocean Ave., tel. 401/466–5670.

Off Soundings Sailboat Race The course is charted from Stonington, Connecticut, to New Harbor. Awards are presented to winning sailors, and everyone celebrates at tent parties throughout the weekend. > Tel. 401/466–2631.

Storm Trysail Race Week Held biennially (in odd-numbered years) since 1963, this is the largest sailing event on the East Coast. More than 200 racing sailboats, ranging in size from 24 feet to 70 feet, compete in daily races—including one around the island, weather permitting. > Tel. 401/466–2982 or 914/834–8857.

JULY

Block Island Bill Fish Tournament Swordfish, blue marlin, white marlin, yellowfin tuna, and mahimahi are the catch in these waters, but it's a tag-and-release tournament. Trophies are awarded for the biggest fish in each category. > Tel. 401/466–2631.

JULY–AUGUST

Block Island Arts & Crafts Guild Fair At these all-day affairs, usually held the third Saturday in July and August on the Block Island Historical Society grounds, many local artists display their work. > Tel. 401/466–2481.

AUGUST

Annual House and Garden Tour Here's your chance to visit some of the lovely historic homes and gardens that make this island so charming. > Tel. 401/466–2481.

Block Island Arts Festival More than 50 artists exhibit their work—jewelry, knitted wear, photography, watercolors, and much more—over a weekend in mid-August. > Narragansett Inn, Ocean Ave., New Harbor, tel. 401/466–2626.

Block Island Triathlon You can show your mettle or meet your match at this annual event, sponsored by the Recreation Department. > Tel. 401/466–3223.

SEPTEMBER

Run around the Block Approximately 700 runners participate in this scenic 15-km road race, held on the first weekend after Labor Day. It begins at Isaac's Corner on Lakeside Drive. > Tel. 800/383–2474 or 401/466–2982, www.blockislandchamber.com.

OCTOBER

Audubon Birding Weekend Bird-watching enthusiasts gather during fall migration. > Tel. 401/949–5454 or 800/383–2474.

WHERE TO STAY

Atlantic Inn On a hillside overlooking the harbor, this restored 1879 Victorian inn has a broad veranda and a row of dormer windows peeping from the mansard roof. Innkeepers Anne and Brad Marthens decorated the rooms, and much of the oak and maple furniture is original to the building. Isolated from the hubbub of the waterfront, you can sit on the veranda and simply enjoy the peace and quiet. The inn's restaurant is among the best on the island. > High St. (Box 1788, 02807), tel. 401/466–5883 or 800/224–7422, fax 401/466–5678, www.atlanticinn.com. 20 rooms, 1 suite. Restaurant, 2 tennis courts, croquet, bar, playground, meeting room; no a/c, no room TVs, no smoking. D, MC, V. Closed Nov.–Mar. CP. $$–$$$$

Barrington Inn Innkeepers Geri Ballard and Mike Shatusky run a tidy, inviting B&B and enjoy helping you plan your days. The inn is in a country setting between Old Harbor and New Harbor. The guest rooms, on two upper floors, are cozy and have delightful views of New Harbor and the Great Salt Pond; three rooms have private decks. You can mingle with the other guests in either of two sitting rooms and have breakfast in the dining room or on the deck. Two adjacent housekeeping apartments are rented only by the week. > Beach St., 02807, tel. 401/466–5510 or 888/279–9400, fax 401/466–5880, www.thebarringtoninn.com. 6 rooms, 2 apartments. Fans, bicycles, boating; no a/c, no room phones, no room TVs, no kids under 12, no smoking. MC, V. Closed Nov.–Mar. CP. ¢–$$

Hotel Manisses Victorian furnishings and interesting knickknacks fill the rooms in this 1872 mansion. Extras include picnic baskets, a small animal farm next door, a complimentary island tour, and afternoon wine and hors d'oeuvres in the parlor or on the porch. Four rooms have enormous bathrooms with whirlpool tubs.

Owners Joan and Justin Abrams, who moved to Block Island in the 1960s, also own the 1661 Inn. > Spring St., 02807, tel. 401/466–2421 or 800/626–4773, fax 401/466–3162, www.blockislandresorts.com. 17 rooms. Restaurant, some in-room VCRs, refrigerators, bar; no a/c, no TV in some rooms, no kids under 12, no smoking. MC, V. BP. **$$$–$$$$**

The Hygeia House Built in 1883 as the homestead of Dr. John C. Champlin, the island's only physician, the inn is now owned and operated by Champlin Starr (the doc's great grandson) and his wife, Lisa. From high on a hill each room offers a water view. Rooms are fairly small but charming, decorated with original or "found" antique furniture and memorabilia. The atmosphere is casual, and at any moment a guest or one of the family might strike up a tune on the parlor's upright piano. > Beach St. (Box 464, 02807), tel. 401/466–9616, www.hygeiahouse.com. 3 rooms, 7 suites. Boating, piano; no a/c, no room phones, no room TVs, no smoking. MC, V. CP. **$$$–$$$$**

The National Hotel One of the largest Victorian hotels facing the ferry landing in Old Harbor is a well-loved waterfront gathering place and lunch spot. Rooms on the island side are cooler and quieter, whereas those on the ocean side have a clear view of the waterfront and all the action. The building doesn't have an elevator, but one room is on the ground floor, designed to be wheelchair-accessible. It's also the only air-conditioned room. > Water St., 02807, tel. 401/466–2901 or 800/225–2449, fax 401/466–5948, www.blockislandhotels.com. 39 rooms, 6 suites. Restaurant, cable TV, bar, taproom; no a/c in some rooms. AE, MC, V. Closed Nov.–Apr. **$$–$$$$**

Old Town Inn Lucinda and David Morrison renovated this old favorite, in a country setting between Old Harbor and New Harbor. The relaxed atmosphere; the sweeping lawn, where kids can play; and the wonderful breakfasts of home-baked bread and pastries, fresh fruit, and hot dishes that David whips up each morning add to the appeal. Rooms are spacious and simply but comfortably decorated. Some have decks, and there's a large sitting room. > Old Town Rd. (Box 1762), 02807, tel. 401/466–5958, fax 401/466–9728, www.oldtowninnbi.com. 10 rooms. Dining room; no a/c, no room phones, no room TVs, no kids under 5, no smoking. MC, V. BP. **$$–$$$**

Rose Farm Inn Accommodations are in two buildings—an original 1897 farm house and the Captain Rose House, which was built in the 1990s. Some rooms have king canopy beds, decks, and double whirlpool tubs. Rooms in the newer house have private entrances; some are wheelchair-accessible, with wide doors and special bathroom accommodations. In the farm house, rooms are accessed through the interior corridors. This is a quiet place, set amid 20 acres of hillside meadows but only a short walk to town and beaches. Breakfast is served in a large enclosed porch area, and complimentary high tea is served each afternoon. > Off High St. (Box E, 02807), tel. 401/466–2034, fax 401/466–2053, www.blockisland.com/rosefarm. 19 rooms, 17 with bath. Dining room, some in-room hot tubs; no a/c, no smoking. AE, D, MC, V. Closed late Oct.–early May. CP. **$$–$$$$**

1661 Inn If your island-vacation fantasy includes lounging in bed while gazing at swans gracefully gliding along the shoreline, consider staying here. You can loll on the inn's expansive deck or curl up in a chair on the lawn. The rooms reflect remarkable attention to detail: floral wallpaper in one room matches the colors of the hand-painted tiles atop its antique bureau; another room has a collection of wooden model ships. Some rooms have a gas fireplace and/or a jetted tub; many have a private deck overlooking the ocean. The owners also operate Hotel Manisses, down the street. > Spring St., 02807, tel. 401/466–2421 or 800/626–4773, fax 401/466–2858, www.blockislandresorts.com. 21 rooms. Some in-room hot tubs, in-room VCRs, refrigerators; no a/c, no smoking. MC, V. BP. **$$$$**

Spring House Hotel The broad white-clapboard Victorian building on 15 acres has a mansard roof (with a cupola) and a sweeping front porch that's a great spot for lunch or simply relaxing. Because of its huge (and beautifully appointed) public rooms, this is a popular venue for special events. Guest rooms, which have whitewashed furniture accentuated with prints and pastel colors, are on the two upper floors; additional rooms are in the hotel's Samuel Mott building, a few yards away. > Spring St., 02807, tel. 401/466–5844 or 800/234–9263, www.springhousehotel.com. 50 rooms, 18 suites. Restaurant, fans, bar, no-smoking rooms; no a/c, no room TVs. AE, MC, V. Closed mid-Oct.–Mar. CP. $$$–$$$$

Weather Bureau Inn A former weather station, this elegant Victorian inn has a formal dining room, fireplaces to read by, and original mahogany paneling to admire. Each of the four rooms is decorated with antique furniture, damask wall or bed coverings, and nautical prints. A batch of chocolate-chip cookies in the parlor, complimentary soft drinks and bottled water, and wine and cheese in the afternoon are offered. The rooftop deck has views of both harbors by day and (with the inn's telescope) the stars at night. > Beach Ave. (Box 281, 02807), tel. 401/466–9977 or 800/633–8624, www.weatherbureauinn.com. 4 rooms. Dining room, boating, dock, mountain bikes; no a/c, no room phones, no room TVs, no smoking. AE, MC, V. Closed mid-Oct.–Mar. BP. $$$–$$$$

WHERE TO EAT

Atlantic Inn On chef Edward Moon's nightly four-course prix-fixe menu, appetizers might include tuna noisette with asparagus and capers or carrot risotto with spring peas and morels. After a palate-cleansing granita or sorbet, the main course might be grilled grouper or tilapia, the chef's signature monkfish rumaki, a perfectly grilled steak, or a vegetarian dish, such as giant tortellini filled with roasted tomatoes and artichokes. Enticing cobblers, tartlets, mousses, and parfaits are often on the dessert list. The wine choices are impressive and include great ports to accompany the cheese course. > High St., Old Harbor, tel. 401/466–5883. D, MC, V. Closed Mon.–Wed. in late May–late June and in early Sept.–mid-Oct. Closed mid-Oct.–late May. No lunch. $$$$

Beachead The food—especially the Rhode Island clam chowder, which has a cloudy broth instead of a dairy base, and the seafood Fra Diavolo, with its just-spicy-enough red sauce—is very good, the price is right, and you won't feel like a tourist at this beachside hangout favored by locals and fishermen. Play pool, catch up on town gossip, or sit at the bar and stare out to sea. The nautical theme includes a 21-pound lobster on the wall, hand-carved beams, and tables made from ship's hatches. The menu and service are unpretentious: steamed lobsters, seafood, steaks, and pastas for dinner; chili, chowder, sandwiches, salads, and burgers for lunch. > Corn Neck Rd., New Harbor, tel. 401/466–2249. Reservations not accepted. MC, V. $–$$

Eli's Though the noise level is high and the napkins are paper, the food makes this restaurant a favorite. Pastas are the menu's mainstays, but the kitchen makes extensive use of local seafood (grilled monkfish, pesto-crusted mahimahi, or freshly caught swordfish), as well as rack of lamb, oven-roasted chicken breast with risotto, and steaks like a 12-ounce filet mignon filled with lobster, mozzarella, and sun-dried tomatoes, topped with a béarnaise sauce. The list of beers and wines is long and interesting. > Chapel St., Old Harbor, tel. 401/466–5230. Reservations not accepted. D, MC, V. Closed Jan., Feb., and Mon.–Wed. in Mar.–May. No lunch. $$–$$$$

Finn's This Block Island institution serves reliably good fried and broiled fish and steamed lobster, as well as excellent chowder and a wonderful smoked bluefish pâté.

Landlubbers can have a steak or a burger platter with coleslaw and french fries. Eat inside or under an umbrella on the patio, or get food to go. Finn's upstairs raw bar is on a deck overlooking Old Harbor. > Ferry Landing, Water St., Old Harbor, tel. 401/466–2473. Reservations not accepted. MC, V. Closed mid-Oct.–mid-May. $–$$

Hotel Manisses Gazebo A glass-enclosed gazebo facing the gardens of the Hotel Manisses is one of the island's finest dining spots. The menu changes to reflect what's fresh and available, which often includes grilled swordfish, cioppino, macadamia-encrusted red snapper, or grilled filet mignon with basil-mashed potatoes. The lobster bisque is a terrific starter, or choose your favorites from the raw bar. In fact, try whatever the chef recommends—if it's seafood, it's most likely right off the boat and prepared with herbs and vegetables from the hotel garden. > Hotel Manisses, Spring St., Old Harbor, tel. 401/466–2421. AE, MC, V. Closed weekdays Nov.–Jan. $$–$$$

The Oar A tuna-salad sandwich made with fresh tuna, lobster roll, clam chowder, peel-and-eat shrimp, perfectly grilled hamburger and fries, fish-and-chips, and other simple fare made special bring locals and out-of-towners alike to the Oar's dining deck, which overlooks all the activity in New Harbor. In the evening, which is only slightly more elaborate, seafood and steaks are served indoors or out. > West Side Rd., New Harbor, tel. 401/466–8820. AE, MC, V. Closed Nov.–Mar. $–$$$

Spring House Dinner in the grand dining room may be wonderful, but lunch on the porch is definitely fabulous. The incomparable view is enhanced only by a perfect Caesar salad, crab cakes, homemade clam chowder, or seared scallops with couscous. Dinner entrées might include roasted halibut with lobster hash, grilled organic chicken with cilantro tomatillo sauce, blackened ahi tuna, or a perfectly grilled steak. No wonder so many people plan to celebrate their special events at this hotel restaurant. > Spring House Hotel, Spring St., Old Harbor, tel. 401/466–5844. AE, MC, V. Closed mid-Oct.–Mar. $$$–$$$$

ESSENTIALS

Getting Here

Most people travel to Block Island via ferry from Galilee/Point Judith, Rhode Island, where frequent year-round service is available. Seasonal ferries also leave daily from New London, Connecticut, and Montauk, New York. Galilee/Point Judith is about an hour farther east of New York City than New London is, but the ferry from New London to Block Island takes two hours, compared with the one-hour car ferry (or 30-minute passenger-only high-speed boat) from Galilee/Point Judith. Plus, ferries at Galilee/Point Judith are far more frequent. In general, ferries are canceled only if the sea is dangerously rough or the wind is stronger than 40 mph—and that's rare.

You can take a bus or train to meet the ferry in New London, which docks next to the bus and train stations. On Friday you have the option of taking an evening ferry that gets you on the island around 9 PM. This is your best bet because trains don't get you to the terminal in time for the morning ferry, and the buses leave the city before 5 AM. If you must travel by bus and can't make either the morning or Friday-evening ferry from New London, consider taking a shuttle bus from Uptown Manhattan to Galilee/Point Judith.

Travel via Montauk isn't practical (unless you start out from eastern Long Island instead of New York City). The ferry trip alone takes 1¾ hours, and the departure time is 9 AM. Trains don't stop near the ferry landing, and the trip from the city—by car or shuttle bus—takes a minimum of 2½ hours.

If you're driving, plan to park in one of the long-term lots ($5–$10 per day); you really don't need a car on the island. Taxis are plentiful at the Old Harbor and New Harbor ferry landings, as well as at the airport. You can either hail a taxi on the road or call ahead for a pickup. Rates are set by the town and involve a zone system. Most rides cost a flat $5.

New England Airlines has regularly scheduled daily flights to Block Island from Rhode Island's Westerly Airport all year. The trip takes about 12 minutes, but it does cost more than the ferry. If you decide to fly, consider that fog can sock in Block Island rather suddenly, grounding or delaying flights.

Because travel to Block Island is more complicated than travel to most other area weekend destinations, you may want to make this trip over a long weekend.

BY BUS

Greyhound Lines has regular service between New York City and New London, Connecticut, where the bus depot is adjacent to the Block Island Ferry dock. To catch the morning ferry, you have to take a bus that leaves Port Authority before 5 AM. From April through October, Adventure Northeast, a shuttle-bus service, runs from Manhattan to the Point Judith ferry terminal, with stops at the New London ferry terminal and Rhode Island's Westerly Airport. The shuttle (reservations required) leaves Manhattan from in front of Fitzpatrick's, on the northwest corner of the 2nd Avenue–85th Street intersection, and from Dublin House, on the north side of 79th Street near Broadway.

LINES **Adventure Northeast Transportation Service** > Tel. 718/601–4707, www.adventurenortheast.com. **Greyhound Lines** > Tel. 800/231–2222, www.greyhound.com.

DEPOTS **New London Bus Depot** > 45 Water St., New London, CT 06320, tel. 860/447–3841.

BY CAR

To get to the New London dock from New York City, take I–95 north to Exit 83 (Downtown New London). At the third light, turn left onto Governor Winthrop Boulevard and proceed straight, over railroad tracks, before turning right onto Ferry Street. The 125-mi trip should take about 2½ hours, depending on traffic.

To get to the Galilee/Point Judith ferry, take I–95 north to Exit 92. Follow Route 2 south and then Route 78 (Westerly Bypass) until you reach U.S. 1. Turn left (north) onto U.S. 1 until you reach the Galilee/Point Judith exit. Bear right onto Route 108 south for about 3 mi and you'll see a right-hand turn for the Block Island Ferry, which docks at the State Pier. Depending on traffic, the trip should take about 3½ hours. Long-term parking is available at lots near the dock.

For a short getaway you're better off walking or bringing or renting a bicycle or moped, or even taking a taxi around the island. Ferry reservations for your car may be difficult in season, and round-trip transportation for your car costs nearly $60.

BY FERRY

Ferries are Block Island's principal links to the mainland. In summer months, Block Island has round-trip ferry service several times daily from Galilee/Point Judith, as well as once or twice daily from New London, Connecticut, and Montauk, New York. From November to June the only ferry service is from Galilee/Point Judith.

Interstate Navigation Co. operates car-passenger ferries to Old Harbor from Galilee/Point Judith, a one-hour trip, for $16.45 round-trip; add $2.25 each way for a bicycle. The ferries run year-round, six or seven times a day in the summer, less frequently in the off-season. All-day, overnight, or long-term parking is available in various lots near the dock for $10 a day. If you bring your car aboard the ferry, the passenger car fee is $25.95 each way; make auto reservations well ahead (months even), as space is limited. Foot passengers cannot make reservations; you should arrive 45 minutes ahead in high season, as the boats do fill up.

Island Hi-Speed Ferry makes six round-trips a day from mid-May through mid-October between Galilee and New Harbor. The trip takes about 30 minutes; the round-trip fare is $26 for adults and $6 for bicycles. Reservations are recommended.

Nelseco Navigation Company operates a 9 AM passenger-car ferry to Old Harbor from New London from mid-June to mid-September; a second ferry leaves at 7:15 PM on Friday. Reservations are advised for the two-hour trip. One-way fares from New London are $15 per adult, $3.50 for bikes, and $28 per passenger car. The dock is 300 yards from the New London Railroad Station, and parking is available at a garage across from the dock.

Viking Ferry Lines operates passenger and bicycle service to New Harbor from Montauk. Ferries leave daily at 9 AM from mid-May through mid-October. The trip, which takes 1¾ hours, costs $25 each way, plus $7 per bicycle.
LINES **Interstate Navigation Company** > Tel. 401/783–4613, www.blockislandferry.com. **Island Hi-Speed Ferry** > Tel. 877/733–9425, www.islandhighspeedferry.com. **Nelseco Navigation Company** > Tel. 860/442–7891, www.blockislandferry.com. **Viking Ferry Lines** > Tel. 516/668–5709, www.montaukferry.com.

BY PLANE
New England Airlines operates scheduled daily flights from Rhode Island's Westerly Airport to Block Island (a 12-minute trip) year-round.
CARRIERS **New England Airlines** > Tel. 401/466–5881 or 800/243–2460, www.ids.net/flybi/nea.
AIRPORTS **Block Island Airport** > Center Rd., tel. 401/466–5511. **Westerly Airport** > 56 Airport Rd., Westerly, RI, tel. 401/596–2357.

BY TRAIN
Amtrak's Northeast Corridor line stops in New London, where the Block Island ferry slip is next to the train station. Some trains also stop in Kingston, which is a 20-minute taxi ride (about $25) to the Block Island ferry dock in Galilee/Point Judith. You may also take the train to Westerly, Rhode Island, and take a short cab ride (about 10 minutes; $15) to the airport.
LINES **Amtrak** > Tel. 800/872–7245, www.amtrak.com.
STATIONS **Kingston Station** > Railroad Ave., Kingston, RI, tel. 401/783–2913. **New London Station** > 27 Water St., New London, CT, tel. 860/446–3929.

Visitor Information

CONTACTS **Block Island Chamber of Commerce** > Water St., Drawer D, 02807, tel. 401/466–2982, www.blockislandchamber.com. **Block Island Tourism Council** > Water St. (Box 356), 02807, tel. 401/466–5200, www.blockislandinfo.com.

Newport

185 mi northeast of New York City

20

Revised by Patricia Earnest

LOCALS CALL IT "THE ISLAND," as though there is no other place quite like it, and that may well be true. Drive around the Newport end of Aquidneck Island, and you are constantly aware of architecture that tells the story of the development of America—Colonial, Federalist, Victorian, the opulent gilded age. And in summer you also see sails everywhere in this East Coast capital of sailing. Newport is a happening place, especially during the busy summer season.

The so-called gilded age was an important boom time for Newport, and the palatial mansions—called "cottages"—built in that era are the town's hallmark today. But there is much more to Newport than mansion-hopping. Recreational sailing is a huge industry in Newport today. Tanned young sailors often fill Newport bars and restaurants, where they talk of wind, waves, and expensive yachts. (Just stroll down Thames Street after dark for a sampling of Newport's nightlife scene.) For those not arriving by water, a sailboat tour of the harbor is a great way to get your feet wet.

Shop-lined cobblestone streets stretch along the dock area and are filled with trendy boutiques, bars, and restaurants. From the harbor, this highly walkable town rises up toward the historic Point and Hill areas with their rich tapestry of architecture. More than 200 pre-Revolutionary War buildings remain in Newport, the most of any city in the United States. Convenient markers in public areas indicate what you are viewing.

The gilded-age mansions are mostly strung along Bellevue Avenue, a fair distance from the center of town; to see the mansions from the ocean side you can stroll along the scenic Cliff Walk. In summer you're likely to be happier if you park the car and purchase a trolley ticket so you can ride around town all day without any parking worries.

Newport in summer can be a challenge, its streets jammed with visitors and the traffic slowed by sightseeing buses (3½ million people visit the city each year). Yet the quality of Newport's sights and its festivals make it worth braving the crowds. In fall and spring you can explore the city without having to stand in long lines, and lodging prices often come down dramatically during these periods. In early winter, the mansions are outfitted in festive holiday decorations, and cozy lodgings beckon you to sit awhile by a fireplace. There's a full calendar of events year-round, so no matter what time of year you choose to visit, there is always something to do and see.

WHAT TO SEE & DO

Astors' Beechwood The original mistress of this oceanfront mansion, Caroline Schermerhorn Astor, was the queen of American society in the late 19th century; her list of "The Four Hundred" was the first social register. Her husband, William Backhouse Astor, was a reserved businessman and a member of one of the wealthiest families in the nation. As you're guided through the Vaux and Downing–designed

Tuscan Revival 1857 mansion, actors in period costume play the family, their servants, and their household guests. The house closes for special events year-round, so call ahead to confirm open days. > 580 Bellevue Ave., tel. 401/846–3772, www.astors-beechwood.com. $15. June–Dec., daily 10–4; Feb.–May, weekends 10–4.

Belcourt Castle Richard Morris Hunt based this 1894 Gothic Revival mansion on Louis XIII's hunting lodge. Built for banking heir Oliver H. P. Belmont, the house is so filled with European and Asian treasures that locals have dubbed it the Metropolitan Museum of Newport. Sip tea and admire the stained glass and carved wood, and don't miss the Golden Coronation Coach. > 657 Bellevue Ave., tel. 401/846–0669, www.belcourtcastle.com. $10. Daily noon–5.

The Breakers It's easy to understand why, in the early 1890s, it took 2,500 workers two years to build the most magnificent Newport palace, the 70-room home of railroad heir Cornelius Vanderbilt II. Among the marvels within the four-story Italian Renaissance–style palace are a gold-ceiling music room, a blue-marble fireplace, and a porch with a mosaic ceiling that took Italian artisans six months, lying on their backs, to install. To build the Breakers today would cost $400 million. > Ochre Point Ave., tel. 401/847–1000, www.newportmansions.org. $15. Daily 9–6.

Chateau-sur-Mer Bellevue Avenue's first stone mansion was built in the Victorian–Gothic style in 1852 for William S. Wetmore, a tycoon involved in the China trade. It was enlarged in the 1870s by Richard Morris Hunt. The Gold Room, by Leon Marcotte, and the Renaissance Revival–style dining room and library, by the Florentine sculptor Luigi Frullini, are sterling examples of the work of leading 19th-century designers. Bedrooms are decorated with wallpaper by Arts and Crafts designers William Morris and William Burges. > Bellevue Ave. at Shepard Ave., tel. 401/847–1000, www.newportmansions.org. $9. Apr.–mid-Nov., daily 10–6.

Chepstow The Italianate villa with a mansard roof isn't as grand as other Newport mansions, but it houses a remarkable collection of art and furniture gathered by the Morris family of New York City. Built in 1861, the home was designed by Newport architect George Champlin Mason. > 120 Narragansett Ave., tel. 401/847–1000 Ext. 165, www.newportmansions.org. $10. June–Sept., daily 10–6.

Cliff Walk The 3½-mi Cliff Walk began as a footpath in the late 1700s. Today you find spectacular views of the ocean and backyard glimpses of many of Newport's mansions. It's also a great place to explore tide pools and to bird-watch. Easton's Beach (also called First Beach) is the beginning of this spectacular path, which runs south along Newport's cliffs to Bailey's Beach. The walk can be accessed from most of the roads running east off Bellevue Avenue. The unpaved sections can be difficult for small children or people with mobility problems. > Memorial Blvd. at Eustis Ave. Free. Daily dawn–dusk.

Easton's Beach Also known as First Beach, this is one of the prettiest beaches in Rhode Island and is popular for its carousel. > 175 Memorial Blvd., tel. 401/846–1398. Parking $10. Daily 8:30–6.

The Elms In designing this graceful 48-room neoclassical mansion, architect Horace Trumbauer paid homage to the style, fountains, broad lawn, and formal gardens of the Château d'Asnières near Paris. The Elms was built for Edward Julius Berwind, a bituminous-coal baron, in 1899. The energy magnate's home was one of the first in the nation to have central heat and to be piped for hot water. The trees throughout the 12-acre backyard are labeled, providing an exemplary botany lesson. > Bellevue Ave., tel. 401/842–0546, www.newportmansions.org. $10. Daily 10–6.

Fort Adams State Park The 105-acre seaside park presents magnificent panoramas of Newport Harbor and is a great place to take sailing or windsurfing lessons; sailboat rentals are also available. The park is home to the legendary Newport Jazz Festival and Folk Festival. Its small beach has a picnic area and lifeguards (in summer), and is fully sheltered from ocean swells. > Harrison Ave. and Ocean Dr., tel. 401/847–2400, www.riparks.com. $12 per car (nonresident). Daily dawn–dusk.

Great Friends Meeting House The oldest Quaker meetinghouse in the country was erected in 1699, when the Friends made up 60% of Newport's population. It has been called the finest medieval structure in America, and its weathered exterior belies the soaring post-and-beam construction of the interior. > 29 Farewell St., tel. 401/846–0813, www.newporthistorical.org. $4. Tours mid-June–Aug., Thurs.–Sat. 10, 11, 1, and 3.

Hunter House The French admiral Charles Louis d'Arsac de Ternay used this 1748 home as his Revolutionary War headquarters. The elliptical arch in the central hall is a typical Newport detail. Pieces made by Newport artisans Townsend and Goddard furnish much of the house, which also contains the first commissioned painting by a young Gilbert Stuart, best known for his portraits of George Washington. > 54 Washington St., tel. 401/847–7516, www.newportmansions.org. $10. June–Sept., daily 10–6.

International Tennis Hall of Fame Museum at the Newport Casino The photographs, memorabilia, and multimedia exhibits at the Hall of Fame provide a definitive and fascinating chronicle of the game's greatest moments and characters. The magnificent, shingle-style Newport Casino, a social club, was designed by Stanford White and built in 1880 for publisher James Gordon Bennett Jr. > 194 Bellevue Ave., tel. 401/849–3990 or 800/457–1144, www.tennisfame.com. $8. Museum and grounds daily 9:30–5.

Isaac Bell House Considered one of the finest examples of American shingle–style architecture, the home, under restoration at this writing, is open to the public as a work in progress. The exterior has been completed; inside, a short film documents the effort to revitalize the McKim, Mead & White design, and you are given a tour of various rooms. Bell, who built the home in 1883, was a wealthy cotton broker. > Bellevue Ave. at Perry St., tel. 401/847–1000, www.newportmansions.org. $10. June–Sept., daily 10–6.

Kingscote The first of the mansions on Bellevue Avenue, this Victorian structure, completed in 1841, was designed by Richard Upjohn for George Noble Jones, a plantation owner from Savannah. (Newport was popular with Southerners before the Civil War.) The Gothic Revival property was sold to David King during the Civil War and expanded under the direction of McKim, Mead & White. Decorated with antique furniture, glass, and Asian art, it contains a cork ceiling and several Tiffany windows. > Bowery St. off Bellevue Ave., tel. 401/847–1000, www.newportmansions.org. $10. June–Sept., daily 10–6.

Marble House Perhaps the most opulent Newport mansion, the Marble House is known for its extravagant gold ballroom. The house was the gift of William Vanderbilt to his wife, Alva, in 1892. Alva divorced William in 1895 and married Oliver Perry Belmont, becoming the lady of Belcourt Castle. When Oliver died in 1908, she returned to Marble House and spent much of her time campaigning for women's rights. The Chinese tea house behind the estate was built in 1913. > Bellevue Ave. near Ruggles St., tel. 401/847–1000, www.newportmansions.org. $10. Mid-Apr.–Dec., daily 10–6; Jan.–mid-Apr., weekends 10–6.

Museum of Newport History at the Brick Market The building, once used for slave trading, houses a city museum with multimedia exhibits that explore Newport's social and economic influences. Antiques, such as the printing press of James Franklin (Ben's brother), inspire the imagination. Built in 1760 and designed by Peter Harrison, who was also responsible for the Touro Synagogue and the Redwood Library, the Palladian-style building served as a theater and town hall. > 127 Thames St., tel.

401/849–0813, www.newporthistorical.org. $5. Apr.–Oct., Mon. and Wed.–Sat. 1–5, Sun. 1–4; Nov.–Mar., Fri. and Sat. 10–4, Sun. 1–4.

Museum of Yachting The museum has four galleries, which include an exhibit about the history of the Vanderbilts (of the Breakers and Marble House fame) and their yachts, many of which were America's Cup contenders and/or winners; the rescue boat used by Ida Lewis, keeper of the Limerock Light from 1860 to 1922, who rescued dozens of men over the years; and a scale model of *Courageous,* an America's Cup contender and the state yacht of Rhode Island. In summer eight wooden yachts constitute a floating exhibition. > Fort Adams State Park, Ocean Dr., tel. 401/847–1018, www.moy.org. $5. Mid-May–Oct., daily 10–5.

Newport Art Museum and Art Association Richard Morris Hunt designed the Stick-style Victorian building that houses this community-supported center for the arts. The galleries exhibit contemporary works by New England artists. > 76 Bellevue Ave., tel. 401/848–8200, www.newportartmuseum.com. $6. Memorial Day–Columbus Day, Mon.–Sat. 10–5, Sun. noon–5; rest of yr, Mon.–Sat. 10–4, Sun. noon–4.

Rosecliff Newport's most romantic mansion was built for Mrs. Hermann Oelrichs in 1902; her father had amassed a fortune from Nevada silver mines. Architect Stanford White modeled the palace after the Grand Trianon at Versailles. Rosecliff has a heart-shaped staircase, and its 40 rooms include the Court of Love and a grand ballroom. Its grand ballroom has appeared in several movies, including *True Lies* and *The Great Gatsby.* > Bellevue Ave. at Marine Ave., tel. 401/847–5793, www.newportmansions.org. $10. Apr.–Nov., daily 10–6.

Rough Point The late tobacco heiress and preservationist Doris Duke owned this mansion, which is open for small group tours that leave from the Newport County Convention Center and Visitor's Bureau (23 America's Cup Avenue). The 1889 Gothic-style mansion, with 105 rooms, was built in the English-manor style for an heir to the Vanderbilt railroad fortune. The furnishings range from the grand to the peculiar (count the mother-of-pearl bedroom suite among the latter), but Duke's taste in art, especially English portraiture, was pretty sharp: of all the Newport mansions, Duke's has the best art collection. You can purchase same-day tickets at the visitors bureau; advance reservations are available on-line. > Bellevue Ave. at Ocean Dr., tel. 401/845–9124, www.newportrestoration.com. $25. Tours Tues.–Sat. every 20 min 10–3:20.

Samuel Whitehorne House Museum The owner of this mansion, one of the few Federal-style structures in Newport, went bankrupt before construction was completed in 1811. It has been restored and houses the Doris Duke collection of 19th-century Newport furniture, plus silver and pewter of Newport origin. > 416 Thames St., tel. 401/849–7300, www.newportrestoration.com. $8. Apr.–Oct., Mon., Thurs., and Fri. 11–4, weekends 10–4.

Touro Synagogue The oldest surviving synagogue in the United States—dedicated in 1763—was designed by Peter Harrison. Although the building is simple on the outside, the interior is quite elaborate, and it may have served as an inspiration to Thomas Jefferson in the building of Monticello. One of the oldest Torahs in North America is on display. Tours start every 30 minutes; there are no tours on Saturday or Jewish holidays. > 85 Touro St., tel. 401/847–4794 Ext. 23, www.tourosynagogue.org. Free. July and Aug., Sun.–Fri. 10–5; May, June, Sept., and Oct., weekdays 1–3, Sun. 11–3.

Trinity Church This Colonial beauty was built in 1726 and modeled after London churches designed by Sir Christopher Wren. A special feature of the interior is the three-tier wineglass pulpit, the only one of its kind in America. The lighting, woodwork, and palpable feeling of history make attending Episcopal services here an unforgettable experience. Famous folks associated with the church include George Washington, who worshiped in pew 81; Handel, who tested the organ before it was sent from England; and Bishop Desmond Tutu, who preached here in 1987. > Queen Anne Sq., tel. 401/846–0660, www.trinitynewport.org. $2 donation. Tours May–mid-June and mid-Oct.–late Oct., weekdays 10–1; mid-June–early July and early Sept.–mid-Oct., weekdays 10–4; early July–early Sept., Mon.–Sat. 10–4; and Sun. year-round after 10 AM service.

Wanton-Lyman-Hazard House Newport's oldest residence dates from the mid-17th century. The dark-red building was site of the city's Stamp Act riot of 1765; after the British Parliament levied a tax on most printed material, the Sons of Liberty stormed the house, which was occupied by the English stamp master. The house contains period artifacts, and there's a Colonial-style garden. > 17 Broadway, tel. 401/846–0813, www.newporthistorical.org. $4. Mid-June–Aug., Wed.–Sat. 10–4 or by appointment.

Tours

Classic Cruises of Newport You can take a trip around Newport Harbor or Narragansett Bay in either a sailing schooner or a former rum-running motor yacht. Tours on the schooner are $25 and last about 1½ hours; tours on the motor yacht are $17 and last about 1¼ hours (cocktail cruises on either boat are a bit more). Schooner tours are year-round, but there are no motor-yacht tours in winter. > Bannister's Wharf, America's Cup Ave., tel. 401/849–3033 or 800/395–1343, www.cruisenewport.com.

Newport Historical Society Guided walking tours of Historic Hill leave from the Museum of Newport History Thursday, Friday, and Saturday mornings at 10 from May through August. Other walks are conducted throughout the year by appointment. The walk costs $8 and includes museum admission. > 82 Touro St., tel. 401/846–0813, www.newporthistorical.org.

Newport on Foot From April through October experts in local history lead 90-minute walking tours of Newport. Tours cover about 1 mi at an easy pace and are geared to slowest in the group. Meet at the Gateway Visitor Center at 23 America's Cup Avenue. The walk costs $8. Call for times. > Tel. 401/846–5391.

Newport Walks Several 90-minute tours are offered, including a "Newport 101" tour offered Thursday to Sunday in July at 10:30 and 1:30. Lantern-led evening ghost tours are given every night at 8:15 from May through Halloween; cemetery tours are offered at 5 PM on Saturday in July and August. "Newport 101" and ghost tours leave from Queen Anne Square on Thames Street; cemetery tours leave from the Gateway Visitor Center (23 America's Cup Avenue). All tours are $18; reserve at the visitor center. > Tel. 401/841–0494 or 866/334–4678, www.newportwalks.com.

Old Colony and Newport Railroad A meandering rail journey in one of two turn-of-the-20th-century train coaches pulled by a vintage diesel engine lasts 80 minutes and takes you through the naval base and along the coast of Narragansett Bay. You're told about the historical, cultural, and environmental aspects of the west shore of Aquidneck Island and have views of beaches and boats, including U.S. fleet carriers. Tickets are $6.50 for regular class, $10 for first class. Trains roll on Sunday at 11:45 and 1:45. > 19 America's Cup Ave., tel. 401/624–6951 or 401/683–4549, www.ocnrr.com.

Viking Tours of Newport Year-round trolley tours of Newport can include a visit to up to two of the mansions. The cost is $19.50 to $42, depending on the options. Hour-long Newport Harbor tours aboard the *Viking Queen* are conducted from mid-May through mid-October at 10:30, noon, and 1:30; from July to September, there is an additional tour at 3. The cost is $10, and boats leave from the Goat Island Marina next to the Hyatt Regency. Trolley tours leave from the Gateway Visitor Center. > Gateway Visitor Center, 23 America's Cup Ave., tel. 401/847–6921.

Sports

BOATING

Newport is New England's biggest boating center. If you don't arrive by sailboat, it's still possible to rent one for an hour or a day to explore the magnificent harbor area. Adventure Sports rents sailboats, kayaks, and canoes. Sail Newport rents sailboats by the hour.

EQUIPMENT **Adventure Sports** > The Inn at Long Wharf, 142 Long Wharf, tel. 401/849–4820. **Sail Newport** > Fort Adams State Park, tel. 401/846–1983.

FISHING

Striped bass and bluefish can be found in the waters around Newport. Saltwater Edge sells both surf- and fly-fishing gear, gives lessons, and conducts guided trips. A half-day guided trip is $195 for one, plus $75 for each additional person. Charters are $295 for a half-day for two people. Fishin' Off runs trips on a 36-foot Trojan.

EQUIPMENT & GUIDES **Fishin' Off** > American Shipyard, Goat Island Causeway, tel. 401/849–9642. **Saltwater Edge** > 561 Thames St., tel. 401/842–0062, www.saltwateredge.com. **Sam's Bait & Tackle** > 36 Aquidneck Ave., tel. 401/849–5909.

Shopping

Newport's wide variety of individually owned boutiques, galleries, and antiques stores is a major draw. Many are on Thames Street; others are on Spring Street, Franklin Street, and at Bowen's and Bannister's wharves. The Brick Market area—between Thames Street and America's Cup Avenue—has more than 40 shops. Bellevue Avenue just south of Memorial Boulevard (near the International Tennis Hall of Fame) contains a strip of pricey shops with high-quality merchandise.

Aardvark Antiques The store specializes in architectural pieces and stained glass and also carries unique fountains and garden statuary. > 475 Thames St., tel. 401/849–7233.

Angela Moore Moore designs jewelry and other accessories that have been featured in *Vogue*, *InStyle*, and other fashion publications. > 119 Bellevue Ave., tel. 401/849–1900.

The Armory Almost 125 dealers carry antiques, china, and estate jewelry. > 365 Thames St., tel. 401/848–2398.

Arnold Art Store and Gallery The gallery exhibits and sells marine-inspired paintings and prints. > 210 Thames St., tel. 401/847–2273.

MacDowell Pottery Some of the New England potters whose works are showcased here are local. > 140 Spring St., tel. 401/846–6313.

Michael Hayes The upscale clothier sells togs for men and women, including the Tommy Bahama line, as well as for children. > 204 Bellevue Ave., tel. 401/846–3090.

Thames Glass The dramatic blown-glass pieces are designed by Matthew Buechner and created in the adjacent studio. > 688 Thames St., tel. 401/846–0576.

Save the Date

JANUARY–FEBRUARY

Newport Winter Festival New England's largest winter extravaganza encompasses 150 individual events ranging from sand- and ice-sculpture contests to a citywide scavenger hunt. > Tel. 401/847–7666, www.newportevents.com.

MARCH

St. Patrick's Day Celebration A citywide celebration of this Irish holiday takes place at City Hall, including the longest continuing St. Patrick's Day parade in New England. A food festival celebrates Newport's connection with Kinsale, its sister city in Ireland. > Tel. 401/845–9123, www.gonewport.com.

MAY

Newport Spring Boat Show New England's largest boat show for new and used boats is held each year at the Newport Yachting Center; there's also a unique marine flea market with gadgets and gizmos galore. > Newport Yachting Center, off America's Cup Ave., tel. 401/846–1115, www.newportspringboatshow.com.

JUNE

Newport International Polo Series The Newport Polo Club sponsors this season opener each June, which features the equestrian sport of polo played by Team USA against international rivals. > Tel. 401/847–7090, www.newportinternationalpolo.com.

Newport Flower Show at Rosecliff The 1902 gilded-age mansion is bedecked with floral displays; there are also gardening lectures and demonstrations. > Bellevue Ave. at Marine Ave., tel. 401/847–1000, www.newportmansions.org.

JULY

Black Ships Festival Numerous Japanese cultural events are held all across the city in mid-July to commemorate Commodore Matthew C. Perry's 1854 expedition, which opened trade with Japan. > Tel. 401/846–2720, www.newportevents.com.

Miller Lite Hall of Fame Tennis Championships Top pros compete in the only U.S. men's tournament of the ATP Tour played on grass courts. > International Tennis Hall of Fame, 194 Bellevue Ave., tel. 401/849–6053, www.tennisfame.com.

Newport Music Festival Mid-July sees two weeks of chamber music in and around the mansions. There are morning, afternoon, and evening concerts. > Tel. 401/849–8048 or 800/326–6030, www.newportmusic.org.

AUGUST

JVC Newport Jazz Festival Legendary performers and rising stars participate in this world-renowned event. Most concerts are in Fort Adams State Park, overlooking Newport Harbor. > Tel. 401/847–3700, www.festivalproductions.net.

SEPTEMBER

Newport International Boat Show Hundreds of sail- and powerboats and accessories are available at the Northeast's largest in-water boat show. > Tel. 401/846–1115, www.newportboatshow.com.

OCTOBER

Oktoberfest This three-day festival at the Newport Yachting Center mid-October celebrates all things German, with Bavarian music, dancers, food, a biergarten, and a marketplace. > Newport Yachting Center, off America's Cup Ave., tel. 401/846–1600, www.newportfestivals.com.

NOVEMBER–DECEMBER

Christmas at the Newport Mansions Marble House, the Elms, and the Breakers are open and decorated for the holiday season. > Tel. 401/847–1000, www.newportmansions.org.

WHERE TO STAY

Abigail Stoneman Inn The grand house, designed and built in 1866 by George Champlin Mason, has an impressive collection of Newport women artists' works. You're pampered with a choice of 17 different pillows, elaborate bath amenities, and more than a dozen bottled waters. Each room has a fireplace and a two-person whirlpool tub. Personal service is a hallmark here. > 102 Touro St., 02840, tel. 401/847–1811 or 800/845–1811, fax 401/848–5850, www.abigailstonemaninn.com. 5 rooms. In-room hot tubs, some kitchens, cable TV, in-room VCRs; no kids under 13, no smoking. AE, MC, V. BP. **$$$$**

Admiral Fitzroy Inn An 1854 Victorian provides a restful retreat amid Newport's bustling waterfront district. Period antiques decorate the rooms, each of which has either an antique brass or hand-carved wood bed. Two rooms have private decks with harbor views. > 398 Thames St., 02840, tel. 401/848–8000 or 866/848–8780, fax 401/848–8006, www.admiralfitzroy.com. 17 rooms. Some in-room hot tubs, cable TV, refrigerators, meeting room; no smoking. AE, D, MC, V. BP. **$$–$$$$**

Best Western Mainstay Inn The two-story budget lodging is near the beach and 1 mi from downtown Newport. Interior corridors connect all the rooms here. > 151 Admiral Kalbfus Rd., 02840, tel. 401/849–9880 or 800/528–1234, fax 401/849–4391, www.bestwestern.com. 165 rooms. Restaurant, room service, in-room data ports, cable TV, pool, bar, business services, no-smoking rooms. AE, D, DC, MC, V. EP. **¢–$$**

Castle Hill Inn & Resort On a 40-acre peninsula overlooking Narragansett Bay and the Atlantic, this turreted 1874 Victorian inn and its adjacent beach houses have everything you could want, including marble showers, fireplaces, and period furnishings. The beach- and harbor-house rooms are more modern. A full English tea is served each afternoon. Hiking trails lead to the Castle Hill Lighthouse and a private beach. > 590 Ocean Ave., 02840, tel. 401/849–3800 or 888/466–1355, fax 401/849–3838, www.castlehillinn.com. 23 rooms, 2 suites. Restaurant, in-room data ports, some in-room hot tubs, some kitchenettes, some refrigerators, some in-room VCRs, massage, hiking, beach, bar, laundry service; no smoking. AE, D, DC, MC, V. BP. **$$$$**

The Chanler The hostelry overlooks First Beach, right by the start of the Cliff Walk. Its rooms are spectacular, all with views of the Atlantic or the beach. Rooms are oversize, with fireplaces and wet bars, and range in style from Gothic to Early American to French provincial. The restaurant overlooks the ocean and has two outdoor terraces. > 117 Memorial Blvd., 02840, tel. 401/847–1300, fax 401/848–5850, www.thechanler.com. 15 rooms, 5 suites. Restaurant, in-room hot tubs, refrigerators, cable TV, in-room VCRs, sauna, bar, meeting room; no smoking. AE, MC, V. BP. **$$$$**

Cliffside Inn Grandeur and comfort come in equal supply at this swank Victorian home on a tree-lined street near the Cliff Walk. The rooms contain Victorian antiques; the more than 100 paintings by artist Beatrice Turner, who lived in the house for many years and painted self-portraits, are a signature touch. The Governor's Suite has a two-sided fireplace, a whirlpool bath, a four-poster king-size bed, and a brass birdcage shower. Ten other rooms also have working fireplaces. > 2 Seaview Ave., 02840, tel. 401/847–1811 or 800/845–1811, fax 401/848–5850, www.cliffsideinn.com. 8 rooms, 8 suites. In-room data ports, some in-room hot tubs, cable TV, in-room VCRs; no kids under 13, no smoking. AE, D, MC, V. BP. **$$$–$$$$**

Elm Tree Cottage Owner Priscilla Malone's concern for guests is evident—she accommodates special-breakfast requests and provides turn-down service, bubble bath, tub pillows, and other amenities like razors and toothbrushes. Most rooms have fireplaces. Complimentary sherry and a concert-grand-player piano set the tone. Breakfast seating is at your own private table. > 336 Gibbs Ave., 02840, tel. 401/849–1610 or 888/356–8733, fax 401/849–2084, www.elm-tree.com. 5 rooms, 1 suite. Some cable TV, lounge; no TV in some rooms, no kids under 14, no smoking. Closed mid-Nov.–mid-Feb. AE, MC, V. BP. **$$–$$$$**

Francis Malbone House The design of this stately painted-brick house is attributed to Peter Harrison, the architect responsible for Touro Synagogue and the Redwood

Library. A lavish inn with period reproduction furnishings, the 1760 structure was tastefully doubled in size in the mid-1990s. The rooms in the main house are all in corners (with at least two windows) and look out over the courtyard or across the street to the harbor. Most rooms have working fireplaces. > 392 Thames St., 02840, tel. 401/846–0392 or 800/846–0392, fax 401/848–5956, www.malbone.com. 18 rooms, 2 suites. In-room data ports, some in-room hot tubs, some refrigerators, cable TV, business services; no kids under 13, no smoking. AE, MC, V. BP. $$$–$$$$

Hotel Viking An inn built in 1926 expressly for the guests of mansion owners, the redbrick Viking is elegantly situated at the north end of Bellevue Avenue. The wood paneling and original chandeliers evoke the hotel's sophisticated history. The stately rooms, with reproduction Colonial furniture and appointments (draperies and spreads), resemble the grand homes of Colonial merchant seamen. > 1 Bellevue Ave., 02840, tel. 401/847–3300 or 800/556–7126, fax 401/848–4864, www.hotelviking.com. 218 rooms, 4 suites. Restaurant, indoor pool, hot tub, sauna, bar, meeting rooms, no-smoking rooms. AE, D, DC, MC, V. EP. $$$$

Hyatt Regency Newport On Goat Island across from the Colonial Point District, the Hyatt has great views of the harbor and the Newport Bridge. Most rooms have water views. Although the hotel is a 15-minute walk to Newport's center, bike and moped rentals are nearby. All rooms have oak furnishings and multicolor jewel-tone fabrics. > 1 Goat Island, 02840, tel. 401/851–1234 or 800/532–1496, fax 401/846–7210, www.hyatt.com. 264 rooms. Restaurant, tennis court, indoor pool, saltwater pool, hair salon, health club, spa, boating, racquetball, meeting room, no-smoking rooms. AE, D, DC, MC, V. EP. $$–$$$$

Ivy Lodge The only B&B in the mansion district, this grand (though small by Newport's standards) shingled Victorian has gables and a Gothic turret. The home has 11 fireplaces and large and lovely rooms. The defining feature is a Gothic-style entryway with a three-story turned-baluster staircase and a dangling wrought-iron chandelier. In summer you can relax in wicker chairs on the porch. > 12 Clay St., 02840, tel. 401/849–6865, fax 401/849–2919, www.ivylodge.com. 7 rooms, 1 suite. Dining room, some in-room data ports, some in-room hot tubs, some refrigerators, cable TV, some in-room VCRs; no smoking. AE, D, MC, V. BP. $$$$

La Farge Perry The B&B is named for renowned painter and stained-glass artist John La Farge and his wife, the niece of the famous Commodore Matthew C. Perry. At the top of the "Hill," the inn is quiet yet close to attractions. Rooms include antique pieces; one has a canopy bed. The full breakfast is cooked to order. > 24 Kay St., 02840, tel. 401/847–2223 or 877/847–1100, fax 401/849–3422, www.lafargeperry.com. 5 rooms. In-room hot tubs, refrigerators, in-room VCRs; no kids under 12, no smoking. AE, D, DC, MC, V. BP. $$$–$$$$

Newport Marriott An atrium lobby with marble floors and a nautical theme unfolds as you enter this hotel on the harbor at Long Wharf. Rooms that don't border the atrium overlook the city or the waterfront. Fifth-floor rooms facing the harbor have sliding French windows that open onto large decks. Rates vary greatly according to season and location. > 25 America's Cup Ave., 02840, tel. 401/849–1000 or 800/228–9290, fax 401/849–3422, www.marriott.com. 312 rooms, 7 suites. Restaurant, room service, in-room data ports, cable TV with movies, indoor pool, health club, hot tub, sauna, racquetball, bar, laundry facilities, meeting rooms, no-smoking rooms. AE, D, DC, MC, V. EP. $$–$$$$

Newport Harbor Hotel & Marina This hotel in downtown Newport has panoramic views of yachts in the harbor from the sundeck. Ask for a room with a balcony and a view of the 60-slip marina. From May to October former America's Cup boats are available for guest charters and daily sunset sails. > 49 America's Cup Ave., 02840, tel. 401/847–9000 or 800/955–2558, fax 401/849–6380, www.newporthotel.com. 132 rooms, 1 suite. Restaurant, room service, in-room data ports, cable TV with movies and video games, indoor pool, sauna, bar, dry cleaning, laundry service, Internet, business services, meeting rooms, no-smoking rooms. AE, D, DC, MC, V. EP. $$–$$$$

Sanford-Covell Villa Marina The impressive waterfront Victorian with a majestic 35-foot entrance hall was built in 1869 by architect William Ralph Emerson. A saltwater lap pool, dock with seating, and wraparound porch add to the inn's charm, as do original details such as parquet floors, walnut wainscoting, and frescoes. > 72 Washington St., 02840, tel. 401/847–0206, fax 401/848–5599, www.sanford-covell.com. 5 rooms. Dining room, some cable TV, pool, laundry facilities, some pets allowed; no a/c, no room phones, no TV in some rooms, no smoking. No credit cards. CP. $$–$$$$

Vanderbilt Hall Hotel The luxury hotel, a short walk from the harbor, was built in 1909 as a YMCA. A butler greets you on arrival, a musician plays nightly on the inn's grand piano, and a classy billiard room beckons. Room 35 has a king-size bed and three windows with views of Newport Harbor and Trinity Church; suites have office space and sitting rooms. All rooms have antique furnishings. > 41 Mary St., 02840, tel. 401/846–6200 or 888/826–4255, fax 401/846–8701, www.vanderbilthall.com. 42 rooms, 9 suites. Restaurant, room service, in-room data ports, some in-room hot tubs, cable TV, indoor pool, gym, hot tub, massage, sauna, steam room, billiards, laundry service, business services; no kids under 12, no smoking. AE, D, DC, MC, V. $$$$

The Victorian Ladies Inn During warm-weather months, breakfast is served in the beautiful garden of this Victorian inn close to the beach. Rooms contain antique or reproduction furniture, and many have four-poster beds. > 63 Memorial Blvd., 02840, tel. 401/849–9960, fax 401/849–9960, www.victorianladies.com. 11 rooms. Cable TV, library; no phones in some rooms, no kids under 10, no smoking. Closed Jan. MC, V. BP. $$–$$$$

WHERE TO EAT

Asterix An auto-repair garage before Danish chef John Bach-Sorensen took it over, the restaurant has a concrete floor painted to look like it's been covered with expensive tiling. Asian twists enliven the French-influenced Mediterranean fare, accompanied by a carefully selected menu of wines, brandies, and aperitifs. Sunday brunch is served year-round. > 599 Thames St., tel. 401/841–8833. AE, D, DC, MC, V. No lunch. $$–$$$

The Black Pearl At this dignified, converted dock shanty, popular with yachters, clam chowder is sold by the quart. Dining is in the casual tavern (¢–$$) or the formal Commodore's Room. The latter serves an appetizer of black-and-blue tuna with red-pepper sauce; the French and American entrées include duck breast with green-peppercorn sauce. A third choice in season is to sit at the outdoor patio and bar. > Bannister's Wharf, tel. 401/846–5264. Jacket required (Commodore's Room). AE, MC, V. Reservations essential (Commodore's Room). $$–$$$$

Brick Alley Pub The lines start forming early at this midtown favorite. A bar, four dining rooms, plus a brick-walled patio offer lots of seating. A 1938 red Chevrolet truck stands in one room, and artifacts and memorabilia of old Newport are everywhere. The diverse menu includes ultimate nachos, which are breathtaking in size. Kids under nine have a free beverage and dessert and a selection from a treasure chest. > 140 Thames St., tel. 401/849–6334. AE, D, DC, MC, V. $–$$$

Cafe Zelda At this restaurant you rub elbows with sailors and, possibly, the fisherman who brought in the fresh catch. The 1895 brick building, once a brewery, is now an elegant restaurant, but you can enjoy lighter fare, too. Menu favorites include striped bass with tomato-basil beurre blanc and balsamic chicken with spinach-herb gnocchi. Desserts are wonderful. You can eat at the busy mahogany bar, too. > 528 Thames St., tel. 401/849–4002. AE, MC, V. $$–$$$

Clarke Cooke House–Skybar A 1743 sea captain's house in the heart of the waterfront is really three restaurants. First there's the elegant and formal third-floor Skybar with two dining areas; a trellised, protected porch; and the Gilbert Stuart Room, where crystal, silver, lavish floral displays, and waiters in white tie set the tone for the superb menu. Downstairs is the Boom Boom Room with dancing. Favorites are rack of lamb *persillade*, with potato-turnip gratin and minted tarragon glaze, and lobster, either sautéed with pepper sauce or in the shell. Jackets are suggested for men. > Bannister's Wharf, tel. 401/849–2900. Closed Sun.–Thurs. Nov.–May. No lunch weekdays. AE, D, DC, MC, V. $$$–$$$$

LaForge Casino Restaurant The casual but upscale restaurant, part of the Newport Casino, was built in the 1880s and overlooks the grass courts of the International Tennis Hall of Fame. In summer might see tennis players in period costumes hitting the ball in a game of court tennis. It's a well-known lunch destination for those in search of lobster rolls or a lobster salad. The dinner menu includes steaks, a fabulous baked stuffed lobster, and simpler pub fare such as shepherd's pie. > 186 Bellevue Ave., tel. 401/847–0418. AE, MC, V. $–$$$

Le Bistro This intimate establishment, known for the lighter cuisines of the south of France, has been a staple of Newport dining for more than two decades. Choose the fresh local seafood, Australian rack of lamb, or the sea scallops paella. The menu includes vegetarian options. > 41 Bowen's Wharf, tel. 401/849–7778. AE, D, DC, MC, V. $$–$$$

The Mooring Here is the quintessential Newport dining experience: great seafood, prepared both traditionally or inventively, plus a stellar view of Newport's boats, boats, and more boats. The seafood chowder at this family-oriented restaurant has won the local cook-off so many times that it was removed from further competition. Popular choices include the seafood scampi and lobster. In fine weather you can dine on the enclosed patio overlooking the harbor; on chilly winter evenings, take advantage of the open fire in the sunken interior room. > Sayer's Wharf, tel. 401/846–2260. Closed Mon. and Tues. Nov.–Mar. AE, D, DC, MC, V. $–$$$

Puerini's The aroma of garlic and basil greets you as you enter this laid-back neighborhood Italian restaurant. Lace curtains veil windows, and black-and-white photographs of Italy cover the soft-pink walls. The long and intriguing menu includes green noodles with chicken in marsala sauce, tortellini with seafood, and cavatelli with four cheeses. The wine list is extensive. > 24 Memorial Blvd. W, tel. 401/847–5506. No lunch. Reservations not accepted. MC, V. $–$$

Restaurant Bouchard A 1785 post-and-beam house is home to the restaurant of classically trained chef Albert Bouchard. His presentations include the no-work (for you) Lobster Cardinal, with a truffled cognac sauce and Gruyère topping. A diminutive bar and fireplace add to the style of this upscale yet homey restaurant. > 505 Thames St., tel. 401/846–0123. Closed Tues. No lunch. AE, D, MC, V. $$$

Salvation Cafe Thai, Mexican, Indian, vegetarian, Japanese, sushi, and other ethnic cuisines are all deftly prepared at this storefront that has two funky courtyard patios. Inside there's a stainless-steel horseshoe bar and sectional sofa. The dining room mixes local art with flotsam from flea markets. The pad thai gets raves. > 140 Broadway, tel. 401/847–2620. No lunch. AE, MC, V. $–$$

Scales & Shells The open and airy dining room at this restaurant is boisterous and fun. The signature dish is the lobster *fra diavlo,* a 1½-pound lobster plus mussels, clams, and calamari served with a spicy marinara sauce over linguini. Toro tuna, sushi-grade tuna marinated in soy, lemon, and garlic and wood-grilled, is also very good. A smaller, second-floor dining area called Upscales has more-intimate dining. > 527 Thames St., tel. 401/846–3474. Closed Mon. Jan.–Apr. No lunch. **$–$$$**

White Horse Tavern The 1673 building is now home to one of Newport's finest restaurants. Oak-beam ceilings, a cavernous fireplace, and uneven plank floors epitomize Newport's Colonial charm. The fare is suave American cuisine, including local seafood and fancier dishes like beef Wellington, along with more exotic entrées such as cashew-encrusted venison tenderloin topped with apple-cider demiglace. > Marlborough and Farewell Sts., tel. 401/849–3600. Reservations essential. AE, D, DC, MC, V. No lunch Mon. and Tues. **$$$–$$$$**

ESSENTIALS

Getting Here

Driving is the most convenient way to get to Newport from New York City. There is no direct bus service to Newport from New York City, but you can take a bus to Providence, where you need to take a shuttle service from the Providence Bus Terminal to Kennedy Plaza in downtown Providence. From here you can catch a Rhode Island Public Transit Authority bus to Newport for less than $2.

Parking and driving can be a problem in downtown Newport, although most lodging properties do have parking for their guests. Once in Newport, you can take local transportation to all the attractions.

BY BUS

From April through October, Adventure Northeast, a shuttle-bus service, runs from Manhattan to Newport. It leaves from in front of Fitzpatrick's, on the northwest corner of the 2nd Avenue–85th Street intersection, and from Dublin House, on 79th Street near Broadway; reservations are required. The trip takes 3½ to 4 hours; the round-trip fare is $109. Otherwise, you can take a bus to Providence and then transfer to a local bus.

Greyhound Bus Lines leaves a dozen times a day from Manhattan's Port Authority Bus Terminal to the Providence Bus Terminal. The trip takes anywhere from 4 hours and 10 minutes to 6 hours, depending on the departure and arrival times you choose; round-trip fare is $145. Bonanza Bus Lines leaves Port Authority five times daily for Providence. The trip takes 3¾ hours and costs $59 round-trip.

A shuttle service connects the Providence Bus Terminal with Kennedy Plaza in downtown Providence, where you can catch a local bus operated by the Rhode Island Public Transit Authority (RIPTA) for the 70-minute trip to Newport. The RIPTA bus stops at the Gateway Visitor Center (23 America's Cup Avenue) in Newport and costs less than $2.

LINES **Adventure Northeast Transportation Service** > Tel. 718/601–4707, www.adventurenortheast.com. **Bonanza Bus Lines** > Tel. 800/556–3815, www.bonanzabus.com. **Greyhound Bus Lines** > Tel. 800/231–2222,

www.greyhound.com. **Rhode Island Public Transit Authority (RIPTA)** > Tel. 401/847–0209, 800/244–0444 in Rhode Island, www.ripta.com.
DEPOTS **Providence Bus Terminal** > Bonanza Way at Washington and Dorrance Sts., Providence, tel. 401/751–8800.

BY CAR
From New York City, the quickest route by car is to take Interstate 95 east to Route 138, at Exit 3A in Rhode Island, and proceed to U.S. 1. Turn left onto U.S. 1 north and continue to the exit for the Jamestown and Newport bridges. After crossing both bridges, take the first exit and bear right at the end of the ramp, onto Farewell Street. Continue to the second traffic light and turn right onto America's Cup Avenue, where you can see the visitor center on the right. Public parking is behind it. The trip takes 3½ to 4 hours, depending on the season and traffic conditions.

With the exception of Ocean Drive, Newport is a walker's city. In summer, traffic thickens, and the narrow one-way streets can constitute a difficult and challenging maze. If you're not staying in the historic part of Newport, it's worth parking in a pay lot and leaving your car behind while you visit in-town sights. One such lot is at the Gateway Visitor Center (23 America's Cup Avenue). Leave your car here and purchase a RIPTA one-day pass. For $5 per adult or $10 for families (two adults and related children), you can ride the trolleys around town all day and pay only $1 for your parking. This pass also gives you discounted admission to many area attractions.

Visitor Information

The Newport County Convention Center and Visitor's Bureau operates the Gateway Visitor Center, where you can buy bus- and boat-tour tickets and get information about the mansions and other sights.
INFORMATION **Newport County Convention Center and Visitor's Bureau** > 23 America's Cup Ave., 02840, tel. 401/849–8048 or 800/976–5122, www.gonewport.com.

The Southern Berkshires

Great Barrington is about 140 mi north of New York City;
Lenox is 12 mi north of Great Barrington

21

Revised by Elizabeth Gehrman

SINCE THE LATE 1800s, when the families of the industrialist "robber barons" escaped New York City by fleeing to Berkshires mansions they called cottages, the southern Berkshires have served as a summer playground for New Yorkers as well as for Bostonians. (Great Barrington is almost the same distance from Boston as it is from New York City.)

Today the area is a hotbed of cultural activity in summer. The famed Tanglewood music festival, a fixture here for decades and the summer home of the Boston Symphony Orchestra, draws half a million visitors yearly to Lenox. Booking a room in Lenox—or in any of the nearby communities, for that matter—can set you back dearly during this busy season, particularly during the festival. If you visit during the off-season, however, you can still appreciate Lenox's grand architecture and refined restaurants as well as the deeply wooded, parklike surroundings laced with miles of hiking trails and scenic back roads.

Another major hub is tiny Lee. Although it doesn't cater quite as much to visitors as some of its neighbors do, its small but bustling downtown contains a mix of touristy and workaday shops, and it can be a quiet retreat from the hordes. Still, because Lee is one of the two Berkshires exits from the Massachusetts Turnpike (I–90), travel services such as chain motels and family restaurants are plentiful here.

Stockbridge, home to the decades-old Berkshire Theatre Festival, has had many artistic and literary inhabitants, including sculptor Daniel Chester French, writers Norman Mailer and Robert Sherwood, and, fittingly enough, painter Norman Rockwell, who lived here from 1953 until his death in 1978. James Taylor sang about the town in his hit "Sweet Baby James," and balladeer Arlo Guthrie, in his famous Thanksgiving anthem "Alice's Restaurant," claims to have tossed a mountain of garbage from the back of his Volkswagen bus and down a Stockbridge hillside. Even when it's overrun with summer throngs, Stockbridge keeps its composure, neither contrived nor commercial, and with it the reassuring promise that there is a place where Rockwell's art seems to dwell in life.

Great Barrington has no arts festival to pull in visitors, but, like much of the Berkshires region, it gets vacationers and second-home owners from both Boston and New York; this is why the *New York Times* is found on local coffee-shop counters alongside the *Boston Globe,* and restaurants deliver complex, toothsome fare. Although Great Barrington is the largest town in the region's southern half, its population is less than 8,000. Nevertheless, the vibe here is busy and cosmopolitan, in part because the stores, restaurants, and other services are more typical of towns three or four times larger. Other highlights include a large arts community, whose works are often on display at the numerous galleries in the area, and proximity to a full four-season roster of recreational activities, from hiking to skiing. Nearby West Stockbridge has a more industrial past. And though it sees a fair share of summertime visitors, its hardware store, market, and other local shops seem to suggest that it's not about to become a boutiques-laden tourist trap anytime soon.

WHAT TO SEE & DO

GREAT BARRINGTON

Bartholomew's Cobble South of Great Barrington, Bartholomew's Cobble is a natural rock garden beside the Housatonic River (the Native American name means "place beyond the mountains"). Trees, ferns, and wildflowers fill the 329-acre site, which includes 5 mi of hiking trails. The visitor center holds a natural-history museum. > 105 Weatogue Rd., Sheffield, tel. 413/229–8600, www.thetrustees.org. $4. Park daily. Visitor center Apr.–Nov., daily 9–4:30; Dec.–Mar., Tues.–Sat. 9–4:30.

Beartown State Forest The forest's more than 12,000 acres of mixed hardwoods are a rainbow of color come autumn, but any time of year there's activity worth pursuing here, from cross-country skiing in winter to swimming at Benedict Pond in summer. A dozen primitive campsites offer proximity to the pond. > 69 Blue Hill Rd., off Rte. 23, Monterey, tel. 413/528–0904, 877/422–6762 camping reservations, www.mass.gov. $5. Daily.

Monument Mountain Reservation One of a small series of hills breaking up the broad expanse of the Housatonic River valley, this mountain's exposed rock ledges at its 1,735-foot peak provide exceptional views over the meandering river, the forested ranges on either side of the valley, and the scattered farms below. A single trail loops around the base, with a spur to the top. The mountain has literary associations, too: Nathaniel Hawthorne and Herman Melville picnicked here in 1850. It's about 5 mi from downtown. > U.S. 7, Great Barrington, tel. 413/298–3239, www.thetrustees.org. Free. Daily 9–5.

Mount Washington State Forest The 400-acre park is in the southwest corner of Massachusetts, 16 mi southwest of Great Barrington and on the New York border. The main attraction is **Bash Bish Falls,** which cascades 80 feet into a clear natural pool. To reach the falls, you have to hike down a steep trail into a gorge. Nearby is a free but primitive camping area open year-round. > East St. off Rte. 41, Mt. Washington, tel. 413/528–0330, www.mass.gov. Free. Daily.

LENOX

Berkshire Scenic Railway Museum A restored 1903 railroad station in Lenoxdale, about 2 mi from Lenox, contains displays of antique rail equipment, vintage exhibits, and a large working model railway. A permanent exhibit called "Gateway to the Gilded Age" shows photographs of the robber barons on the way to their "cottages" in a restored 1927 rail car. You can take a 2½-hour round-trip on the museum's diesel engine, which runs through the woods and along the river to Stockbridge on the historic New Haven Railway's Housatonic Valley Line. > 10 Willow Creek Rd., Lenoxdale, tel. 413/637–2210, www.berkshirescenicrailroad.org. Museum free, train ride $12. May–Oct., weekends 9:30–4; call for train schedule.

Frelinghuysen Morris House & Studio Left just as it was when the American abstract artists Suzy Frelinghuysen and George L. K. Morris occupied it, this sleek modernist home on 46 verdant acres displays their artwork as well as those of contemporaries including Pablo Picasso, Georges Braque, and Juan Gris. Guided tours are given hourly. > 92 Hawthorne St., Lenox, tel. 413/637–0166, www.frelinghuysen.org. $9. Thurs.–Sun. 10–3.

The Mount Novelist Edith Wharton, the first woman to win a Pulitzer Prize, was also an expert decorator whose book *The Decoration of Houses* is credited with establishing interior design as a profession in this country. She designed this 1902 mansion as her summer residence, and changing exhibits continue to make use of her ideas. Tours are conducted of the home and grounds; afterward, linger over a light lunch on the terrace while enjoying the view of 3 acres of formal gardens. > Plunkett St. and U.S. 7, Lenox, tel. 413/637–1899 or 888/637–1902, www.edithwharton.org. $16. May–Oct., daily 9–5.

Pleasant Valley Wildlife Sanctuary Covering more than 1,200 acres in the valley of Yokun Brook and on the surrounding slopes of Lenox Mountain, this sanctuary, run by the Massachusetts Audubon Society, is the picture of tranquility. It includes a hemlock gorge, a limestone cobble, a hummingbird garden, and precisely mapped walking trails. > 472 W. Mountain Rd., Lenox, tel. 413/637–0320, www.massaudubon.org. $4. Columbus Day–late June, Tues.–Sat. 9–5, Sun. 10–4; rest of yr, Tues.–Sat. 9–5, Sun. 10–4, Mon. 9–4.

Tanglewood For more than 60 years the Boston Symphony Orchestra has made its summer home at this scenic hilltop estate named after a series of stories by Nathaniel Hawthorne. During the summer season you can take a free walking tour of the grounds on Wednesday morning or, if you have concert tickets, at 12:30 before the Sunday concerts; a few late-afternoon tours are given on days of evening concerts. Call for the schedule. > 297 West St., Lenox, tel. 413/637–5165, www.bso.org. Free. Tours June–Aug., Wed. at 10:30, Sun. at 12:30; call for other times.

Ventfort Hall Built in 1893 as the summer cottage of Sarah Morgan, the sister of highfalutin financier J. P. Morgan, Ventfort Hall contains the **Museum of the Gilded Age,** which explores the role of Lenox and the Berkshires as the definitive mountain retreat during that fabled era. After being abandoned for a quarter-century, the Elizabethan revival mansion was saved from the wrecking ball in 1994 by the Ventfort Hall Association, which is heading up ongoing restoration efforts. > 104 Walker St., Lenox, tel. 413/637–3206, www.gildedage.org. $8. May–Oct., tours daily on the hr 10–2; call for winter hrs.

STOCKBRIDGE

Berkshire Botanical Garden The 15 landscaped acres here contain perennial and annual beds with some 2,500 varieties. Of note are a flower-fringed pond, a terraced herb garden, and floral display gardens of plants that thrive in the Berkshires. Picnicking is encouraged. > Rtes. 102 and 183, Stockbridge, tel. 413/298–3926, www.berkshirebotanical.org. $7. May–Oct., daily 10–5.

Berkshire Center for Contemporary Glass You can watch glassblowers create magnificent pieces and, in summer, create your own paperweight. This handsome gallery also displays and sells the works of some of the country's foremost artists working in glass. > 6 Harris St., West Stockbridge, tel. 413/232–4666. Free. Memorial Day–Dec., daily 10–6.

Chesterwood In the late 1800s and early 1900s, this landscaped estate was the summer home of Daniel Chester French, one of America's most acclaimed sculptors. Tours take in both the house and studio, where you can view a scaled-down version of his statue of Abraham Lincoln in the Lincoln Memorial. The exterior of the house, which was built after the studio, incorporates Colonial revival elements and has many windows (to take advantage of the views). > 4 Williamsville Rd., Stockbridge, tel. 413/298–3579, www.chesterwood.org. $10. May–Oct., daily 10–5.

Children's Chime Tower The tower stands near the site of the 18th-century missionary settlement of Christian Indians dedicated in 1878 to the memory of the Rev. Dudley Field, a Stockbridge resident and father of U.S. Supreme Court justice Stephen Field. The chimes are rung every evening from "apple blossom time until frost." > Main St., Stockbridge.

Mission House With its bright palette of interior colors and elaborately scrolled Connecticut Valley front doorway, this meticulously restored home, presided over by both a Christian missionary and a stern Calvinist preacher in its day, may alter a few preconceptions about Colonial aesthetics. It also contains the area's best exhibit on local Indian history. > Main St., Stockbridge, tel. 413/298–3239, www.thetrustees.org. $5. Memorial Day–Columbus Day, daily 10–5.

Naumkeag Stanford White designed this Berkshire cottage for Joseph Choate, a politically well-connected lawyer and McKinley's ambassador to the court of St. James. The house provides a glimpse into the gracious living of the industrial boom known as the gilded era of the Berkshires in the late 19th century. > Prospect Hill Rd., Stockbridge, tel. 413/298–3239, www.thetrustees.org. $10. Memorial Day–Columbus Day, daily 10–5.

Norman Rockwell Museum The largest public collection of the beloved artist and longtime local's work is on display in this spacious and sunlit museum. The 36-acre grounds, which welcome picnickers, also contain Rockwell's freestanding studio, moved here from its original location in town. > Rte. 183, Stockbridge, tel. 413/298–4100, fax 413/298–4142, www.nrm.org. $12. Nov.–Apr., weekdays 10–4, weekends 10–5; May–Oct., daily 10–5.

October Mountain State Forest The state's largest park has more than 16,000 acres of deep forest in the center of the Berkshires. Snowmobiling is popular and, except during deer-hunting season, the forest is an ideal place for experienced hikers to commune with nature. A 46-site campground has full bathhouses and a dumping station for RVs. > 256 Woodland Rd., Lee, tel. 413/243–1778, 877/422–6762 campground reservations, www.mass.gov. Free. Daily.

Sports

BIKING

The Ashuwillticook (pronounced *ash*-oo-will-ti-cook) Rail Trail runs from the Pittsfield-Cheshire town line north through Adams. Part of the trail is paved. It traces the old rail line and passes through rugged woodland and by Cheshire Lake. This is also a great venue for strolling, jogging, in-line skating, and cross-country skiing. The Berkshire Visitors Bureau distributes a free Berkshire Bike Touring Route, which describes a series of relatively short excursions along area roads.

GOLF

Cranwell Resort, Spa & Golf Club This full-service, 380-acre resort includes a championship golf course and the largest golf school in the United States. Green fees are $84 for 18 holes; resort guests get a discount. > 55 Lee Rd., Lenox, tel. 413/637–1364 or 800/272–6935, www.cranwell.com.

Egremont Country Club The 18-hole course ranks among the most challenging and scenic in western Massachusetts. Green fees are $40 on weekends, $25 on weekdays. > Rte. 23, Great Barrington, tel. 413/528–4222, www.egremontcountryclub.com.

SKIING

Butternut Basin The ski resort has multiple chairlifts, full snowmaking capabilities, a ski school, and a racing program. With more than half its 22 trails designed for intermediate-level skiers, Butternut is known for its beautiful cruising runs. Snowboarders are welcome. Lift tickets cost $32 to $43 a day during the December–March ski season. > Rte. 23, Great Barrington, tel. 413/528–2000 or 800/438–7669, www.butternutbasin.com.

Canterbury Farm The spectacular, high-country property in Becket has 12 mi of groomed cross-country-ski trails and offers lessons and rental equipment. You can ski across a nearby lake or take to some 2,000 acres of unmaintained trails that surround the farm. A day ticket costs $12 during the December–March ski season. > Fred Snow Rd., Becket, tel. 413/623–0100, www.canterbury-farms.com.

Catamount The two-dozen trails here are almost evenly split among beginner, intermediate, and expert runs, with some vertical double–black diamond terrain for the truly fearless. Half the trails are open for night skiing. Day lift tickets cost $19 to $40, and the season runs from December through April. > Rte. 23, South Egremont, tel. 413/528–1262 or 800/342–1840, www.catamountski.com.

Shopping

Berkshire County Massachusetts Antiques Dealers Association The stretch of U.S. 7 from Sheffield to Great Barrington has the best concentration of antiques stores in the Berkshires. For a listing and map of more than 60 antiques and collectibles shops, send an SASE to the Berkshire County Massachusetts Antiques Dealers Association. > Box 130, Sheffield 01257, tel. 413/229–3070, www.berkshireantiquesandart.com.

Prime Outlets at Lee Bargain-basement prices at about five dozen shops, including Coach, J. Crew, Geoffrey Beene, and Anne Klein, make this a good rainy-day destination. The outlets are open weekdays until 9, Sunday until 6. > U.S. 20, at Exit 2 off I–90, Lee, tel. 413/243–8186.

Save the Date

ONGOING

Shakespeare and Co. Shakespeare's plays and others are performed at several theaters in and around Lenox, both indoors and out, from May through November. > Tel. 413/637–3353 tickets, www.shakespeare.org.

JUNE–AUGUST

Jacob's Pillow Dance Festival In the 1930s Ted Shawn, a pioneer in men's modern dance, purchased a farm in Becket to serve as a dance school. Now it hosts the oldest dance festival in America, with ballet, jazz, and modern-dance performances on the schedule. > 358 George Carter Rd., Becket, tel. 413/243–0745, www.jacobspillow.org.

JUNE–SEPTEMBER

Berkshire Theatre Festival The second oldest summer theater in the nation—it was founded in 1928—inhabits an 1887 building designed by McKim, Mead & White as a casino, in Stockbridge. Four shows are produced here each season; previous stars have included Gene Hackman, Al Pacino, Joanne Woodward, and Calista Flockhart. > Box 797, Main St., Stockbridge, tel. 413/298–5536, www.berkshiretheatre.org.

JULY–AUGUST

Aston Magna Festival The annual festival has garnered international recognition for its contribution to the popularization of early music using historically accurate instruments and performance practices. The festival takes place on five successive Saturdays at St. James Church in Great Barrington. > Tel. 413/528–3595 or 800/875–7156, www.astonmagna.org.

Tanglewood The Tanglewood Institute was founded by Serge Koussevitzky in 1938 as a summer school for talented young composers and conductors. Today the 500-acre property in Lenox is one of the world's premier cultural centers, presenting many styles of music, from orchestral to contemporary jazz. > 297 West St., Lenox, tel. 617/266–1492 or 888/266–1200, 617/266–1200 tickets, www.tanglewood.org.

AUGUST

Berkshire Crafts Fair This established juried retail crafts show at the Monument Mountain Regional High School in Great Barrington spotlights the works of 95 exhibitors. > Tel. 413/528–3346 Ext. 28, www.berkshirecraftsfair.org.

SEPTEMBER

Apple Squeeze Festival The event cheerfully ushers in autumn and the first apple pressing for cider. For one weekend Lenox Village is transformed into a country fair with sidewalk sales, singers, bands, crafts demonstrations, face painting, a giant pumpkin weigh-off, a children's dog show, a 5K run, and lots and lots of apples. > Tel. 413/637–3646 Lenox Chamber of Commerce, www.lenox.org.

Tub Parade A procession of horse-drawn carriages in Lenox re-creates the parades of decorated "tubs" (pony carts) begun by the "cottagers" of the 1890s to celebrate the end of summer. High tea and tours of Ventfort Hall follow. > Tel. 413/637–3646 Lenox Chamber of Commerce, www.lenox.org.

Lee Founders Weekend Vintage cars, swing bands, Italian food, a Latino festival, and a parade mark this annual celebration throughout Lee on the last weekend of the month. Other highlights include antiques and crafts sales and Revolutionary and Civil War displays. > Tel. 413/243–0852 Lee Chamber of Commerce, www.leechamber.org.

OCTOBER

Berkshire Botanical Garden Harvest Festival Started in 1934, this is the longest-running and best-known community event in the Berkshires. It remains old-fashioned and family-oriented, with rides, games, food, music, crafts, and a giant tag sale. > Rtes. 102 and 183, Stockbridge, tel. 413/298–3926, www.berkshirebotanical.org.

DECEMBER

Historic Inn & House Tour Lenox's fabled old mansions are open late in the month for this one-day inn and house tour, which includes high tea at Ventfort Hall. > Tel. 413/637–3646 Lenox Chamber of Commerce, www.lenox.org.

Stockbridge Main Street at Christmas Early in the month downtown is decked out in Norman Rockwell–era finery for this weekend festival that kicks off on Saturday with house tours, a reading by actors from the Berkshire Theater Festival, and caroling, followed by a candlelight walk to the holiday concert. > Tel. 413/298–5200 Stockbridge Chamber of Commerce, www.stockbridgechamber.org.

WHERE TO STAY

GREAT BARRINGTON

The Old Inn on the Green and Gedney Farm Though this lodging consists of five distinctive properties, one thing all the rooms have in common is that they are bright, well appointed, and luxurious. From the 1760 Old Inn, with its welcoming two-story plantation porch, to Gedney Farm's two turn-of-the-20th-century Normandy-style barns and the ultradeluxe Thayer House, you find authentic restoration, antiques such as four-poster queen beds, fireplaces, and whirlpool tubs. The restaurant is well worth a visit, too. > Rte. 57, New Marlborough 01230, tel. 413/229–3131 or 800/286–3139, fax 413/229–8236, www.oldinn.com. 37 rooms, 5 suites. Restaurant, dining room, some fans, in-room data ports, some in-room hot tubs, pool, hiking, taproom, library, meeting rooms; no a/c in some rooms, no TV in some rooms, no smoking. AE, MC, V. CP. $$$–$$$$

Race Brook Lodge This brookside compound of haylofts, ice houses, and hoop sheds, along with a late-1700s brick Federal-style house, has simple and understated furnishings. Rooms shy away from frills and pastels; most walls are white, although some have hand-stenciled designs, and quilts cover many beds. Several buildings contain just three or four guest rooms, making them ideal for families or friends traveling together. The lodge keeps technology at bay, but a phone, TV, data port, and fax machine are available on the premises. > 864 S. Undermountain Rd., Sheffield 01257, tel. 413/229–2916 or 888/725–6343, fax 413/229–6629, www.rblodge.com. 26 rooms, 2 with shared bath; 8 suites. Restaurant, some kitchens, pool, hiking, lounge, meeting rooms, some pets allowed (fee); no room phones, no room TVs, no smoking. MC, V. BP. $–$$

Thornewood Inn River, field, and mountain views are what you see from this turn-of-the-20th-century Dutch Colonial inn and carriage house. Canopy beds, flowered wallpaper, and lace outfit the rooms, some of which have whirlpool tubs or fireplaces. In summer the inn offers live jazz on weekends, and on-staff massage therapists are available by appointment throughout the year. > 453 Stockbridge Rd., Great Barrington 01230, tel. 413/528–3828 or 800/854–1008, fax 413/528–3307, www.thornewood.com. 12 rooms, 3 suites. Restaurant, cable TV, pool, massage, bar, business services, meeting room; no kids under 12 July and Aug., no smoking. AE, D, MC, V. BP. $–$$$

Wainwright Inn The incredible three-story Victorian, built in 1766 by a captain in the Revolutionary War, has been admirably restored by current owners Robert and Marja Tepper. During the warm-weather months, flower baskets adorn the building's gingerbread-laced wraparound porches, where wicker seating invites lingering; indoors, antique furnishings are homey rather than overwrought, and some rooms have fireplaces. Dinner is available on request in winter. > 518 S. Main St., Great Barrington 01230, tel. 413/528–2062, fax 413/644–6410, www.wainwrightinn.com. 7 rooms, 2 suites. Dining room, cable TV, piano, baby-sitting, Internet; no kids under 8, no smoking. MC, V. BP. $–$$$

LEE

Ashley Inn The bed-and-breakfast, an 1874 classical revival home built for shoe merchant A. P. Hollenbeck, showcases a large collection of clocks, Santa statuettes, and other antiques. Its four rooms are simple yet welcoming, with bright linens and subtle wallpapers. A front porch with a swing completes the picture of an old family homestead. > 182 W. Park St., Lee 01238, tel. 413/243–2746, fax 413/243–2489, www.ashleyinn.com. 4 rooms. Dining room; no room phones, no room TVs, no kids under 16, no smoking. AE, D, MC, V. BP. $–$$

Federal House With soaring columns and a Greek Revival facade, the well-maintained 1824 house cuts a dashing figure along Route 102, and its airy porches are ideal for whiling away a warm afternoon. Antiques fill the rooms, many of which have working fireplaces; all have original wide-plank pine floors and plush down comforters for cool nights. > 1560 Pleasant St., South Lee 01260, tel. 413/243–1824 or 800/243–1824, fax 413/243–1828, www.federalhouseinn.com. 10 rooms. Dining room, in-room data ports, cable TV; no kids under 12, no smoking. AE, D, MC, V. BP. $$$–$$$$

Historic Merrell Inn Built in the 1780s as a private residence, this carefully kept inn has some good-size rooms, several with working fireplaces, and an unfussy yet authentic style. Breakfast—maybe homemade blueberry pancakes or basil-and-cheese omelets—is served in the original dining room, which has a fireplace. VCRs are available on request, and a refrigerator stocks free soft drinks and bottled water. The Riverview Suite is a good option for families with infants because it's in a separate wing. From the property you can hike over to Beartown State Forest, which the inn borders. > 1565 Pleasant St., South Lee 01260, tel. 413/243–1794 or 800/243–1794, fax 413/243–2669, www.merrell-inn.com. 9 rooms, 1 suite. Dining room, cable TV; no smoking. AE, MC, V. BP. $–$$$$

LENOX

Blantyre Modeled after a castle in Scotland, this elegant 1902 manor house sits amid nearly 100 acres of manicured lawns and woodlands. Formality accompanies the grandeur; men, for instance, must wear jacket and tie for dinner here. Guest rooms are lavishly decorated and have hand-carved four-poster beds. > 16 Blantyre Rd., off U.S. 20, 01240, tel. 413/637–3556, fax 413/637–4282, www.blantyre.com. 15 rooms, 9 suites. Restaurant, dining room, room service, some in-room hot tubs, some refrigerators, cable TV, some in-room VCRs, 4 tennis courts, pool, gym, hot tub, massage, sauna, croquet, hiking, dry cleaning, laundry service, Internet, meeting rooms; no kids under 12, no smoking. AE, DC, MC, V. CP. Closed early Nov.–early May. $$$$

Rookwood Inn Although it feels quite secluded, this huge Queen Anne Victorian is one block from the center of Lenox. Families are welcome, and afternoon refreshments are served. Many rooms have built-ins or fireplaces, and all are tastefully furnished with antiques, including four-poster beds, wing chairs, roomy armoires, and spindle-leg side tables. Some have fireplaces, whereas others offer private porches. > 11 Old Stockbridge Rd., 01240, tel. 413/637–9750 or 800/223–9750, fax 413/637–1352, www.rookwoodinn.com. 21 rooms, 6 suites. Dining room, in-room data ports, library, piano, baby-sitting, Internet; no TV in some rooms, no smoking. AE, D, DC, MC, V. BP. $$–$$$$

Summer White House This dignified house, which dates from 1885, was one of the original Berkshire cottages, and its many porches are an inviting feature. Rooms, furnished with antiques and reproductions, are named after first ladies. Guests have access to the tennis court and indoor pool at a nearby sister property. > 17 Main St., 01240, tel. 413/637–4489, fax 413/637–4489, www.summerwhitehouse.com. 7 rooms. Dining room, cable TV, library, piano; no kids under 12, no smoking. D, MC, V. CP. $$$

Yankee Inn Custom-crafted Amish canopy beds, ornamental fireplaces, and high-quality fabrics distinguish the top rooms at this immaculate hotel, one of several modern lodgings along U.S. 7. The more economical rooms are motel-style, with exterior corridors and little panache, but all are tidy and have useful amenities such as coffeemakers. > 461 Pittsfield Rd., 01240, tel. 413/499–3700 or 800/835–2364, fax 413/499–3634, www.yankeeinn.com. 96 rooms. In-room data ports, some in-room hot tubs, some refrigerators, cable TV, 2 pools (1 indoor), gym, hot tub, lounge, meeting room, no-smoking rooms. AE, D, MC, V. CP. $–$$$$

STOCKBRIDGE

Card Lake Inn Originally a stage-coach stop, the inn has brass beds with quilts, Colonial furniture, and original 1805 floorboards. The restaurant has an outdoor café where you can have breakfast; an English-style tavern is also on the premises. > 29 Main St., West Stockbridge 01266, tel. 413/232–0272, fax 413/232–0294, www.cardlakeinn.com. 10 rooms, 2 with shared bath; 2 suites. Restaurant, pub, business services; no room phones, no room TVs, no kids June–Oct. D, MC, V. BP. $–$$

Spa Options

THE BERKSHIRES ARE HOME to Canyon Ranch, one of the best known destination spas in North America, and the Kripalu Center, a yoga-focused facility. At the Cranwell Resort, in Lenox, you don't have to commit to a weekend program to take advantage of the extensive spa facilities.

Canyon Ranch in the Berkshires. The centerpiece of this world-class destination spa on 120 woodland acres is an 1897 mansion that is a replica of the Petit Trianon in Versailles. Two floors of guest rooms flank the mansion's elegant lobby and are more functional, contemporary—New England style, with flower-print fabric and big windows. Upon arrival you consult with a program coordinator and a nurse who map out a plan of activities; there are more than 250 daily classes, outings, and workshops from which to choose, so you need the help. Rates are all-inclusive, including some spa treatments, with a three-night minimum. > 165 Kemble St., Lenox 01240, tel. 413/637–4100 or 800/742–9000, fax 413/637–0057, www.canyonranch.com. 126 rooms, 24 suites. Dining room, some refrigerators, 6 tennis courts, 2 pools (1 indoor), hot tub, fitness classes, health club, massage, sauna, spa, boating, bicycles, basketball, hiking, racquetball, squash, volleyball, cross-country skiing, library, dry cleaning, laundry facilities, Internet, business services, meeting rooms; no kids under 14, no smoking. AE, D, MC, V. All-inclusive. $$$$

Cranwell Resort, Spa & Golf Club. The historic Gilded Age estate on 380 rolling acres has commanding views of the southern Berkshire foothills, one of the largest spas in the Northeast, and a major golf school. Five separate buildings house the guest rooms; those in the mansion are the most deluxe, with 19th-century antiques and reproductions. A handful of activities—fitness and aquatic classes, yoga, guided hikes, and biking in summer and fall; snowshoe treks and cross-country skiing in winter—is offered each day, and personal trainers are available for one-on-one consultations. > 55 Lee Rd., Lenox 02140, tel. 413/637–1364 or 800/272–6935, fax 413/637–4364, www.cranwell.com. 107 rooms. 3 restaurants, room service, some in-room data ports, cable TV, 18-hole golf course, putting green, 4 tennis courts, 2 pools (1 indoor), fitness classes, health club, spa, mountain bikes, hiking, cross-country skiing, no-smoking rooms. AE, DC, MC, V. EP. $$$$

Kripalu Center for Yoga and Health. The nonprofit retreat center, in a former Jesuit seminary on 300 wooded acres adjacent to the Tanglewood grounds, aims to help you achieve peace of mind and to gain insights about healthy lifestyles via a program combining yogic practices with contemporary wisdom about holistic health. Participants—who can number as many as 450 at a time—start their mornings with yoga and meditation followed by a breakfast eaten in silence. (Meals are vegetarian and served buffet-style.) Evening programs include concerts, lectures, and other entertainment. The accommodations are basic, but the location, high in the Berkshires, is spectacular. > Box 793, Lenox 01240, tel. 413/448–3152 or 800/741–7353, fax 413/448–3384, www.kripalu.org. 180 rooms and 150 dormitory beds. Dining room, lake, massage, bicycles, hiking; no room phones, no room TVs, no smoking. MC, V. $$$$

Inn at Stockbridge Posh rooms with antiques and down comforters grace this 1906 Georgian revival inn. All bedrooms are large, but the Cottage House suites are especially airy and spacious. Some rooms have gas fireplaces or canopy beds; all have modern amenities such as CD players. A wine-and-cheese hour is set up each evening. > 30 East St., Stockbridge 01262, tel. 413/298–3337 or 888/466–7865, fax 413/298–3406, www.stockbridgeinn.com. 8 rooms, 8 suites. Some in-room hot tubs, cable TV, in-room VCRs, pool, gym, massage, library, piano, recreation room, Internet; no kids under 12, no smoking. AE, D, MC, V. BP. **$$–$$$$**

Red Lion Inn An inn since 1773, the Red Lion has hosted five presidents and many celebrities over the years. It consists of a large main building—where many rooms are small and furnishings are slightly shabby-chic—and several more-up-to-date structures, including a former firehouse. Owned and operated by the Fitzpatrick family since 1968, the inn has an impressive collection of antiques and china and a sweeping front porch ideal for cocktails and people-watching. > 30 Main St., Stockbridge 01262, tel. 413/298–5545, fax 413/298–5130, www.redlioninn.com. 83 rooms, 14 with shared bath; 25 suites; 1 cottage (May–Oct.). 2 restaurants, room service, some in-room hot tubs, some kitchens, some refrigerators, cable TV, some in-room VCRs, pool, gym, massage, pub, piano, laundry service, business services, meeting room; no smoking. AE, D, DC, MC, V. **$–$$$**

Williamsville Inn Each room in this 1797 farmhouse is furnished with antiques. From June through October, the gardens of the 10-acre property display works by internationally renowned sculptors. Play areas for children have been designated indoors and out. The restaurant is notable. Master chef and owner Erhard Wendt runs a culinary school here as well. > Rte. 41, West Stockbridge 01266, tel. 413/274–6118, fax 413/274–3539, www.williamsvilleinn.com. 15 rooms, 1 suite. Restaurant, tennis court, pool, baby-sitting, playground, Internet; no room phones, no room TVs, no smoking. AE, MC, V. BP. **$$–$$$**

WHERE TO EAT

GREAT BARRINGTON

Castle Street Café Exposed brick, hand-blown glass lamps, original art, and William Gottlieb's famous photos of jazz legends add up to urbane contemporary elegance, which appropriately echoes the sophisticated menu and acclaimed wine list. The dinner menu focuses on hearty American fare, including such dishes as chicken breast stuffed with spinach and Portobello mushrooms and smothered in shiitake mushroom sauce; steak au poivre with straw potatoes; and roasted salmon and root vegetables. The bar serves a lighter menu, usually with live piano music in the backdrop. > 10 Castle St., tel. 413/528–5244. Closed Tues. No lunch. AE, D, MC, V. **$–$$$**

Pearl's With its pressed-tin ceilings, tall booths, exposed-brick walls, and well-coiffed crowd, this spot adds a dash of big-city atmosphere to the Berkshires. The menu updates the old bigger-is-better steak-house tradition. Call ahead for a table on weekends, or simply hobnob and sip one of the well-chosen wines and creative drinks at the elegant bar. > 47 Railroad St., tel. 413/528–7767. AE, MC, V. No lunch Sun.–Fri. **$$–$$$$**

Union Bar and Grill The ultramodern eatery serves an eclectic, globally influenced American cuisine, from quesadillas and barbecued ribs to pan-roasted halibut, grilled salmon, and other selections finished with truffles, wild mushrooms, and similarly fancy ingredients. It's known for pastas, pizza, and martinis. > 293 Main St., tel. 413/528–6228. No lunch weekdays. MC, V. **$$–$$$**

Verdura With all the culinary hot spots that have opened in the Berkshires in the past few years, this restaurant stands out as much as anything for its understated decor, youthful and friendly staff, and superbly executed Tuscan cooking. Recommended are the saffron–lobster risotto and grilled, prosciutto-wrapped brook trout. > 44 Railroad St., tel. 413/528–8969. AE, MC, V. **$–$$$**

LEE
Morgan House Inn Don't be misled by the homey Colonial decor of this 1817 stage-coach inn: the regional American menu is decidedly upscale. Filet mignon, New York strip steak, and lamb tournedos are among the house specialties. > 33 Main St., Lee, tel. 413/243–3661. AE, MC, V. **$–$$**

Sullivan Station Mesclun salads, whole-grain bread, and ample vegetables freshen the traditional menu at this restaurant in a converted depot decked out with railroad memorabilia. The burgers, mixed grill, seafood platter, veal Parmesan, turkey club, and vegetarian pasta are best bets. > Railroad St., Lee, tel. 413/243–2082. AE, D, MC, V. **$–$$**

Sweet Basil The traditional red-sauce Italian fare at this laid-back trattoria in South Lee is reasonably priced and includes seafood, chicken with pesto over linguine, and calamari marinara. This is one of the few good restaurants with a children's menu in these parts. > 1575 Pleasant St., South Lee, tel. 413/243–1114. AE, MC, V. No lunch. **$$**

LENOX
Blantyre Indulge in an elaborate prix-fixe dinner in the formal restaurant of this luxury inn. Cocktails are served in two sitting rooms and on the garden terrace, and after-dinner drinks are offered in the Main Hall amid the soothing strains of classical harp music. The kitchen puts a contemporary spin on Continental cuisine and avoids heavy sauces. > 16 Blantyre Rd., tel. 413/637–3556. Reservations essential. Jacket and tie. Closed Nov.–Apr. and Mon. No lunch Sept.–June. AE, DC, MC, V. **$$$$**

Café Lucia Homemade ravioli with fresh tomatoes, garlic, and basil is just one of the impeccably executed northern Italian dishes, which change seasonally. Make your reservations up to a month ahead during Tanglewood season, especially if you want to sit on the inviting covered deck. > 80 Church St., tel. 413/637–2640. Reservations essential. AE, DC, MC, V. Closed Mon. and, in Nov.–June, Sun. No lunch. **$$–$$$$**

Church Street Cafe A little more relaxed both in style and ambience than its nearby competitors, Church Street Cafe presents a no-less ambitious and intriguing menu of creative globally inspired dishes, from punchy tortilla soup to roasted Japanese sea bass with shrimp ravioli. In warm weather you can dine on a tree-shaded outdoor deck. > 65 Church St., tel. 413/637–2745. MC, V. **$$–$$$**

Panda House When you need a break from Continental and standard New England fare, this spacious restaurant fits the bill with its efficient service and lengthy menu of Mandarin, Hunan, and Cantonese dishes. > 664 Pittsfield-Lenox Rd., tel. 413/499–0660. AE, D, MC, V. **$–$$**

The Village Inn The menu changes seasonally, but favorite dishes include Shaker pot roast and sautéed shrimp over angel-hair pasta. The restaurant, in a 1771 inn, has antiques, a working fireplace, and a garden view. > 16 Church St., tel. 413/637–0021. No lunch. D, DC, MC, V. **$$–$$$**

STOCKBRIDGE

Michael's At this relaxed and family-friendly traditional restaurant just off the main street, house specialties such as chicken marsala, chicken Dijon, grilled eggplant with feta cheese, and shrimp scampi are diverse enough to satisfy most cravings but familiar enough not to intimidate. > 5 Elm St., tel. 413/298–3530. AE, D, MC, V. **$–$$**

Once Upon a Table The atmosphere is casual yet vaguely romantic at this little place in an alley off Stockbridge's main street. The Continental and new American fare includes seasonal dishes, with appetizers such as escargot potpie and entrées that include seared crab cakes with horseradish-cream as well as lobster ravioli. > 36 Main St., tel. 413/298–3870. Reservations essential. MC, V. No dinner Mon.–Wed. in Jan.–Mar. **$$–$$$**

Red Lion Inn Dining Room The formal, antiques- and pewter-filled main dining room of the region's most famous inn, a giant and rambling clapboard 1773 building, serves expertly prepared New England cuisine that is at once both deeply traditional yet thoroughly contemporary in its use of (and respect for) fresh top-quality ingredients. > 30 Main St., tel. 413/298–5545. AE, D, DC, MC, V. **$$–$$$**

WEST STOCKBRIDGE

Card Lake Inn Chicken with grilled vegetables, pork chops, roast beef, and the other basic New England dishes cater more to the landlubber, but seafood specials such as baked scrod are occasionally offered. The restaurant, like the 1805 inn itself, is filled with antiques, and its linen tablecloths, dim lighting, and substantial fare make it the perfect ending to a cool autumn day spent leaf-peeping. > 29 Main St., tel. 413/232–0272. Closed Mon. and Tues. MC, V. **$–$$**

Rouge A contemporary French restaurant in an 1870s Colonial house with a patio overlooking the Williams River, Rouge has many tempting signature dishes, including braised free-range duck and shredded-potato cake as well as steak au poivre and watercress salad with cognac sauce. For starters consider a *rouge et noir* (red and black) martini, made of Godiva liqueur, raspberry vodka, and raspberry coulis. > 3 Center St., tel. 413/232–4111. Closed Mon. and Tues. No lunch. MC, V. **$$–$$$**

Truc Orient Express White-linen elegance, a formal note not often associated with Vietnamese restaurants in the Northeast, suits the level of cooking here, which seems more appropriate to an imperial household than a small Berkshire village. The Happy Pancake combines onion and mushroom with chicken, shrimp, or pork cooked in a golden brown batter; other selections range from duck and fried whole fish to vegetarian dishes. > 3 Harris St., tel. 413/232–4204. Closed Sept.–June and Tues. No lunch. AE, D, MC, V. **$–$$**

Williamsville Inn The intimate 1797 farmhouse with Early American furnishings and handsome fireplaces in two candlelit dining rooms has a varied menu that combines elements of French country fare with intriguing international flavors and preparations. The three- to five-course prix-fixe menu includes entrées such as sautéed halibut with tomato-zucchini gratin and caper vinaigrette; coq au vin with pearl onions, mushrooms, bacon, and garlic-mashed potatoes; and pan-seared duck breast with green-pepper sauce, mixed summer vegetables, and duchess potatoes. > Rte. 41, tel. 413/274–6118. No lunch. AE, MC, V. **$$$$**

ESSENTIALS

Getting Here

You can take a bus to the Berkshires, but having a car here is preferable because the region is spread out and public-transit options are limited.

BY BUS

Bonanza Bus Lines operates scheduled daily bus service between New York City's Port Authority terminal and the Berkshires, including Great Barrington, Stockbridge, Lee, and Lenox.

LINES **Bonanza Bus Lines** > Tel. 800/556–3815 or 888/751–8800, www.bonanzabus.com.

BY CAR

If you're staying in Lee or Lenox, take the New York State Thruway (I–87) north to eastbound I–90, which turns into the Massachusetts Turnpike, to Lee (Exit 2), or the slower but more scenic Taconic State Parkway north to eastbound Route 295 to Route 41 north. Either way brings you to U.S. 20 north, which leads to Lee, Lenox, and the Berkshires' main north–south road, U.S. 7. To reach Stockbridge, south of the turnpike, head for Route 102 west, which eventually leads to West Stockbridge.

For Great Barrington, head north on the Hutchinson River Parkway to I–684 north and proceed to Route 22 north. Continue parallel to the New York–Massachusetts border to Route 23 east (at Hillsdale), which takes you to Great Barrington. You can also take the Taconic State Parkway north to Route 23 east.

Visitor Information

CONTACTS **Berkshire Visitors Bureau** > Berkshire Common, plaza level, West St. at U.S. 7, Pittsfield 01201, tel. 413/443–9186 or 800/237–5747, www.berkshires.org. **Lee Chamber of Commerce** > Box 345, Lee 01238, tel. 413/243–0852, www.leechamber.org. **Lenox Chamber of Commerce** > The Curtis, 5 Walker St., Lenox 01240, tel. 413/637–3646, www.lenox.org. **Stockbridge Chamber of Commerce** > 6 Elm St., Stockbridge 01262, tel. 413/298–5200, www.stockbridgechamber.org. **Southern Berkshires Chamber of Commerce** > 362 Main St., Great Barrington 01230, tel. 413/528–1510, www.southernberkshirechamber.com.

The Northern Berkshires

Pittsfield is about 165 mi north of New York City; North Adams is 21 mi north of Pittsfield

22

Revised by Elizabeth Gehrman

THE STORY OF THE NORTHERN BERKSHIRES is the story of a rebound. The far western edges of Massachusetts, not settled by Europeans until after the French and Indian War, in the mid-1700s, saw boom times beginning after the Civil War, when early industrialization made its way here. In the southern Berkshires were the so-called "cottages" of the New Yorkers who owned the manufacturing facilities. In the north there was mostly manufacturing.

By the end of World War II, northern Berkshires towns such as Pittsfield and North Adams were important suppliers of textiles, plastics, and electronics, and residents were flush, or at least secure. Then the economy began to wane as industry changed, jobs moved out of the area, and, in the 1970s, corporate downsizing began. Nearly three decades later, the northern Berkshires are on the upswing, but art and tourism are the driving forces this time.

The Massachusetts Museum of Contemporary Art, better known as Mass MoCA, opened in North Adams in 1999. The world's largest modern-art gallery, Mass MoCA was created from 13 acres of renovated factory buildings. It is leading the way not only for a revitalization of North Adams—where the conversion of mills and factory buildings into artists' studios and residences has led to preservation efforts and a small explosion in trendy shops and eateries—but of surrounding towns like Pittsfield, as well.

Pittsfield, the seat of Berkshire county and the region's largest and most commercial community, became a significant industrial center after inventor William Stanley moved his electric-generator factory here in the late 1800s. Stanley's company eventually became General Electric, whose plant for the testing and manufacture of transformers, electrical components, and industrial plastics for many decades dominated the economic life of the city. Although Pittsfield remains a workaday city without the monied urbanity of Great Barrington or the rural demeanor of other nearby towns, signs of a turnaround—new shops, restaurants, and preservation efforts—abound today and are seen as signaling the beginning of a renaissance. Indeed, the Berkshire Museum, the Berkshire Opera Company, and Arrowhead, the home of writer Herman Melville, make Pittsfield worth adding to your itinerary.

Dalton's claim to fame, at least among Berkshires residents, is that it's the home of paper manufacturer Crane & Co., which was started by Zenas Crane in 1801. The company is perhaps most famous as the maker of the paper on which U.S. currency is printed. But this tiny postage stamp of a town has other delights, including Holiday Farm, for mountain biking, and Wahconah Falls State Park. Perhaps the best thing about Dalton is its proximity to other Berkshires attractions, both north and south. It is convenient to Tanglewood Music Festival, the Jacob's Pillow Dance Festival, antiques shops, outdoors activities, historic Shaker Village, Mass MoCA, and more, without the crowds those attractions can draw.

Two exceptional art collections make Williamstown, which is tucked into the far northwestern corner of the state and is home to Williams College, worth the extra miles. A combined trip to Mass MoCA, the Sterling and Francine Clark Art Institute, and the Williams College Museum of Art would be any art lover's dream. And because it has just one main drag that caters to hip, upscale students and their families, it's really the perfect place—especially in summer—for a quiet getaway. The same cannot be said for the southern Berkshires.

WHAT TO SEE & DO

DALTON
Crane Museum of Paper Making Exhibits in the handsomely restored Old Stone Mill (dating to 1844) trace the history and art of fine papermaking from 1801 to the present. Because the museum's owner, Crane & Co., has supplied all the paper for U.S. currency since 1879, there's a display of banknotes from around the world as well. > W. Housatonic St., off Rte. 9, tel. 800/268–2281, www.crane.com. Free. June–mid-Oct., weekdays 2–5.

Holiday Farm Crane family descendants own this 2,000-acre working organic farm, which has a sugar house, a beautiful daffodil field in season, a stable offering English and Western riding lessons, hiking trails, mountain biking, a small store, and a five-bedroom cottage to rent. > Holiday Cottage Rd., tel. 413/684–0444 general information, 413/684–9963 or 413/655–0285 riding lessons, www.holidayfarm.com. Free; private riding lessons $45 per hr or $25 per ½ hr, group lessons $25 per person. Farm daily 8–6; riding lessons May–Nov., Mon.–Sat. 9–8.

Wahconah Falls State Park For a refreshing break in warm weather, nothing beats Wahconah Falls, however you choose to get back to nature—fishing, hiking, picnicking, or swimming in the cool pools below its three babbling waterfalls. > Off Rte. 9/8A about 8 mi east of Dalton, tel. 413/442–8992, www.state.ma.us/dem. Free. Daily.

NORTH ADAMS
Contemporary Artists Center The 130,000-square-foot historic Beaver Mill, which occupies 27 acres of woodland adjacent to Natural Bridge State Park, houses this artists' residence and studio and its affiliated Dark Ride Project, an art exhibit where viewers take a 10-minute ride on a Disney-like "Sensory Integrator." In this light-filled atelier you can tour many art studios and admire work in virtually every medium. The CAC also hosts workshops and presents art in several galleries. > 189 Beaver St., off Rte. 8 north of Rte. 2, North Adams, tel. 413/663–9555, www.thecac.org. Free. May–Oct., daily; hrs vary according to event (call ahead).

Massachusetts Museum of Contemporary Arts The sprawling complex, known as Mass MoCA, is the largest center for contemporary arts in the United States. Its 27 buildings, from the 19th century, once housed the now-defunct Sprague Electric Co. Six of the factories have been transformed into more than 250,000 square feet holding galleries, studios, performance venues, cafés, and shops. Its size—one gallery is 40 feet high and another the size of a football field—enables the museum to display monumental-scale works such as Robert Rauschenberg's ¼ *Mile* or 2 *Furlong Piece*. The complex also encompasses theaters, rehearsal studios, and outdoor performance spaces for video, film, dance, and music. > 87 Marshall St., North Adams, tel. 413/664–4481 or 413/662–2111, www.massmoca.org. $9. June–Aug., daily 10–6; Sept.–May, Wed.–Mon. 11–5.

Mohawk Trail State Forest About 15 mi east of North Adams, this state forest occupies the remote mountainous reaches of the upper Deerfield River valley. It's noted for its exceptional catch-and-release trout fishing, rough trails enjoyed by orienteers, and fire roads favored by snowmobilers. The park includes a campground that's open May through Columbus Day. Cross-country skiing is a cold-weather option. > Rte. 2, Charlemont, tel. 413/339–5504, www.state.ma.us/dem. $5 per vehicle. Park daily.

Natural Bridge State Park The marble arch in this 49-acre park, the site of a marble quarry from 1810 through the mid-20th century, is the only natural bridge in North America caused by water erosion. The 30-foot span crosses a narrow 500-foot-deep chasm containing numerous faults and fractures, as well as some 19th-century graffiti. The park includes picnic sites, hiking trails, and well-maintained rest rooms. > Rte. 8 north of Rte. 2, North Adams, tel. 413/663–6392, www.state.ma.us/dem. $2 per vehicle. Daily 8:30–5.

Savoy Mountain State Forest In its more than 11,000 acres of deeply wooded, flat-topped foothills, Savoy Mountain contains two cold swimming ponds, more than 60 mi of trails and fire roads, and a 45-site campground (open Memorial Day through Columbus Day) with showers, rest rooms, and four cabins. The park is southeast of North Adams. > 260 Central Shaft Rd., Savoy, tel. 413/663–8469, www.state.ma.us/dem. Memorial Day–Columbus Day $5 per vehicle. Park daily.

Western Gateway Heritage State Park The old Boston and Maine freight yard sets the scene for shops, a pub-restaurant, and a visitor center with exhibits that trace the tremendous impact of rail travel as well as the effect of the 4½-mi Hoosac Tunnel on the region's industrialization in the 19th century. A 30-minute documentary film looks at the intense labor that went into the building of the tunnel. > 115 State St., Bldg. 4, North Adams, tel. 413/663–6312, www.state.ma.us/dem. Free. Daily 10–5.

PITTSFIELD

Arrowhead From 1850 to 1863, Herman Melville and his family lived in this 40-acre farm. Here Melville wrote *Moby Dick* and other works; his study appears as if he might shortly return to pick up his pen. As headquarters to the Berkshire County Historical Society, the property also offers, in the barn, excellent changing exhibits about local history. Tours are on the hour. > 780 Holmes Rd., tel. 413/442–1793, fax 413/443–1449, www.berkshirehistory.org. $7. Memorial Day–Oct., daily 9:30–5; or by appointment.

Berkshire Museum Three floors of this museum, opened in 1903, house exhibits displaying a varied and sometimes curious collection of objects relating to history, the natural world, and art. Toys designed by artist Alexander Calder share the space with 26 tanks of sea creatures and a 10-foot-high, 26-foot-long "Wally" the Stegosaurus. At the Dino Dig, kids and adults can dig together for replica dinosaur bones before heading over to the ancient-civilization displays of Roman and Greek jewelry and an Egyptian mummy. > 39 South St., tel. 413/443–7171, www.berkshiremuseum.org. $7.50. Mon.–Sat. 10–5, Sun. noon–5.

Canoe Meadows Wildlife Sanctuary The three branches of the Housatonic River converge just north of this Massachusetts Audubon Society property. A pair of small brooks join the river here, too, as it flows through wetlands bordered by woods and fields. A few miles of trails offer access to the sanctuary's various habitats, which provide refuge for a sizable amount of wildlife. > Holmes Rd., tel. 413/637–0320, www.massaudubon.org. $3. Tues.–Sun. 7 AM–dusk.

Hancock Shaker Village This was the third of 13 communities founded in the nation by the United Society of Believers in Christ's Second Appearing, or Shakers. At its peak in the 1840s, the village had almost 300 inhabitants, who made their living farming, selling seeds and herbs, making medicines, and producing crafts. After 170 years—a small miracle considering its population's vow of celibacy (they took in orphans to maintain their constituency)—the whole village was converted into a museum dedicated to interpreting the order's agrarian lifestyle, domestic industry, and enduring design skills. The site contains a farm, some period gardens, a museum shop with reproduction Shaker crafts, a picnic area, a café, and interesting buildings, such as the round stone barn and the laundry and machine shop. From October to late May you take a 90-minute guided tour (call for tour times); the rest of the year you tour on your own. > U.S. 20 at Rte. 41, tel. 413/443–0188 or 800/817–1137, www.hancockshakervillage.org. $15 Memorial Day–late Oct., $12 rest of yr. Memorial Day–late Oct., daily 9:30–5; late Oct.–late May, daily 10–3.

Herman Melville Memorial Room The Berkshire Athenaeum, Pittsfield's public library, contains this admirable collection of primary-research materials; family memorabilia, such as the author's customs-house badge; and the earliest portrait of Melville. > 1 Wendell Ave., tel. 413/499–9486. Free. Sept.–June, Mon.–Thurs. 9–9, Fri. 9–5, Sat. 10–5; July and Aug., Mon., Wed., and Fri. 9–5, Tues. and Thurs. 9–9, Sat. 10–5.

WILLIAMSTOWN

Chapin Library of Rare Books and Manuscripts Original copies of the four founding documents of the United States—the Declaration of Independence, the Articles of Confederation, the Constitution, and the Bill of Rights—share this space with 50,000 books and 50,000 prints, letters, and documents, including a book from the era of Charlemagne, examples of 16th-century printing, and Americana dating back to Columbus's day. > Williams College, Stetson Hall, Main St., Williamstown, tel. 413/597–2462, www.williams.edu. Free. Weekdays 10–noon and 1–5.

Ioka Valley Farm Established in the 1930s, this 600-acre farm 13 mi from Williamstown is one of the best-known pick-your-own farms in the Berkshires. You can pick strawberries from mid-June to early July and pumpkins in the fall; choose Christmas trees in winter; and sit in on maple-sugaring from mid-February to early April. In summer, hayrides, pedal tractors, and a petting zoo with pigs, sheep, goats, and calves draw the little ones to Uncle Don's Barnyard. > 3475 Rte. 43, Hancock, tel. 413/738–5915, www.taconic.net/Iokavalleyfarm. Farm free, Uncle Don's Barnyard $6.50. Daily, but hrs vary seasonally (call ahead).

Mount Greylock State Reservation The highest point in Massachusetts, Mount Greylock has an elevation of 3,491 feet and a 100-mi view from atop the 105-foot War Memorial Tower at its summit. As the name suggests, however, the peak is buried in clouds more often than not. The Appalachian Trail cuts through the middle of the reservation, north to south. Hiking trails range in difficulty from easy ½-mi walks to challenging 7-mi climbs to the summit. Mountain biking, back-country skiing (for experts), and snowmobiling are allowed, with some restrictions. Picnic sites and campsites also are available. > Rockwell Rd., Lanesborough, tel. 413/499–4262 or 413/499–4263, www.state.ma.us/dem. $2 per vehicle. Daily sunrise–½ hr after sunset; visitor center mid-May–mid-Oct., daily 9–5, mid-Oct.–mid-May, daily 9–4.

Sterling and Francine Clark Art Institute The museum is most famous for its collection of impressionist works, including more than 30 paintings by Pierre-Auguste Renoir. But the Clark's exceptional collection includes much more, from the European baroque to Winslow Homer, with sidelines in American silver and old-master prints and drawings. The art-history library is considered to be among the finest in the nation. > 225 South St., Williamstown, tel. 413/458–2303, www.clarkart.edu. Mid-

June–Oct., $10; Nov.–mid-June, free. Mid-June–Labor Day, daily 10–5; early Sept.–mid-June, Tues.–Sun. 10–5.

Williams College Graceful 19th-century architecture fills the picture-book campus of this small liberal-arts institution. The school shares its campus and its origin with the town, both having been named after the same generous 18th-century militia colonel who commanded a frontier garrison a few miles to the east. Befitting a school with a highly respected art-history department, **Williams College Museum of Art** (tel. 413/597–2429, www.wcma.org) has an 11,000-work collection spanning centuries, but its real strength is in modern art. Changing exhibits and site-specific installations of contemporary work across a wide spectrum of styles, media, and themes are another hallmark. > 880 Main St., Williamstown, tel. 413/597–3131, www.williams.edu. Free. Museum Tues.–Sat. 10–5, Sun. 1–5.

Sports

BOATING

Pleasant canoe trips in the Berkshires include Lenox to Dalton (19 mi), Lenox to Stockbridge (12 mi), Stockbridge to Great Barrington (13 mi), and, for experts, Great Barrington to Falls Village (25 mi). The Housatonic River flows south from Pittsfield between the Berkshire Hills and the Taconic Range through Connecticut, where it eventually empties into the Long Island Sound.

Onota Boat Livery rents all kinds of boats and canoes, provides dock space on Onota Lake, and sells fishing tackle and bait. U-Drive Boat Rentals rents boats on Pontoosuc Lake.

RENTALS **Onota Boat Livery** > 463 Pecks Rd., Pittsfield, tel. 413/442–1724. **U-Drive Boat Rentals** > 1651 North St., Pittsfield, tel. 413/442–7020.

GOLF

Wahconah Country Club This semiprivate club has an 18-hole, par-71 course with a good restaurant. Nonmember greens fees are $65 weekdays and $75 weekends. > 15 Orchard Rd., Dalton, tel. 413/684–1333.

Waubeeka Golf Links The 18-hole, par-72 course is open to the public and rents golf clubs. Greens fees are $33 weekdays and $42 weekends. > U.S. 7 and Rte. 43, South Williamstown, tel. 413/458–8355.

MOUNTAIN BIKING

The gently rolling Berkshire Hills are excellent cycling terrain; the Mount Greylock State Reservation has some of the area's best mountain-bike trails. Mountain Goat Bicycle Shop rents mountain bikes and also conducts free hiking tours in the area.

Holiday Farm Every Wednesday evening mountain bikers converge to navigate the varied terrain at this 2,000-acre working farm. (Admission to the race is $7.) This is also a venue for one of the annual 24 Hours of Adrenalin races (www.24hoursofadrenalin.com), which are held in several states and Canadian provinces and are popular with enthusiasts. > Holiday Cottage Rd., Dalton, tel. 413/684–0444, www.holidayfarm.com. Daily 8–6.

Jiminy Peak Lift-serviced mountain biking is one of the summer and fall activities at this resort 10 mi northwest of Pittsfield. From late May through Columbus Day you can hit the trails, which range from beginner to advanced in difficulty, from 11 until dusk. The lift fee is $20 for the day. Special programs include children's biking workshops. Miniature golf, hiking, an alpine slide, and a climbing wall are among the other warm-weather activities. > 37 Corey Rd., Hancock, tel. 413/738–5500, 800/882–8859 outside MA, www.jiminypeak.com.

Mount Greylock State Reservation Many of the trails at the reservation are suitable for mountain biking; the range of difficulty covers beginner to expert. > Rockwell Rd., Lanesborough, tel. 413/499–4262 or 413/499–4263, www.state.ma.us/dem. $2 per vehicle. Daily sunrise–½ hr after sunset; visitor center mid-May–mid-Oct., daily 9–5, mid-May–mid-Oct., daily 9–4.

RENTALS **Mountain Goat Bicycle Shop** > 130 Water St., Williamstown, tel. 413/458–8445, www.themountaingoat.com.

SKIING

Bousquet Ski Area The ski area has more than 20 trails, running the gamut from beginner to black diamond. The peak vertical drop is 750 feet. Lift tickets cost $25 a day. > Dan Fox Dr. off U.S. 7, Pittsfield, tel. 413/442–8316, fax 413/445–4534, www.bousquets.com.

Brodie Mountain The 1,250-foot vertical drop here is the region's greatest. Brodie has 28 trails, mostly for advanced intermediates, and more than 15 mi of cross-country trails. The resort offers hotel and condo accommodations, year-round camping, and an indoor racket club. It's 8 mi north of Pittsfield. Lift tickets cost $30–$38. > U.S. 7, New Ashford, tel. 413/443–4752, 413/443–4751 recorded ski conditions, www.skibrodie.com.

Jiminy Peak This full-scale, 40-trail resort 10 mi northwest of Pittsfield has slopeside condos, an inn, restaurants, weekend entertainment, a conference center, a health club, and a range of family ski programs. The 1,140-foot vertical drop provides some challenging expert runs, but two-thirds of the terrain is for beginning and intermediate skiers, with strong emphasis on the comfortable middle range. A day pass costs $49, a night pass $32. > 37 Corey Rd., Hancock, tel. 413/738–5500, 800/882–8859 outside MA, www.jiminypeak.com.

WHITE-WATER RAFTING

The rapids in the Zoar Gap section of the Deerfield River, which runs parallel to Route 2 near Charlemont and is controlled by dam, are rated class II and III, considered good options for beginners. Other sections of the river are more challenging.

Zoar Outdoor Half-day trips are a good introduction to white-water rafting or kayaking on the Deerfield River for adults and children as young as seven. > Rte. 2, Charlemont, tel. 800/532–7483, www.zoaroutdoor.com.

Save the Date

APRIL

Jazztown At this weeklong festival in Williamstown, you might encounter improvisational luminaries such as Billy Taylor and Wynton Marsalis, as well as students from Williams College. Swing and hip-hop dance classes are also offered. Performances and classes take place all over town, but most events are at the Clark Art Institute or Williams College. > Tel. 800/214–3799.

JUNE–JULY

Berkshire Opera Performers from the Metropolitan Opera, New York City Opera, and other notable companies spend time here as guest performers and artists in residence. The repertoire leans toward bel canto and contemporary, intimate pieces, as well as the occasional better-known works such as *La Traviata*. Venues include the Mahaiwe Performing Arts Center in Great Barrington and Williams College's Chapin Hall. > Tel. 413/442–9955, 413/442–0099 box office, www.berkshireopera.org.

JUNE–AUGUST

Williamstown Theatre Festival Some of America's finest actors appear on the Main Stage at the Williamstown Playhouse each summer, where five productions are mounted; experimental works-in-progress are performed on the smaller Nikos Stage. > Tel. 413/597–3399 information, 413/597–3400 box office, www.wtfestival.org.

JULY

Susan B. Anthony Celebration The town of Adams hosts events like a biathlon, a lawn party, and a cemetery tour as part of the five-day celebration that begins the Saturday before the first full weekend in August. > Tel. 413/663–3735.

SEPTEMBER–OCTOBER

South Mountain Concerts Chamber-music concerts are held in the historic Temple of Music built in 1918. > South Mountain, U.S. 7 and 20, 2 mi south of Pittsfield, tel. 413/442–2106.

OCTOBER

Fall Foliage Festival This nine-day event early in the month includes children's activities, a pet show, a car show, bazaars, community suppers, a parade, and the Mount Greylock Ramble, a hike to the top of the highest peak in the state. Various North Adams venues host the events. > Tel. 413/663–3735 Berkshire Chamber of Commerce, www.berkshirebiz.org.

DECEMBER

Community Christmas of Hancock Shaker Village The annual event has become a holiday tradition for many families. Activities include sleigh or wagon rides and children's crafts. The 19th-century brick main house and the round stone barn housing sheep and cows are open. > U.S. 20 at Rte. 41, tel. 413/443–0188 or 800/817–1137, www.hancockshakervillage.org.

WHERE TO STAY

NORTH ADAMS

Holiday Inn Berkshires From the hotel, you're one block to Mass MoCA, a 10-minute drive to Mount Greylock, and a half-hour drive to white-water rafting. > 40 Main St., North Adams 01247, tel. 413/663–6500 or 800/465–4329, fax 413/663–6380, www.ichotelsgroup.com. 86 rooms. Restaurant, in-room data ports, cable TV, indoor pool, gym, hot tub, sauna, steam room, lounge, dry cleaning, laundry facilities, laundry service, business services, no-smoking rooms. AE, D, DC, MC, V. EP. ¢–$$

Porches Inn A complex of once-dilapidated 1890s mill workers' houses, across from Mass MoCA, has been transformed into one of New England's most delightful and quirky small hotels. The decor incorporates homey touches and retro-chic furnishings but avoids a cluttered feel, and the design strikes a perfect balance between high-tech and historic. Some two-room suites have two bathrooms and loft sleeping areas reached by spiral staircases. > 231 River St., North Adams, 01247, tel. 413/664–0400, www.porches.com. 46 rooms, 22 suites. In-room data ports, some in-room hot tubs, some kitchens, pool, hot tub, sauna, bar, baby-sitting, dry cleaning, laundry service, concierge, business services, meeting room, no-smoking rooms. AE, MC, V. CP. $$$–$$$$

PITTSFIELD

Crowne Plaza Pittsfield Two tiers of rooms surround a large, glass-domed pool at this well-maintained 14-story downtown hotel. Most rooms have mountain views. > Berkshire Common, 1 West St., Pittsfield, 01201, tel. 413/499–2000 or 800/227–6963, fax 413/442–0449, www.crowneplaza.com. 177 rooms, 2 suites. 2 restaurants, room service, in-room data ports, pool, gym, hot tub, sauna, bar, dry cleaning, laundry service, business services, meeting room, no-smoking rooms. AE, D, DC, MC, V. **$–$$$**

Dalton House Eclectically decorated, cheerful guest rooms—including two large suites—are spread out in three interconnected buildings surrounded by peaceful gardens and an outdoor pool. Common areas include a living room with a stone fireplace and a sunny breakfast spot. Perhaps the best things about this bed-and-breakfast are its location, convenient to both the northern and southern Berkshires, and the extensive regional knowledge of the friendly and outgoing innkeepers, the Turetsky family. > 955 Main St., Dalton, 01226, tel. 413/684–3854, fax 413/684–0203, www.thedaltonhouse.com. 8 rooms, 3 suites. In-room data ports, cable TV, pool, Internet; no kids under 8, no smoking. AE, MC, V. BP on Sun., CP rest of wk. **$–$$**

Ramada Limited Inn & Suites Pittsfield This Ramada, built in 2001, is one of the chain's newer properties. Although lacking in flair, the furnishings are contemporary. The location puts you within a few miles of Hancock Shaker Village, Tanglewood, the Berkshire Museum, and other attractions. > 1350 W. Housatonic St., Pittsfield, 01201, tel. 413/442–8714, www.ramada.com. 41 rooms, 18 suites. In-room data ports, some microwaves, some refrigerators, cable TV, laundry facilities, business services, meeting rooms, no-smoking rooms. AE, D, DC, MC, V. CP. **$–$$**

WILLIAMSTOWN

Berkshire Hills Motel At this New England–style country motel, the gurgles of Hemlock Brook help soothe you to sleep. The wooded grounds and flower gardens are appealing, and there are two fireplaces as well as a deck for barbecuing and dining. A natural-spring swimming hole is across the street. > 1146 Cold Spring Rd., Williamstown, 01267, tel. 413/458–3950 or 800/388–9677, fax 413/458–5878, www.berkshirehillsmotel.com. 21 rooms. In-room data ports, cable TV, pool; no smoking. AE, D, MC, V. CP. **¢–$$**

Buxton Brook Farm Bed & Breakfast The 1800 Federal-style home is on 70 acres of woods and gardens; the terrace has a wonderful view of Mount Greylock. The B&B has period antiques and is run by an enthusiastic host, Nancy Alden. > 91 Northwest Hill Rd., Williamstown, 01267, tel. 413/458–3621, fax 413/458–3640. 4 rooms, 1 suite. Pool; no kids under 10, no smoking, no TV in some rooms. AE, D, MC, V. BP. **$$–$$$**

1896 House Brookside and Pondside are the two small motel-inns that make up 1896 House, along with the more spacious Barnside, which has six suites. The properties reside on 17 acres with a brook, a spring-fed duck pond, and fishing holes. Brookside's grounds are parklike, with gardens, a gazebo, and an outdoor dining patio. Pondside is a renovated Cape Cod classic, and the more luxurious Barnside offers a large country porch. > 910 Cold Spring Rd., Williamstown, 01267, tel. 413/458–8125 or 888/666–1896, www.1896house.com. 29 rooms, 7 suites. Restaurant, picnic area, in-room data ports, some in-room hot tubs, some refrigerators, cable TV, some in-room VCRs, pool, fishing, bar; no smoking. AE, D, MC, V. CP. **$–$$**

Field Farm Guest House The house, built in 1948, contains a fine collection of art on loan from Williams College. It was donated as part of a land trust by the former owners (art lovers who gave part of their collection to Williams), and the 316-acre property is now run nonprofit as a B&B. The large windows in the guest rooms have expansive views of the grounds. Three rooms have private decks; two rooms have working tile fireplaces. You can prepare simple meals in the pantry. The grounds, open to the public, include a pond, sculptures, a nature center, and 4 mi of walking trails. > 554 Sloan Rd., off Rte. 43, Williamstown, 01267, tel./fax 413/458–3135, www.berkshireweb.com/trustees/field.html. 5 rooms. Dining room, tennis court, pool, fishing; no room phones, no room TVs, no kids under 12, no smoking. D, MC, V. BP. $$

The Orchards Hotel Although it's right on Route 2 and surrounded by parking lots, this thoroughly proper if rather formal hotel compensates for these shortcomings with a beautiful central courtyard with fruit trees and a pond stocked with koi. English antiques furnish most of the rooms, which are spacious. The inner rooms, with one-way windows looking onto the courtyard, are best for summer stays. The outer rooms have less-distinguished views, but their fireplaces add appeal for winter visits. > 222 Adams Rd., Williamstown, 01267, tel. 413/458–9611 or 800/225–1517, fax 413/458–3273, www.orchardshotel.com. 48 rooms, 1 suite. Restaurant, in-room data ports, in-room safes, some refrigerators, in-room VCRs, pool, gym, hot tub, sauna, bar, meeting room, no-smoking rooms. AE, DC, MC, V. $$$–$$$$

River Bend Farm One of the founders of Williamstown built this 1770s Georgian Colonial farmhouse-tavern, now restored with complete authenticity. Some bedrooms have wide-plank walls, curtains of unbleached muslin, and four-poster beds with canopies or comfy rope beds. For the final touch, the jams and jellies served with breakfast are made by the owners, the Loomis family. Because it's so intimate, the River Bend is an ideal location for small family get-togethers or reunions. > 643 Simonds Rd., Williamstown, 01267, tel. 413/458–3121. 4 rooms with shared baths. Fans, horseshoes; no a/c, no room phones, no room TVs, no smoking. No credit cards. Closed Oct.–Mar. CP. $

WHERE TO EAT

NORTH ADAMS

Freightyard Restaurant and Pub In the Heritage State Park, this busy and festive eatery serves half-pound burgers, prime rib, fajitas, and other down-home favorites. Dinner is served until 11 nightly, and the bar keeps going long after that. > Western Gateway Heritage State Park, 115 State St., tel. 413/663–6547. AE, MC, V. ¢–$

Gramercy Bistro Occupying the space of an old downtown diner, this casual, upbeat eatery has a loyal following. The tavernesque space, with a wood-beamed ceiling and walls lined with black-and-white photos of the town, serves eclectic American cuisine with Asian and French influences The wine list includes 100 choices. Weekend brunch is good. > 24 Marshall St., tel. 413/663–5300. AE, MC, V. $–$$

PITTSFIELD

Brewery at 34 Depot Street This casual, family-friendly spot occupies an airy space separated by glass walls from the region's first microbrewery. The ales, lagers, and stouts are all fine accompaniments for the burgers, veggie burritos, ribs, and specialty salads served here. > 34 Depot St., Pittsfield, tel. 413/442–2072. AE, MC, V. ¢–$

Dakota Restaurant As befits the rustic-hunting-lodge decor, with mounted moose and elk heads and canoes slung from the rafters, the menu here features strapping portions of hearty meats and seafood. Known for hand-cut, aged prime beef, wood-grilled meats and fish, and a giant brunch buffet, Dakota also has a kids' menu that includes salad bar, salmon, and chicken teriyaki. > 1035 South St., Pittsfield, tel. 413/499–7900. No lunch. AE, D, DC, MC, V. $–$$

Dalton Restaurant At this casual and homey family-owned diner, pasta, steaks, seafood, and homemade desserts are on the menu. The large portions, low prices, and friendly waitresses keep the locals coming back. > 401 Main St., Dalton, tel. 413/684–0414. MC, V. $

Ozzie's Steak & Seafood The menu focuses largely on steak and seafood, as the name says. But you might not realize that Ozzie's is also a popular nightclub, with open-mike nights and a party deck in summer. The crowd tends to be young and local, and the place gets pretty packed on weekends. > 450 Housatonic St., Dalton, tel. 413/684–1782 or 413/684–3018. AE, D, MC, V. No dinner Sun.–Tues. $–$$$

South Mountain Grill Hardwood abounds in this 225-seat, family-friendly restaurant. Prime rib, steak Neptune (filet mignon topped with lobster meat, asparagus, and hollandaise sauce), and stuffed lobster are the most popular dishes. All booths provide views of the landscaped grounds. > 1015 South St., Pittsfield, tel. 413/499–2075. AE, MC, V. $–$$$

WILLIAMSTOWN

Arugula Cocina Latina The dapper storefront café with a few tables is mainly a lunch spot, although it does serve food until around 9 PM. With contemporary art lining the walls and piped-in Latin music, you'd expect to find this nifty hole-in-the-wall on a side street in Miami. Indeed, the Cuban sandwich is stellar. You can also order empanadas, leafy salads, chorizo sandwiches, rice and beans, and rich, hot white chocolate. > 25 Spring St., Williamstown, tel. 413/458–2152. Closed Mon. AE, D, MC, V. ¢–$

Cold Spring Manor At this mid- to upscale restaurant, you can relax and play chess or backgammon on the stuffed chairs and couches in the wine-and-cheese room, enjoy a drink or light meal while gazing at the fireplace in the lounge, or sit down to linen tablecloths in the formal dining room. Classic comfort favorites such as pot roast, crème brûlée, and key lime pie share the menu with dishes like tender roast duck in blackberry-brandy sauce and broiled salmon in white wine–dill sauce. > 101 North St., Williamstown, tel. 413/458–4000. AE, D, DC, MC, V. Closed Mon. $–$$$

Mezze Bistro The spectacular menu at this contemporary-in-the-country spot, a local favorite, changes often, but don't be surprised to see sashimi with watercress alongside filet mignon with roasted root vegetables. Stars from the theater festival often have cocktails on the outdoor deck. Reservations are necessary in summer. > 16 Water St., Williamstown, tel. 413/458–0123. No lunch. AE, D, MC, V. $$–$$$

Yasmine's Restaurant At this restaurant in one of the area's top hotels, the kitchen turns out globally inspired contemporary American dishes. Combinations such as whole lobster on arugula risotto and salmon spring rolls with shiitake mushrooms alternate with other innovative fare. > The Orchards Hotel, 222 Adams Rd., Williamstown, tel. 413/458–9611. AE, D, DC, MC, V. $$$

ESSENTIALS

Getting Here

Although buses serve the Berkshires, the easiest way to get around and explore the area is by car. This will enable you to hop from town to town and to take advantage of the many parks and outdoor activities.

BY BUS

Bonanza Bus Lines offers daily bus service between New York City's Port Authority terminal and the Berkshires, including Pittsfield, New Ashford (for Brodie Mountain), and Williamstown.

LINES **Bonanza Bus Lines** > Tel. 800/556–3815 or 888/751–8800, www.bonanzabus.com.

BY CAR

Take either the New York State Thruway (I–87) north to eastbound I–90, which turns into the Massachusetts Turnpike, to Lee (Exit 2), or the slower but more scenic Taconic State Parkway north to eastbound Route 295 to Route 41 north. Both ways take you to U.S. 20, which leads to the Berkshires' main north–south road, U.S. 7.

Scenic drives are plentiful in this part of the Berkshires. One especially pretty road, the Mohawk Trail (Route 2) runs across northern Massachusetts and connects Williamstown with North Adams to the east.

Visitor Information

CONTACTS **Berkshire Chamber of Commerce** > 6 W. Main St., North Adams 01247, tel. 413/663–3735, www.berkshirechamber.com. **Berkshire Visitors Bureau** > Berkshire Common, plaza level, West St. at U.S. 7, Pittsfield, 01201, tel. 413/443–9186 or 800/237–5747; Discover the Berkshires Visitor Center, 3 Hoosac St., off Rte. 8, Adams, tel. 413/743–4500 or 800/237–5747, www.berkshires.org. **Mohawk Trail Association** > Box 1044, North Adams, 01247, tel. 413/743–8127, www.mohawktrail.com. **Williamstown Chamber of Commerce** > Rte. 2 at U.S. 7, Box 357, Williamstown, 01267, tel. 413/458–9077 or 800/214–3799, www.williamstownchamber.com.

Index

Notes

Notes

Notes

Notes